DAILY USE OF THE DRUG
CAUSES POISONING

DRUG & DRØP

Vol. 1

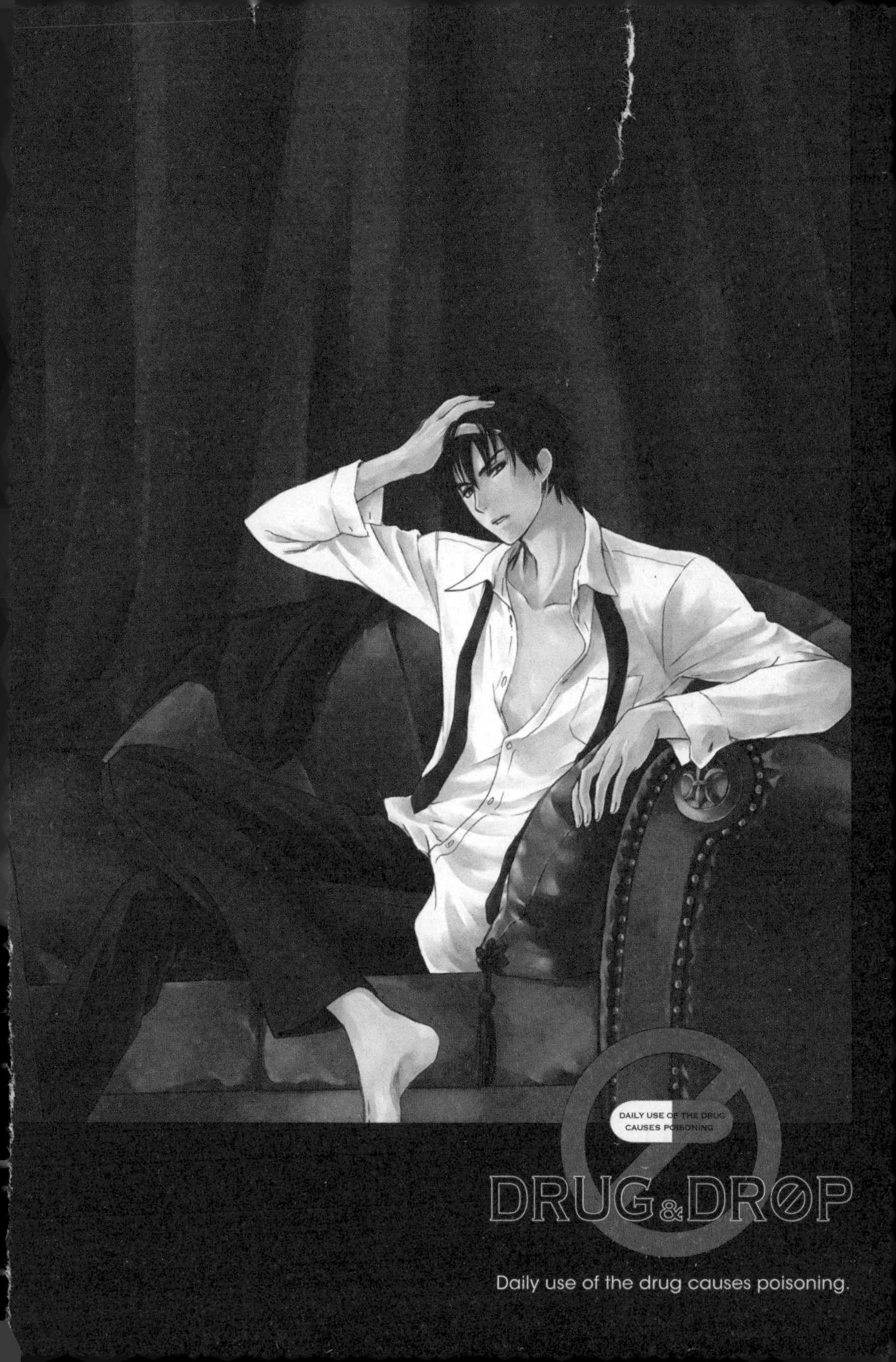
DAILY USE OF THE DRUG
CAUSES POISONING
DRUG & DRØP
Daily use of the drug causes poisoning.

Columbia Global Reports is a publishing imprint from Columbia University that commissions authors to do original on-site reporting around the globe on a wide range of issues. The resulting novella-length books offer new ways to look at and understand the world that can be read in a few hours. Most readers are curious and busy. Our books are for them.

Vigil: Hong Kong on the Brink
Jeffrey Wasserstrom

The Call: Inside the Global Saudi Religious Project
Krithika Varagur

Ghosting the News: Local Journalism and the Crisis of American Democracy
Margaret Sullivan

Carte Blanche: The Erosion of Medical Consent
Harriet A. Washington

Freedomville: The Story of a 21st-Century Slave Revolt
Laura T. Murphy

Reading Our Minds: The Rise of Big Data Psychiatry
Daniel Barron

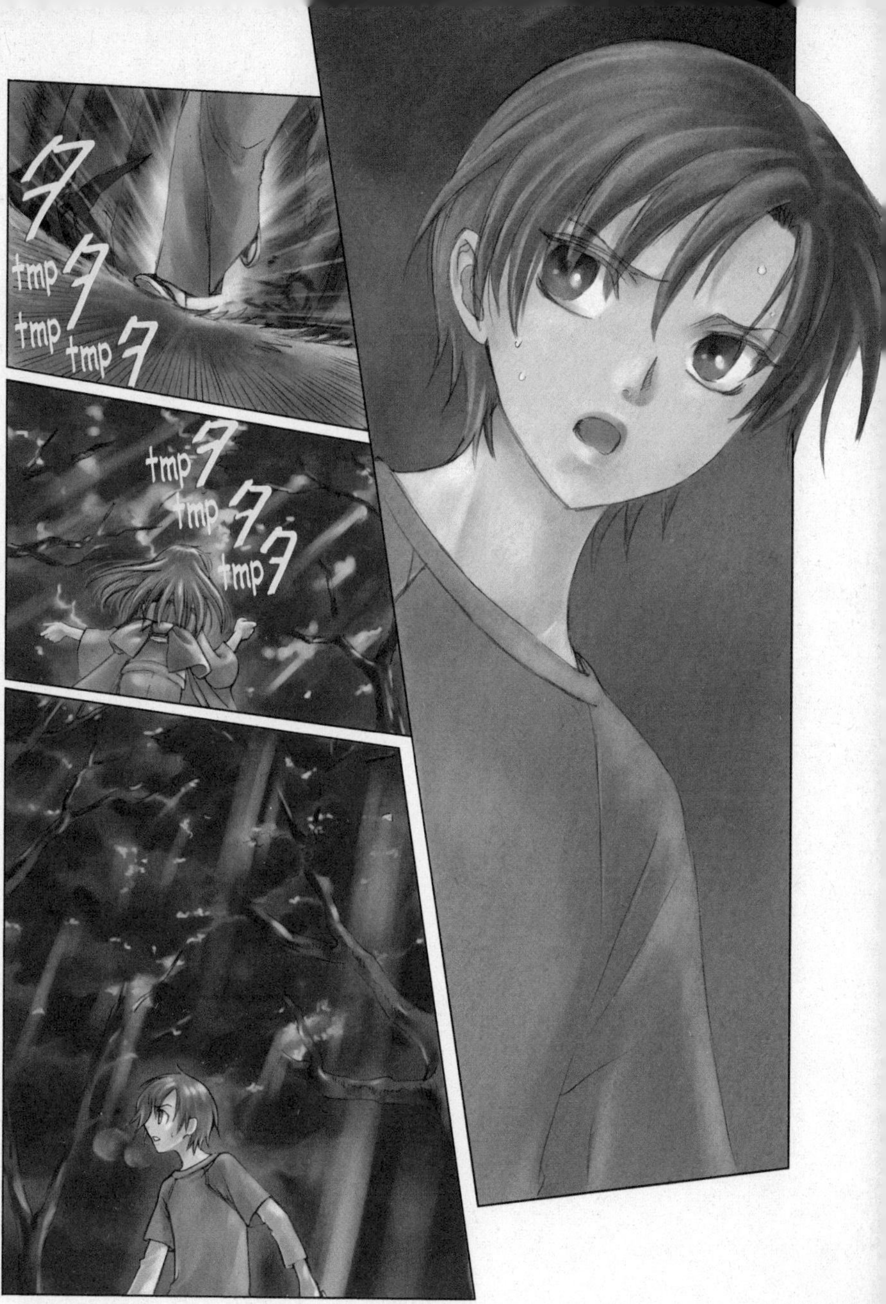
タ
tmp タ
tmp
tmp タ
tmp タ
tmp タ
tmp タ

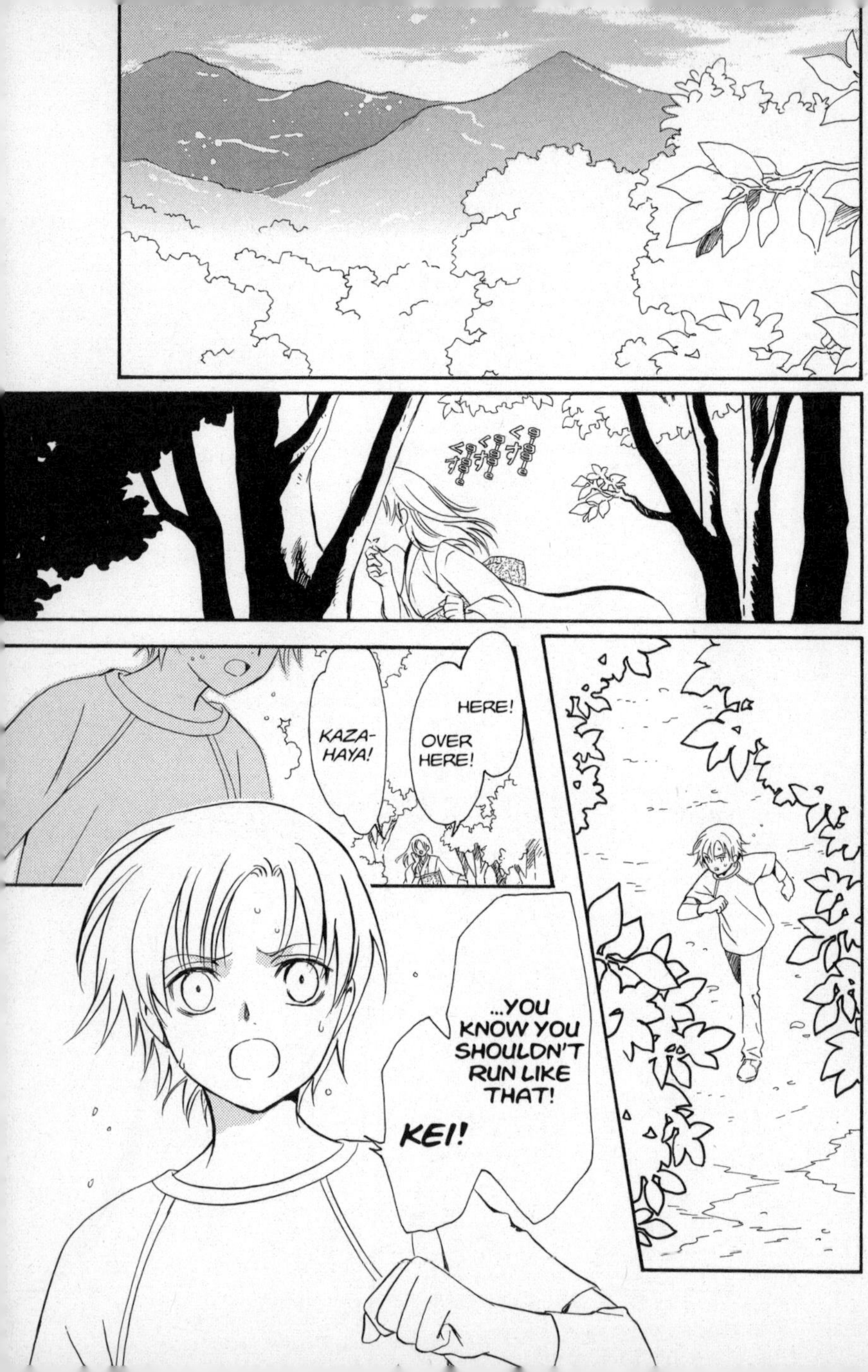
HERE! OVER HERE!
KAZA-HAYA!
...YOU KNOW YOU SHOULDN'T RUN LIKE THAT!
KEI!

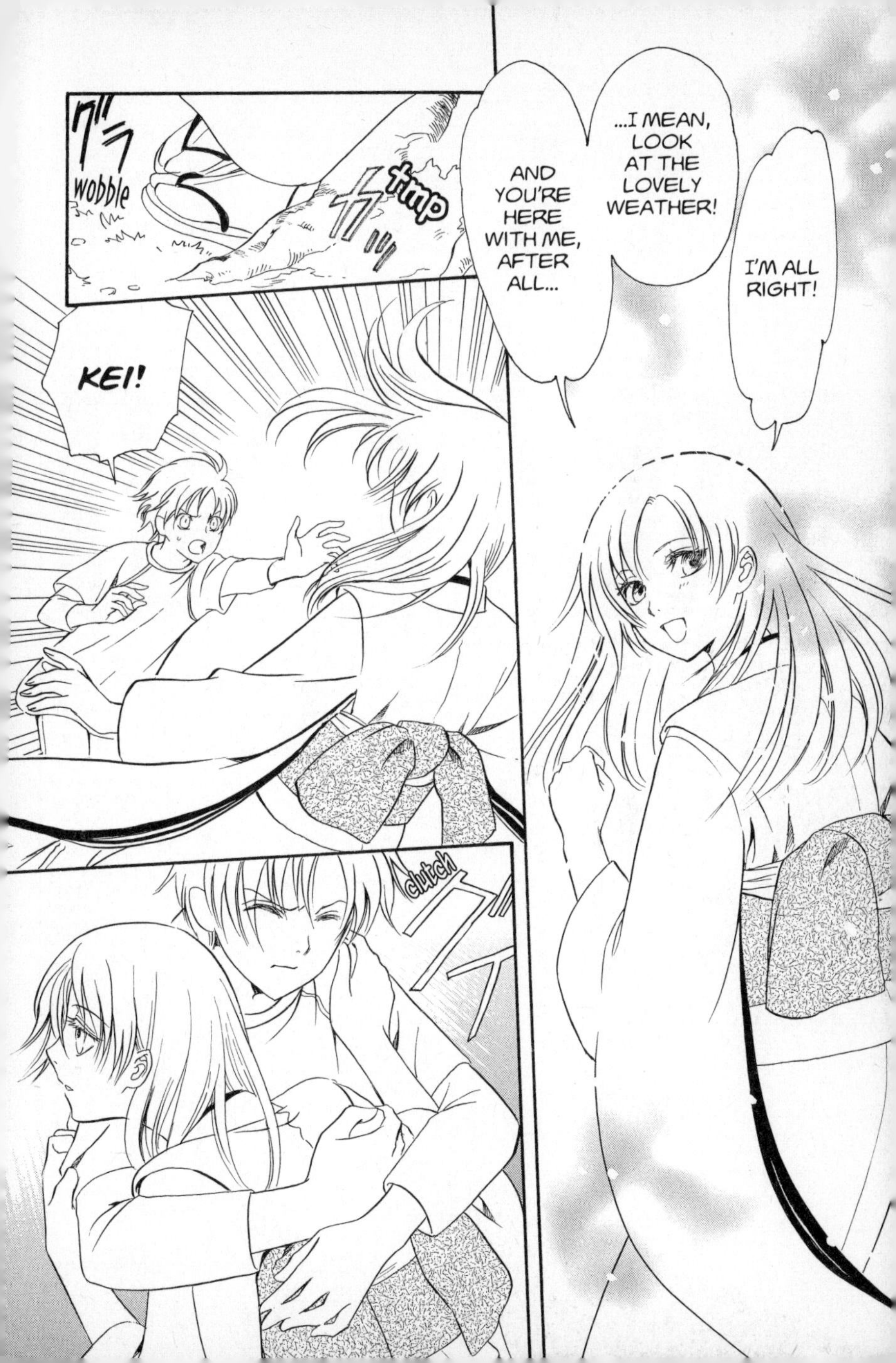
I'M ALL RIGHT!
...I MEAN, LOOK AT THE LOVELY WEATHER!
AND YOU'RE HERE WITH ME, AFTER ALL...
tmp
wobble
KEI!
clutch

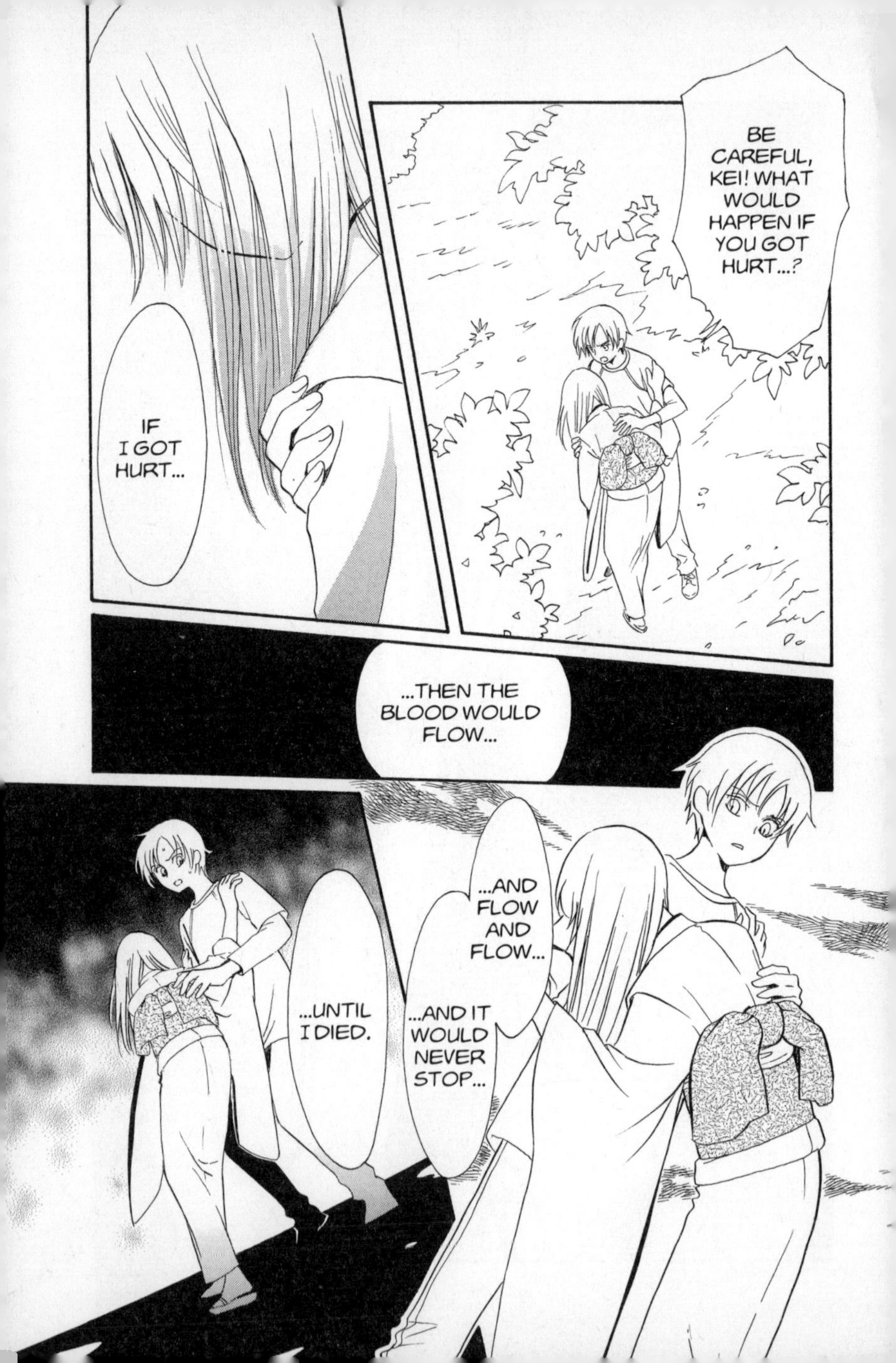
BE CAREFUL, KEI! WHAT WOULD HAPPEN IF YOU GOT HURT...?
IF I GOT HURT...
...THEN THE BLOOD WOULD FLOW...
...AND FLOW AND FLOW...
...AND IT WOULD NEVER STOP...
...UNTIL I DIED.

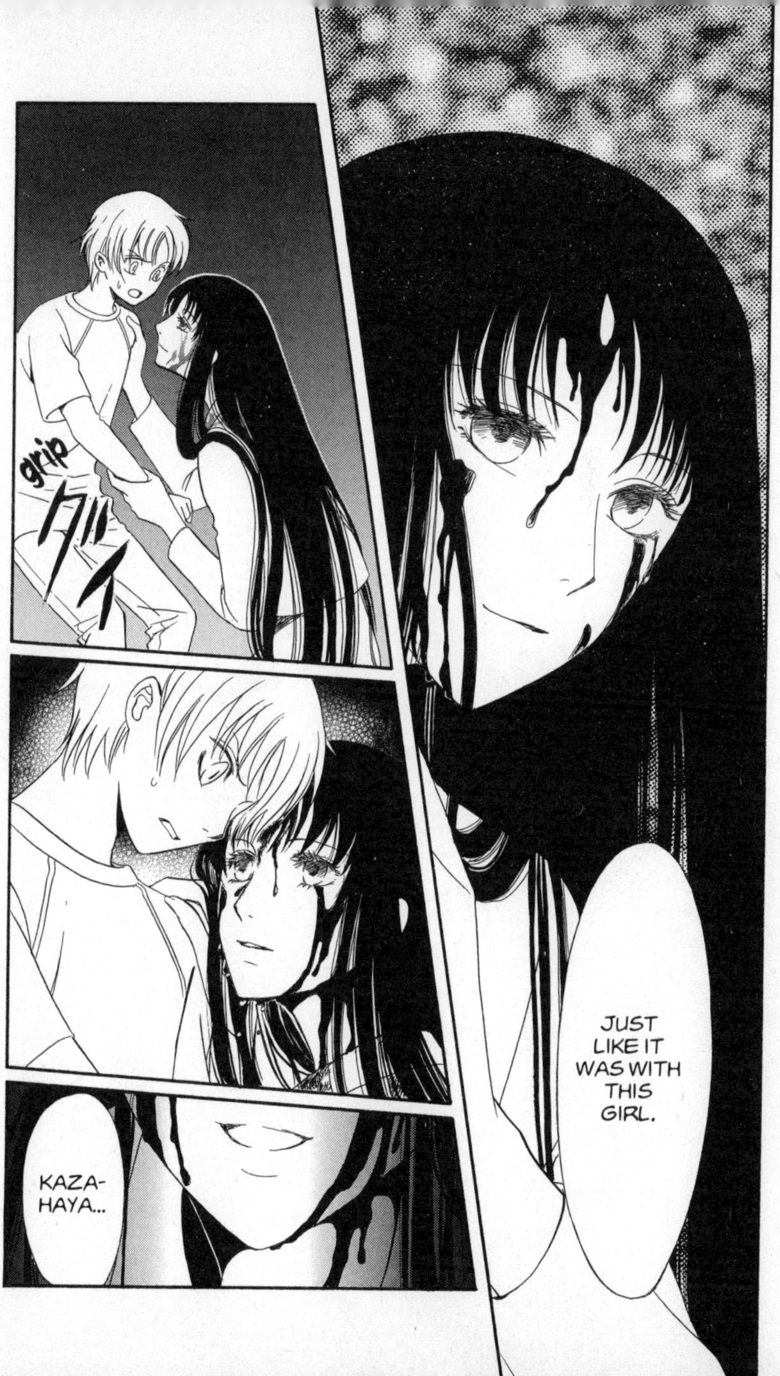
JUST LIKE IT WAS WITH THIS GIRL.
grip
グイ
KAZA-HAYA...

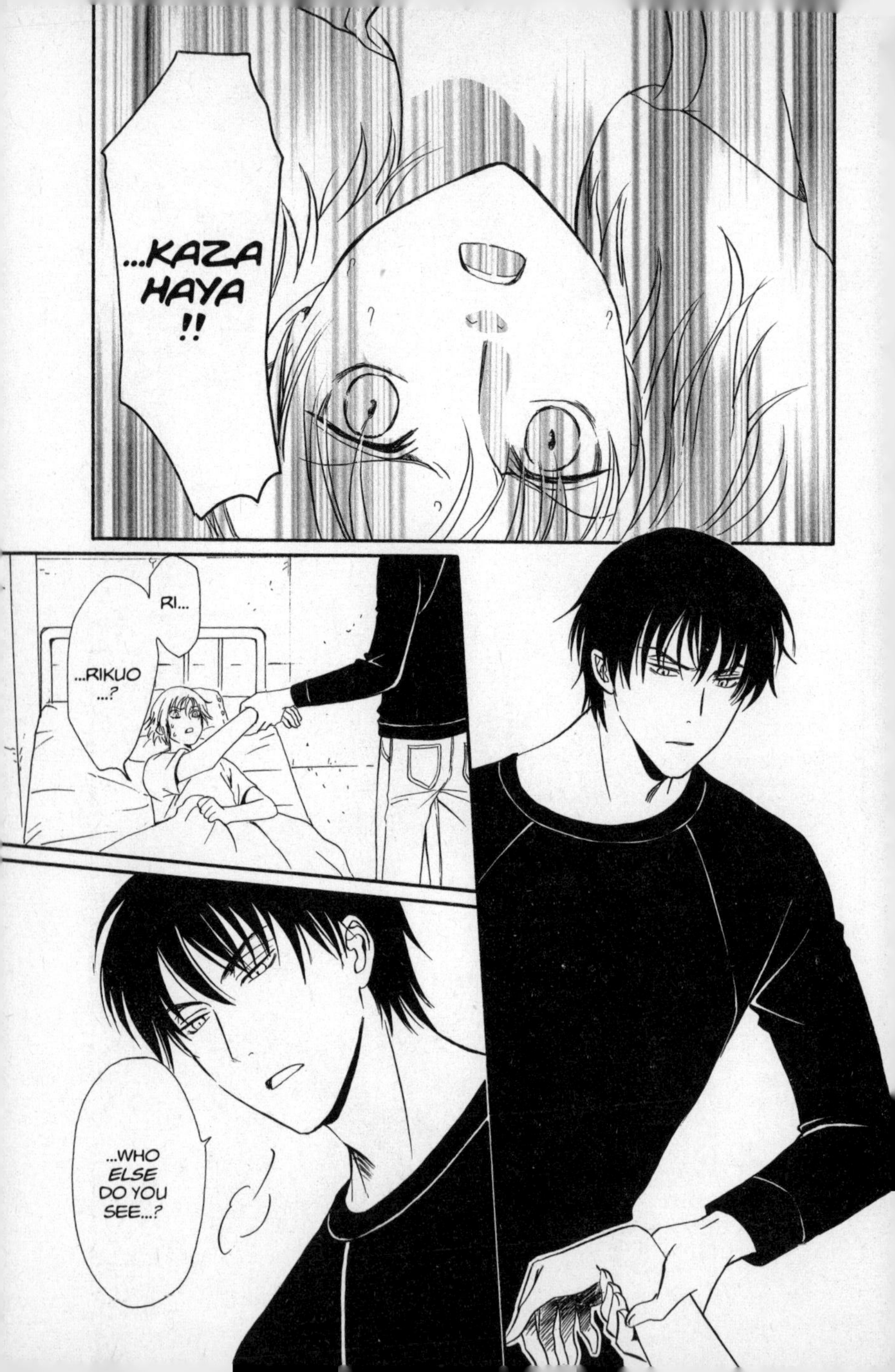
...KAZA HAYA !!
RI...
...RIKUO ...?
...WHO ELSE DO YOU SEE...?

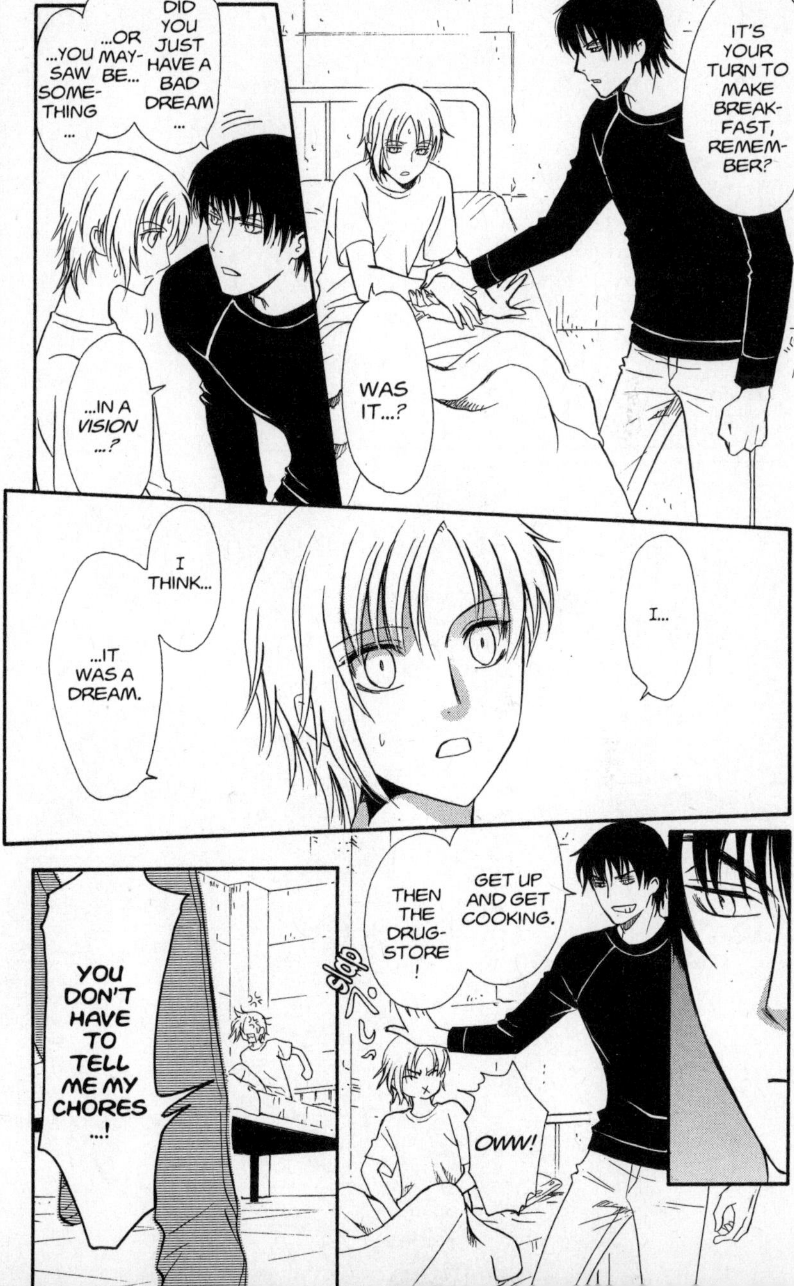

IT'S YOUR TURN TO MAKE BREAKFAST, REMEMBER?
WAS IT...?
DID YOU JUST HAVE A BAD DREAM...
...OR MAYBE...
...YOU SAW SOMETHING...
...IN A VISION...?
I...
I THINK...
...IT WAS A DREAM.
GET UP AND GET COOKING.
THEN THE DRUGSTORE!
slap
OWW!
YOU DON'T HAVE TO TELL ME MY CHORES...!

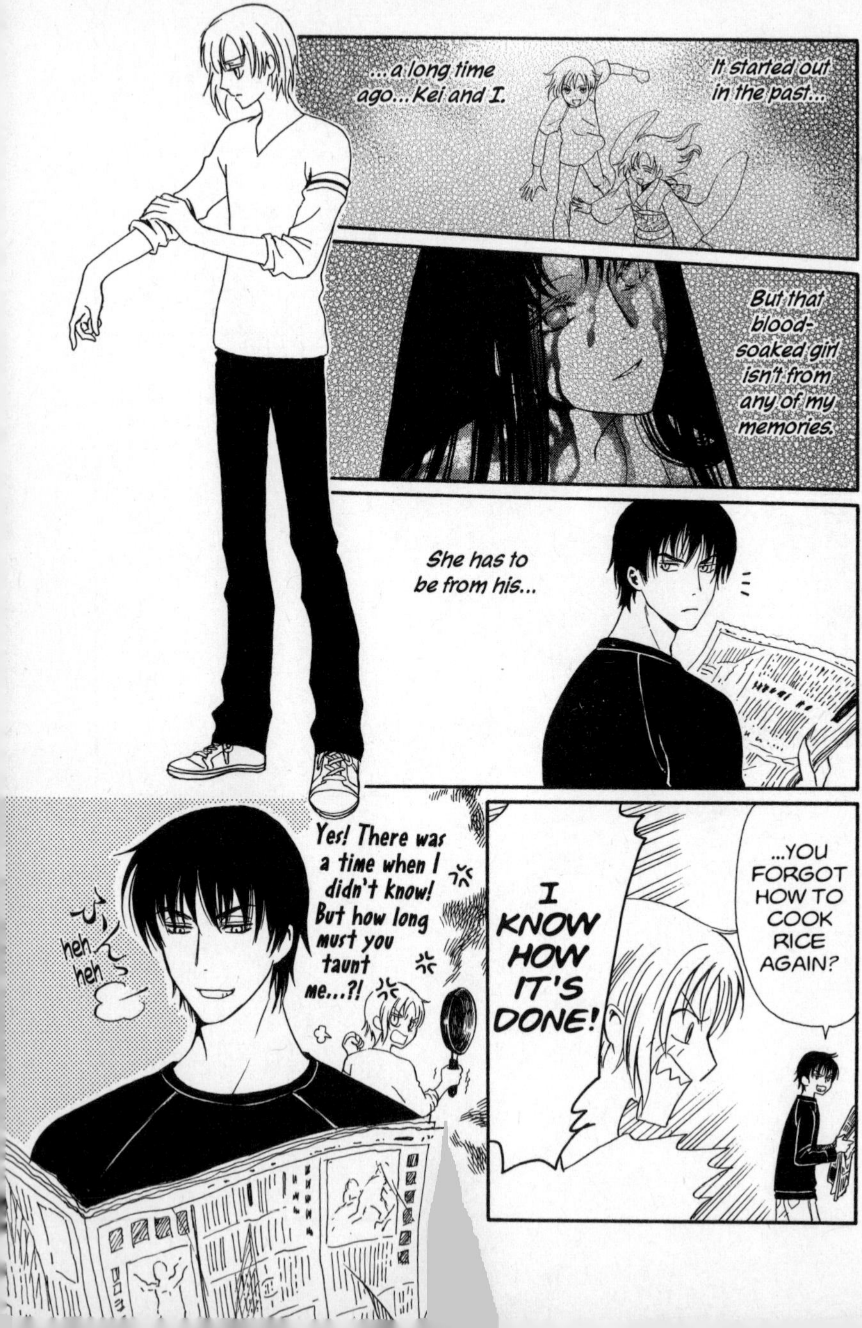
It started out in the past...
...a long time ago...Kei and I.
But that blood-soaked girl isn't from any of my memories.
She has to be from his...
...YOU FORGOT HOW TO COOK RICE AGAIN?
I KNOW HOW IT'S DONE!
Yes! There was a time when I didn't know! But how long must you taunt me...?!
heh heh

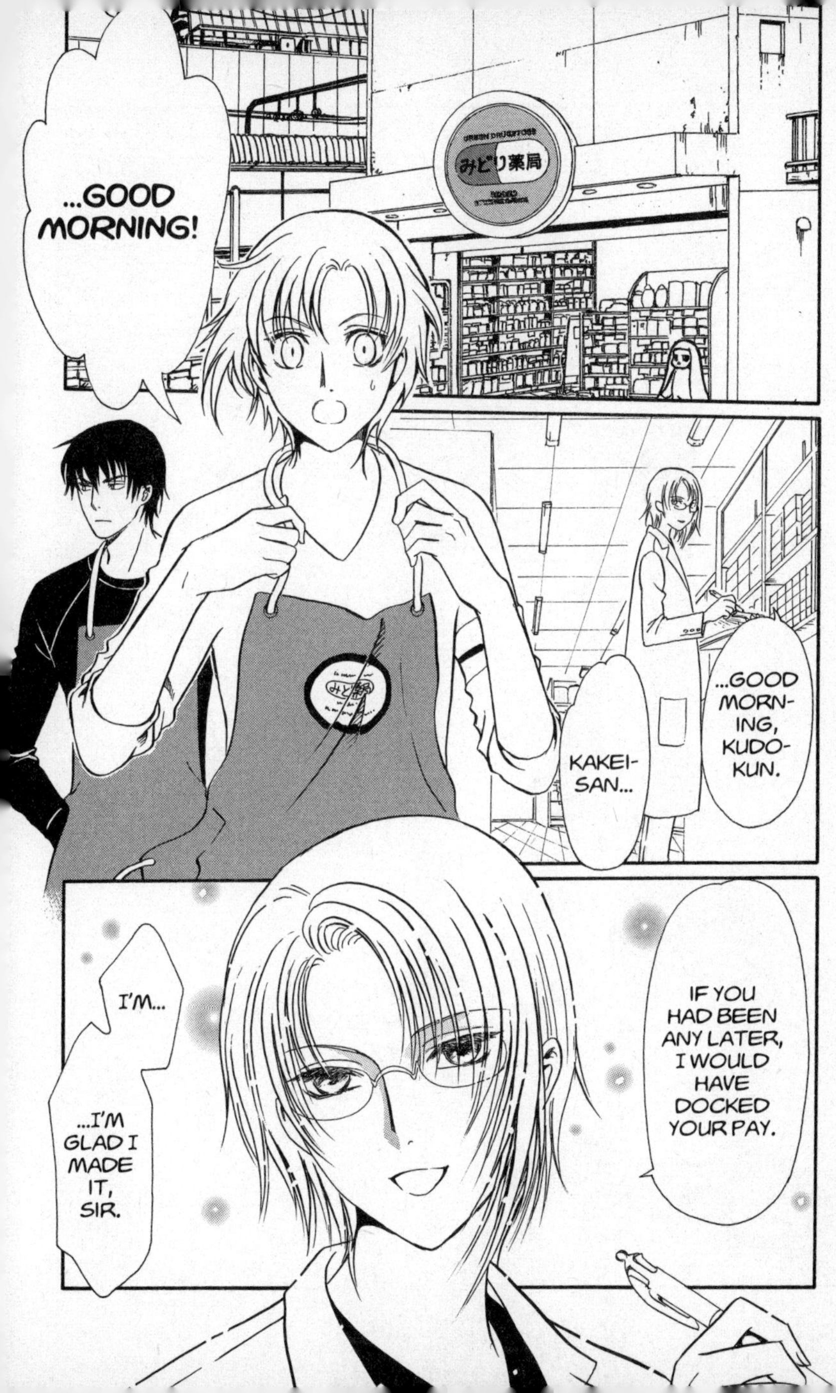
みどり薬局
...GOOD MORNING!
...GOOD MORNING, KUDO-KUN.
KAKEI-SAN...
IF YOU HAD BEEN ANY LATER, I WOULD HAVE DOCKED YOUR PAY.
I'M...
...I'M GLAD I MADE IT, SIR.

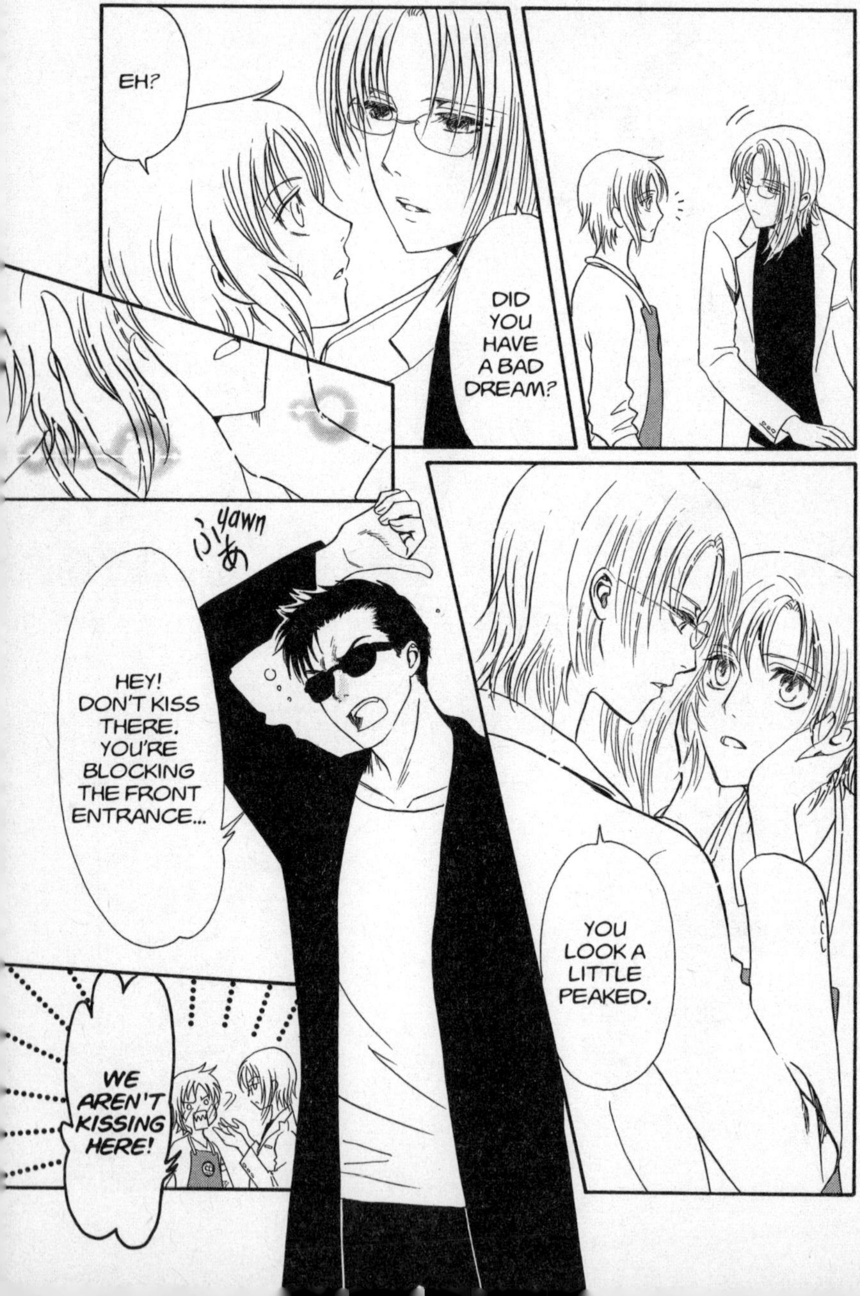
EH?
DID YOU HAVE A BAD DREAM?
YOU LOOK A LITTLE PEAKED.
yawn
ふあ
HEY! DON'T KISS THERE. YOU'RE BLOCKING THE FRONT ENTRANCE...
WE AREN'T KISSING HERE!

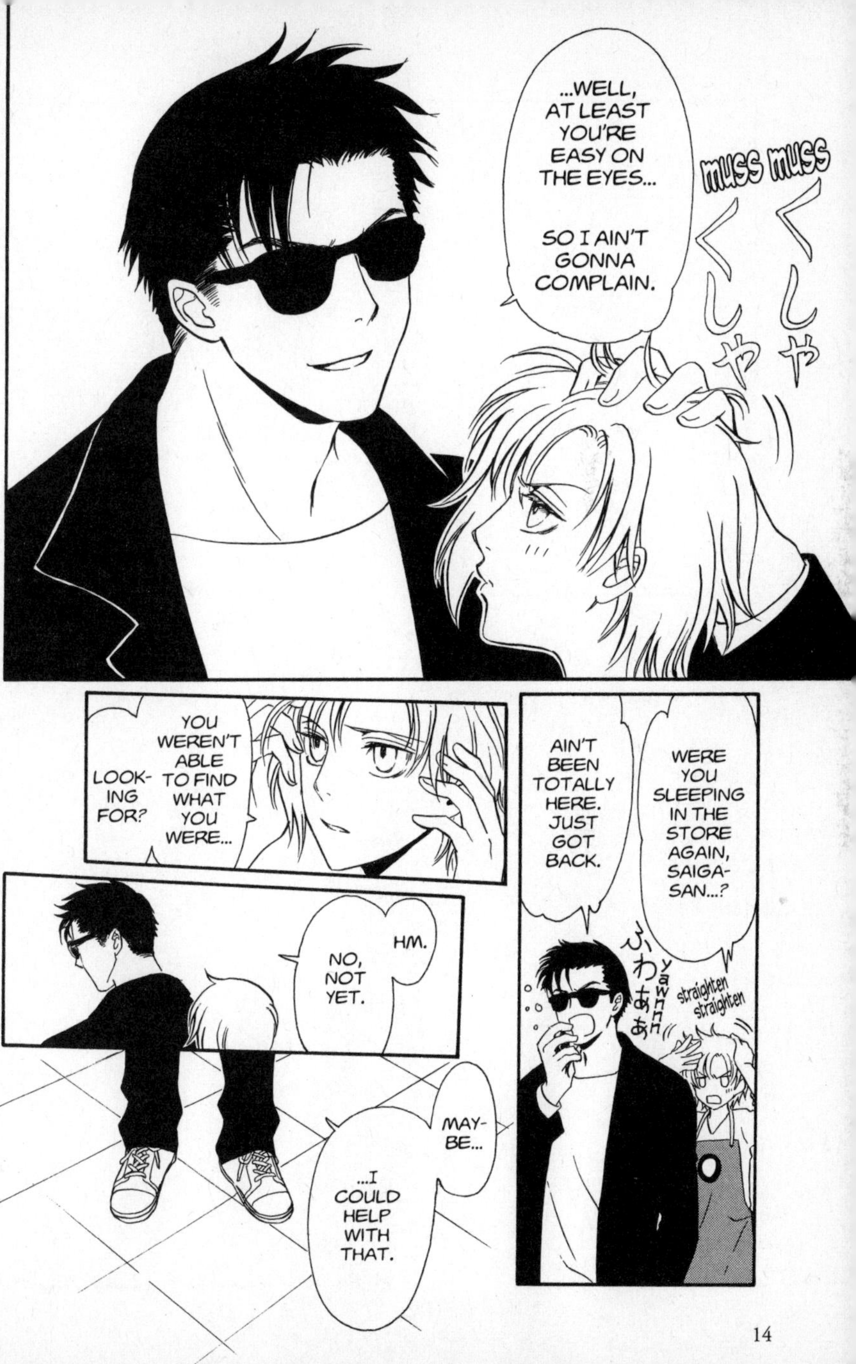
...WELL, AT LEAST YOU'RE EASY ON THE EYES...
SO I AIN'T GONNA COMPLAIN.
muss muss
くしゃくしゃ
WERE YOU SLEEPING IN THE STORE AGAIN, SAIGA-SAN...?
AIN'T BEEN TOTALLY HERE. JUST GOT BACK.
ふわあああ
yawnnn
straighten straighten
YOU WEREN'T ABLE TO FIND WHAT YOU WERE...
LOOK-ING FOR?
HM.
NO, NOT YET.
MAY-BE...
...I COULD HELP WITH THAT.

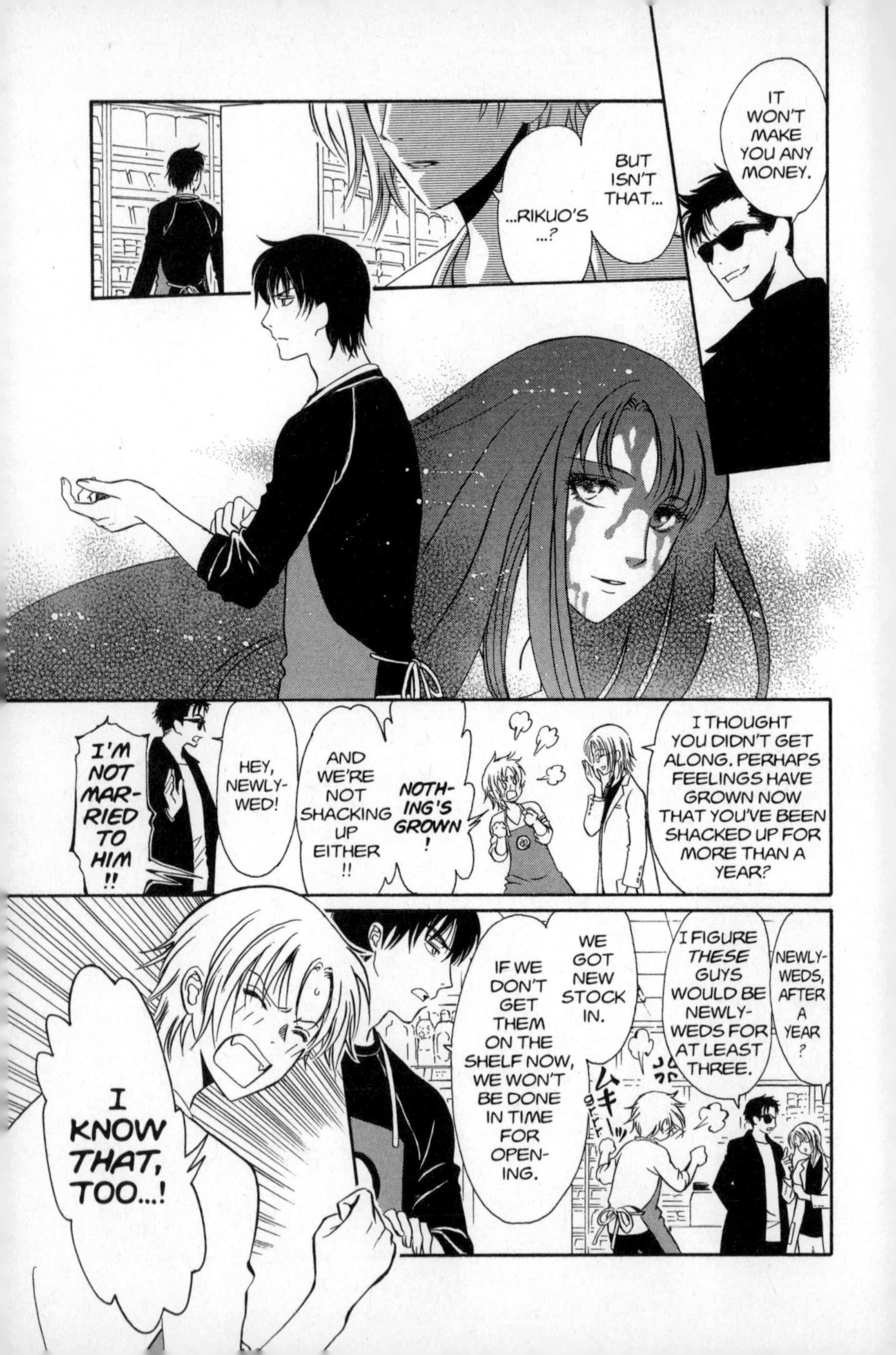
IT WON'T MAKE YOU ANY MONEY.
BUT ISN'T THAT...
...RIKUO'S ...?
I THOUGHT YOU DIDN'T GET ALONG. PERHAPS FEELINGS HAVE GROWN NOW THAT YOU'VE BEEN SHACKED UP FOR MORE THAN A YEAR?
NOTHING'S GROWN!
AND WE'RE NOT SHACKING UP EITHER!!
HEY, NEWLYWED!
I'M NOT MARRIED TO HIM!!
NEWLYWEDS, AFTER A YEAR?
I FIGURE *THESE* GUYS WOULD BE NEWLYWEDS FOR AT LEAST THREE.
ムキーッ
WE GOT NEW STOCK IN.
IF WE DON'T GET THEM ON THE SHELF NOW, WE WON'T BE DONE IN TIME FOR OPENING.
I KNOW THAT, TOO...!

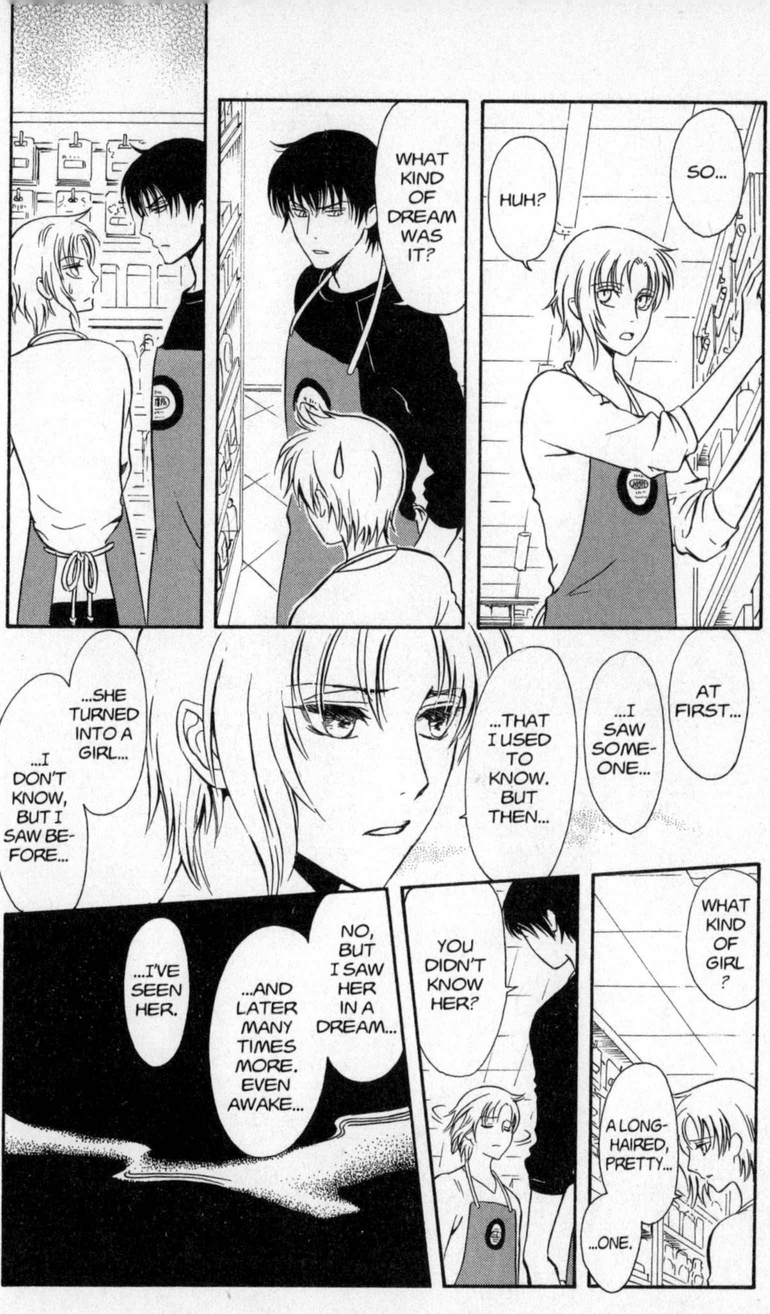
SO...
HUH?
WHAT KIND OF DREAM WAS IT?
AT FIRST...
...I SAW SOME-ONE...
...THAT I USED TO KNOW. BUT THEN...
...SHE TURNED INTO A GIRL...
...I DON'T KNOW, BUT I SAW BE-FORE...
WHAT KIND OF GIRL?
A LONG-HAIRED, PRETTY...
...ONE.
YOU DIDN'T KNOW HER?
NO, BUT I SAW HER IN A DREAM...
...AND LATER MANY TIMES MORE. EVEN AWAKE...
...I'VE SEEN HER.

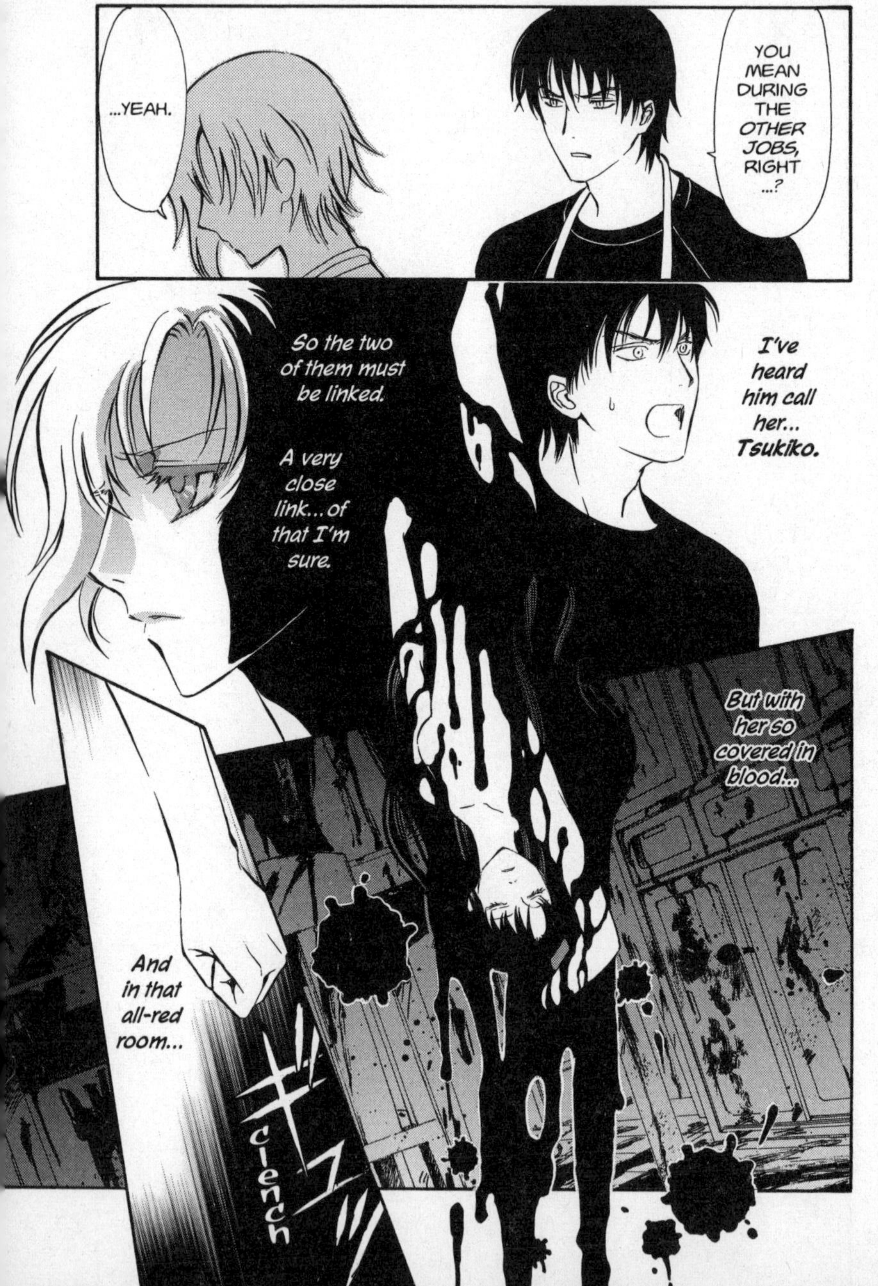
YOU MEAN DURING THE OTHER JOBS, RIGHT ...?
...YEAH.
I've heard him call her... Tsukiko.
So the two of them must be linked.
A very close link... of that I'm sure.
But with her so covered in blood...
And in that all-red room...
clench

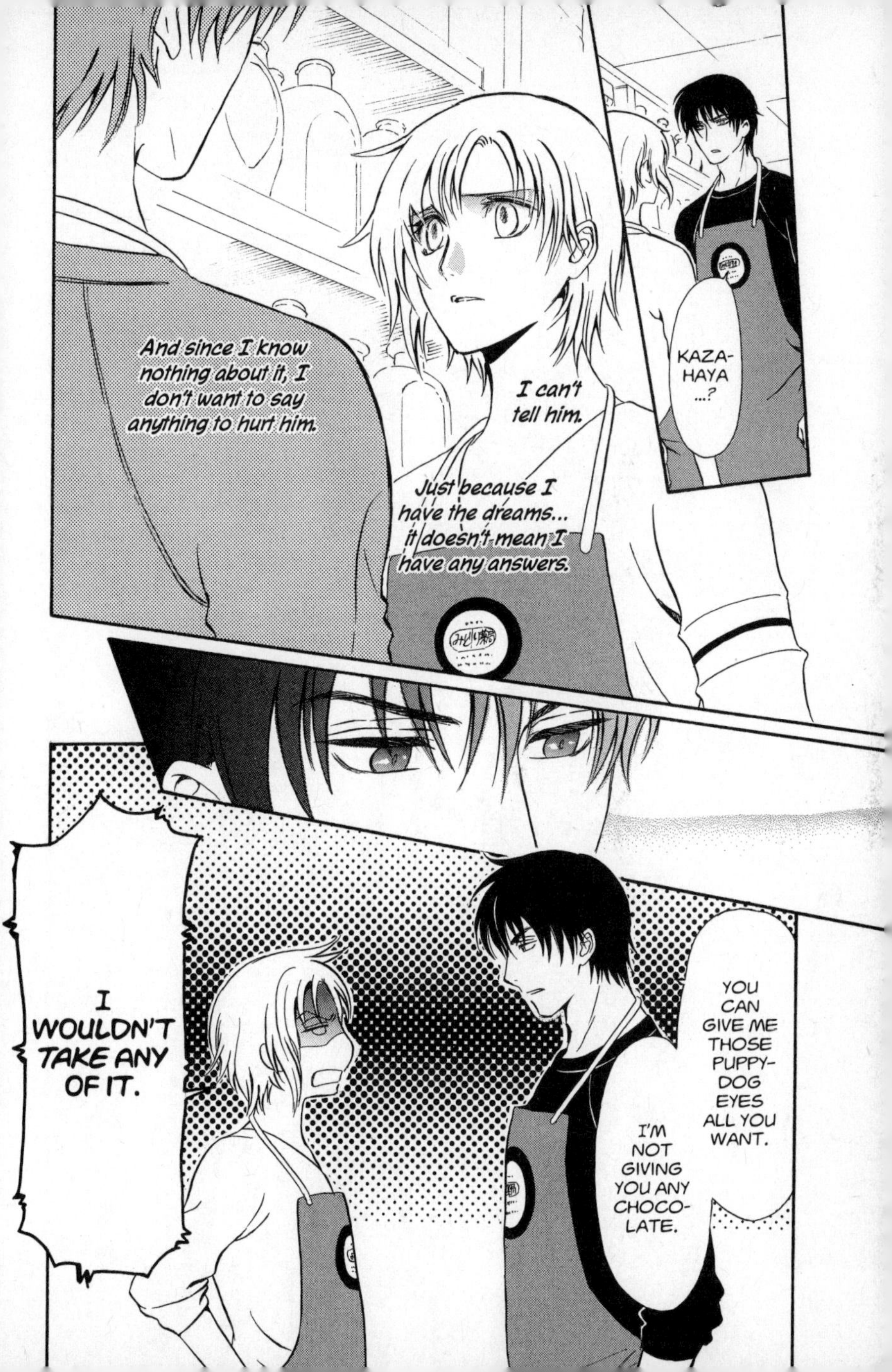
KAZA-HAYA ...?
I can't tell him.
Just because I have the dreams... it doesn't mean I have any answers.
And since I know nothing about it, I don't want to say anything to hurt him.
YOU CAN GIVE ME THOSE PUPPY-DOG EYES ALL YOU WANT.
I'M NOT GIVING YOU ANY CHOCO-LATE.
I WOULDN'T TAKE ANY OF IT.

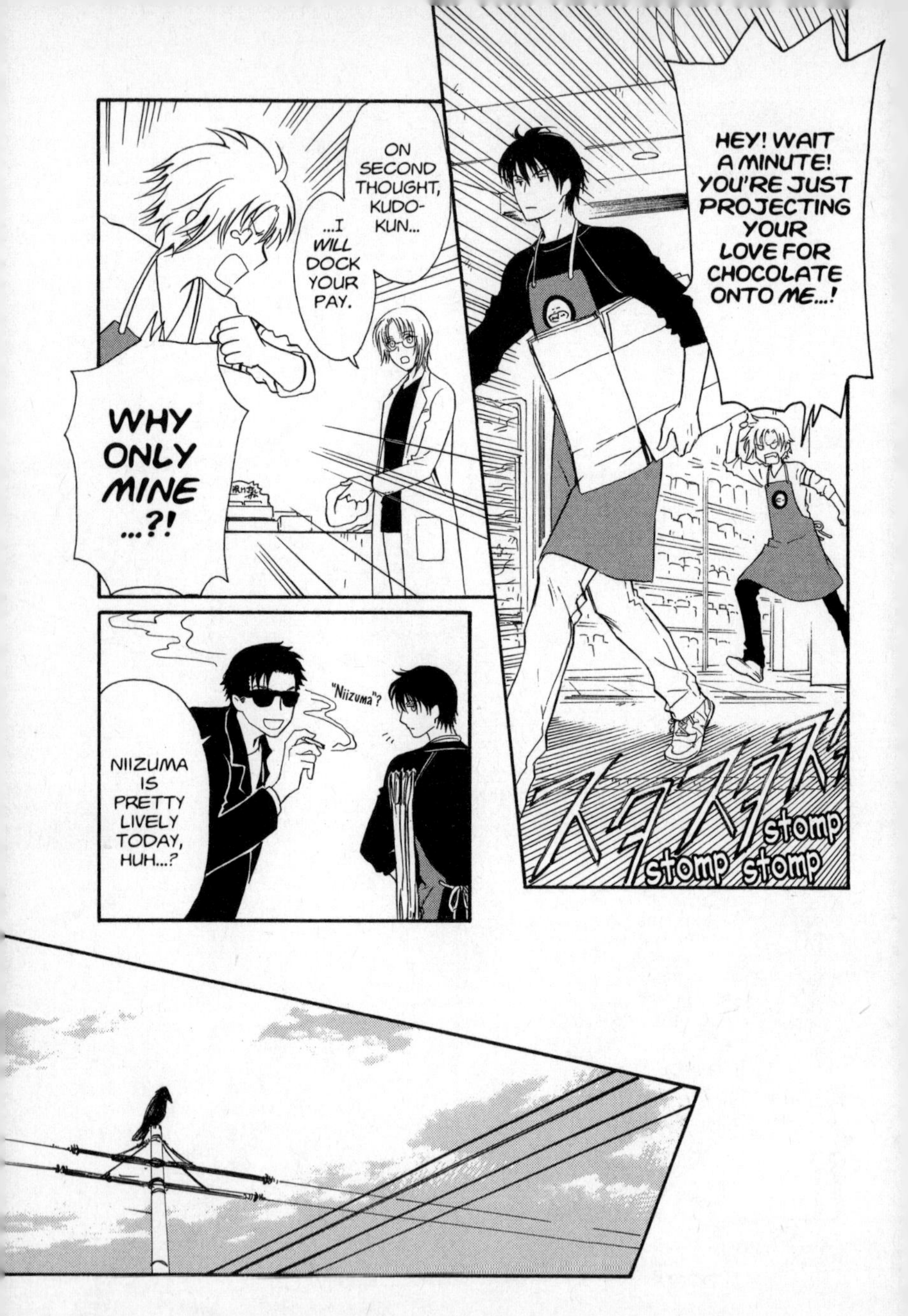
HEY! WAIT A MINUTE! YOU'RE JUST PROJECTING YOUR LOVE FOR CHOCOLATE ONTO ME...!
stomp stomp stomp
ON SECOND THOUGHT, KUDO-KUN...
...I WILL DOCK YOUR PAY.
WHY ONLY MINE ...?!
"Niizuma"?
NIIZUMA IS PRETTY LIVELY TODAY, HUH...?

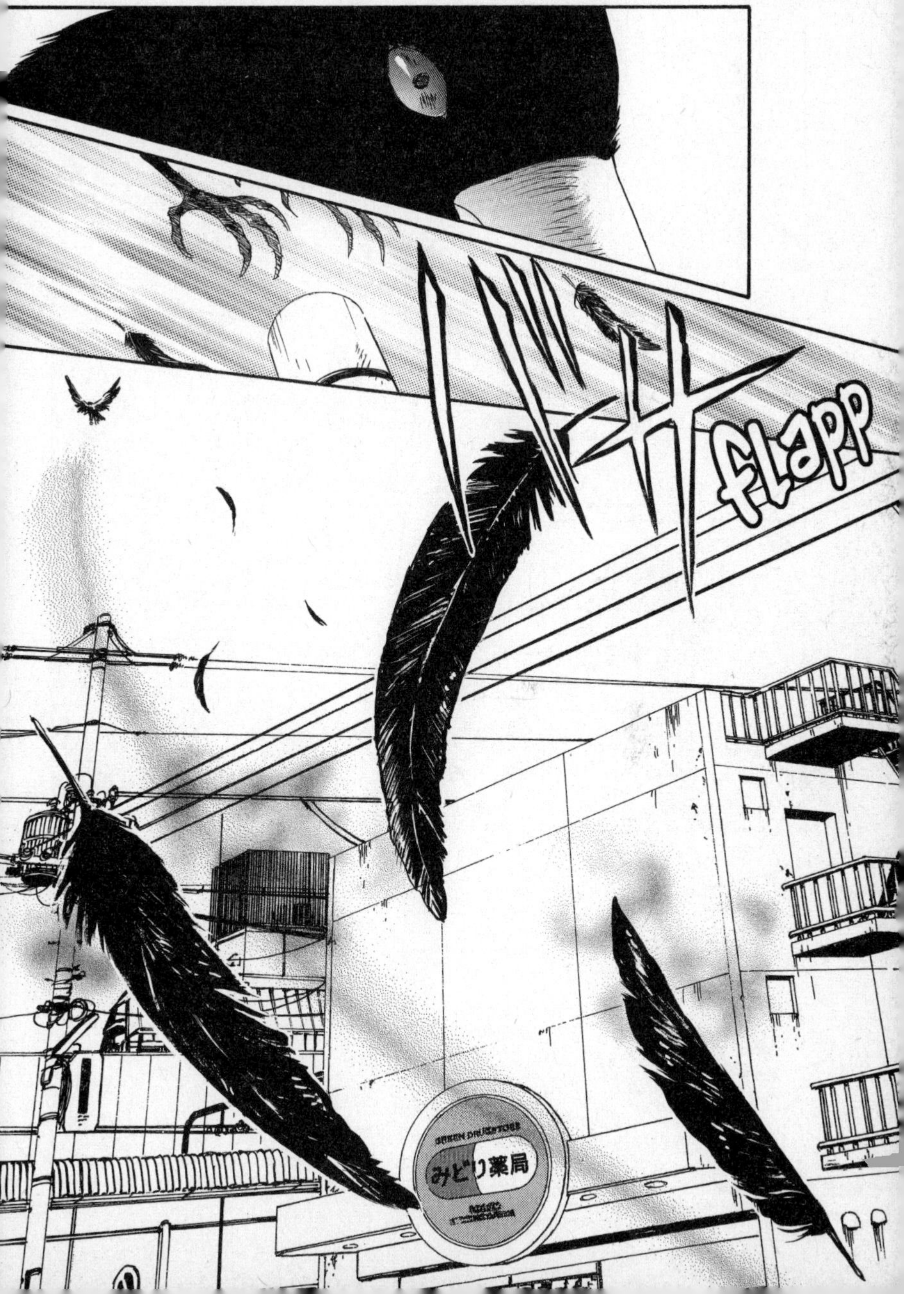
flapp
みどり薬局

DRUG
& DROP

a drugstore with medicine and a danger

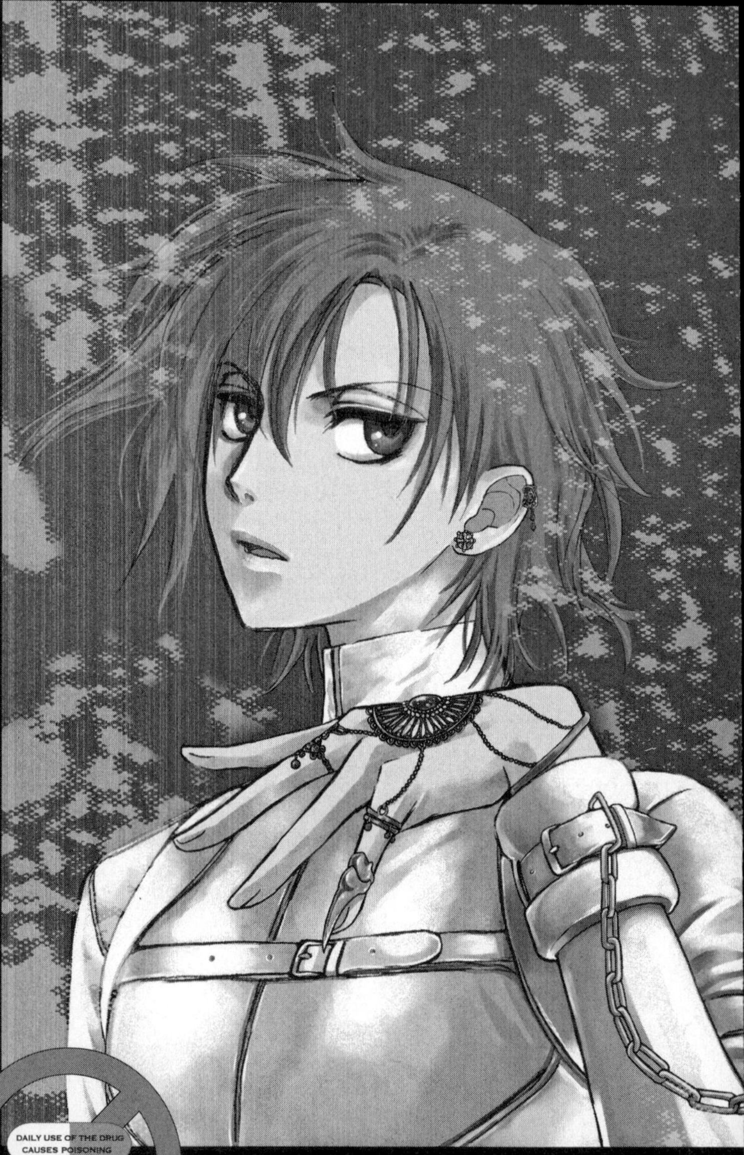

DAILY USE OF THE DRUG
CAUSES POISONING

DRUG & DRØP

Daily use of the drug causes poisoning.

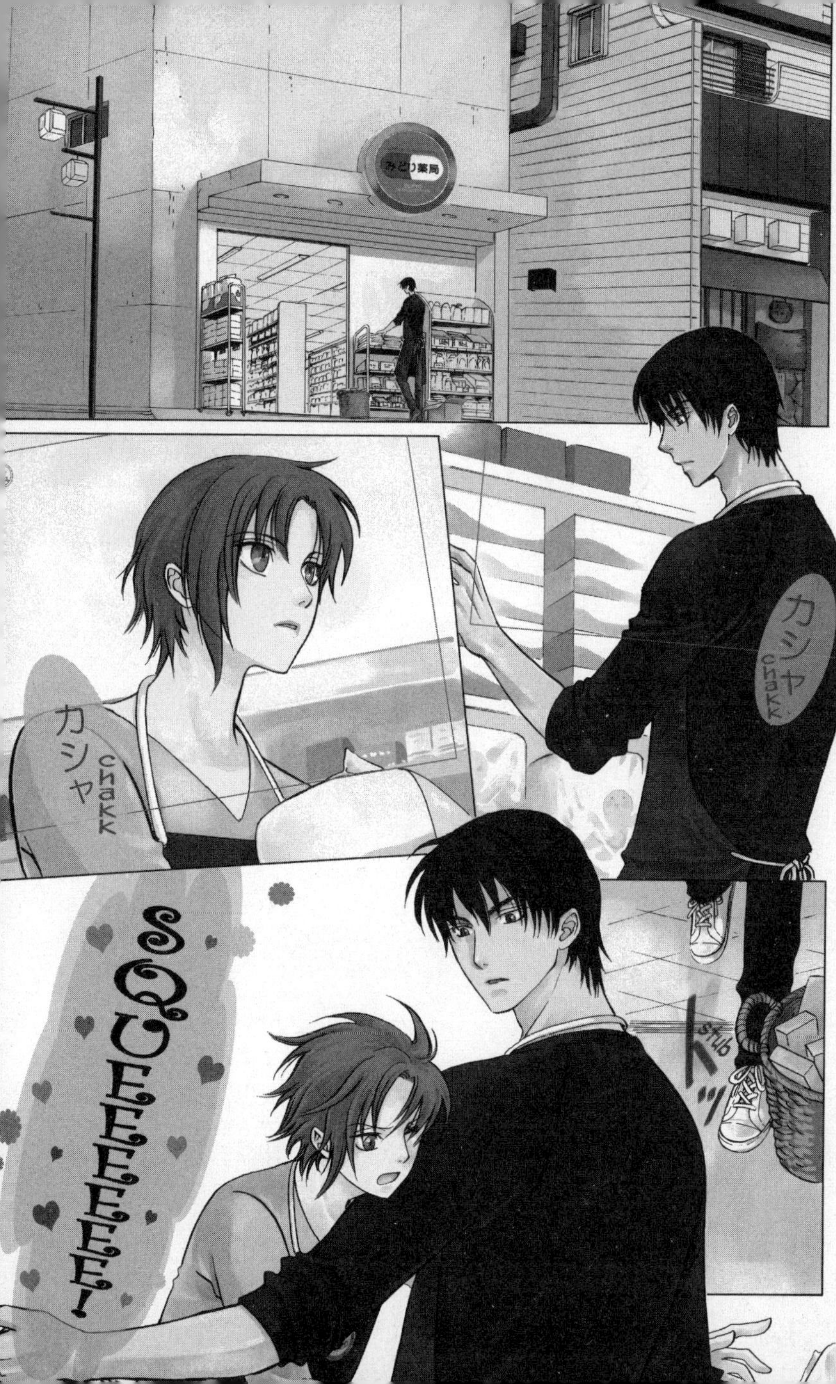
みどり薬局
カシャ
chakk
カシャ
chakk
ドッ
stub
SQUEEEEEEE!

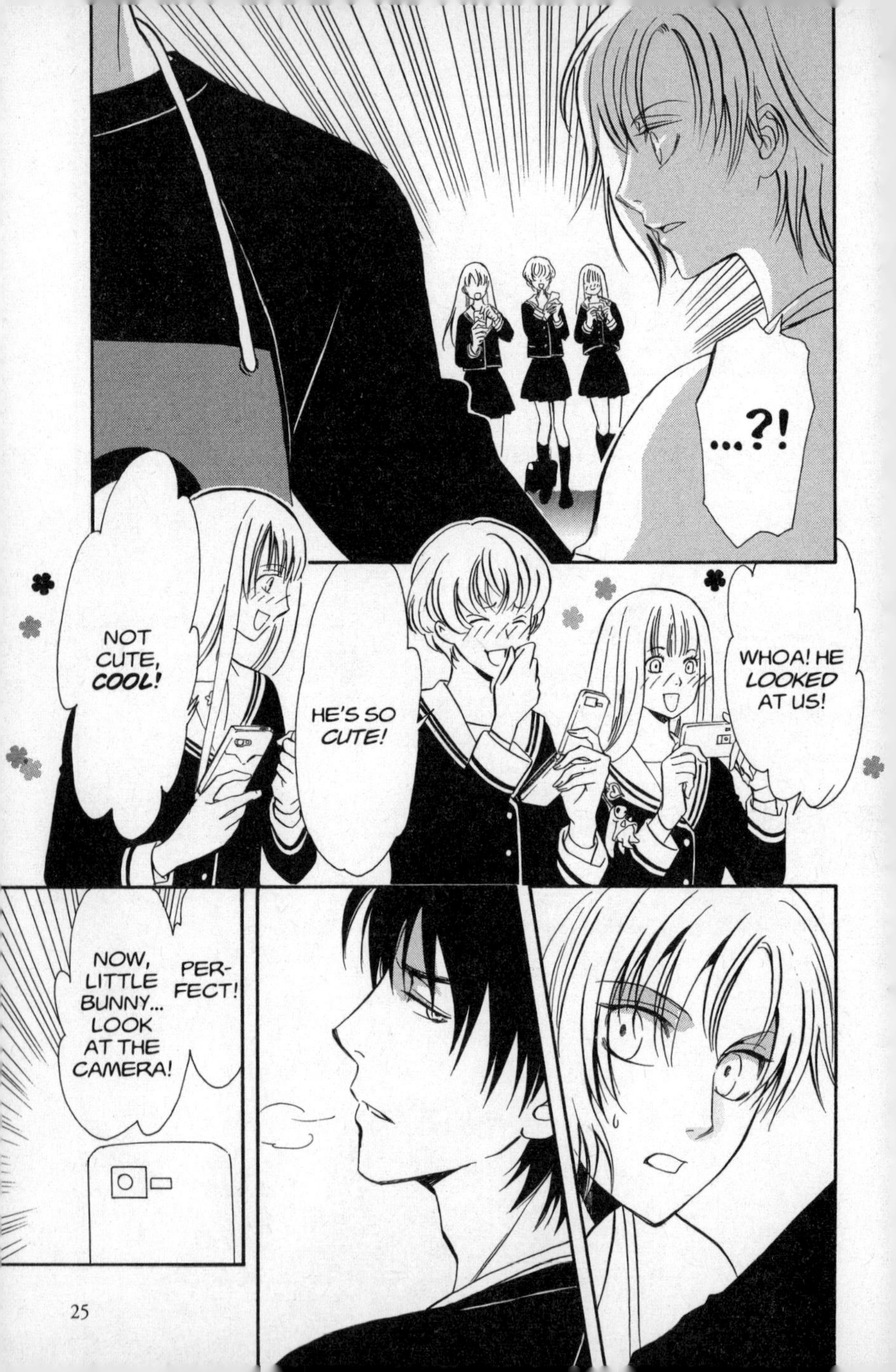
...?!
WHOA! HE LOOKED AT US!
HE'S SO CUTE!
NOT CUTE, COOL!
PER-FECT!
NOW, LITTLE BUNNY... LOOK AT THE CAMERA!

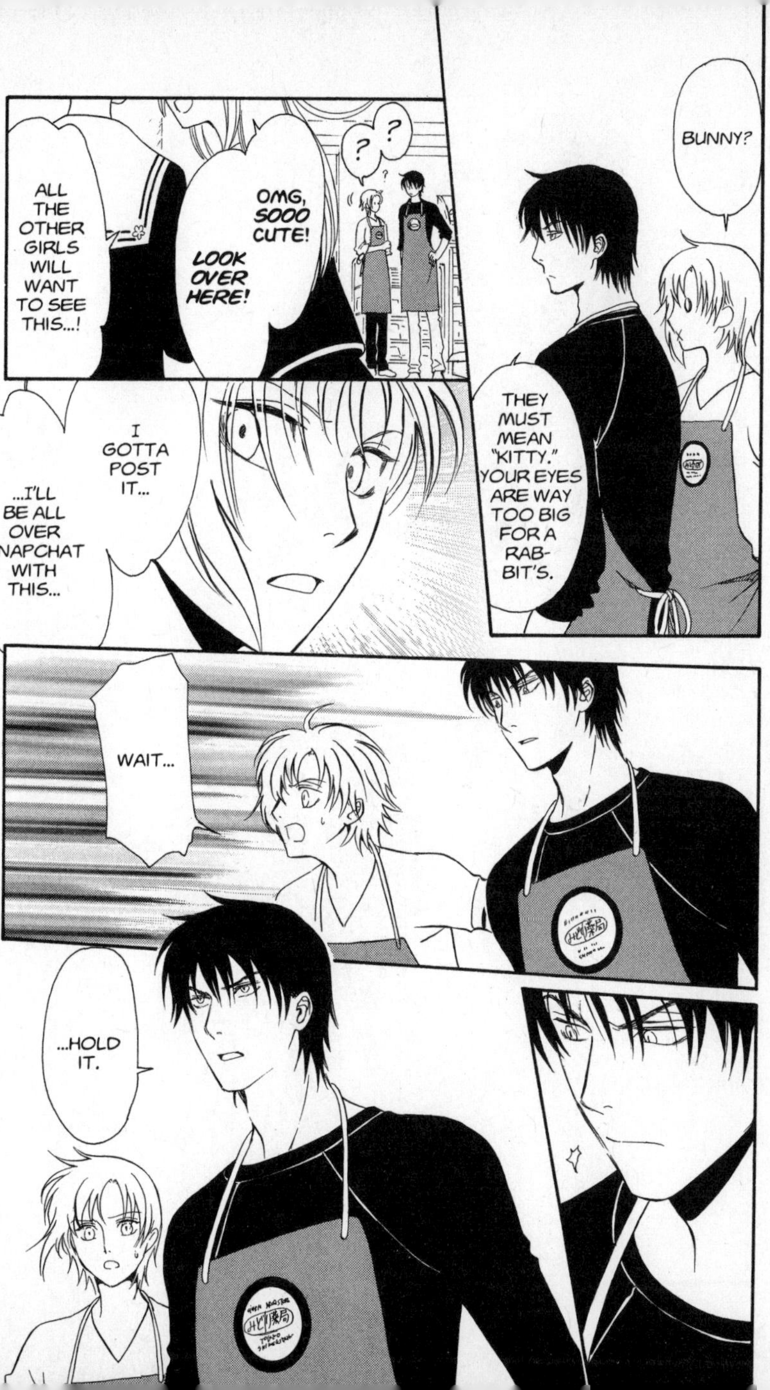
BUNNY?
THEY MUST MEAN "KITTY." YOUR EYES ARE WAY TOO BIG FOR A RAB-BIT'S.
? ?
OMG, SOOO CUTE!
LOOK OVER HERE!
ALL THE OTHER GIRLS WILL WANT TO SEE THIS...!
I GOTTA POST IT...
...I'LL BE ALL OVER SNAPCHAT WITH THIS...
WAIT...
...HOLD IT.

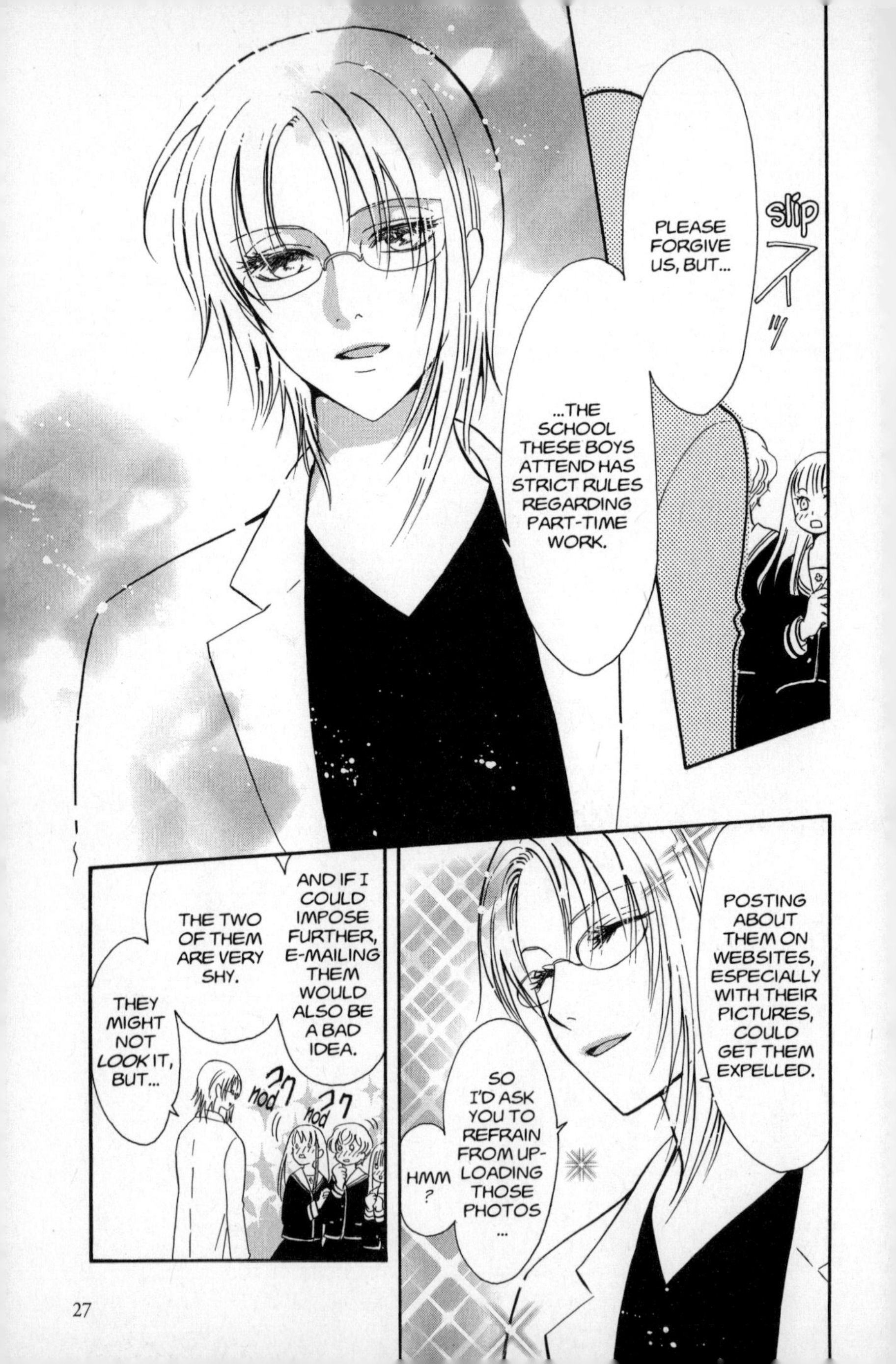

PLEASE FORGIVE US, BUT...
slip
スッ
...THE SCHOOL THESE BOYS ATTEND HAS STRICT RULES REGARDING PART-TIME WORK.
POSTING ABOUT THEM ON WEBSITES, ESPECIALLY WITH THEIR PICTURES, COULD GET THEM EXPELLED.
SO I'D ASK YOU TO REFRAIN FROM UP-LOADING THOSE PHOTOS ...
HMM ?
AND IF I COULD IMPOSE FURTHER, E-MAILING THEM WOULD ALSO BE A BAD IDEA.
THE TWO OF THEM ARE VERY SHY.
THEY MIGHT NOT *LOOK* IT, BUT...
nod
nod

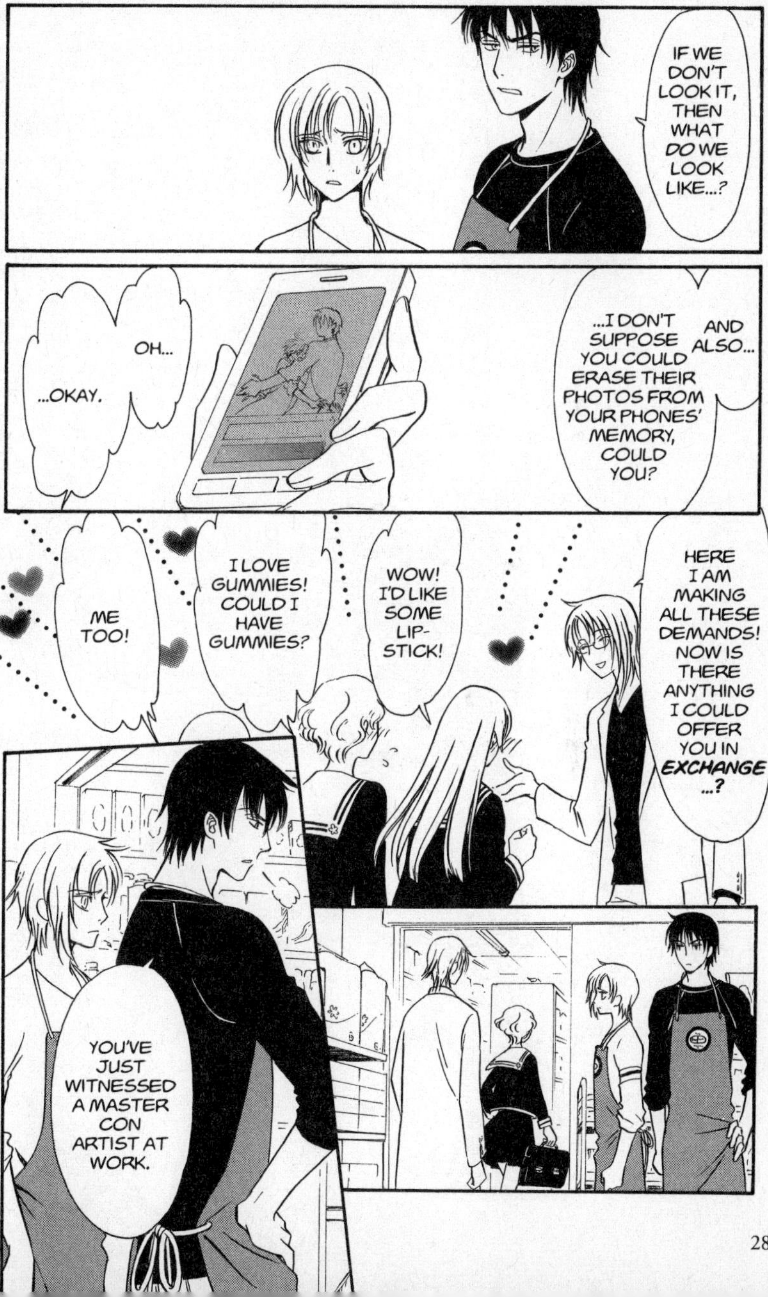
IF WE DON'T LOOK IT, THEN WHAT DO WE LOOK LIKE...?
AND ALSO...
...I DON'T SUPPOSE YOU COULD ERASE THEIR PHOTOS FROM YOUR PHONES' MEMORY, COULD YOU?
OH...
...OKAY.
HERE I AM MAKING ALL THESE DEMANDS! NOW IS THERE ANYTHING I COULD OFFER YOU IN EXCHANGE...?
WOW! I'D LIKE SOME LIP-STICK!
I LOVE GUMMIES! COULD I HAVE GUMMIES?
ME TOO!
YOU'VE JUST WITNESSED A MASTER CON ARTIST AT WORK.

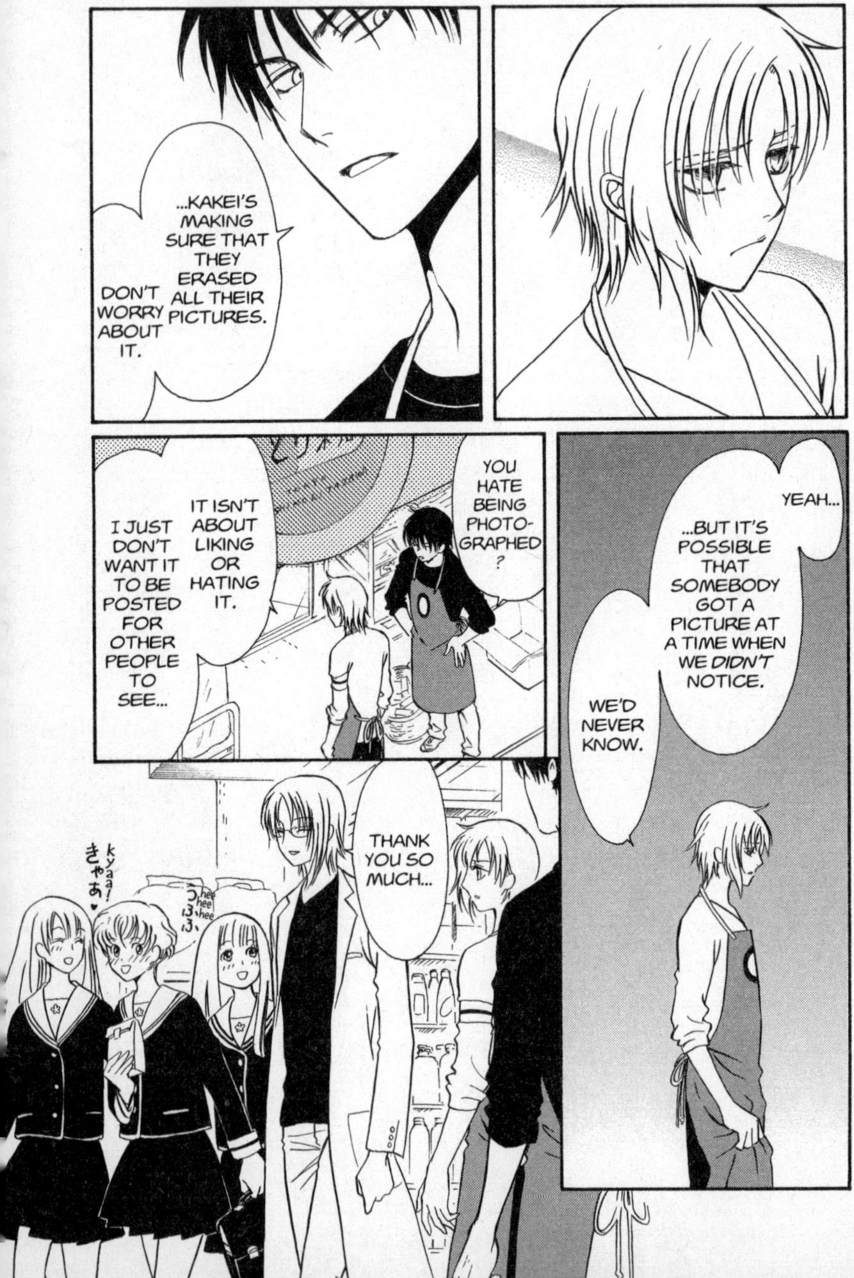
...KAKEI'S MAKING SURE THAT THEY ERASED ALL THEIR PICTURES.
DON'T WORRY ABOUT IT.
YEAH...
...BUT IT'S POSSIBLE THAT SOMEBODY GOT A PICTURE AT A TIME WHEN WE *DIDN'T* NOTICE.
WE'D NEVER KNOW.
YOU HATE BEING PHOTOGRAPHED?
IT ISN'T ABOUT LIKING OR HATING IT.
I JUST DON'T WANT IT TO BE POSTED FOR OTHER PEOPLE TO SEE...
THANK YOU SO MUCH...
ふふ hee hee hee
きゃあ kyaa!

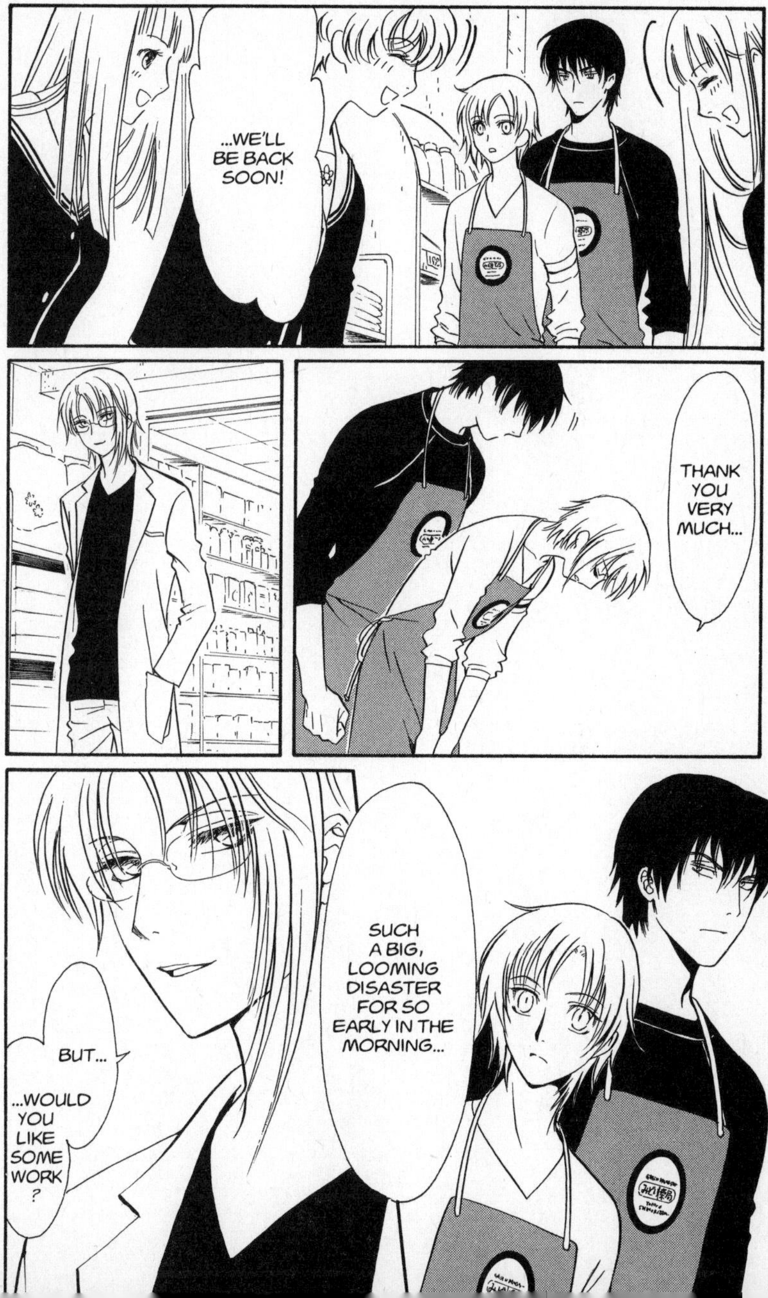
...WE'LL BE BACK SOON!
THANK YOU VERY MUCH...
SUCH A BIG, LOOMING DISASTER FOR SO EARLY IN THE MORNING...
BUT...
...WOULD YOU LIKE SOME WORK?

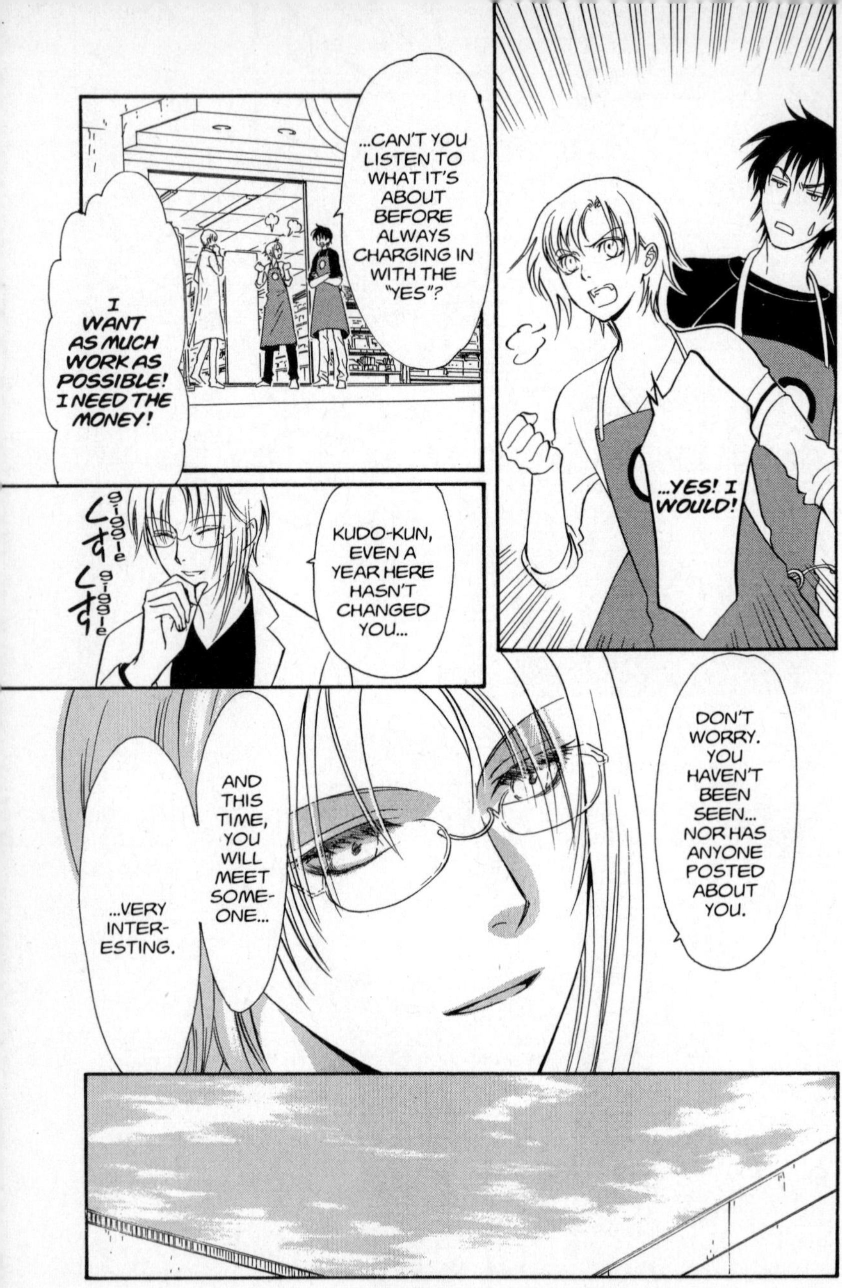
...YES! I WOULD!
...CAN'T YOU LISTEN TO WHAT IT'S ABOUT BEFORE ALWAYS CHARGING IN WITH THE "YES"?
I WANT AS MUCH WORK AS POSSIBLE! I NEED THE MONEY!
KUDO-KUN, EVEN A YEAR HERE HASN'T CHANGED YOU...
くす giggle
くす giggle
DON'T WORRY. YOU HAVEN'T BEEN SEEN... NOR HAS ANYONE POSTED ABOUT YOU.
AND THIS TIME, YOU WILL MEET SOME-ONE...
...VERY INTER-ESTING.

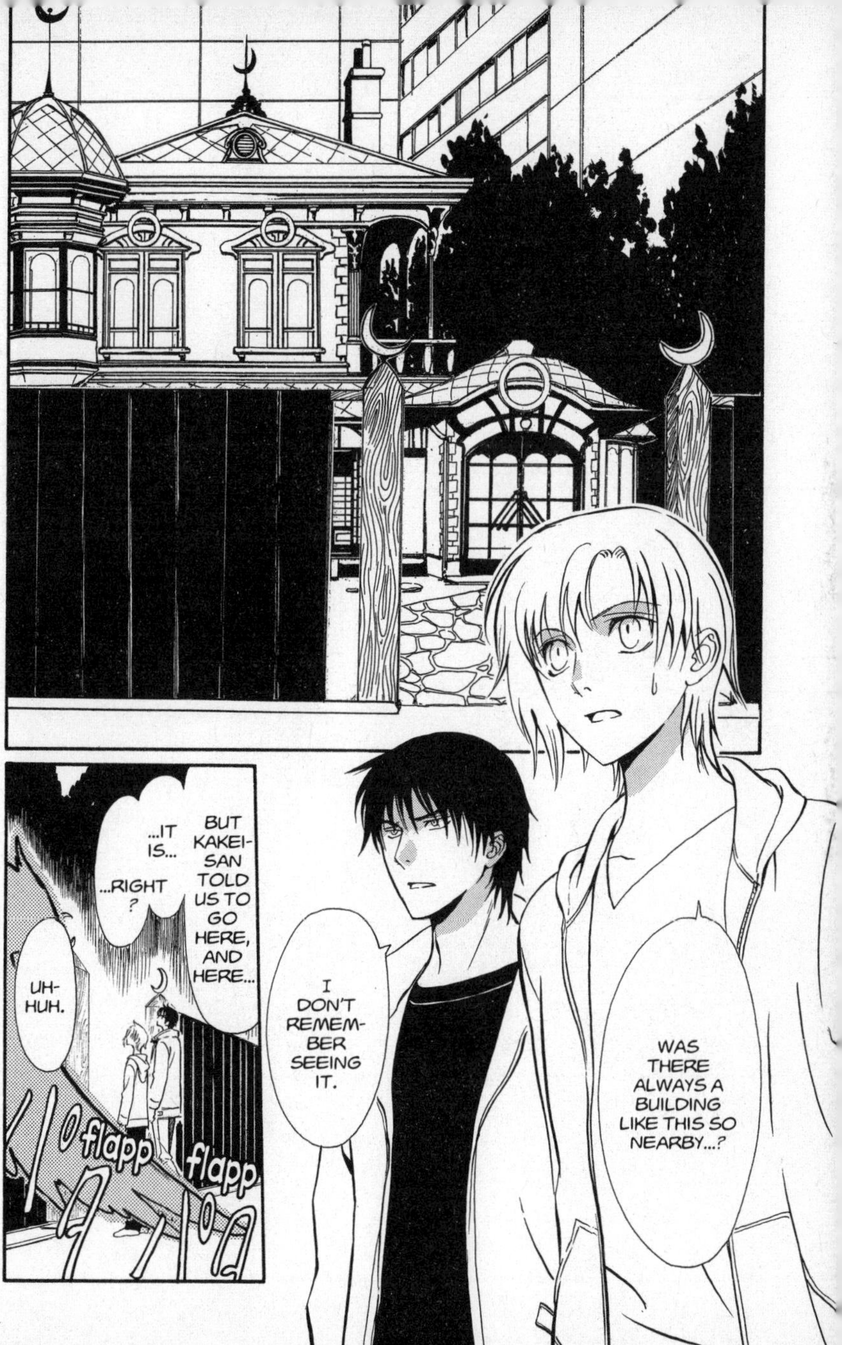
WAS THERE ALWAYS A BUILDING LIKE THIS SO NEARBY...?
I DON'T REMEMBER SEEING IT.
BUT KAKEI-SAN TOLD US TO GO HERE, AND HERE...
...IT IS...
...RIGHT?
UH-HUH.
flapp
flapp

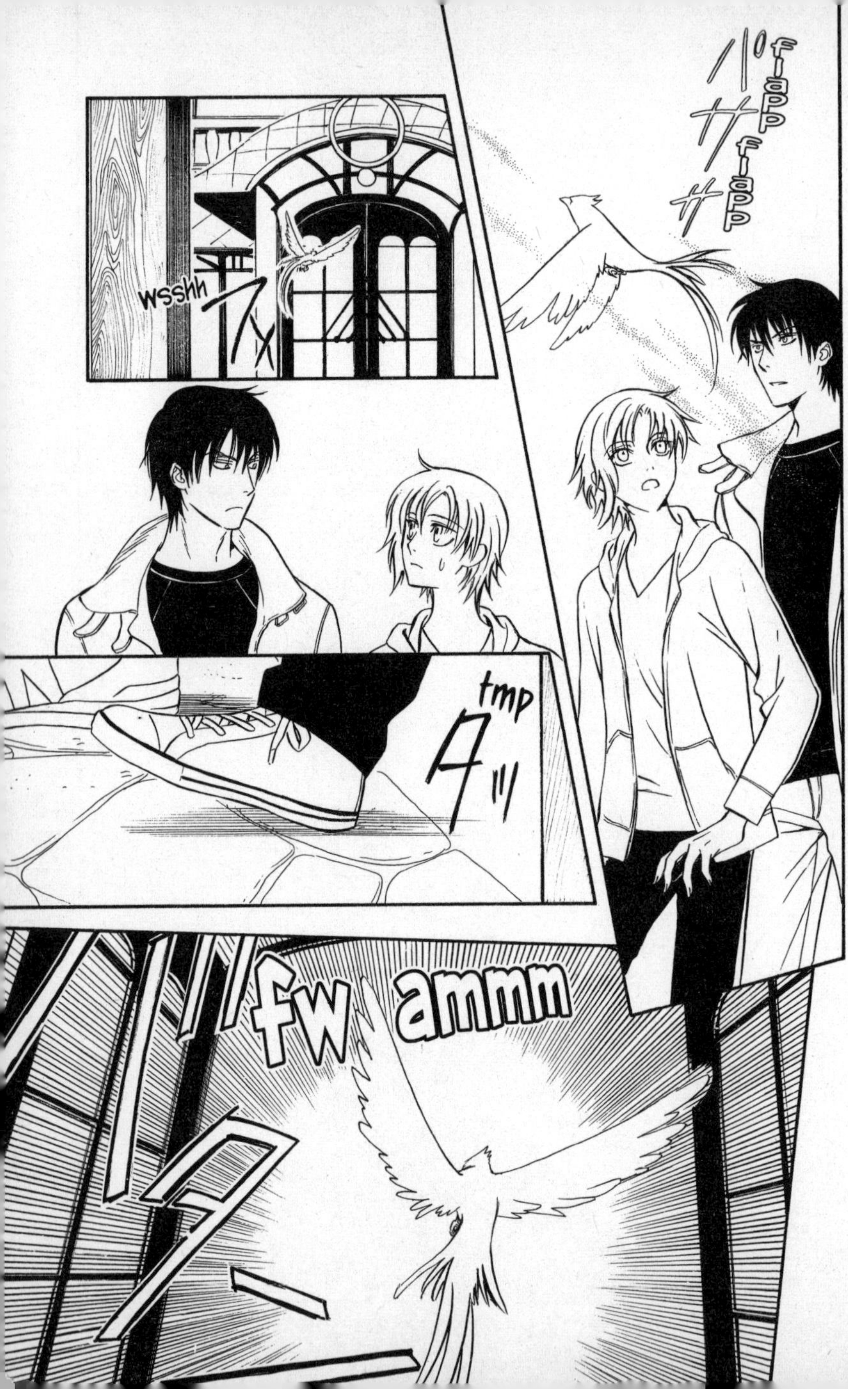
flapp flapp
wsshh
tmp
fw ammm

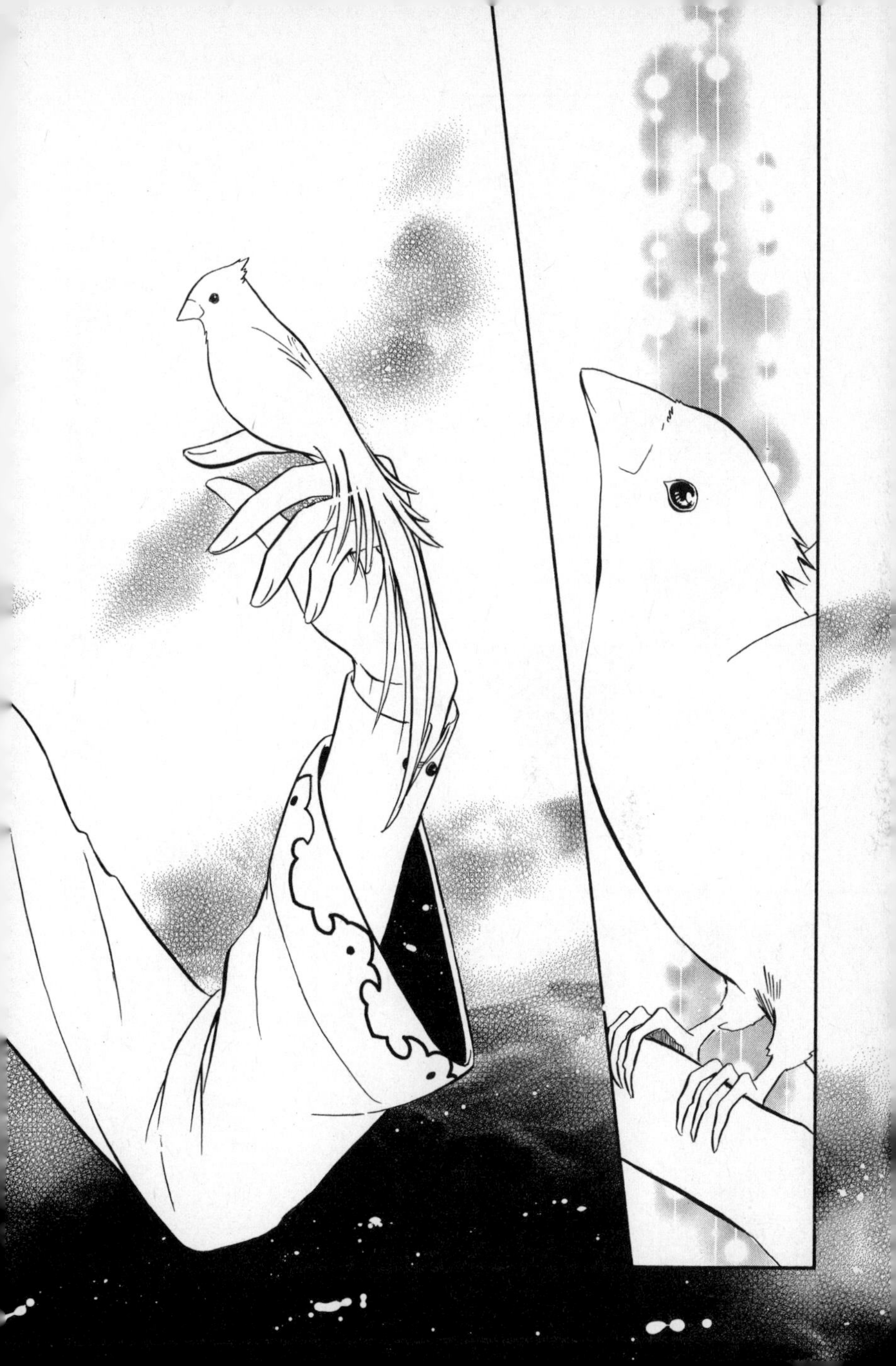

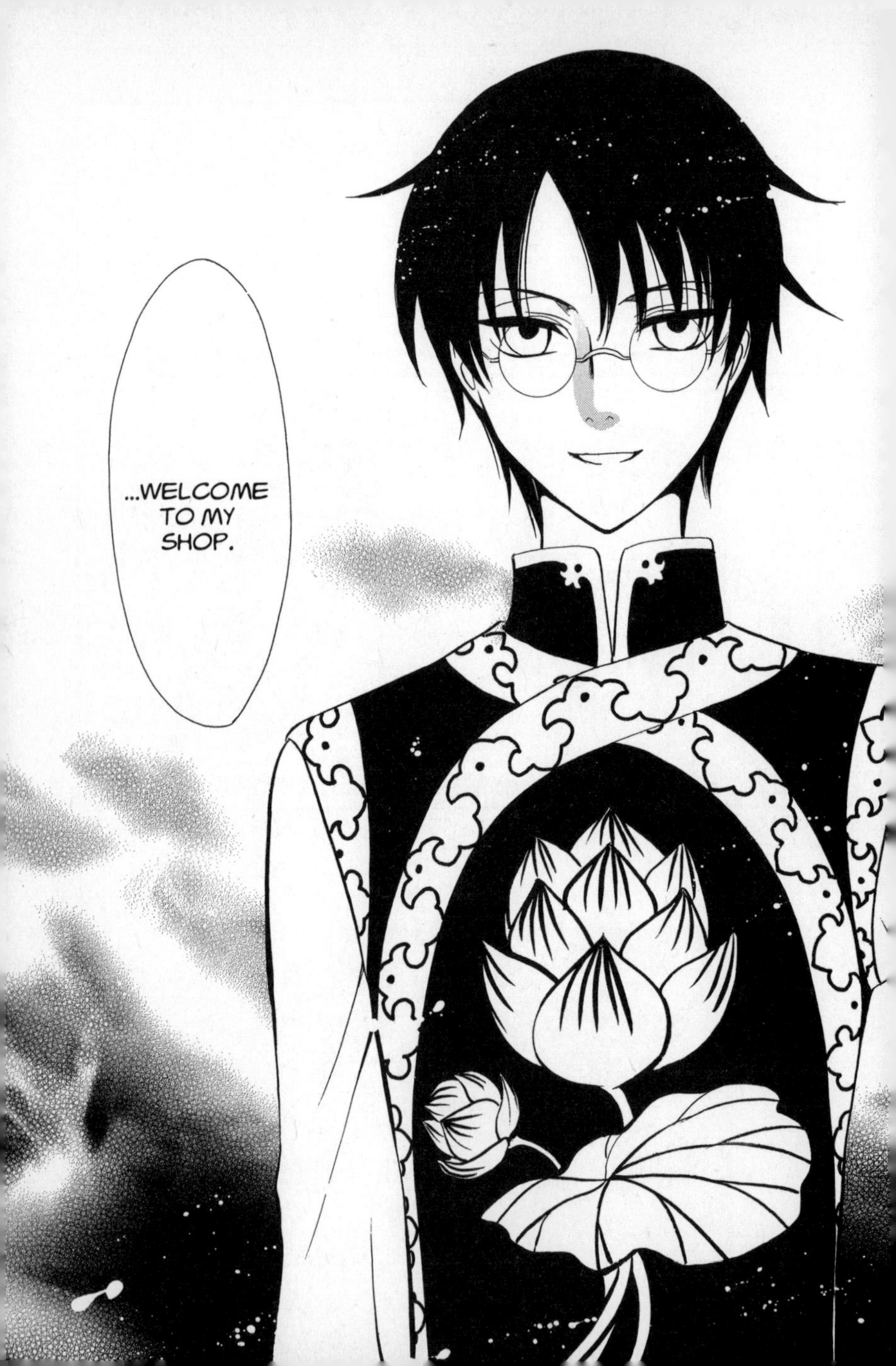
...WELCOME TO MY SHOP.

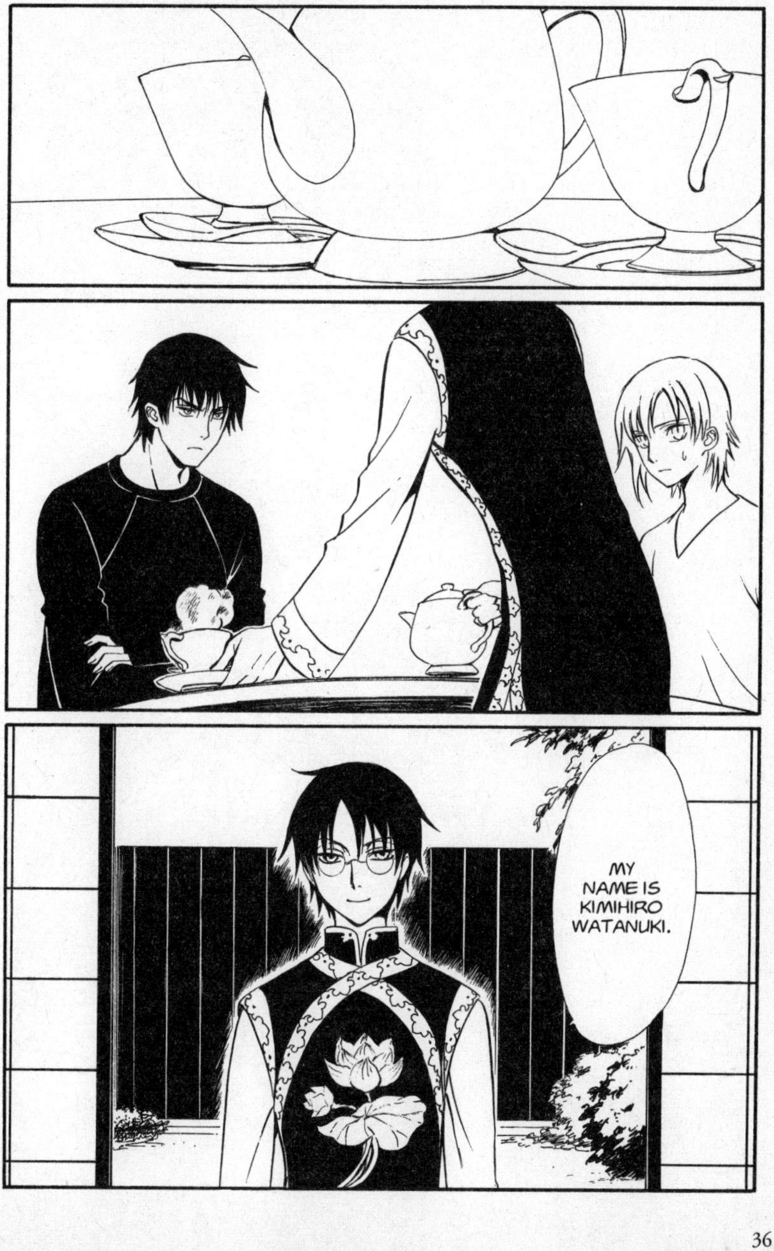
MY NAME IS KIMIHIRO WATANUKI.

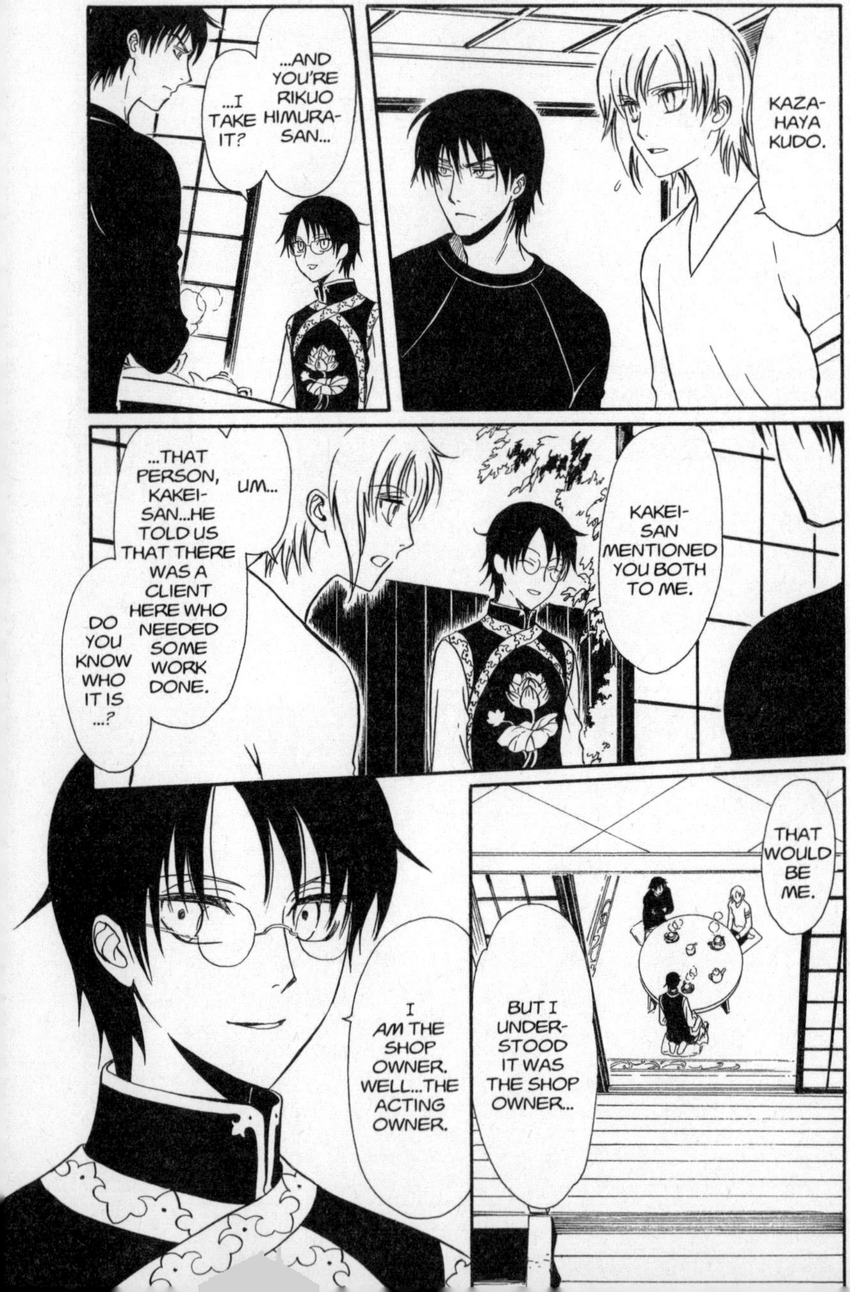
KAZA-HAYA KUDO.
...AND YOU'RE RIKUO HIMURA-SAN...
...I TAKE IT?
KAKEI-SAN MENTIONED YOU BOTH TO ME.
UM...
...THAT PERSON, KAKEI-SAN...HE TOLD US THAT THERE WAS A CLIENT HERE WHO NEEDED SOME WORK DONE.
DO YOU KNOW WHO IT IS ...?
THAT WOULD BE ME.
BUT I UNDERSTOOD IT WAS THE SHOP OWNER...
I AM THE SHOP OWNER. WELL...THE ACTING OWNER.

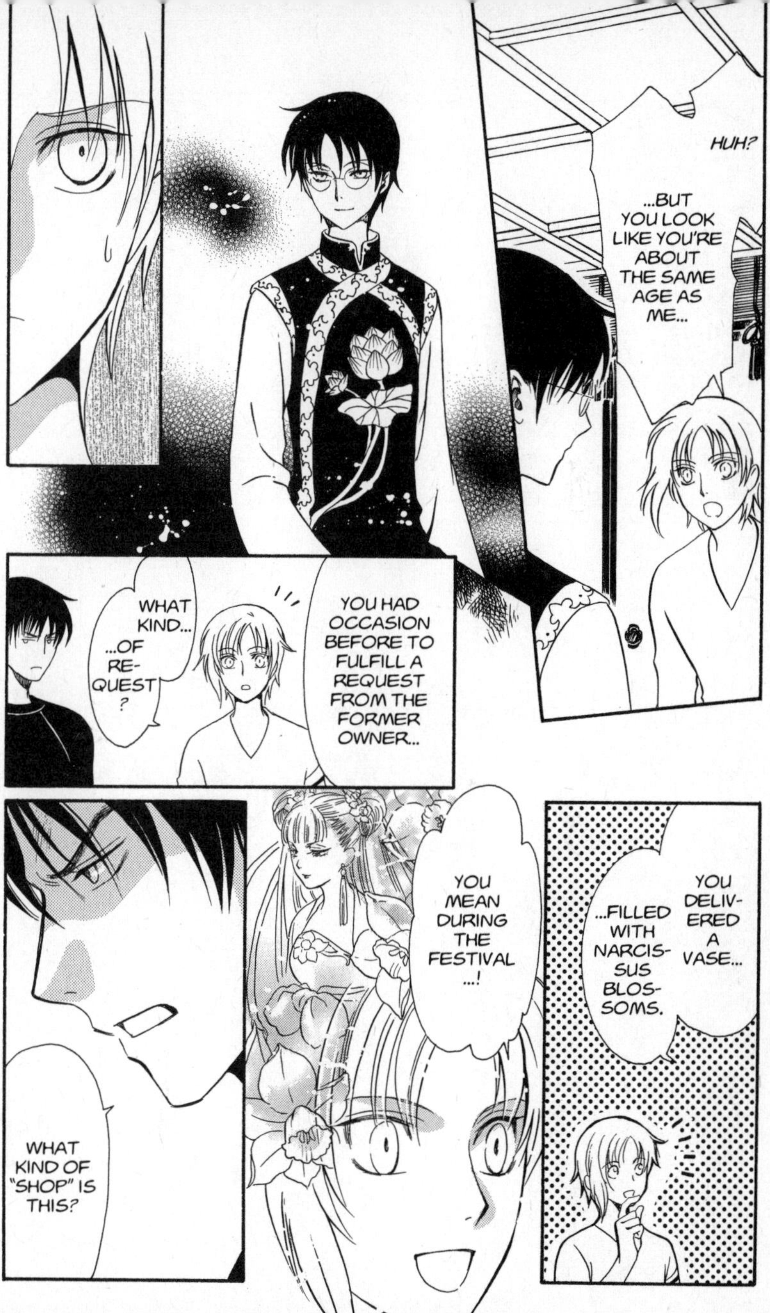
HUH?
...BUT YOU LOOK LIKE YOU'RE ABOUT THE SAME AGE AS ME...
YOU HAD OCCASION BEFORE TO FULFILL A REQUEST FROM THE FORMER OWNER...
WHAT KIND...
...OF RE-QUEST?
YOU DELIV-ERED A VASE...
...FILLED WITH NARCIS-SUS BLOS-SOMS.
YOU MEAN DURING THE FESTIVAL...!
WHAT KIND OF "SHOP" IS THIS?

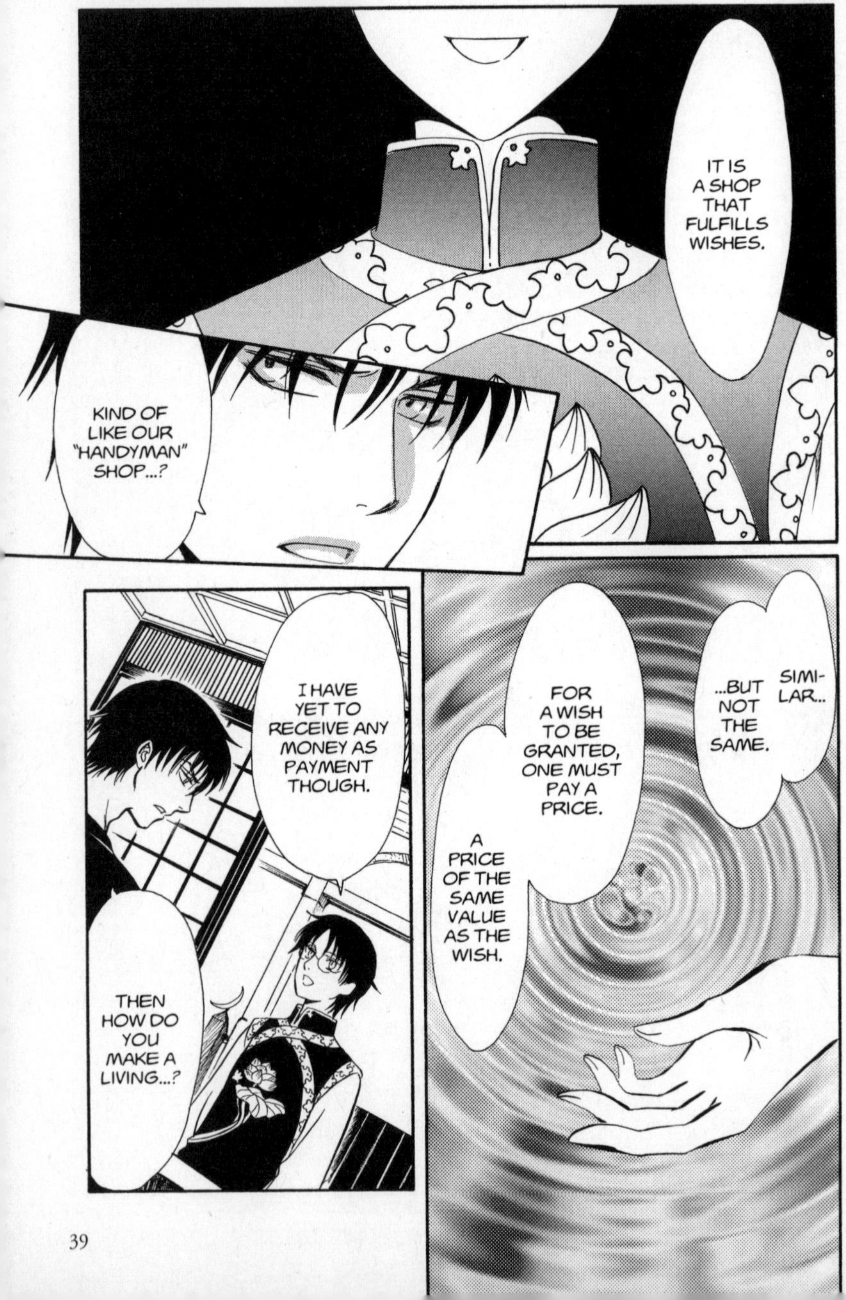
IT IS A SHOP THAT FULFILLS WISHES.
KIND OF LIKE OUR "HANDYMAN" SHOP...?
SIMI-LAR...
...BUT NOT THE SAME.
FOR A WISH TO BE GRANTED, ONE MUST PAY A PRICE.
A PRICE OF THE SAME VALUE AS THE WISH.
I HAVE YET TO RECEIVE ANY MONEY AS PAYMENT THOUGH.
THEN HOW DO YOU MAKE A LIVING...?

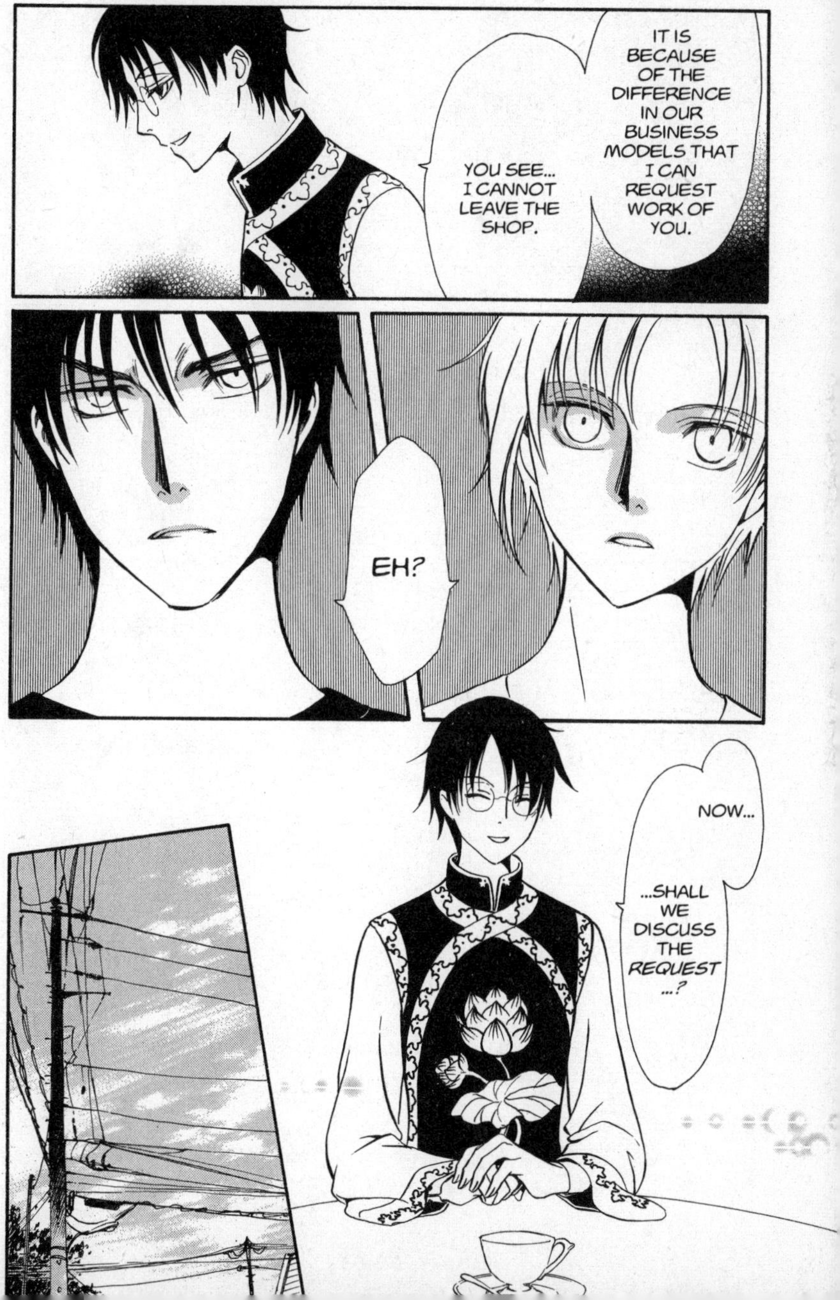
IT IS BECAUSE OF THE DIFFERENCE IN OUR BUSINESS MODELS THAT I CAN REQUEST WORK OF YOU.
YOU SEE... I CANNOT LEAVE THE SHOP.
EH?
NOW...
...SHALL WE DISCUSS THE *REQUEST* ...?

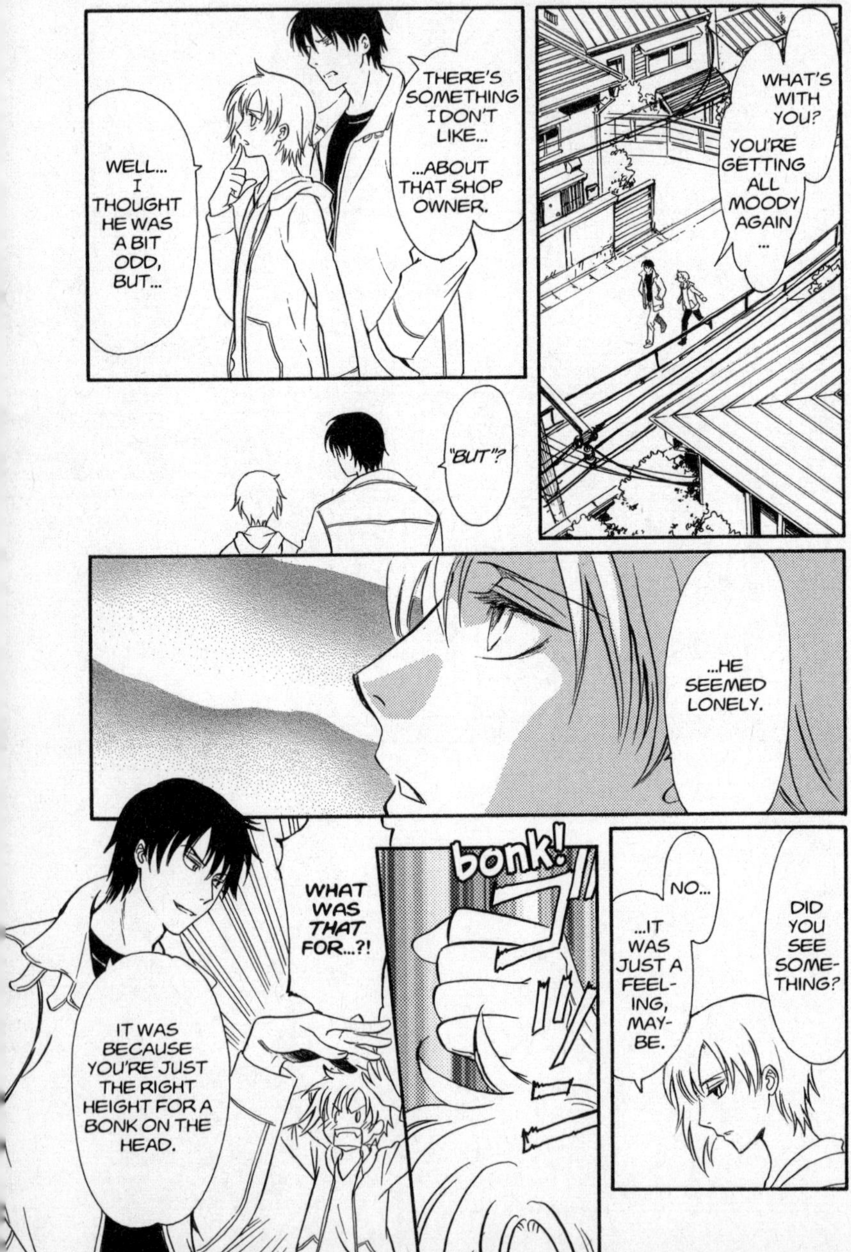
WHAT'S WITH YOU?
YOU'RE GETTING ALL MOODY AGAIN ...
THERE'S SOMETHING I DON'T LIKE...
...ABOUT THAT SHOP OWNER.
WELL... I THOUGHT HE WAS A BIT ODD, BUT...
"BUT"?
...HE SEEMED LONELY.
DID YOU SEE SOME-THING?
NO...
...IT WAS JUST A FEEL-ING, MAY-BE.
bonk!
WHAT WAS THAT FOR...?!
IT WAS BECAUSE YOU'RE JUST THE RIGHT HEIGHT FOR A BONK ON THE HEAD.

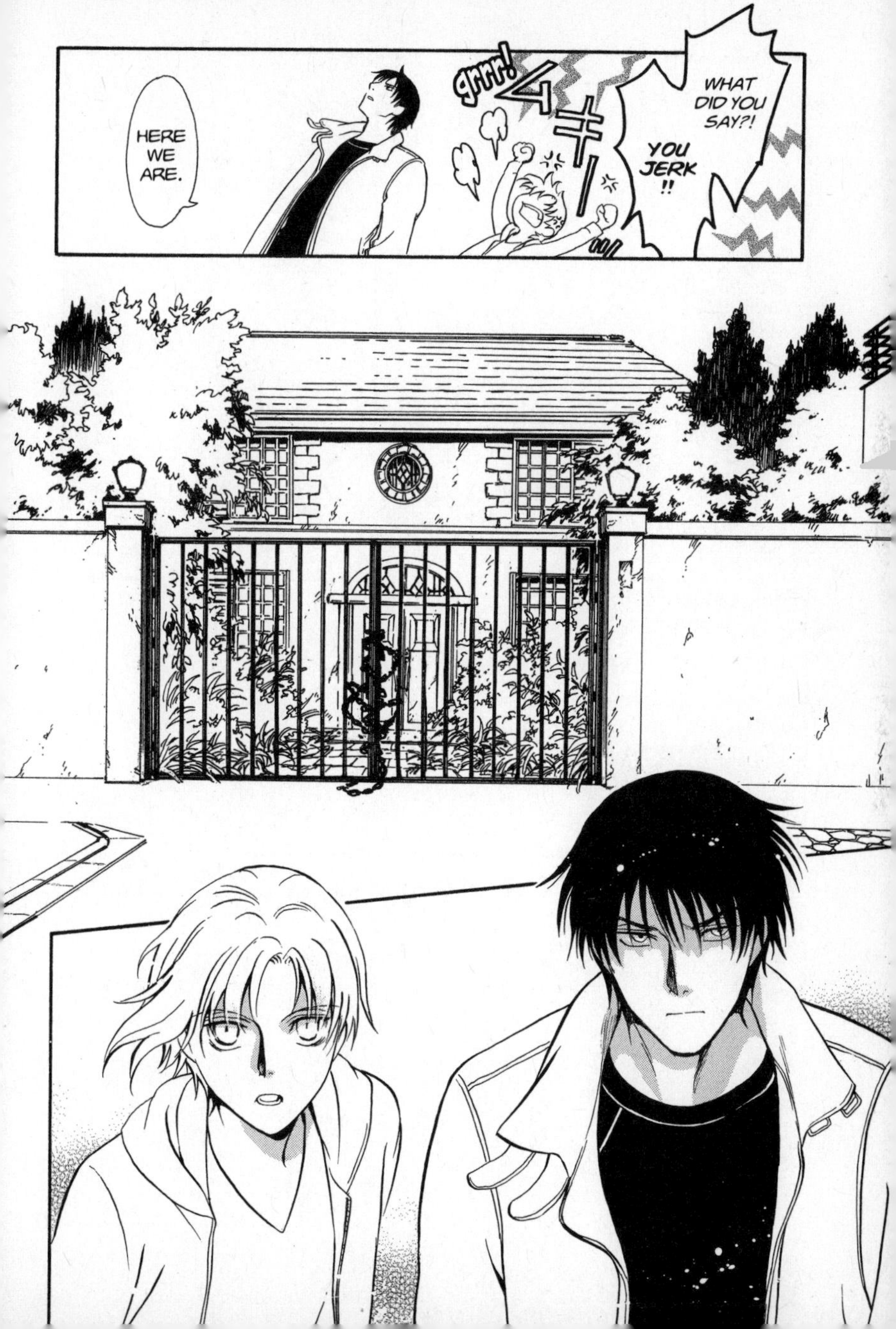

WHAT DID YOU SAY?!
YOU JERK!!
grrr!
HERE WE ARE.

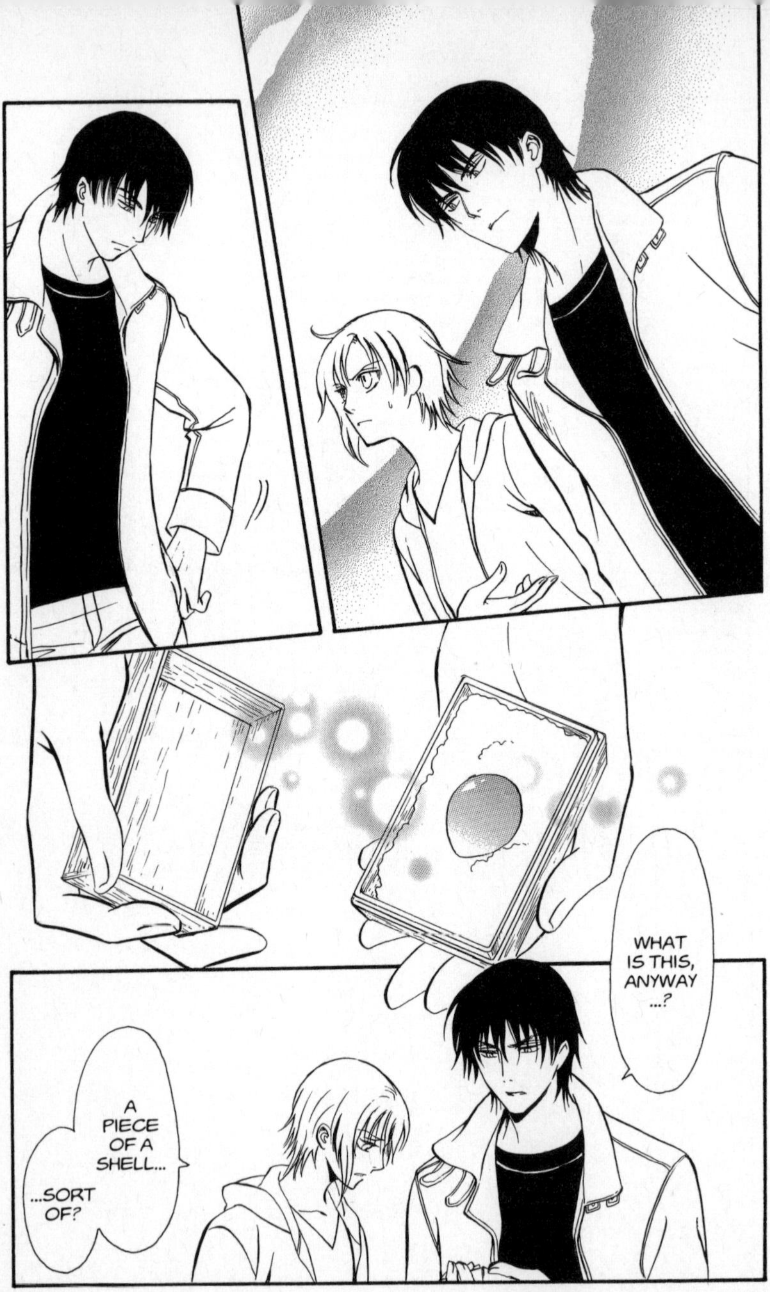
WHAT IS THIS, ANYWAY ...?
A PIECE OF A SHELL...
...SORT OF?

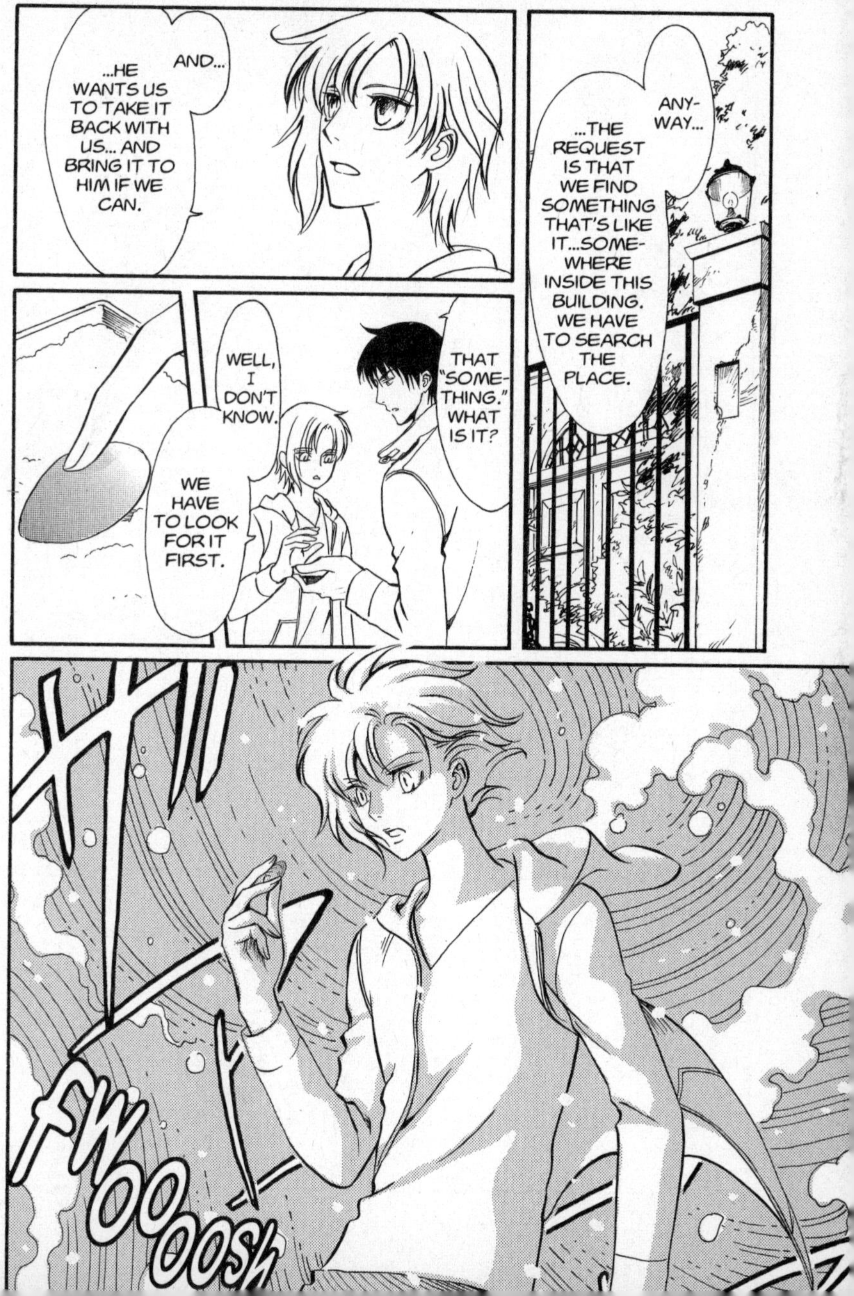
ANY-WAY...
...THE REQUEST IS THAT WE FIND SOMETHING THAT'S LIKE IT...SOME-WHERE INSIDE THIS BUILDING. WE HAVE TO SEARCH THE PLACE.
AND...
...HE WANTS US TO TAKE IT BACK WITH US... AND BRING IT TO HIM IF WE CAN.
THAT "SOME-THING." WHAT IS IT?
WELL, I DON'T KNOW.
WE HAVE TO LOOK FOR IT FIRST.
FWOOOOSH

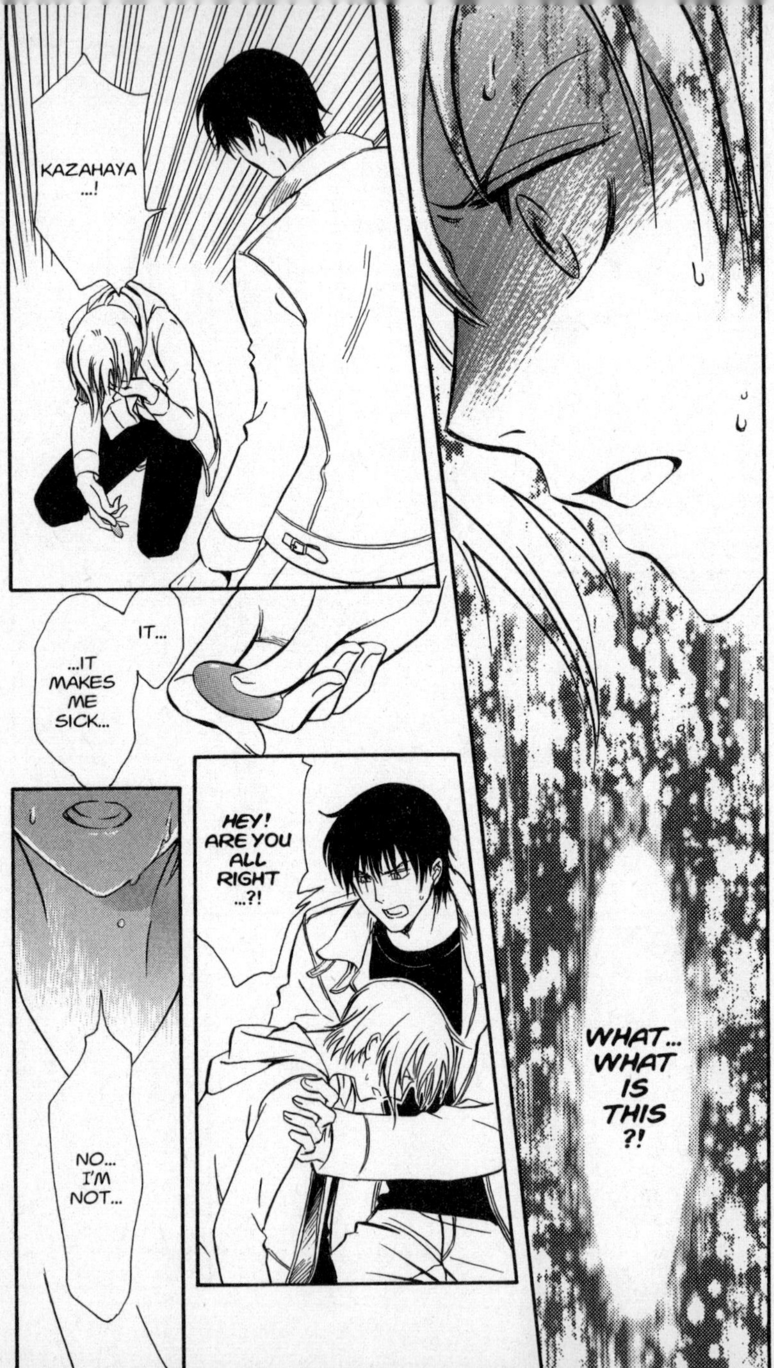
WHAT... WHAT IS THIS?!
KAZAHAYA ...!
IT...
...IT MAKES ME SICK...
HEY! ARE YOU ALL RIGHT ...?!
NO... I'M NOT...

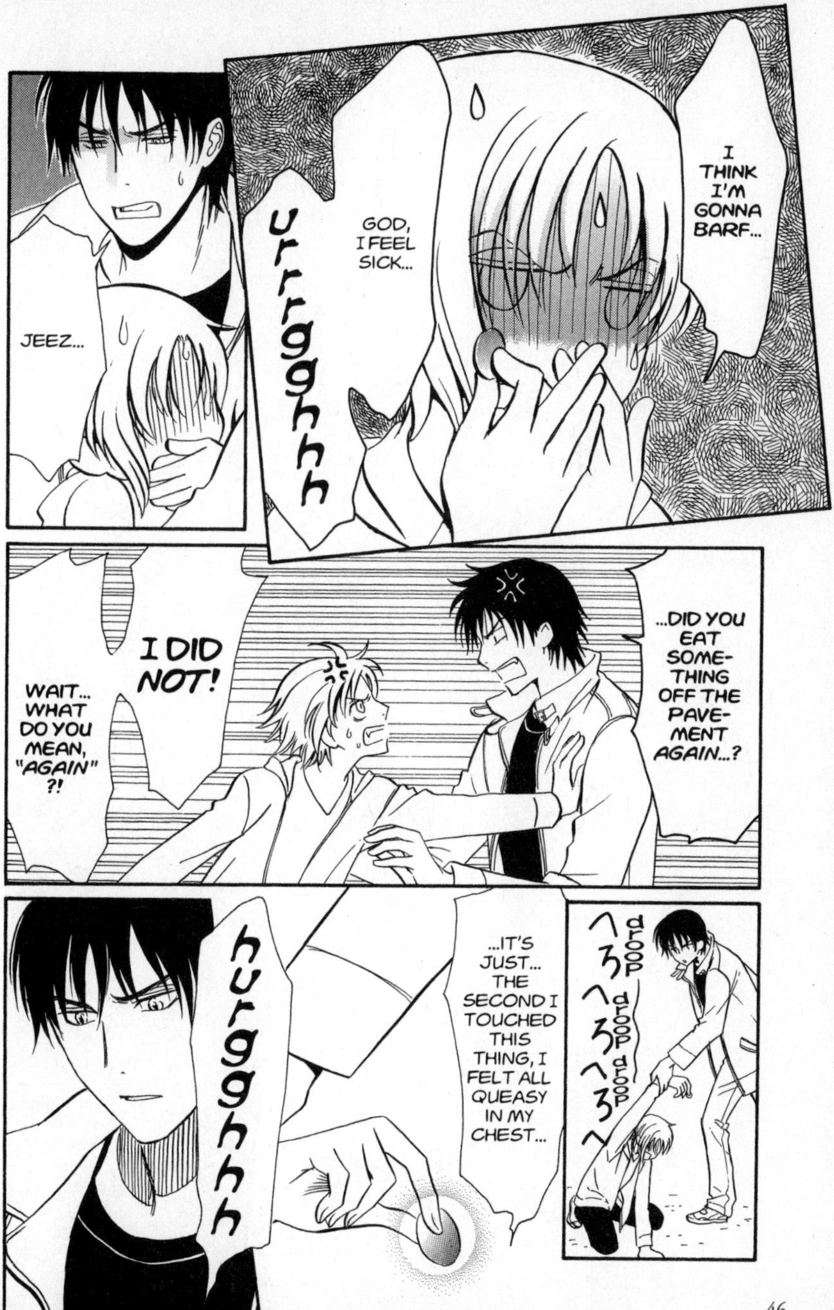
I THINK I'M GONNA BARF...
GOD, I FEEL SICK...
Urrrgghhhh
JEEZ...
...DID YOU EAT SOME-THING OFF THE PAVE-MENT AGAIN...?
I DID NOT!
WAIT... WHAT DO YOU MEAN, "AGAIN"?!
へろへろへろへ
droop droop droop
...IT'S JUST... THE SECOND I TOUCHED THIS THING, I FELT ALL QUEASY IN MY CHEST...
hurgghhhhh

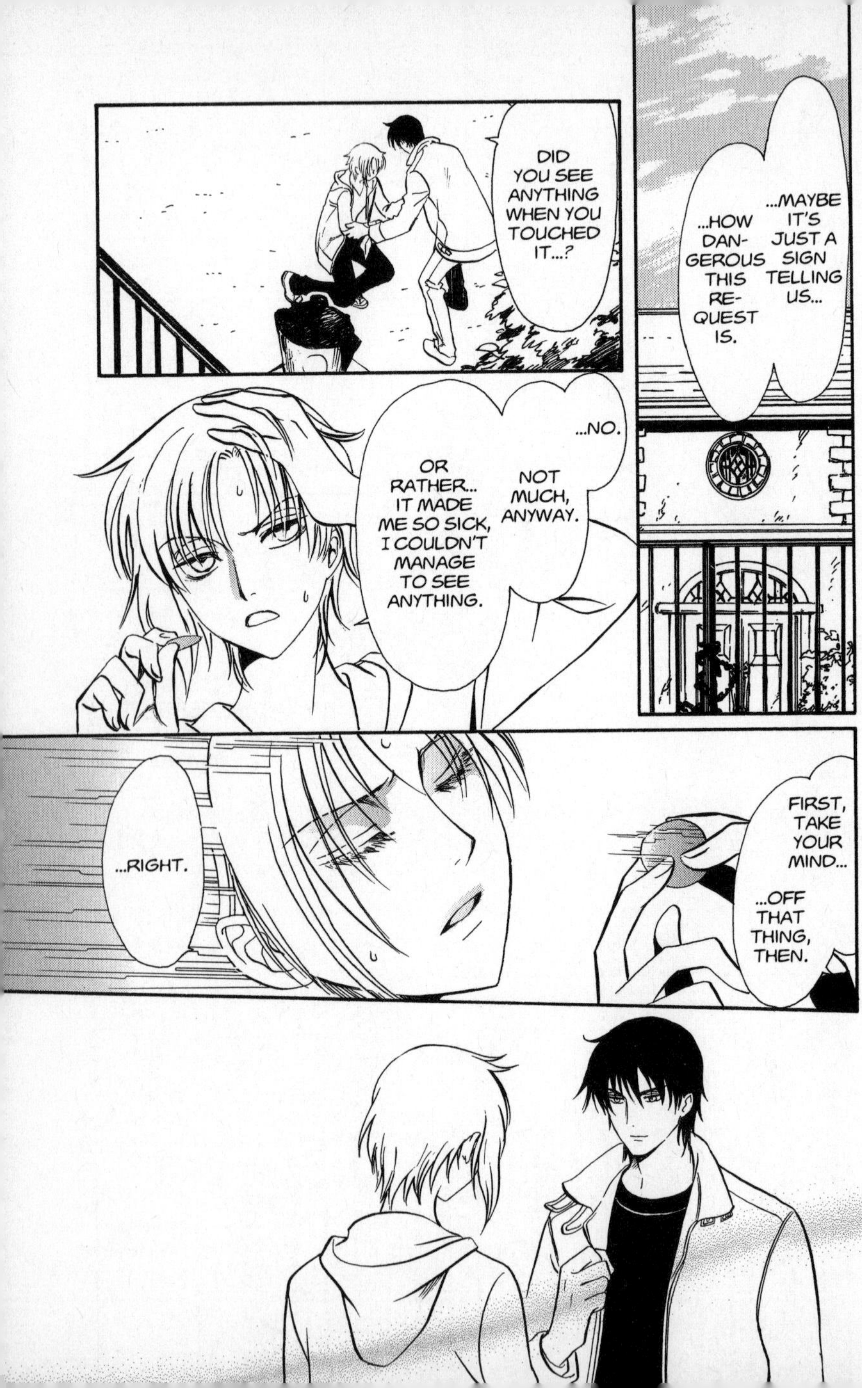
...MAYBE IT'S JUST A SIGN TELLING US...
...HOW DAN-GEROUS THIS RE-QUEST IS.
DID YOU SEE ANYTHING WHEN YOU TOUCHED IT...?
...NO.
NOT MUCH, ANYWAY.
OR RATHER... IT MADE ME SO SICK, I COULDN'T MANAGE TO SEE ANYTHING.
FIRST, TAKE YOUR MIND...
...OFF THAT THING, THEN.
...RIGHT.

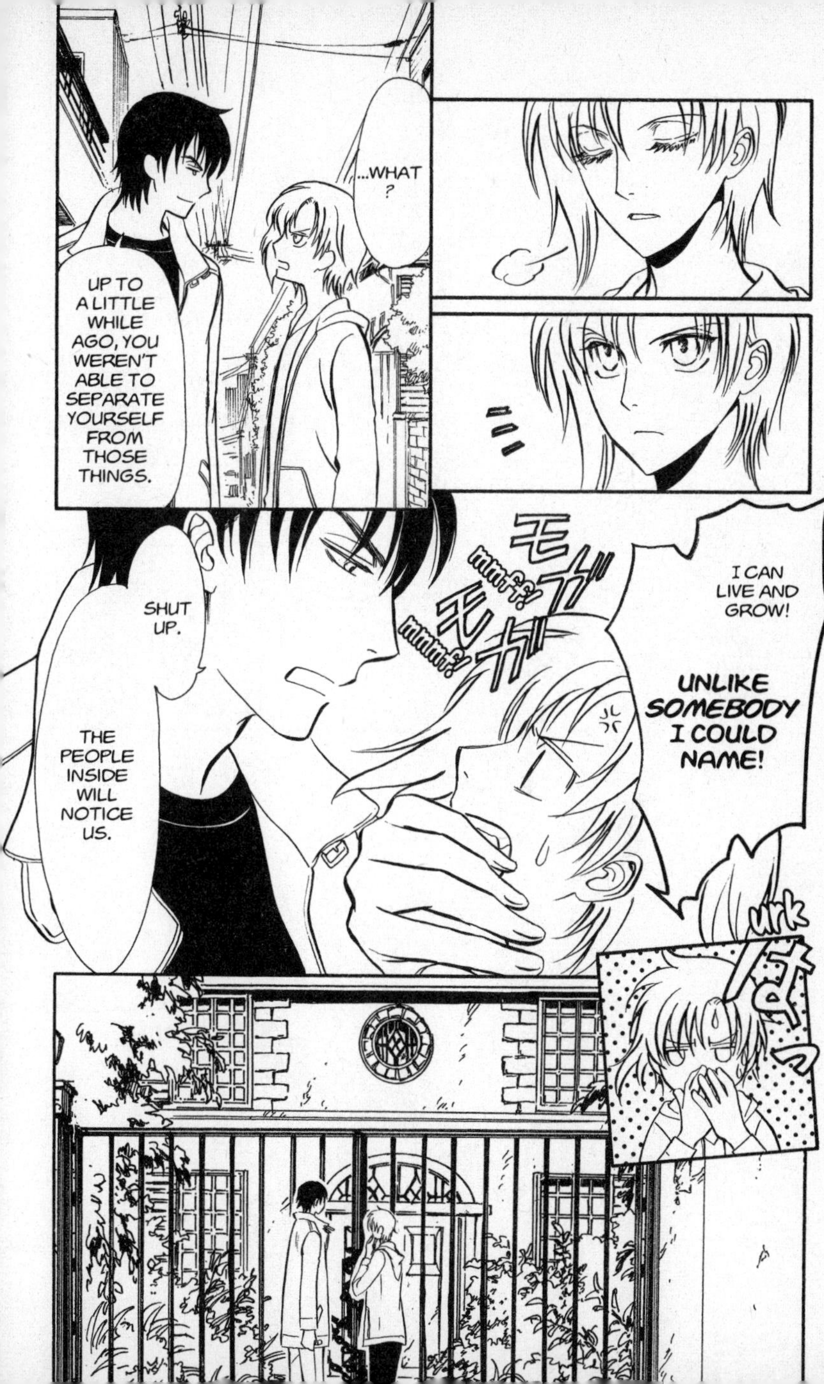
...WHAT ?
UP TO A LITTLE WHILE AGO, YOU WEREN'T ABLE TO SEPARATE YOURSELF FROM THOSE THINGS.
I CAN LIVE AND GROW!
UNLIKE SOMEBODY I COULD NAME!
モガ mmf!
モガ mmmf!
SHUT UP.
THE PEOPLE INSIDE WILL NOTICE US.
はっ urk

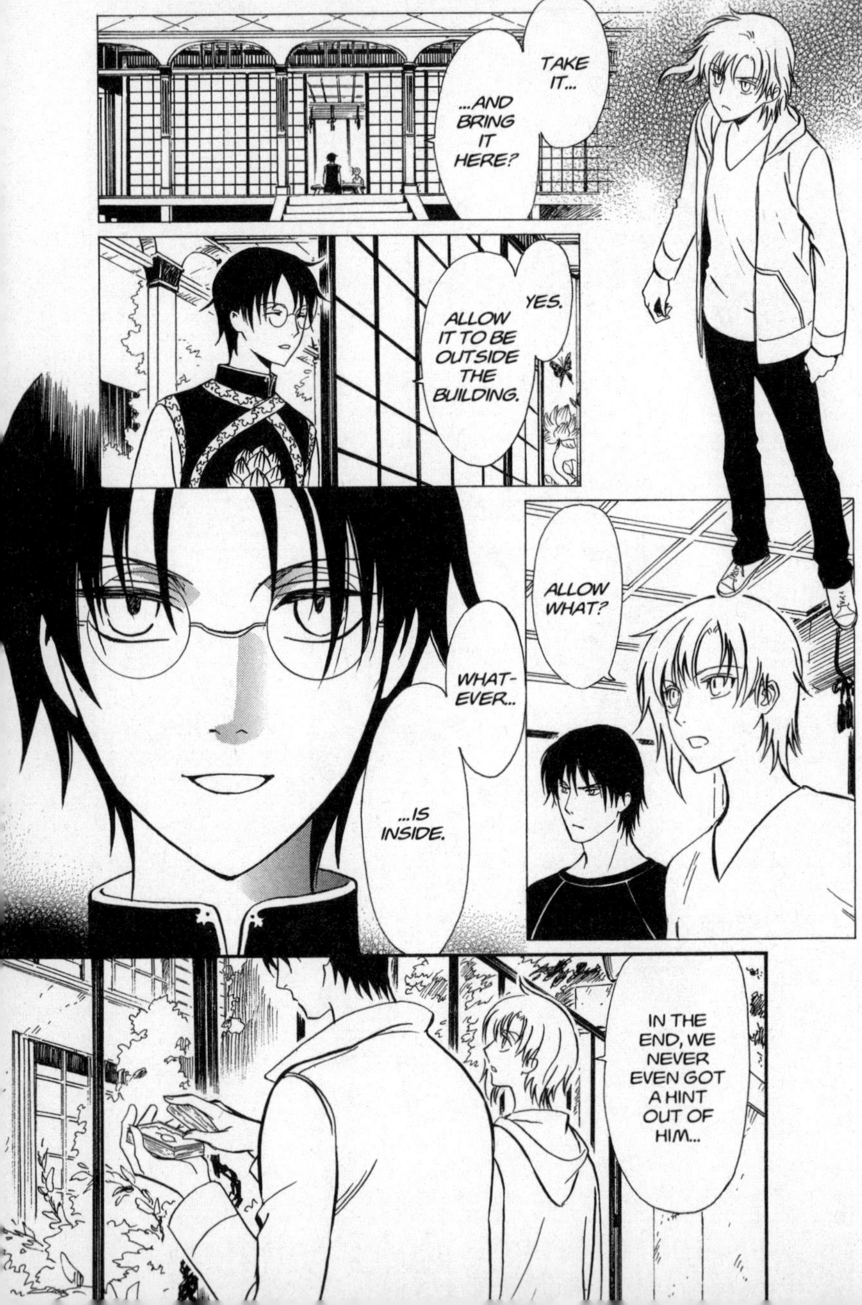
TAKE IT...
...AND BRING IT HERE?
YES.
ALLOW IT TO BE OUTSIDE THE BUILDING.
ALLOW WHAT?
WHAT-EVER...
...IS INSIDE.
IN THE END, WE NEVER EVEN GOT A HINT OUT OF HIM...

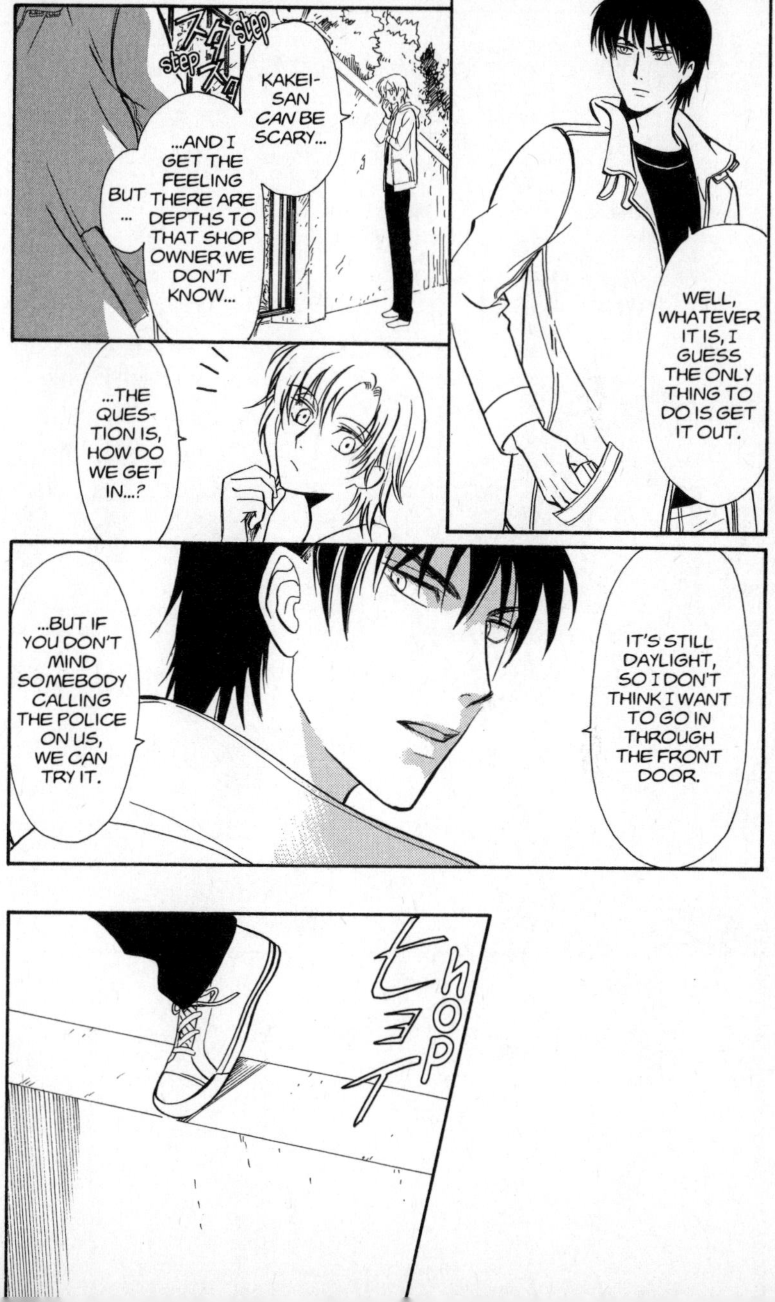
WELL, WHATEVER IT IS, I GUESS THE ONLY THING TO DO IS GET IT OUT.
step
step
KAKEI-SAN CAN BE SCARY...
BUT ...
...AND I GET THE FEELING THERE ARE DEPTHS TO THAT SHOP OWNER WE DON'T KNOW...
...THE QUES-TION IS, HOW DO WE GET IN...?
IT'S STILL DAYLIGHT, SO I DON'T THINK I WANT TO GO IN THROUGH THE FRONT DOOR.
...BUT IF YOU DON'T MIND SOMEBODY CALLING THE POLICE ON US, WE CAN TRY IT.
hop

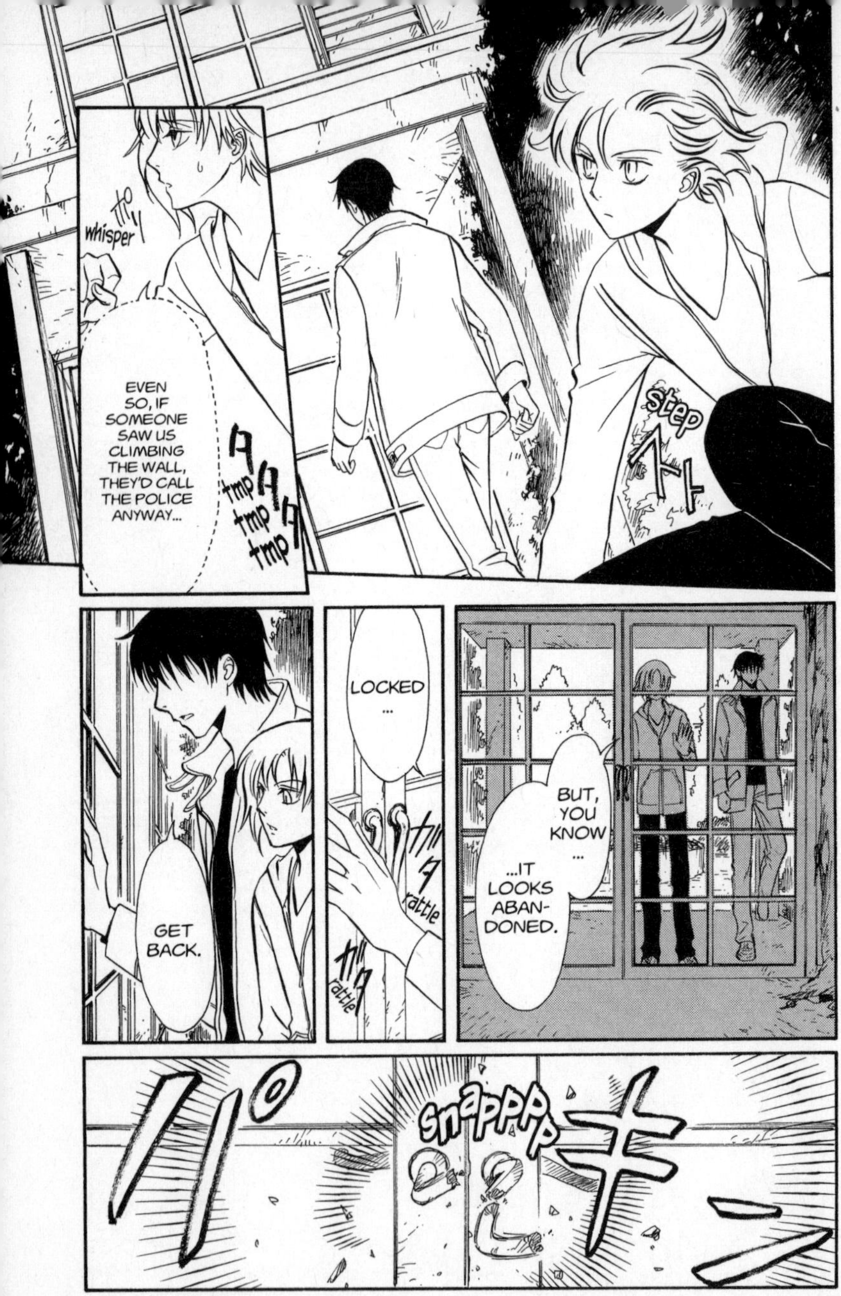
step
whisper
EVEN SO, IF SOMEONE SAW US CLIMBING THE WALL, THEY'D CALL THE POLICE ANYWAY...
tmp tmp tmp
BUT, YOU KNOW...
...IT LOOKS ABAN-DONED.
LOCKED...
rattle
rattle
GET BACK.
snapppp

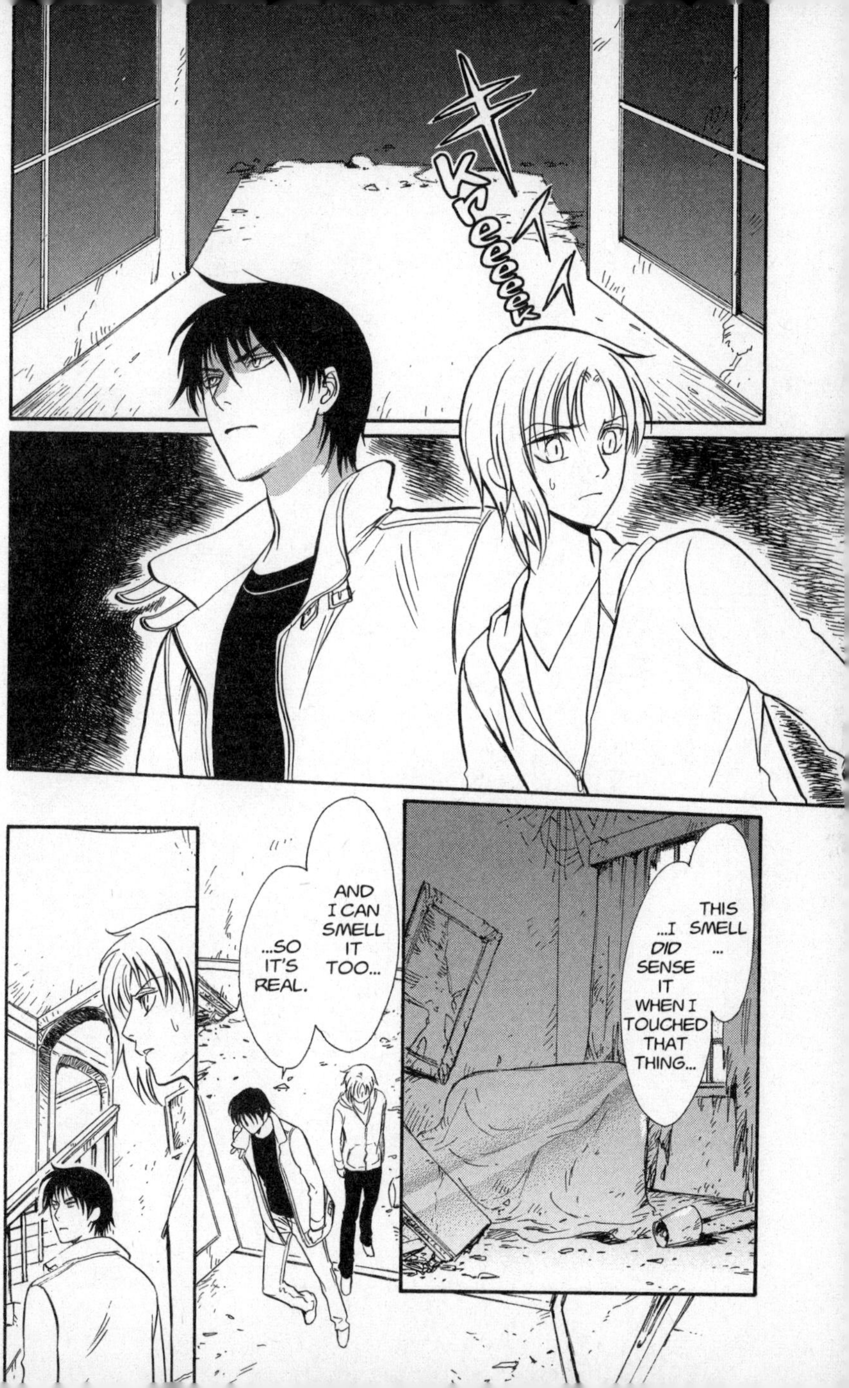

Kreeeeee
THIS SMELL ...
...I DID SENSE IT WHEN I TOUCHED THAT THING...
AND I CAN SMELL IT TOO...
...SO IT'S REAL.

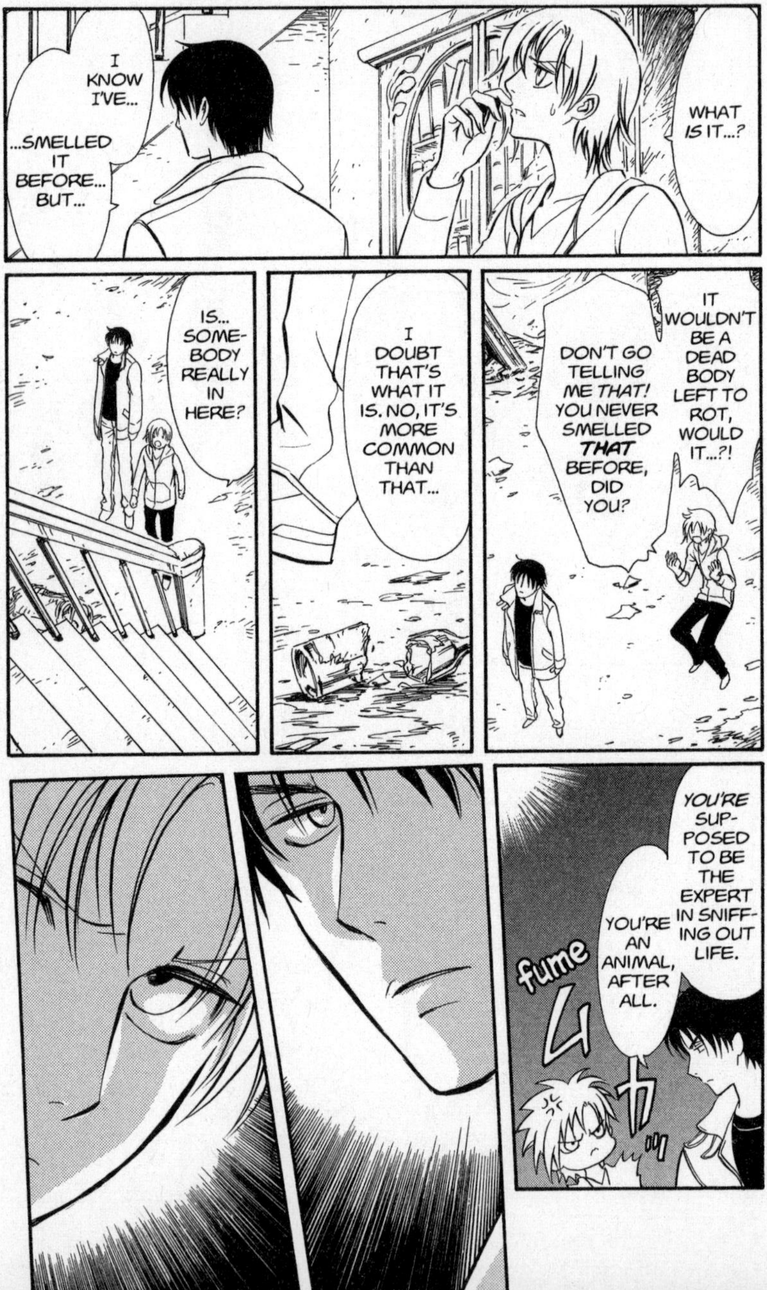
WHAT *IS* IT...?
I KNOW I'VE...
...SMELLED IT BEFORE... BUT...
IT WOULDN'T BE A DEAD BODY LEFT TO ROT, WOULD IT...?!
DON'T GO TELLING ME *THAT*! YOU NEVER SMELLED **THAT** BEFORE, DID YOU?
I DOUBT THAT'S WHAT IT IS. NO, IT'S MORE COMMON THAN THAT...
IS... SOME-BODY REALLY IN HERE?
YOU'RE SUP-POSED TO BE THE EXPERT IN SNIFF-ING OUT LIFE.
YOU'RE AN ANIMAL, AFTER ALL.
fume
ムカッ

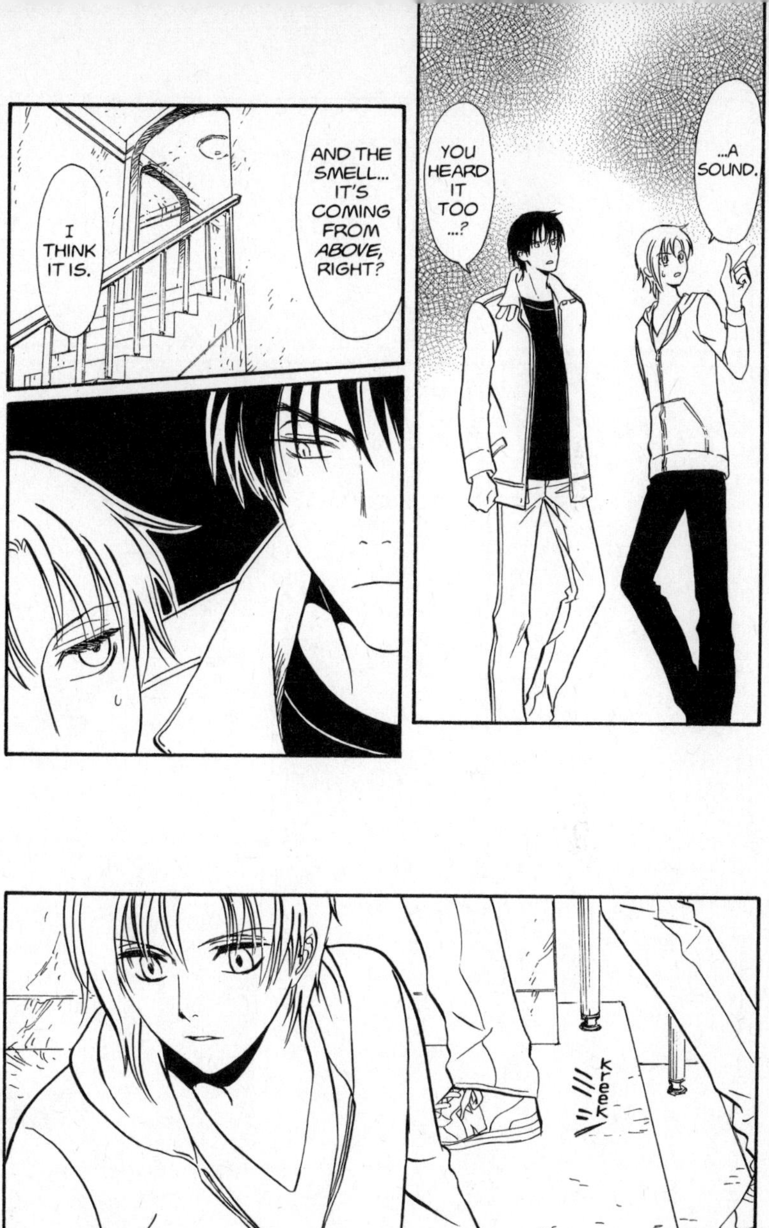
...A SOUND.
YOU HEARD IT TOO ...?
AND THE SMELL... IT'S COMING FROM *ABOVE*, RIGHT?
I THINK IT IS.
kreek

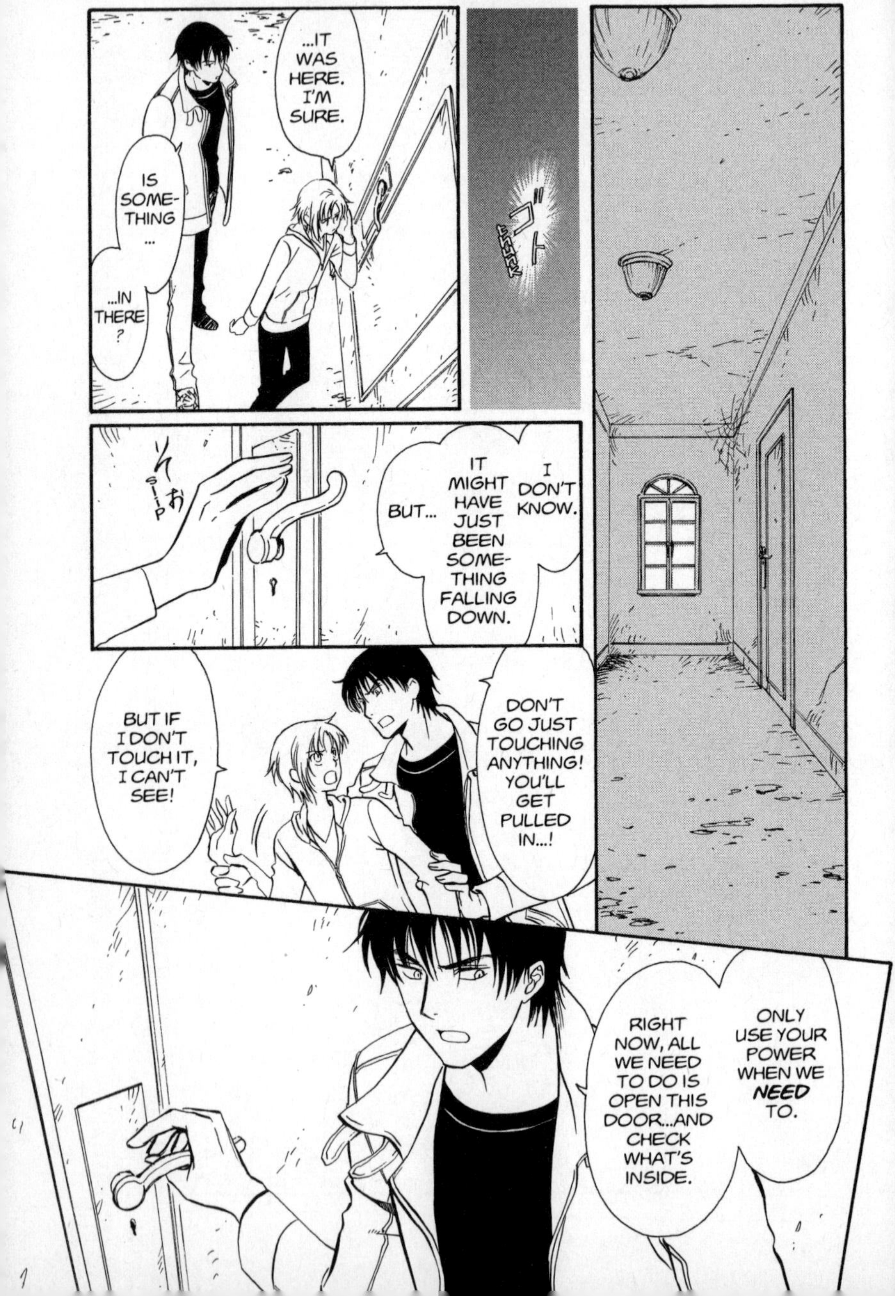
ゴト
...IT WAS HERE. I'M SURE.
IS SOMETHING...
...IN THERE?
I DON'T KNOW.
IT MIGHT HAVE JUST BEEN SOMETHING FALLING DOWN.
BUT...
そお
SLIP
DON'T GO JUST TOUCHING ANYTHING! YOU'LL GET PULLED IN...!
BUT IF I DON'T TOUCH IT, I CAN'T SEE!
ONLY USE YOUR POWER WHEN WE ***NEED*** TO.
RIGHT NOW, ALL WE NEED TO DO IS OPEN THIS DOOR...AND CHECK WHAT'S INSIDE.

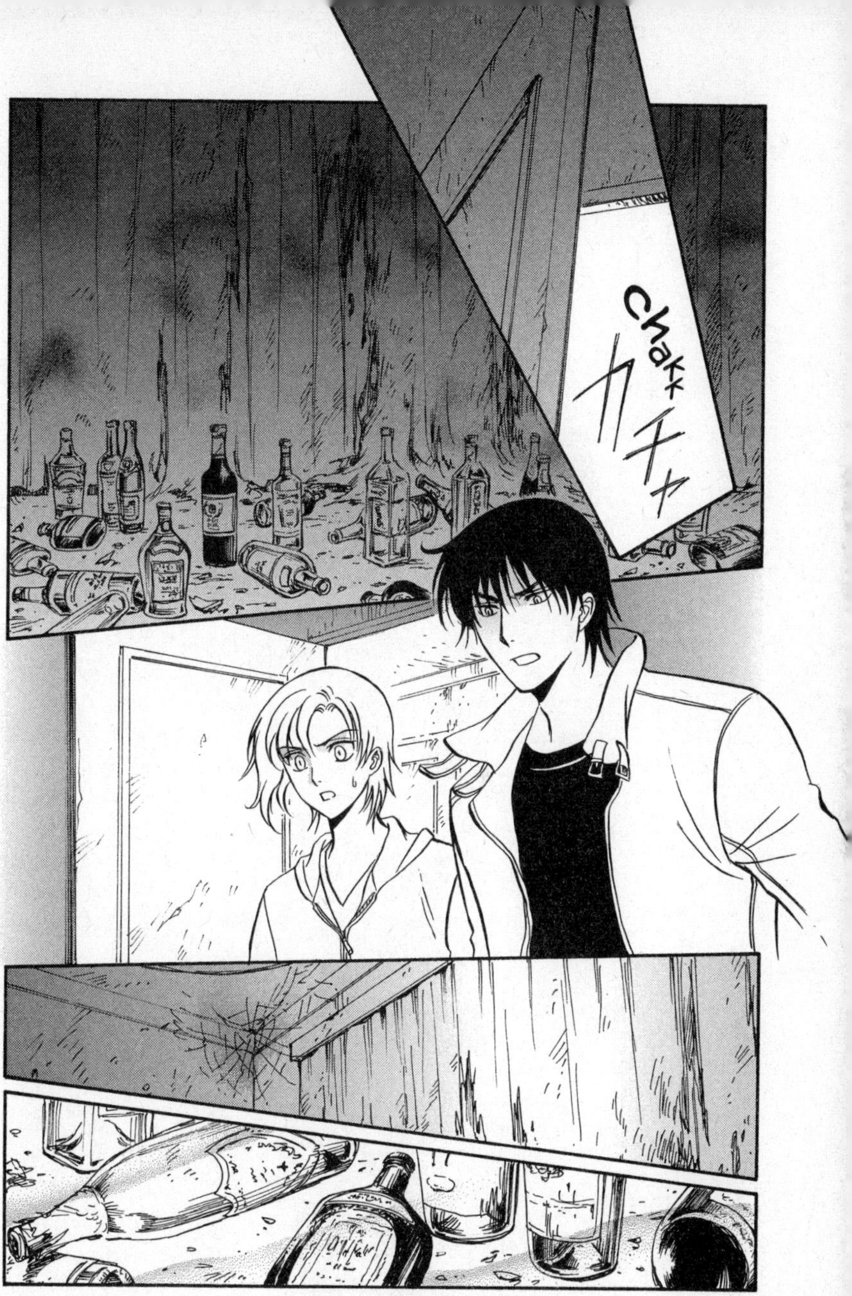
chakk
カチャ

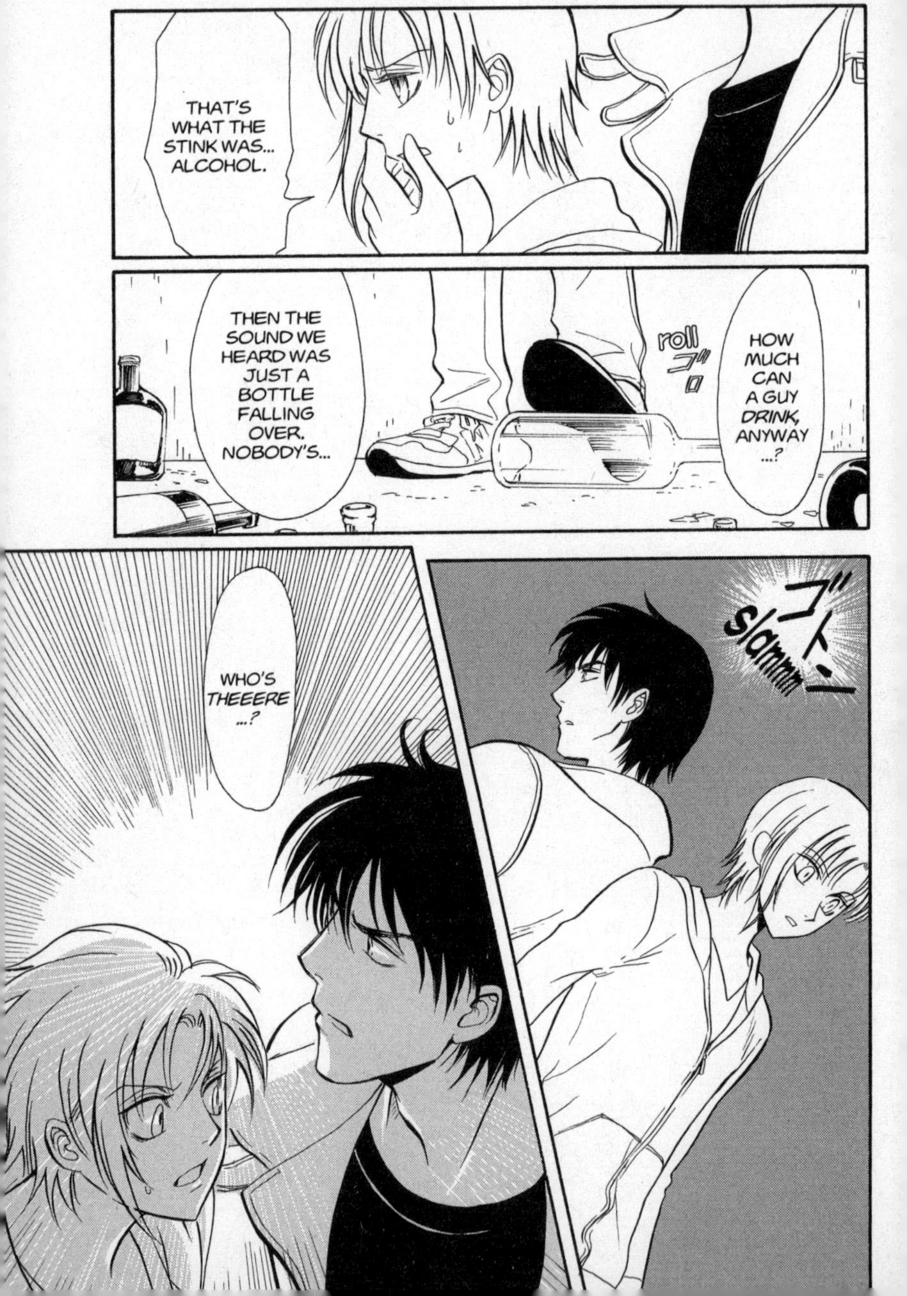
THAT'S WHAT THE STINK WAS... ALCOHOL.
HOW MUCH CAN A GUY DRINK, ANYWAY ...?
ゴロ roll
THEN THE SOUND WE HEARD WAS JUST A BOTTLE FALLING OVER. NOBODY'S...
ゴトン slammm
WHO'S THEEERE ...?

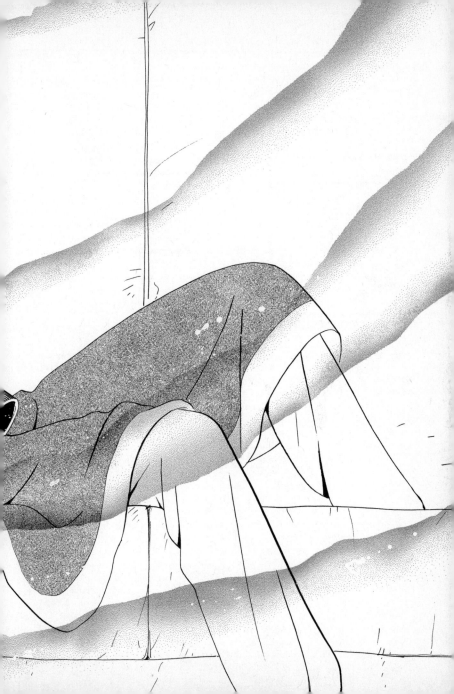

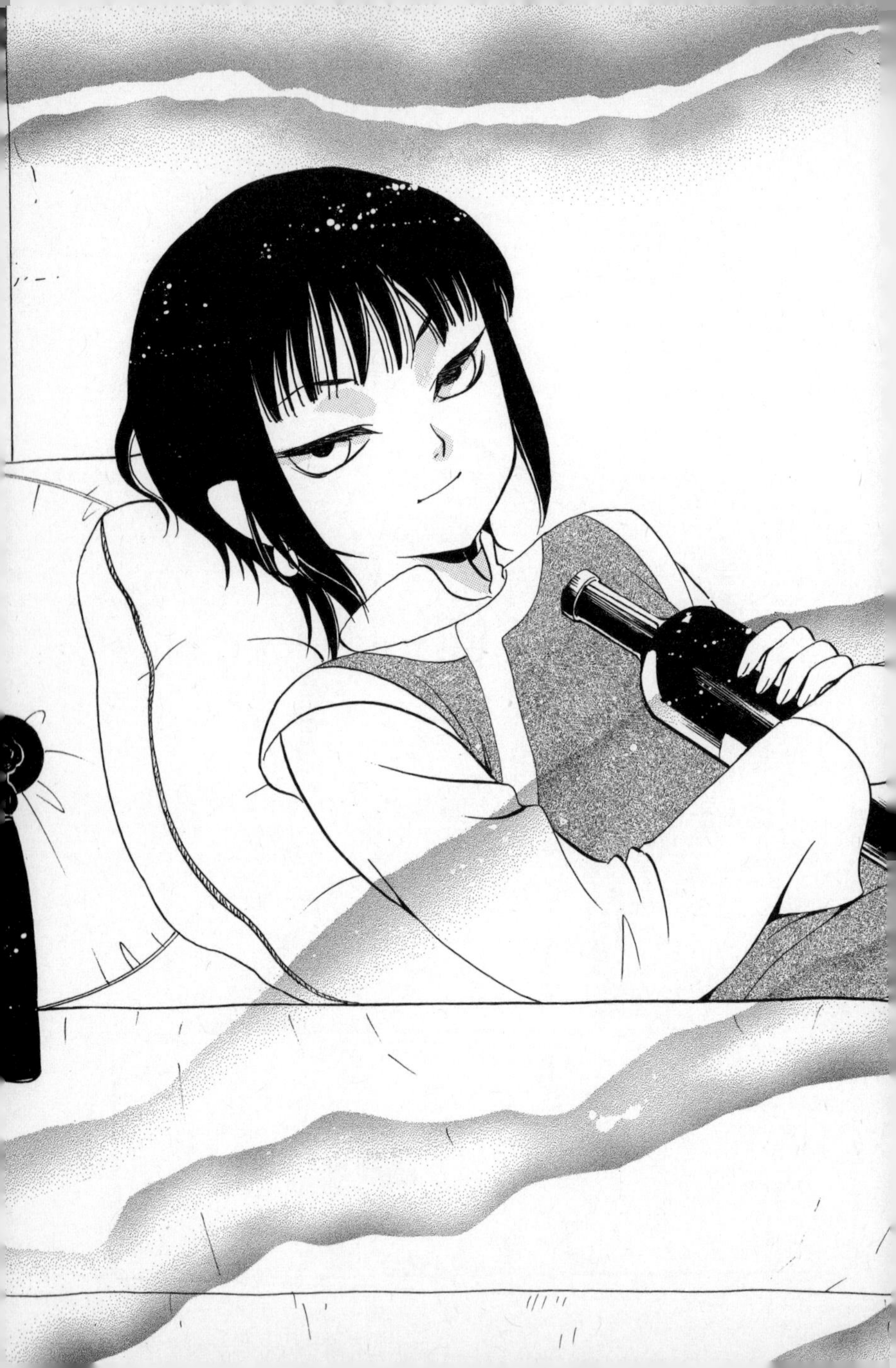

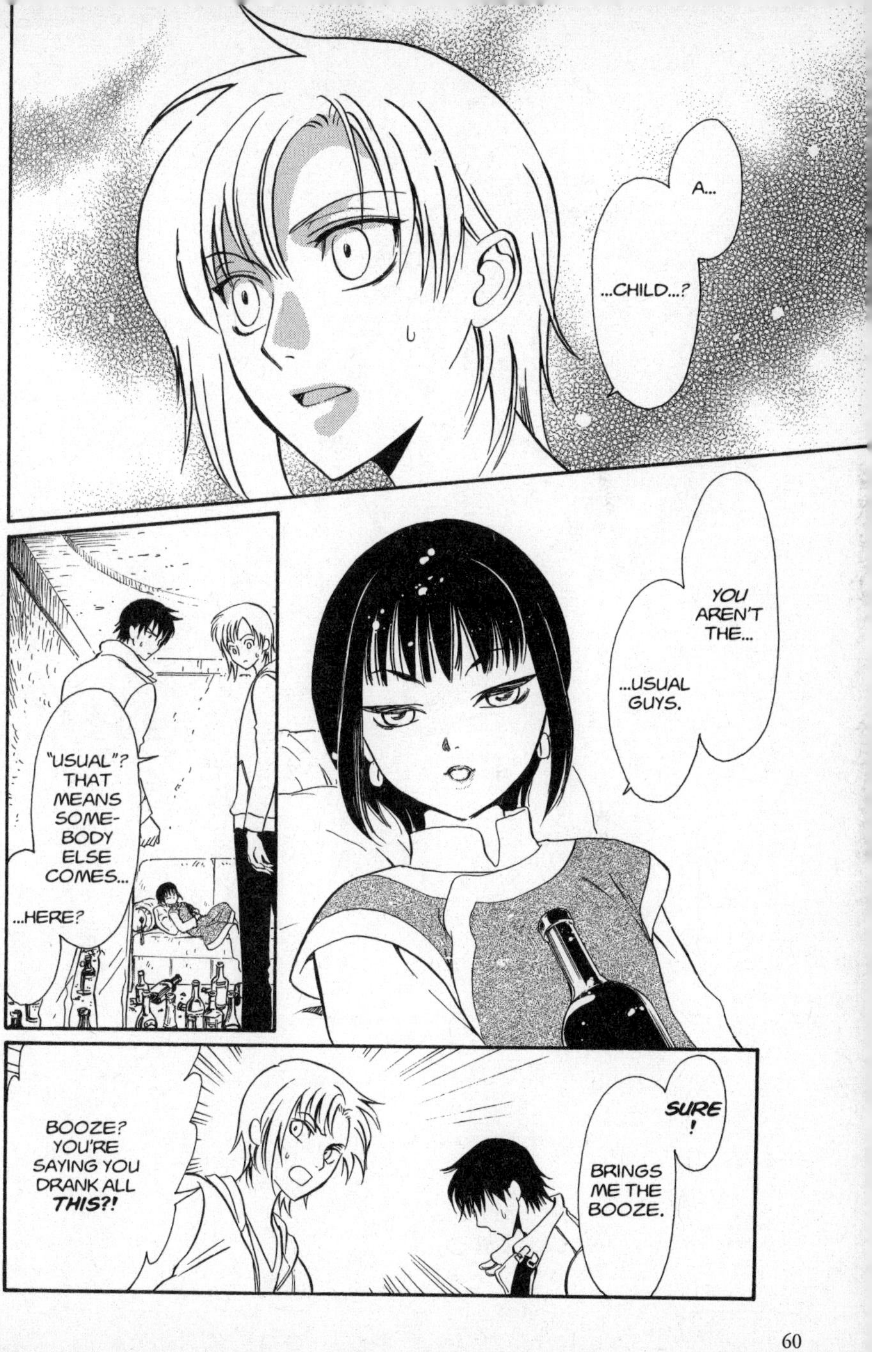
A...
...CHILD...?
YOU AREN'T THE...
...USUAL GUYS.
"USUAL"? THAT MEANS SOMEBODY ELSE COMES...
...HERE?
SURE!
BRINGS ME THE BOOZE.
BOOZE? YOU'RE SAYING YOU DRANK ALL THIS?!

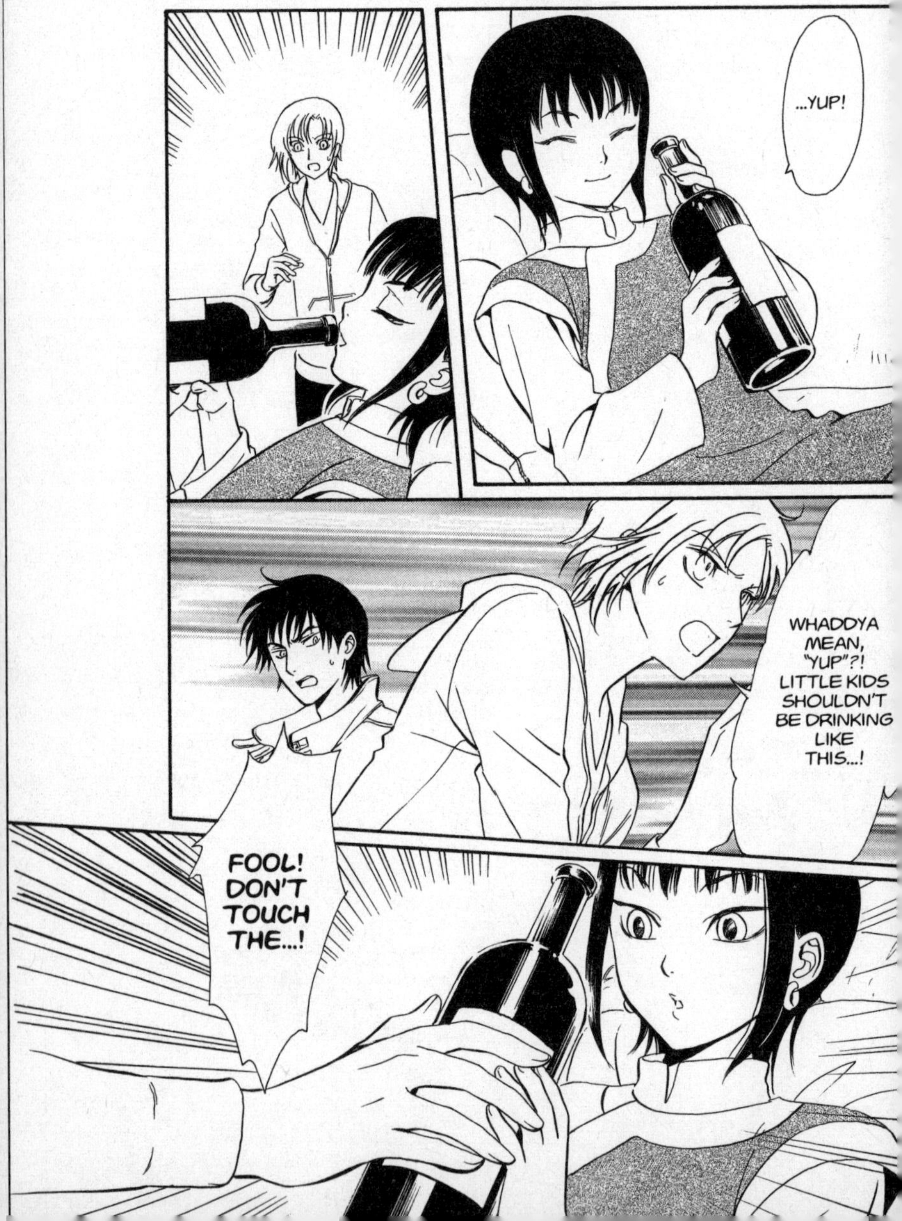
...YUP!
WHADDYA MEAN, "YUP"?! LITTLE KIDS SHOULDN'T BE DRINKING LIKE THIS...!
FOOL! DON'T TOUCH THE...!

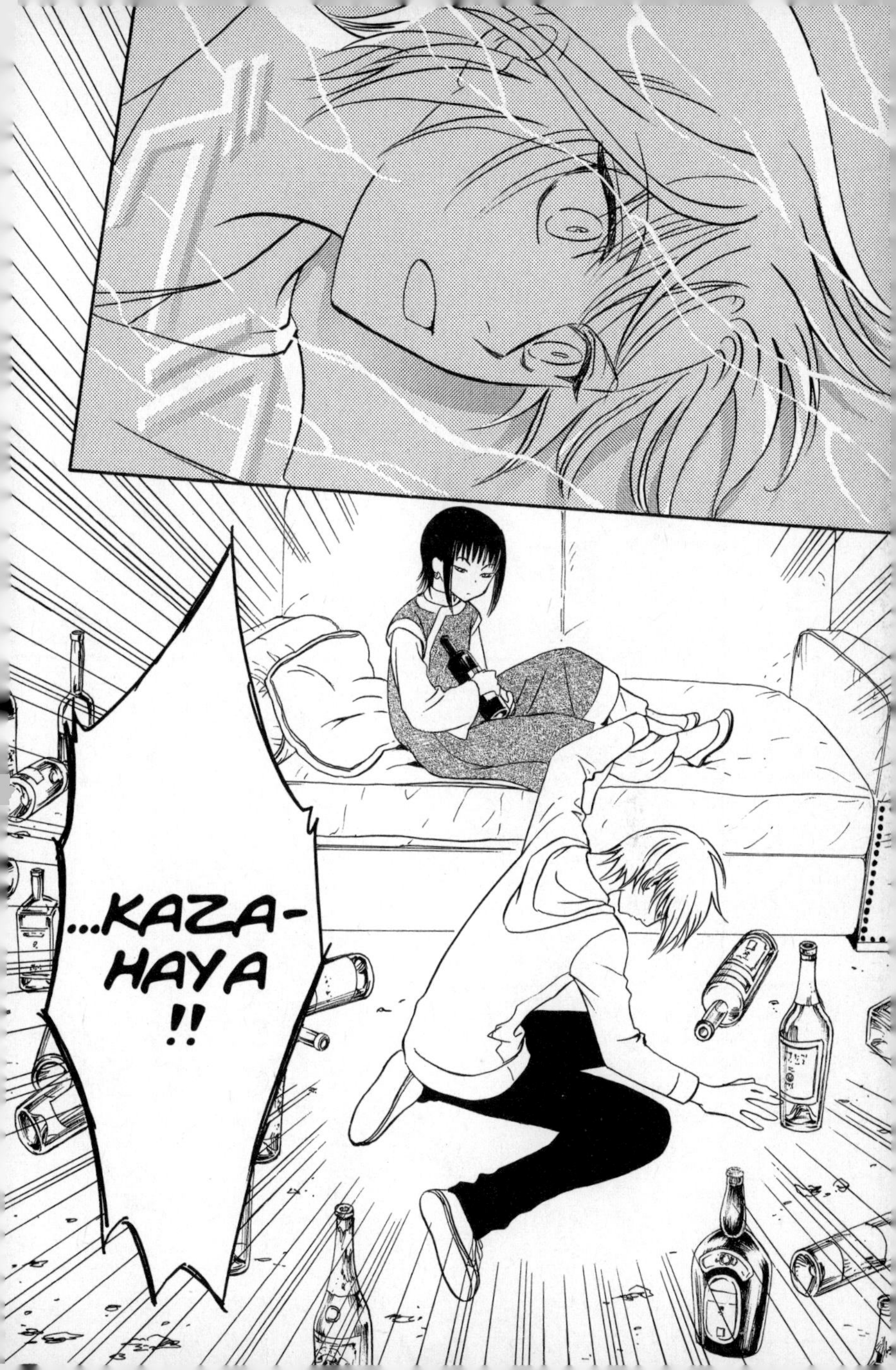
...KAZA-HAYA !!

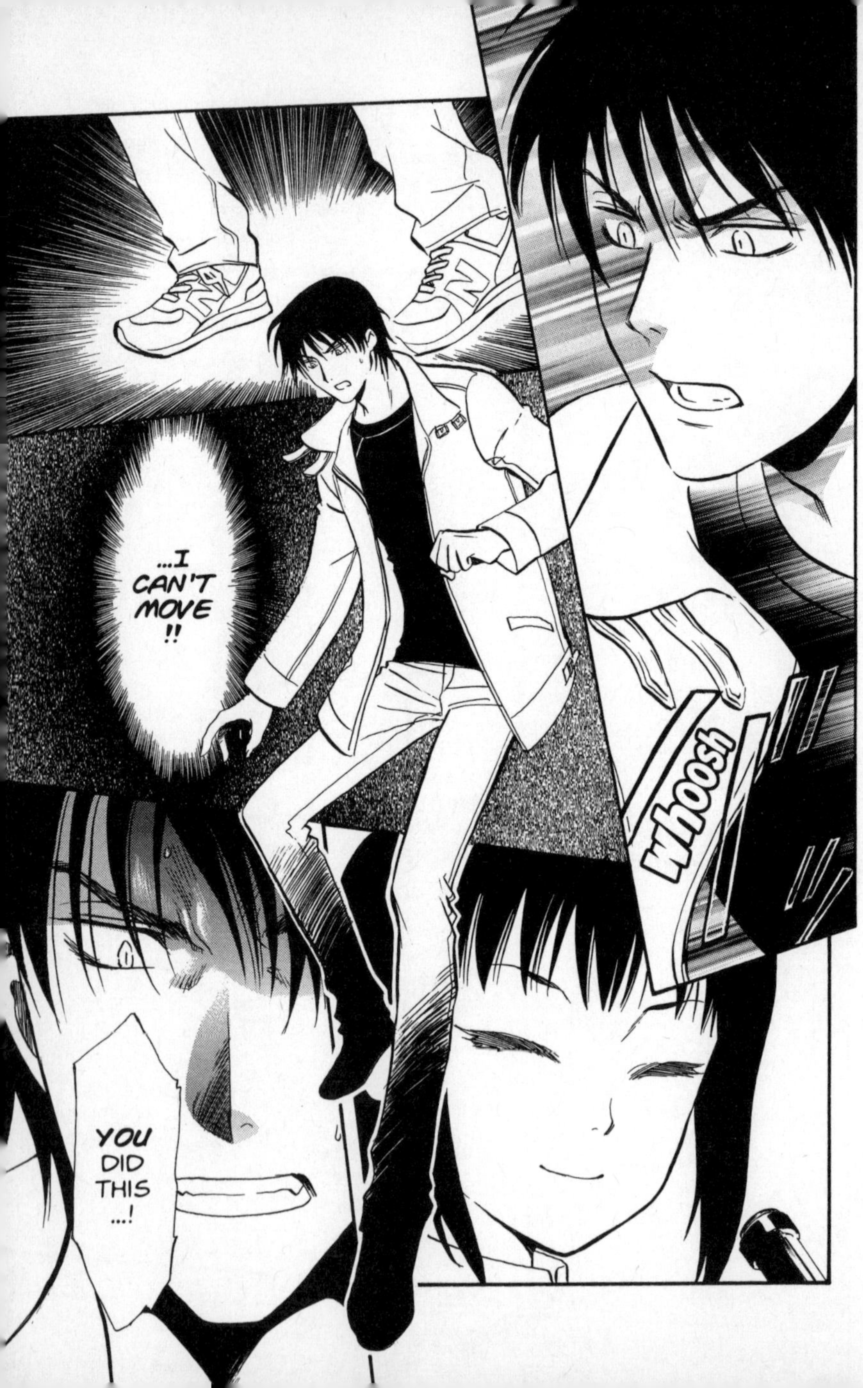
whoosh
...I CAN'T MOVE !!
YOU DID THIS ...!

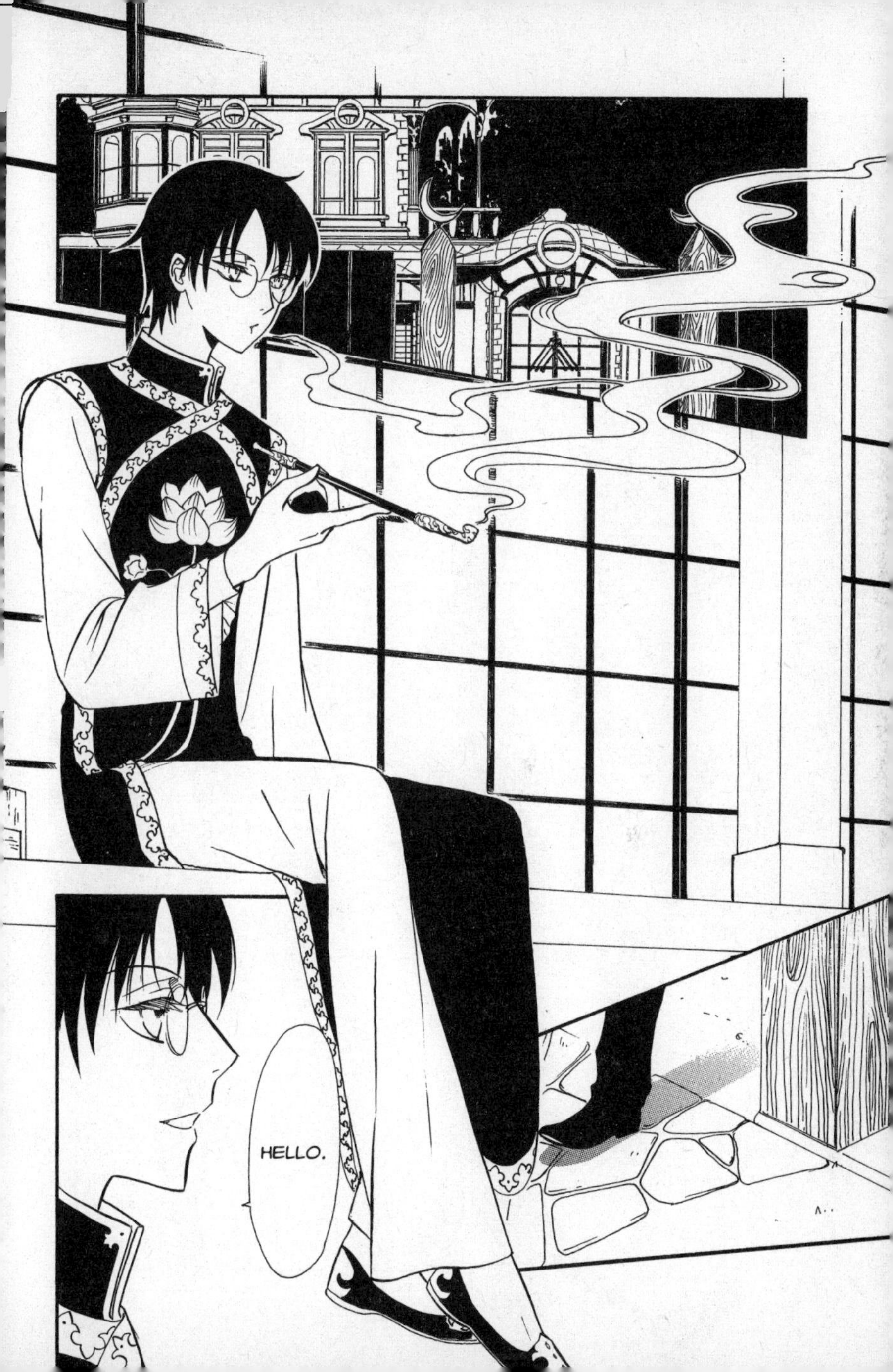
HELLO.

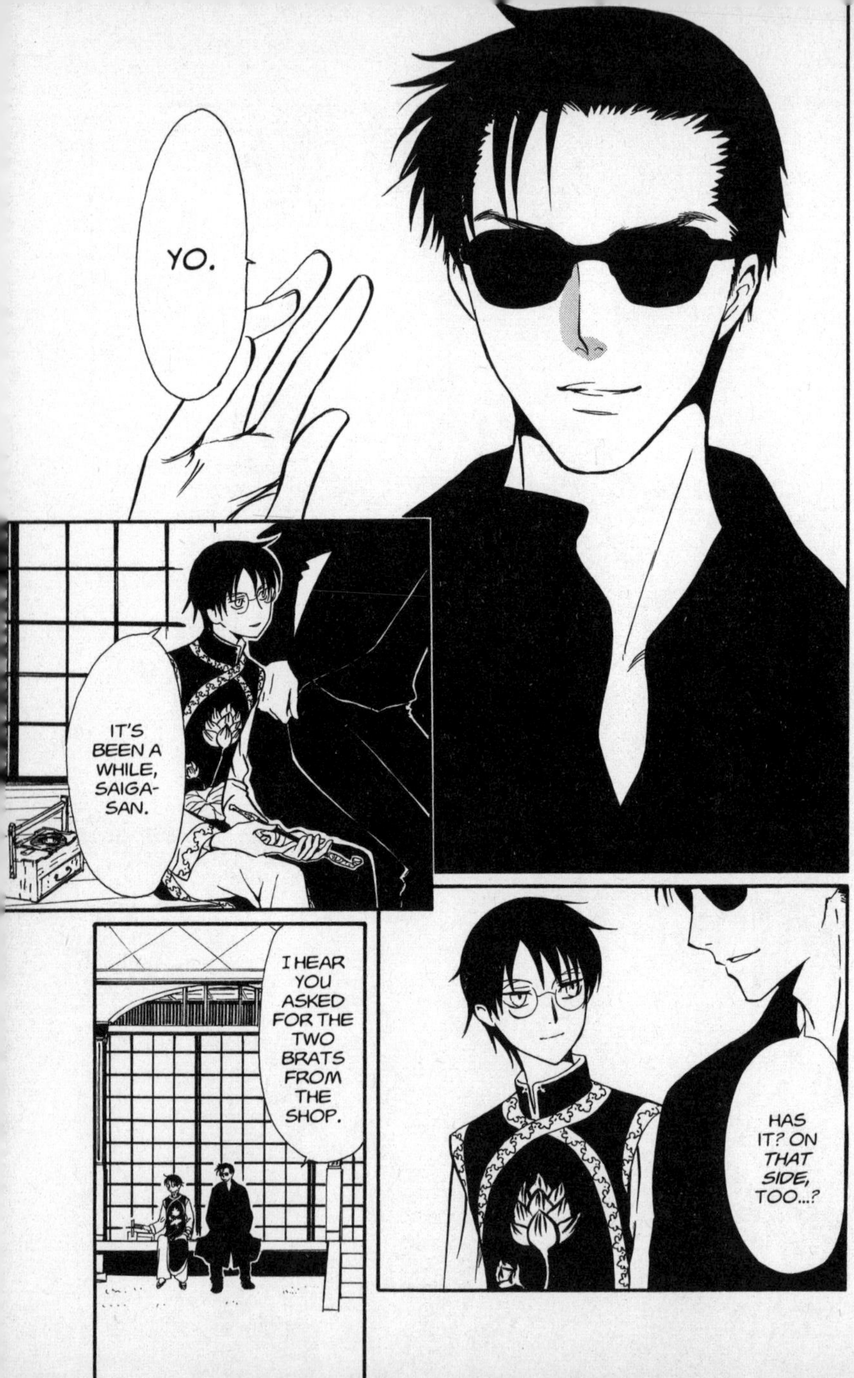
YO.
IT'S BEEN A WHILE, SAIGA-SAN.
HAS IT? ON THAT SIDE, TOO...?
I HEAR YOU ASKED FOR THE TWO BRATS FROM THE SHOP.

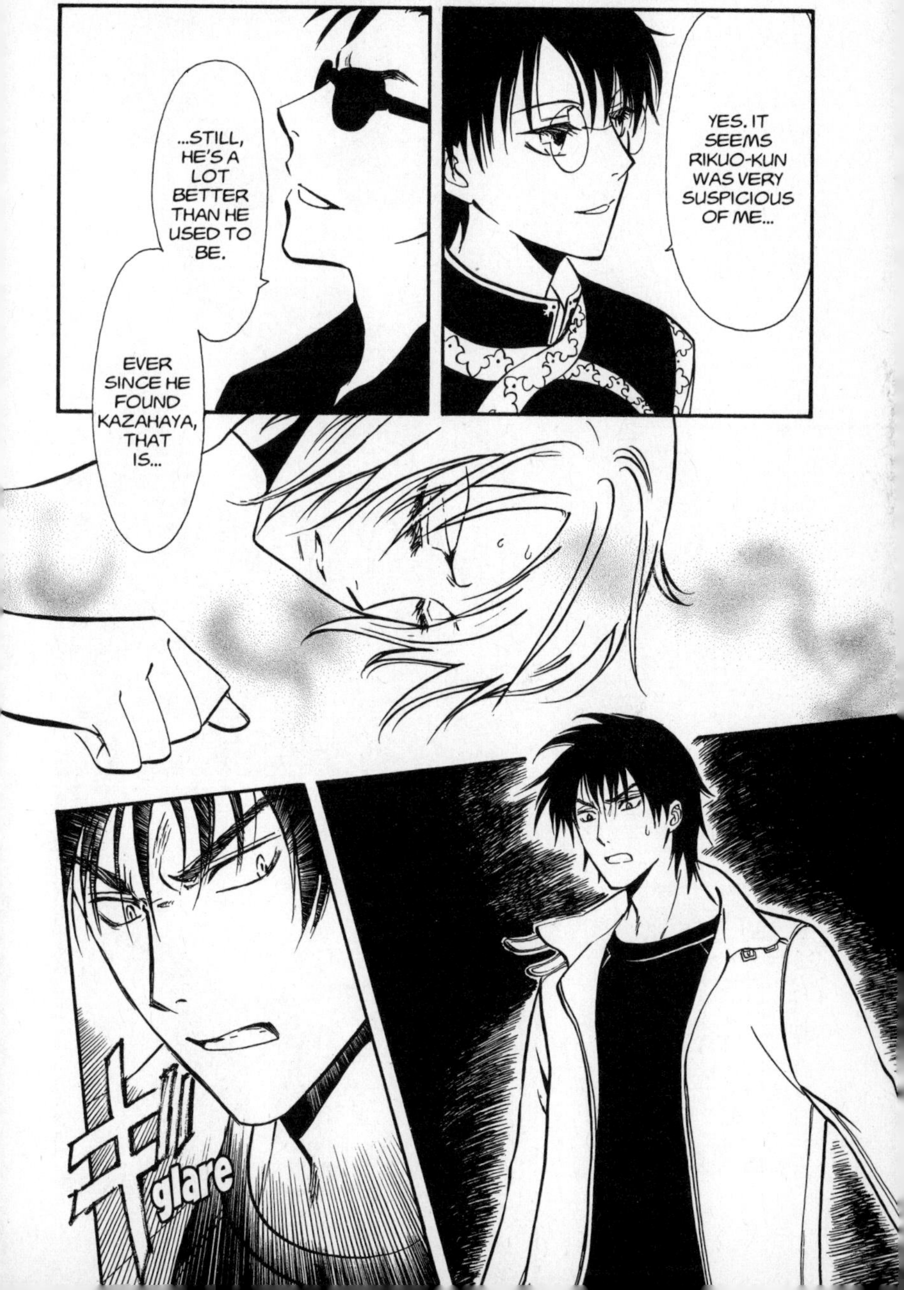
YES. IT SEEMS RIKUO-KUN WAS VERY SUSPICIOUS OF ME...
...STILL, HE'S A LOT BETTER THAN HE USED TO BE.
EVER SINCE HE FOUND KAZAHAYA, THAT IS...
glare

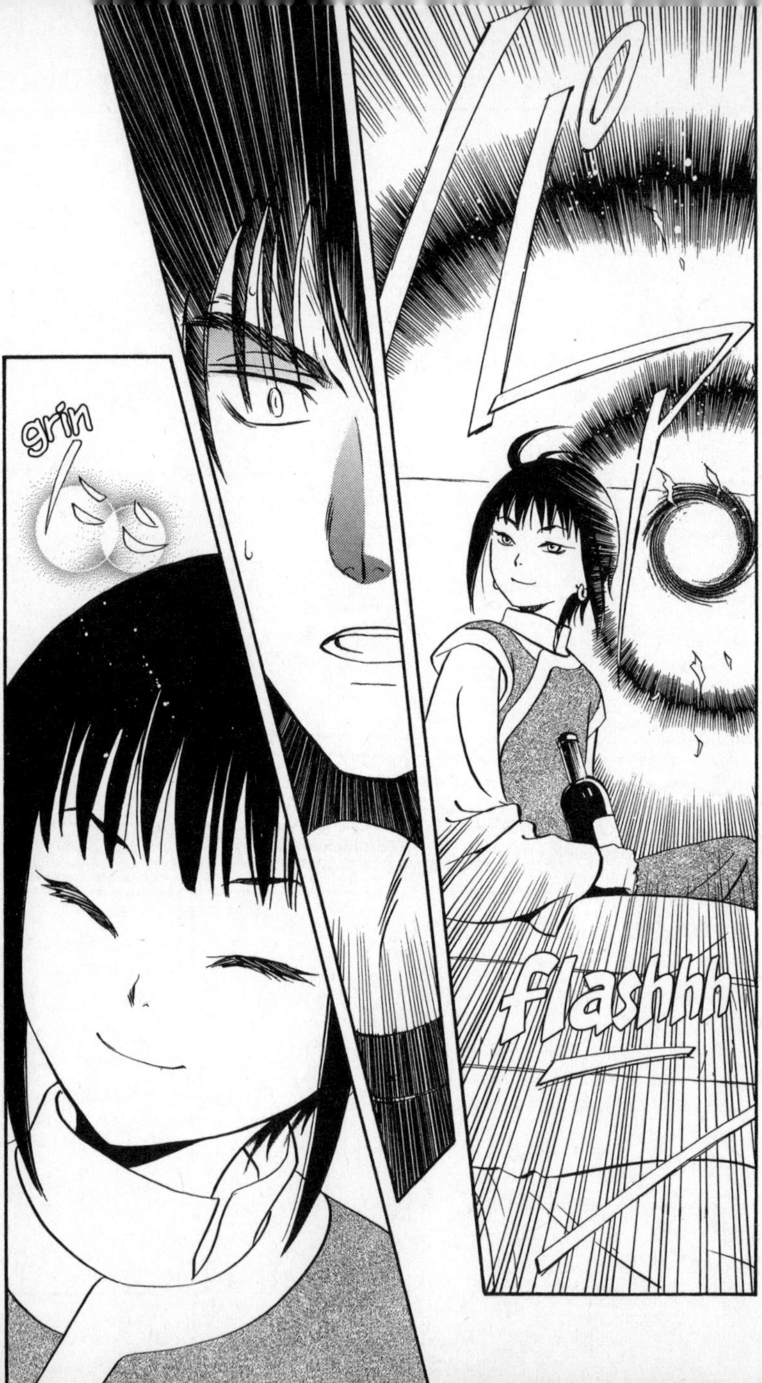
flashhh
grin

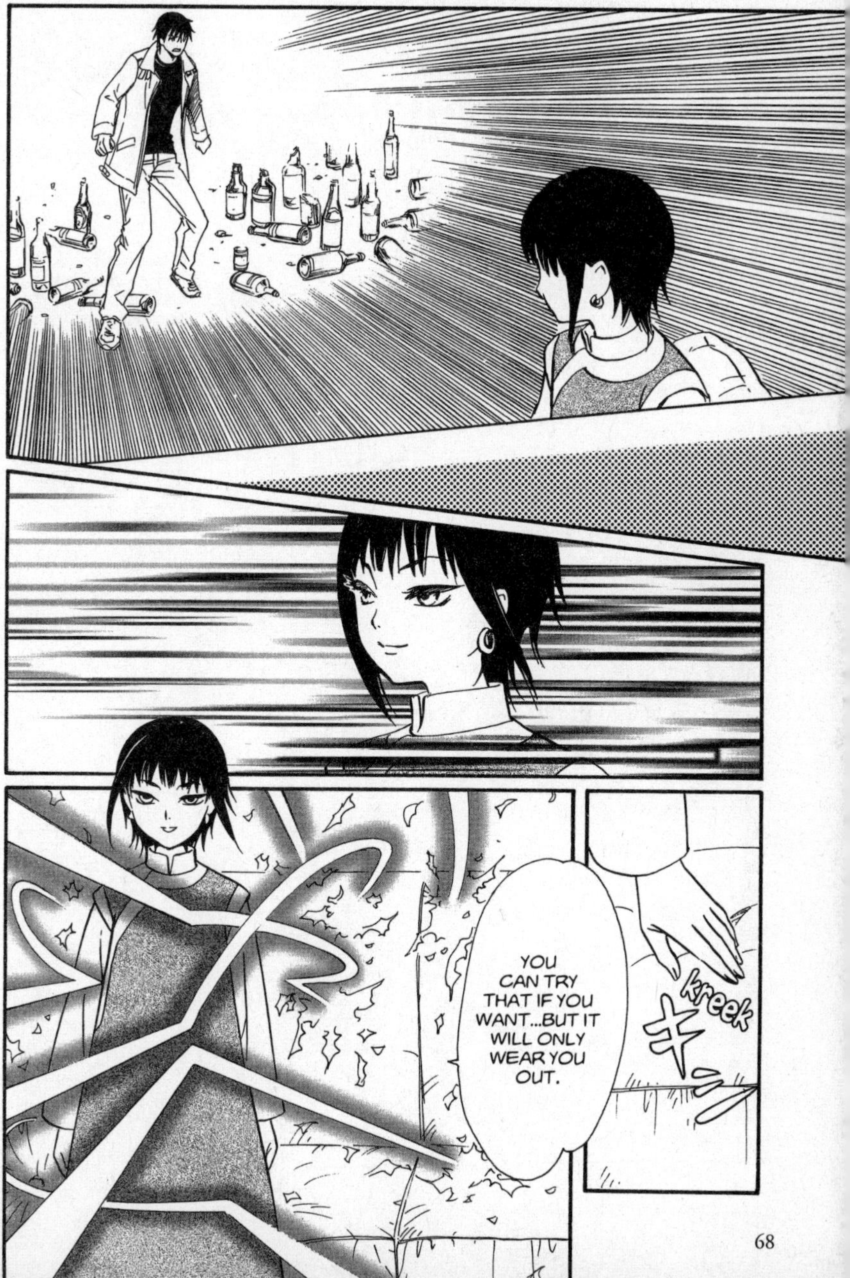
kreek
YOU CAN TRY THAT IF YOU WANT...BUT IT WILL ONLY WEAR YOU OUT.

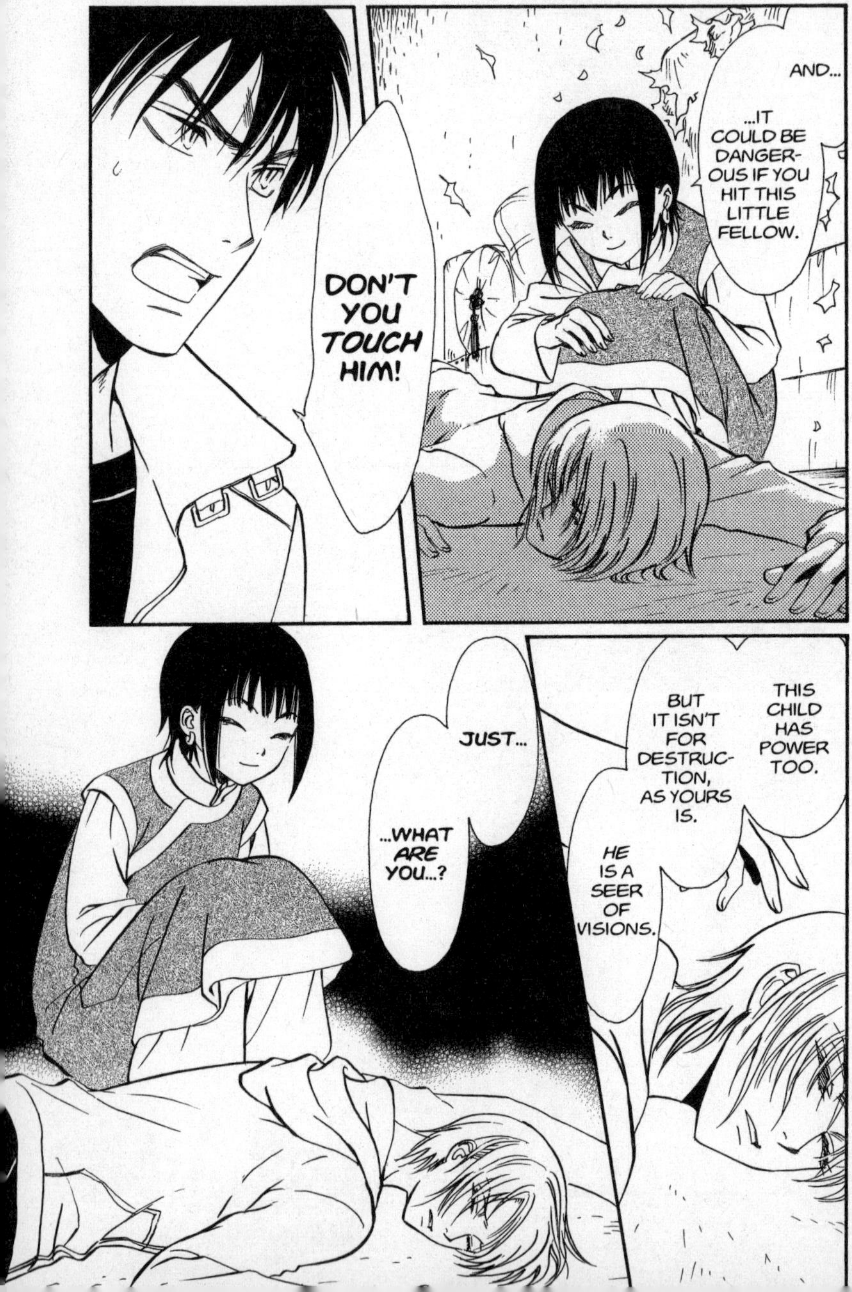
AND...
...IT COULD BE DANGEROUS IF YOU HIT THIS LITTLE FELLOW.
DON'T YOU TOUCH HIM!
THIS CHILD HAS POWER TOO.
BUT IT ISN'T FOR DESTRUCTION, AS YOURS IS.
HE IS A SEER OF VISIONS.
JUST...
...WHAT ARE YOU...?

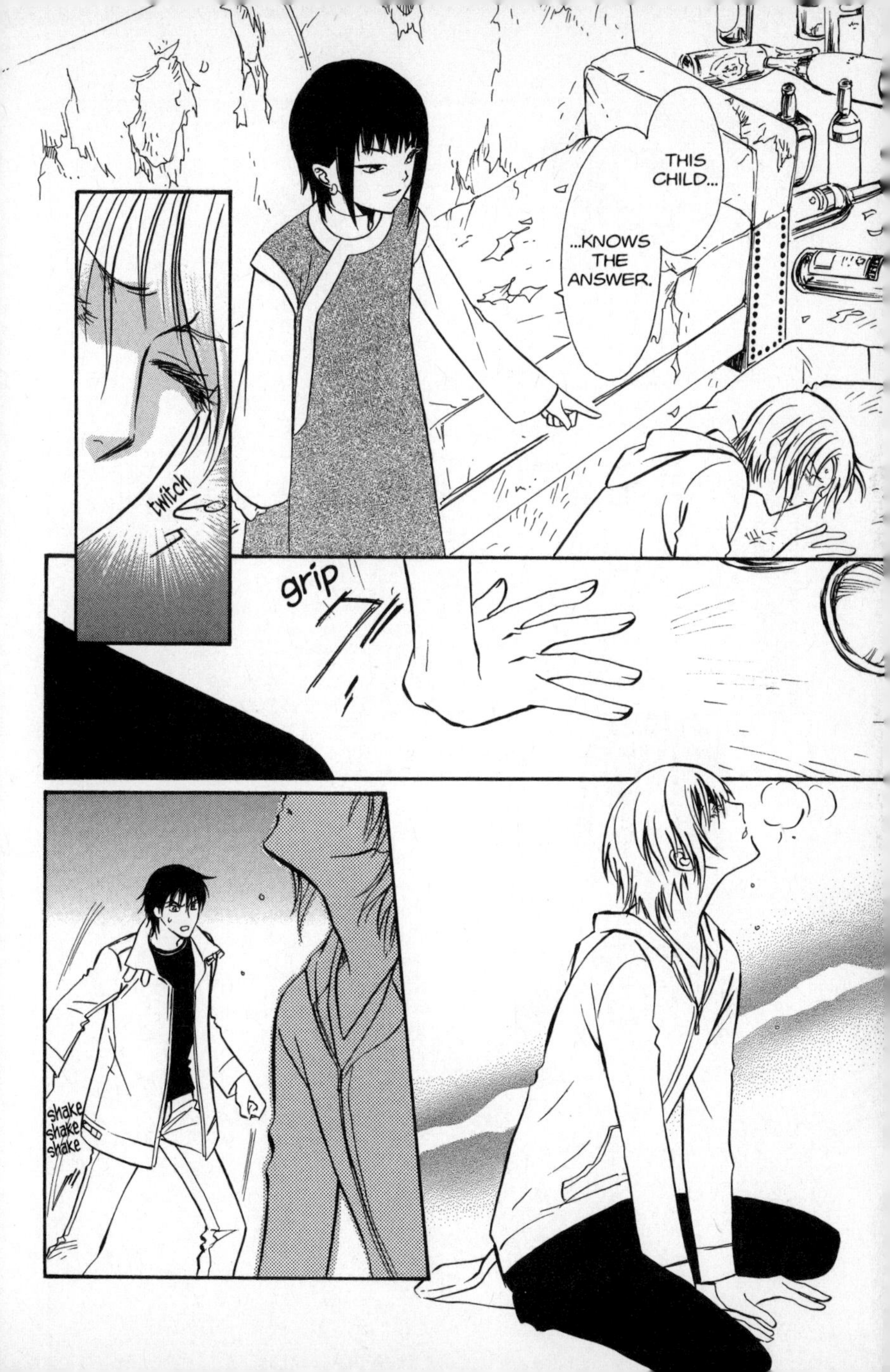
THIS CHILD...
...KNOWS THE ANSWER.
twitch
grip
shake shake shake

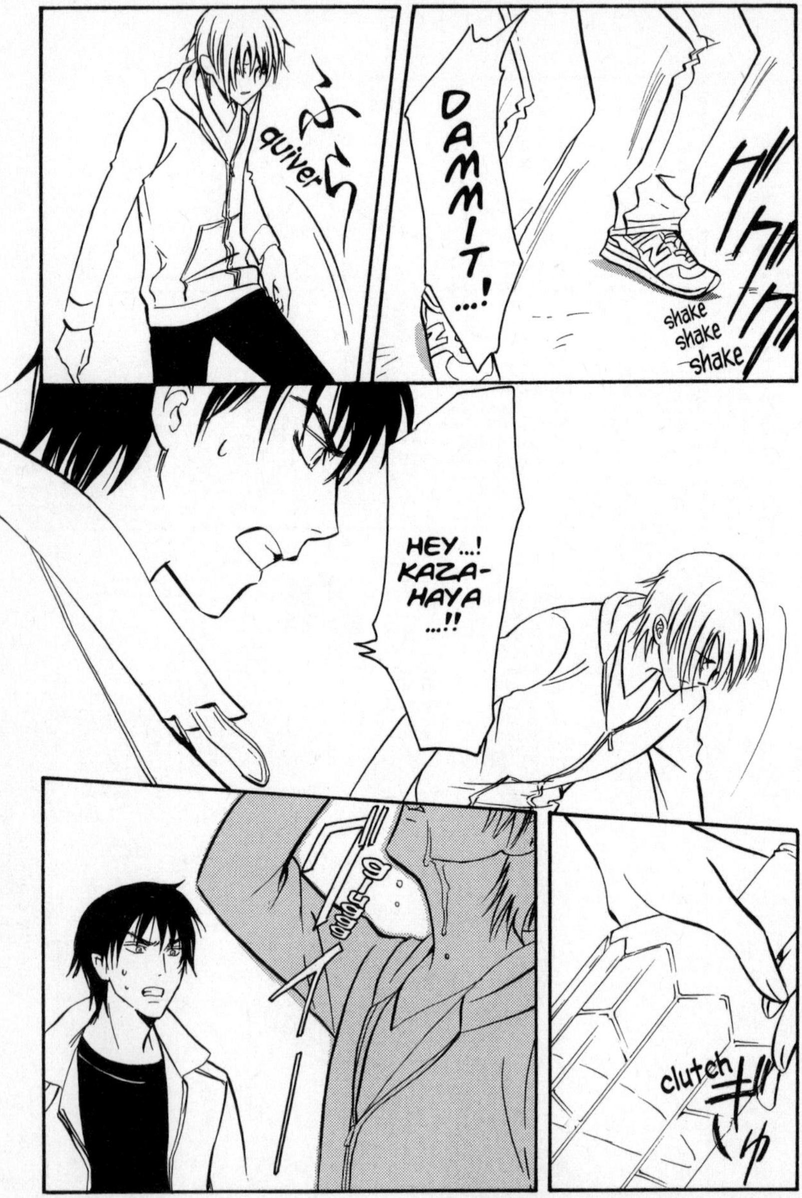
DAMMIT...!
shake
shake
shake
ふら
quiver
HEY...! KAZA-HAYA...!!
clutch

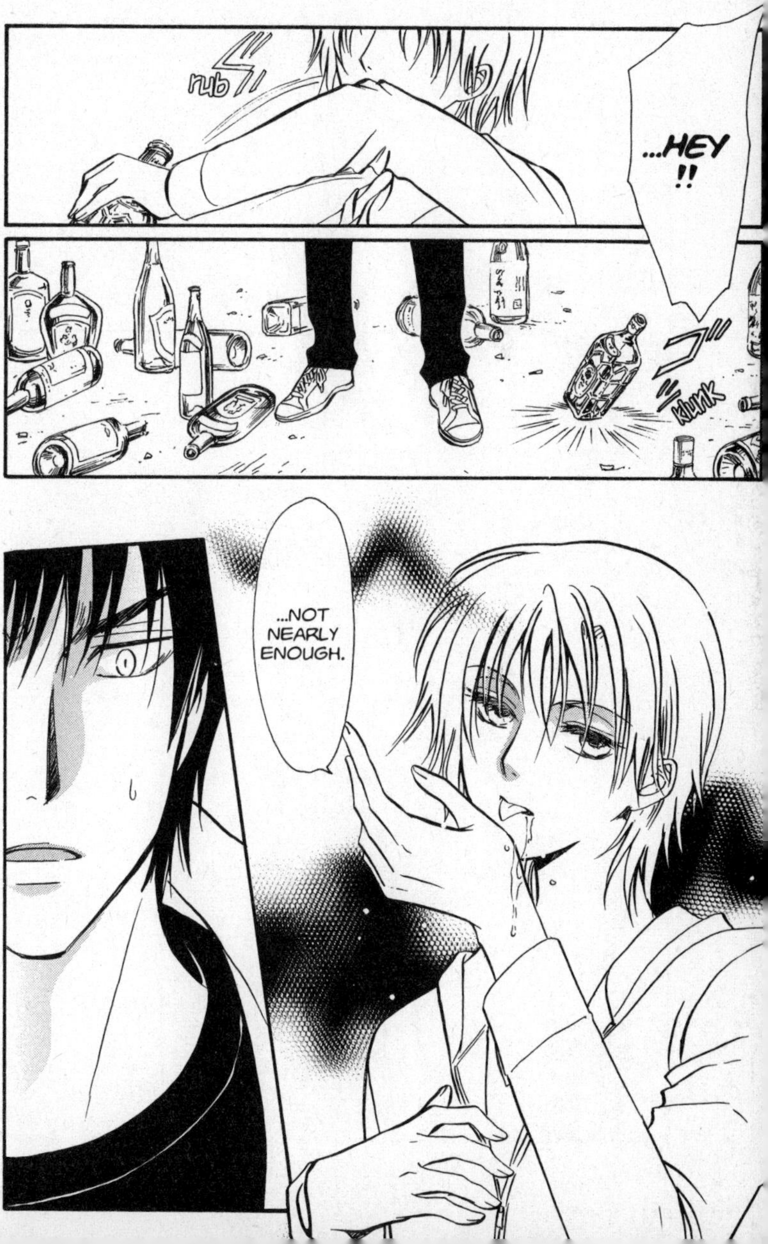
...HEY !!
rub
klunk
...NOT NEARLY ENOUGH.

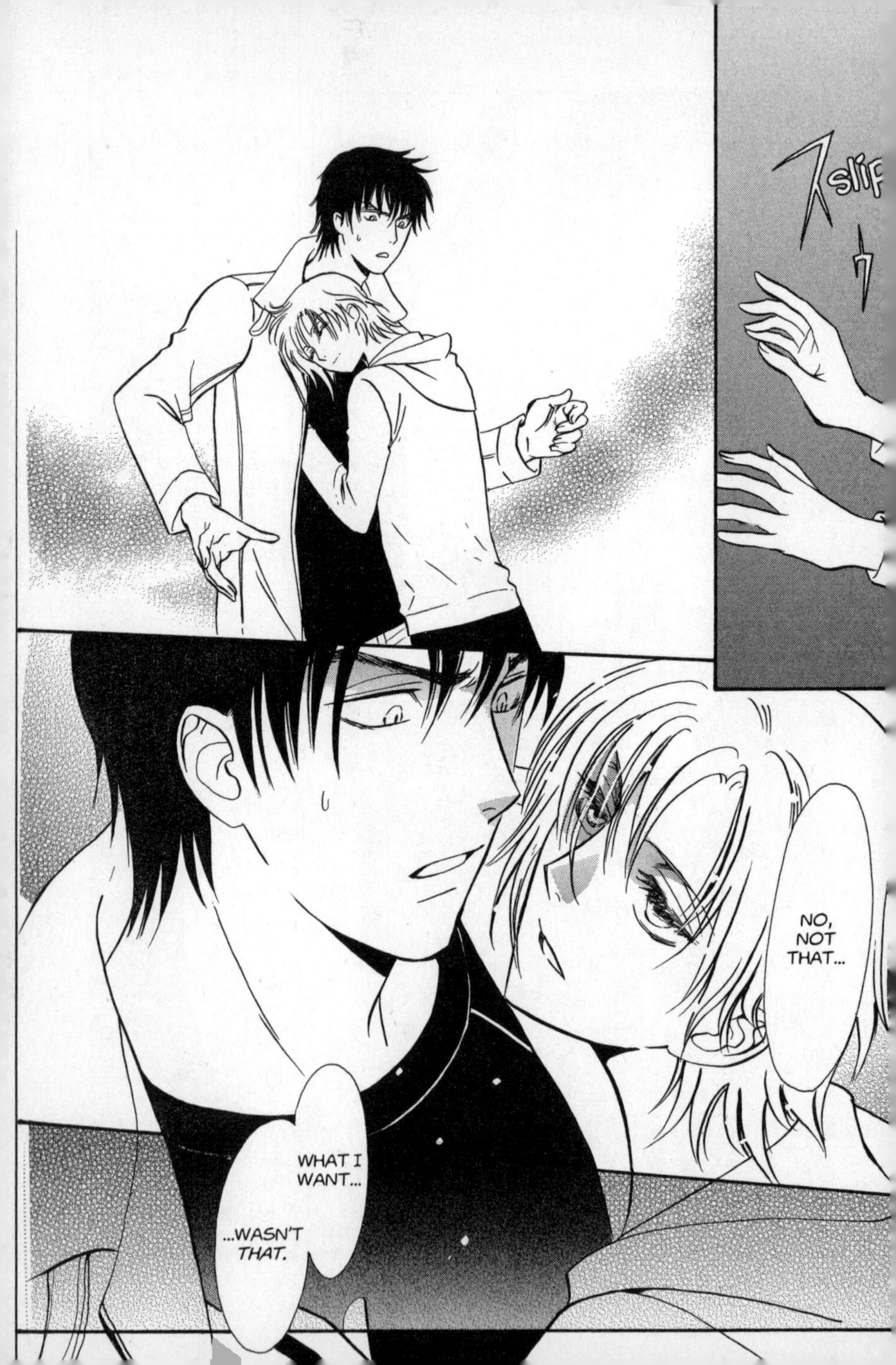
slip
NO, NOT THAT...
WHAT I WANT...
...WASN'T THAT.

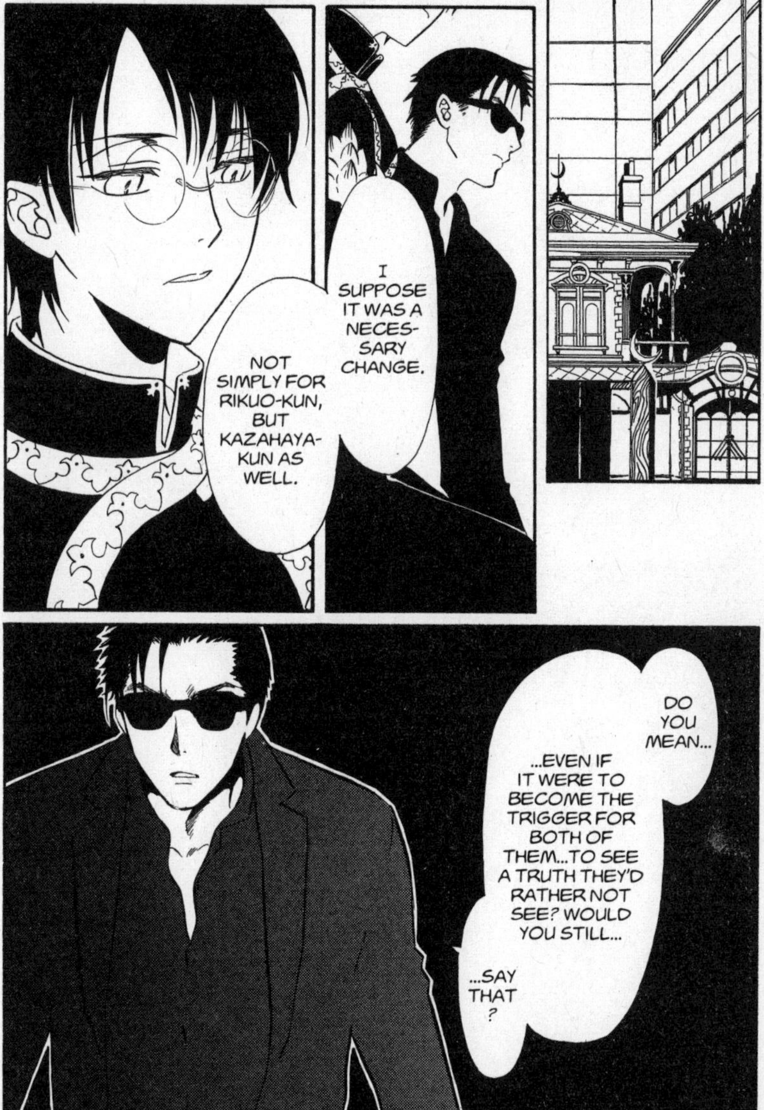
I SUPPOSE IT WAS A NECES-SARY CHANGE.
NOT SIMPLY FOR RIKUO-KUN, BUT KAZAHAYA-KUN AS WELL.
DO YOU MEAN...
...EVEN IF IT WERE TO BECOME THE TRIGGER FOR BOTH OF THEM...TO SEE A TRUTH THEY'D RATHER NOT SEE? WOULD YOU STILL...
...SAY THAT ?

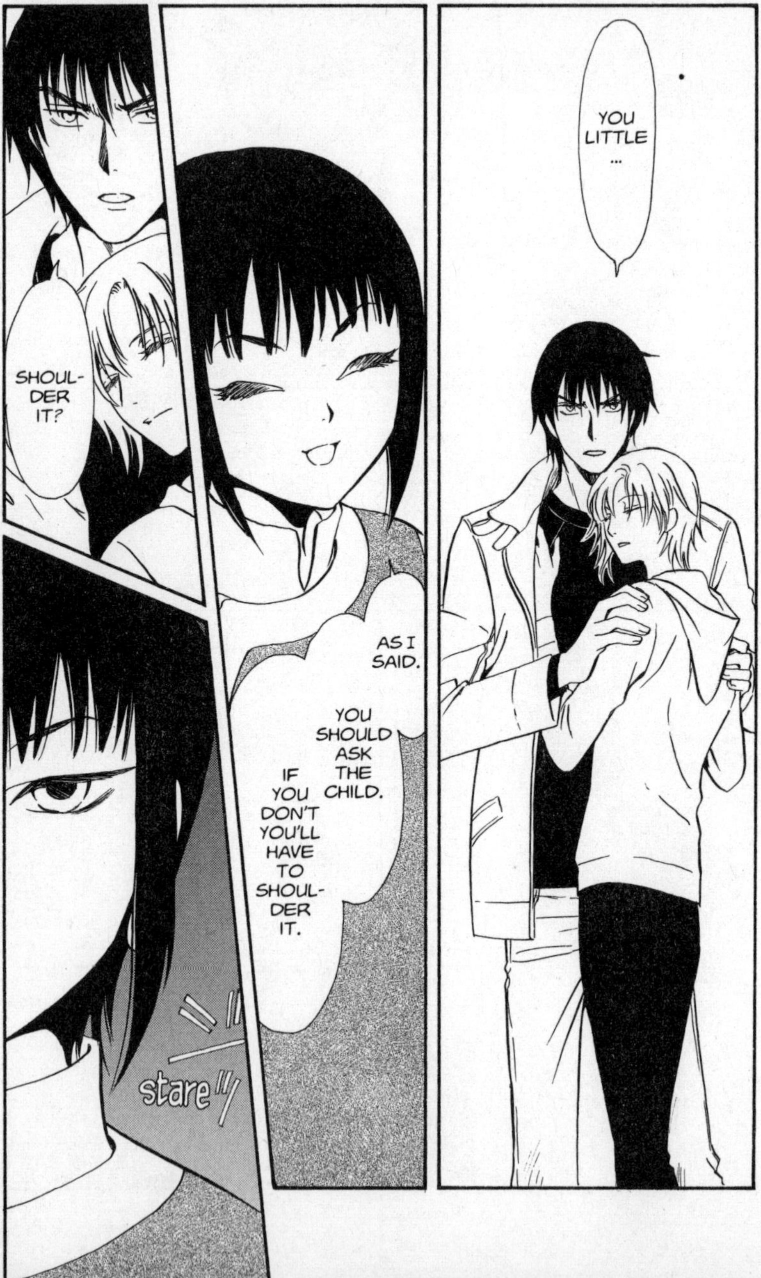
YOU LITTLE ...
AS I SAID.
YOU SHOULD ASK THE CHILD.
IF YOU DON'T YOU'LL HAVE TO SHOULDER IT.
SHOULDER IT?
stare

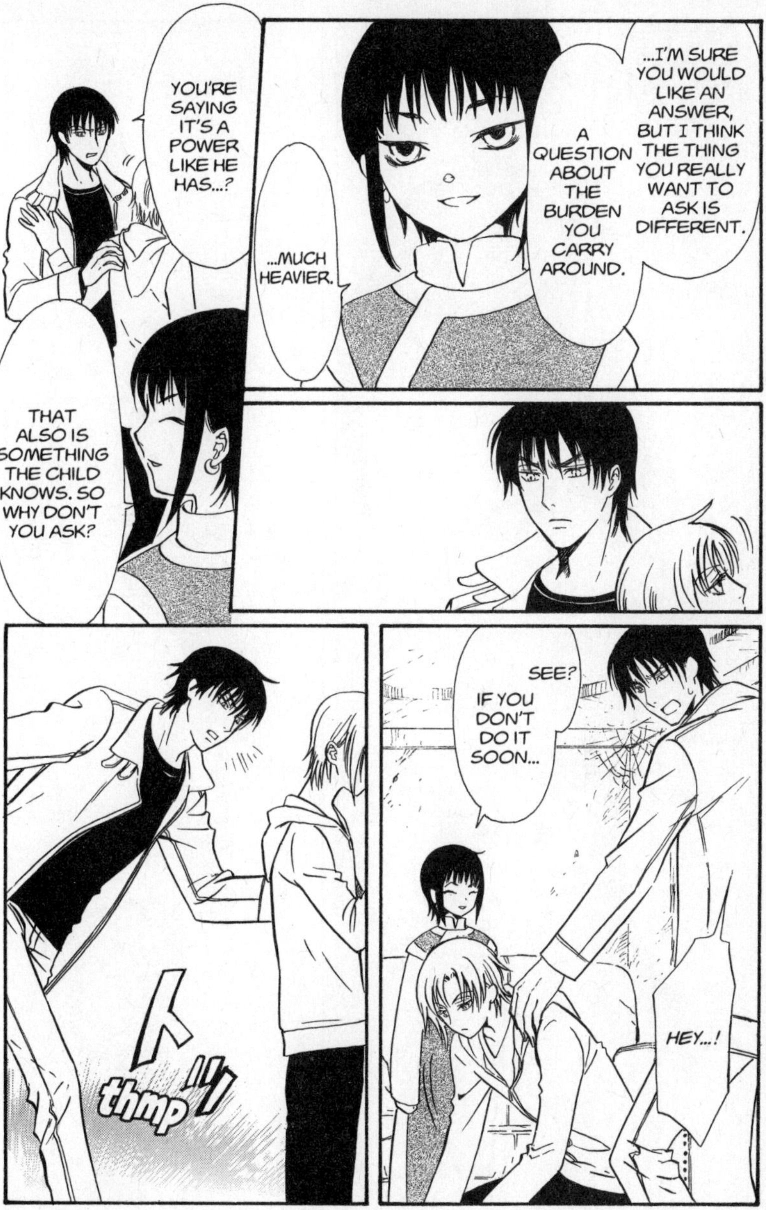

...I'M SURE YOU WOULD LIKE AN ANSWER, BUT I THINK THE THING YOU REALLY WANT TO ASK IS DIFFERENT.
A QUESTION ABOUT THE BURDEN YOU CARRY AROUND.
...MUCH HEAVIER.
YOU'RE SAYING IT'S A POWER LIKE HE HAS...?
THAT ALSO IS SOMETHING THE CHILD KNOWS. SO WHY DON'T YOU ASK?
SEE?
IF YOU DON'T DO IT SOON...
HEY...!
トッ
thmp

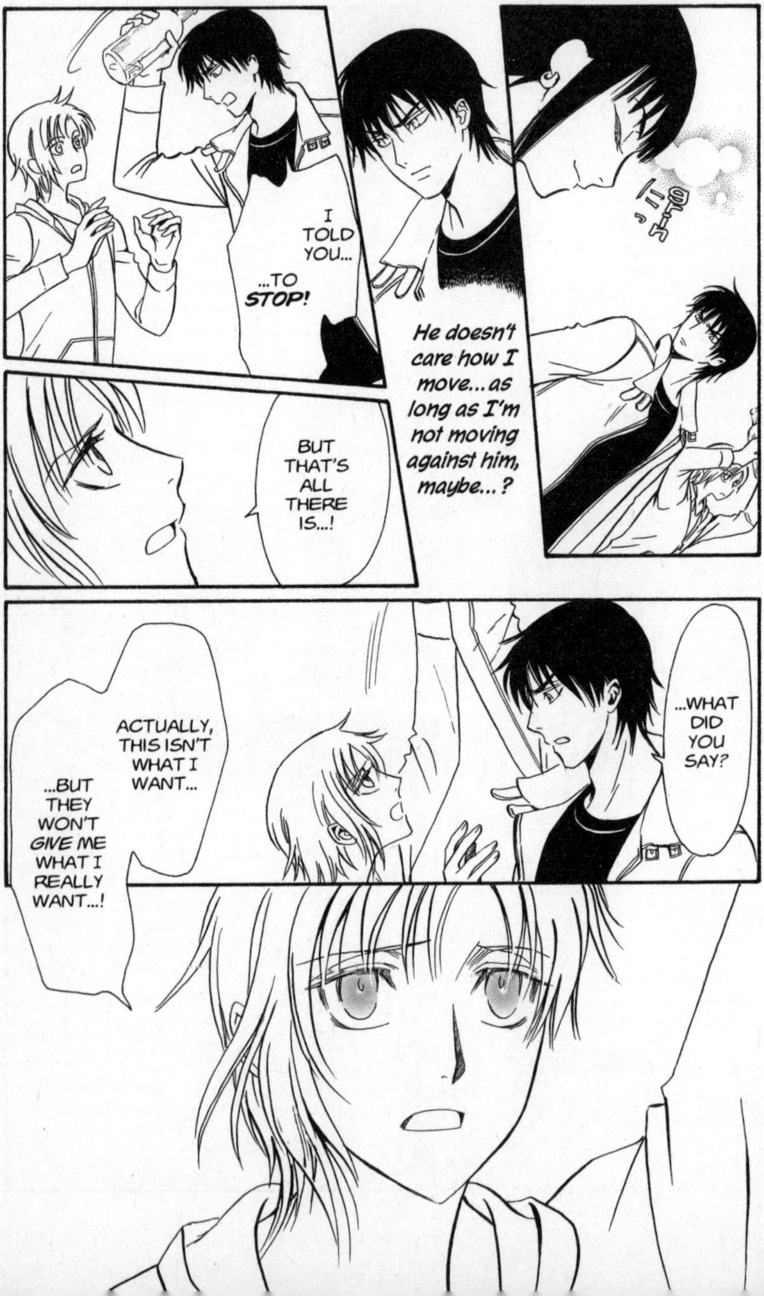
He doesn't care how I move... as long as I'm not moving against him, maybe...?
I TOLD YOU...
...TO STOP!
BUT THAT'S ALL THERE IS...!
...WHAT DID YOU SAY?
ACTUALLY, THIS ISN'T WHAT I WANT...
...BUT THEY WON'T GIVE ME WHAT I REALLY WANT...!

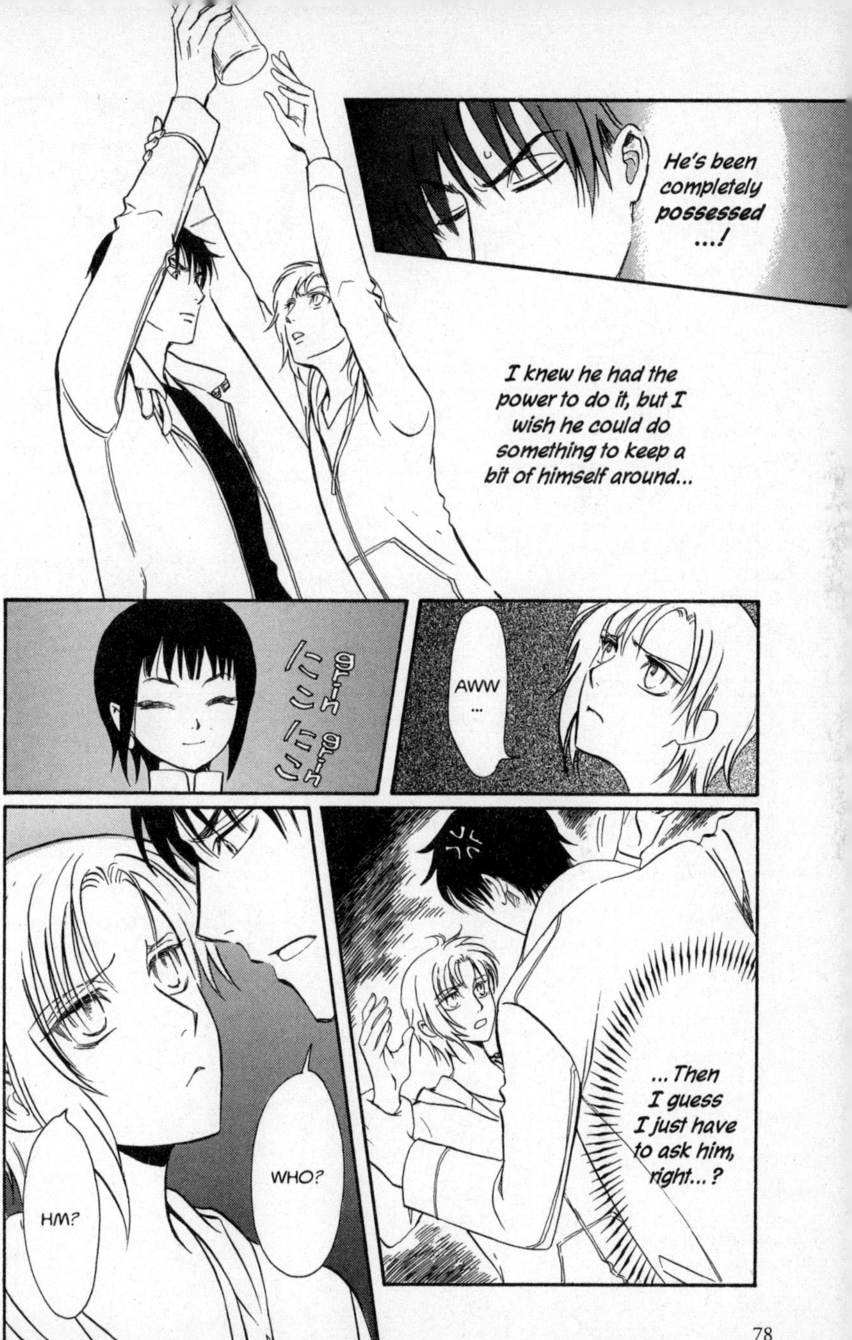
He's been completely possessed ...!
I knew he had the power to do it, but I wish he could do something to keep a bit of himself around...
AWW ...
にこにこ
grin grin
...Then I guess I just have to ask him, right...?
WHO?
HM?

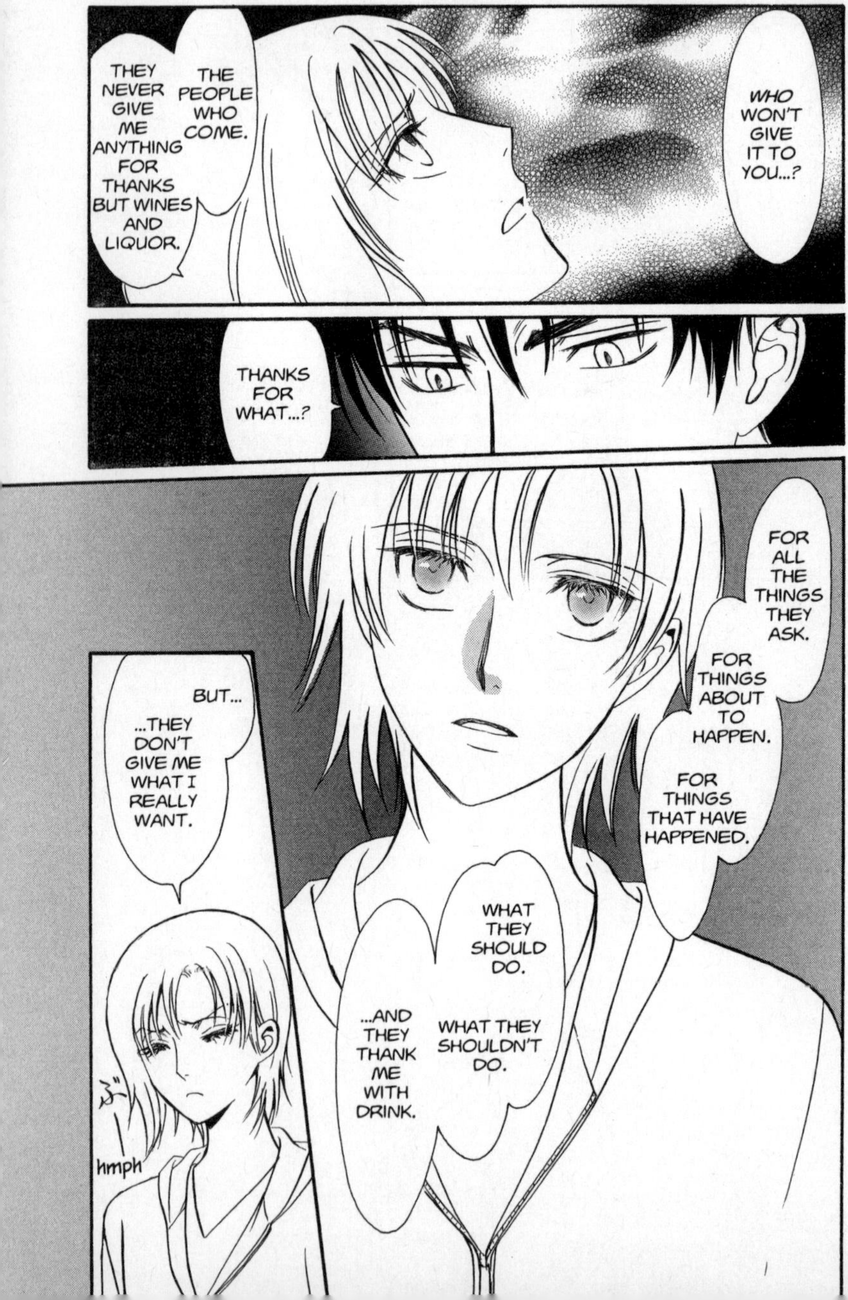
WHO WON'T GIVE IT TO YOU...?
THE PEOPLE WHO COME.
THEY NEVER GIVE ME ANYTHING FOR THANKS BUT WINES AND LIQUOR.
THANKS FOR WHAT...?
FOR ALL THE THINGS THEY ASK.
FOR THINGS ABOUT TO HAPPEN.
FOR THINGS THAT HAVE HAPPENED.
WHAT THEY SHOULD DO.
WHAT THEY SHOULDN'T DO.
...AND THEY THANK ME WITH DRINK.
BUT...
...THEY DON'T GIVE ME WHAT I REALLY WANT.
ぶー
hmph

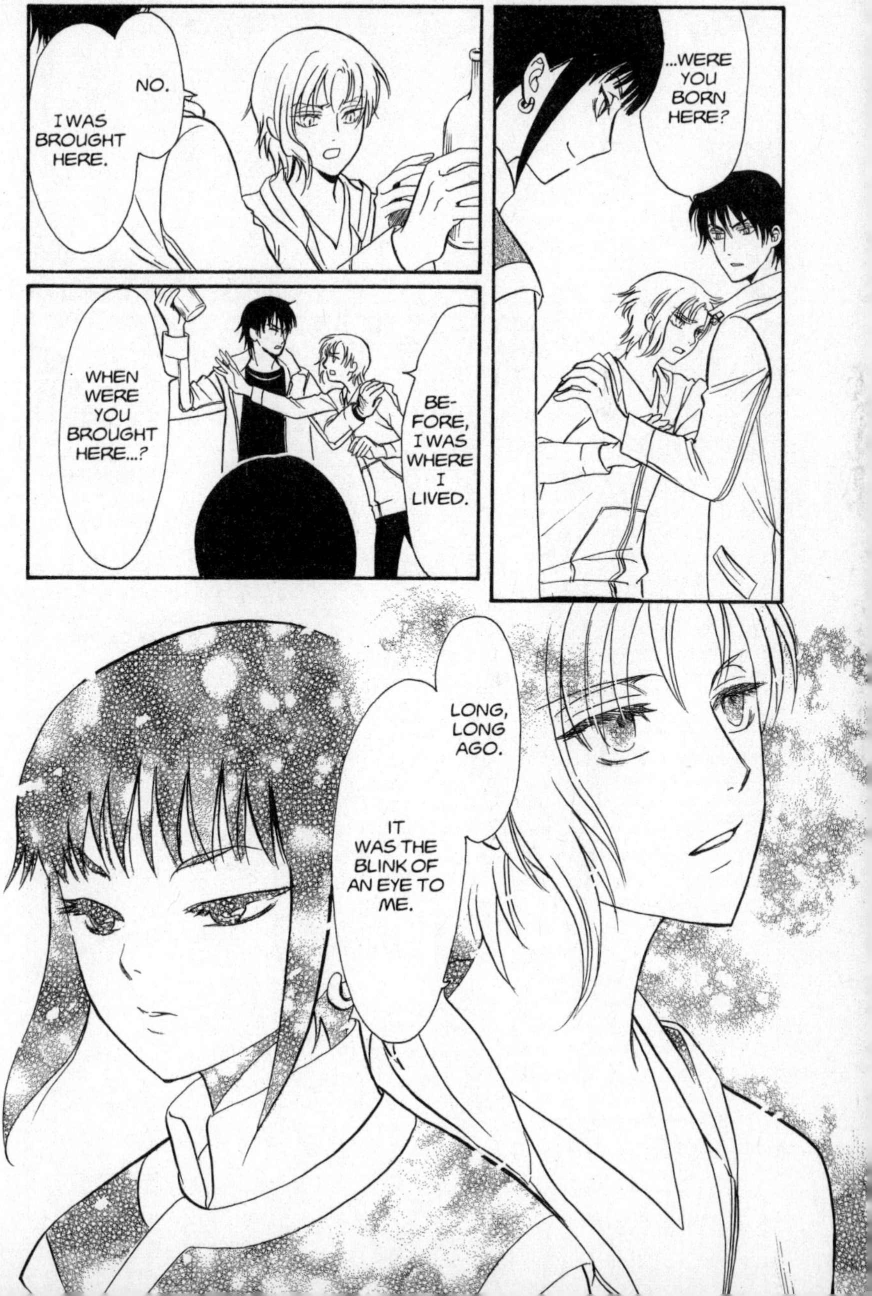
...WERE YOU BORN HERE?
NO.
I WAS BROUGHT HERE.
WHEN WERE YOU BROUGHT HERE...?
BE-FORE, I WAS WHERE I LIVED.
LONG, LONG AGO.
IT WAS THE BLINK OF AN EYE TO ME.

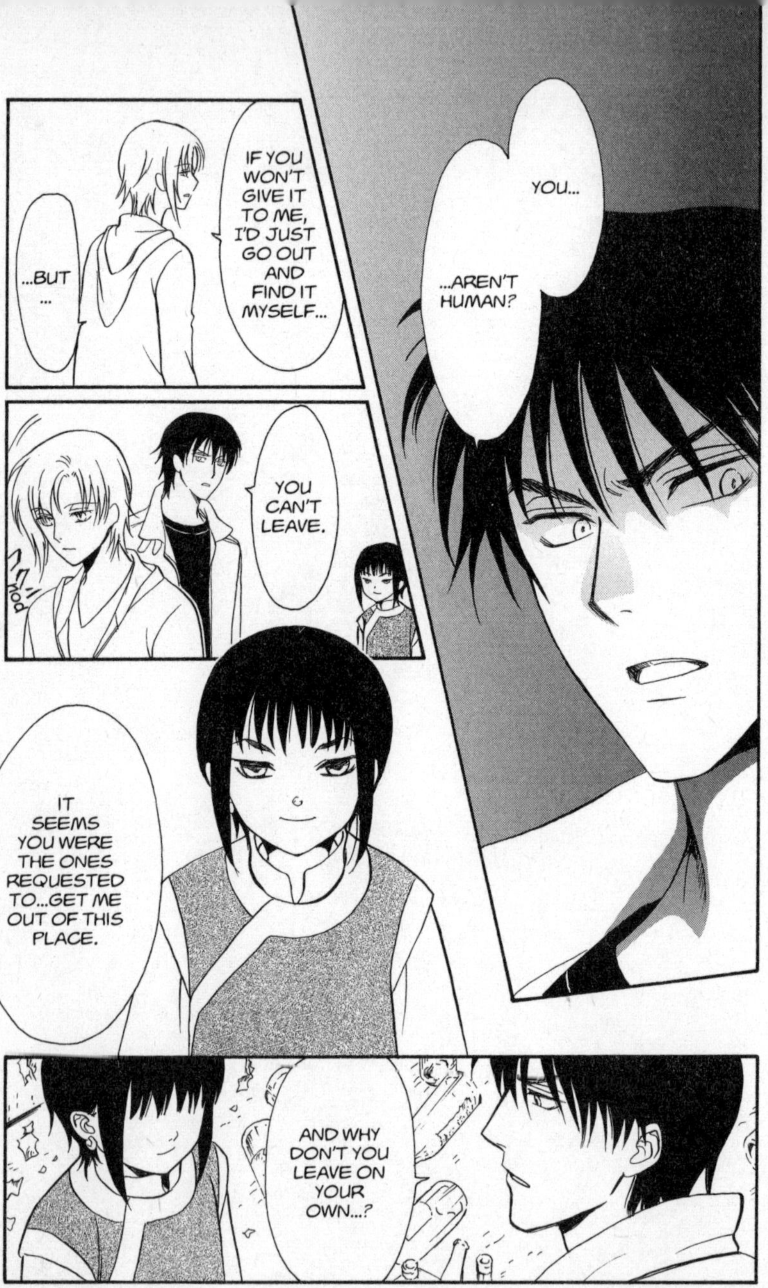
YOU...
...AREN'T HUMAN?
IF YOU WON'T GIVE IT TO ME, I'D JUST GO OUT AND FIND IT MYSELF...
...BUT ...
YOU CAN'T LEAVE.
nod
IT SEEMS YOU WERE THE ONES REQUESTED TO...GET ME OUT OF THIS PLACE.
AND WHY DON'T YOU LEAVE ON YOUR OWN...?

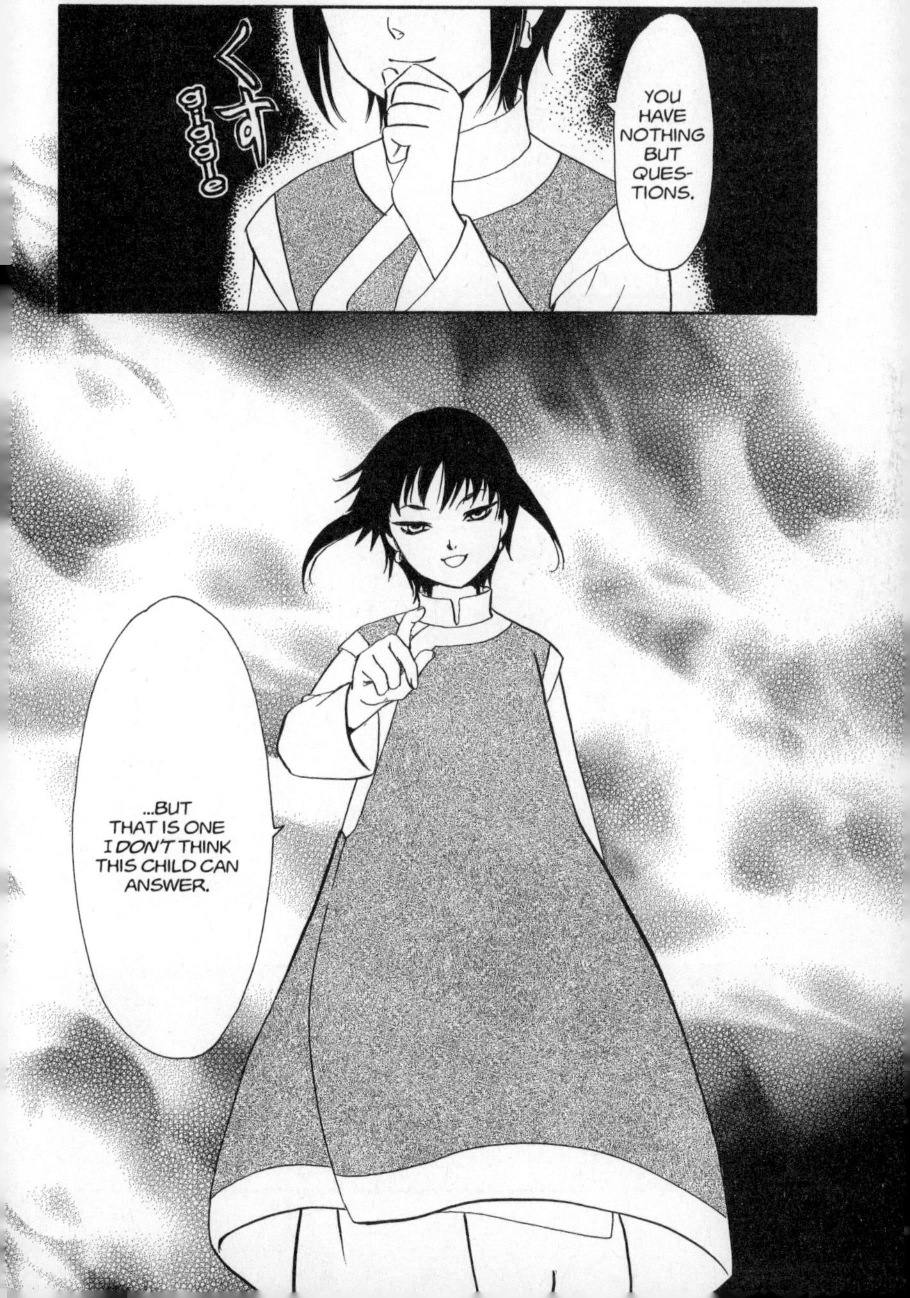
くす
giggle
YOU HAVE NOTHING BUT QUES-TIONS.
...BUT THAT IS ONE I *DON'T* THINK THIS CHILD CAN ANSWER.

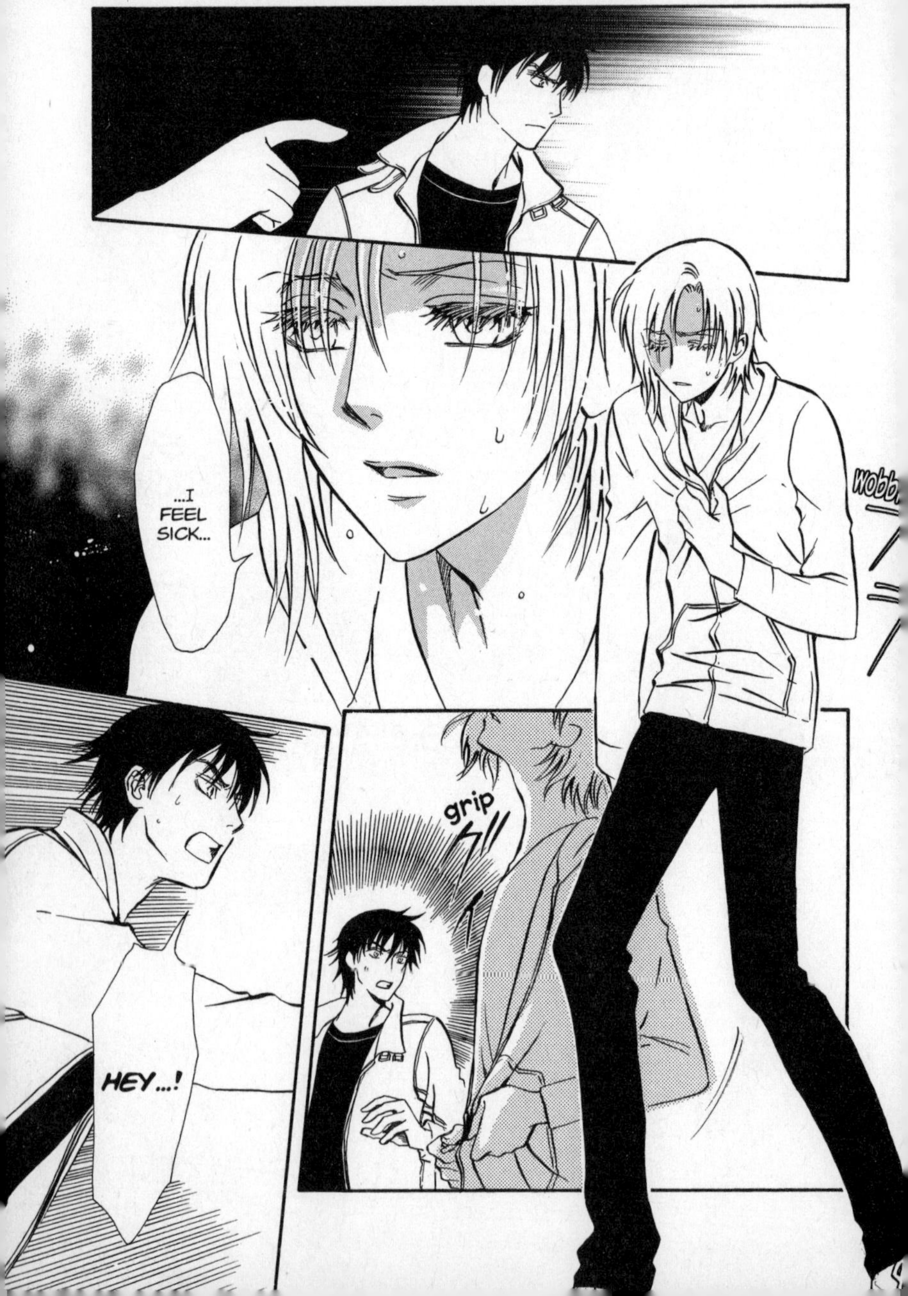
wobb
...I FEEL SICK...
grip
HEY...!

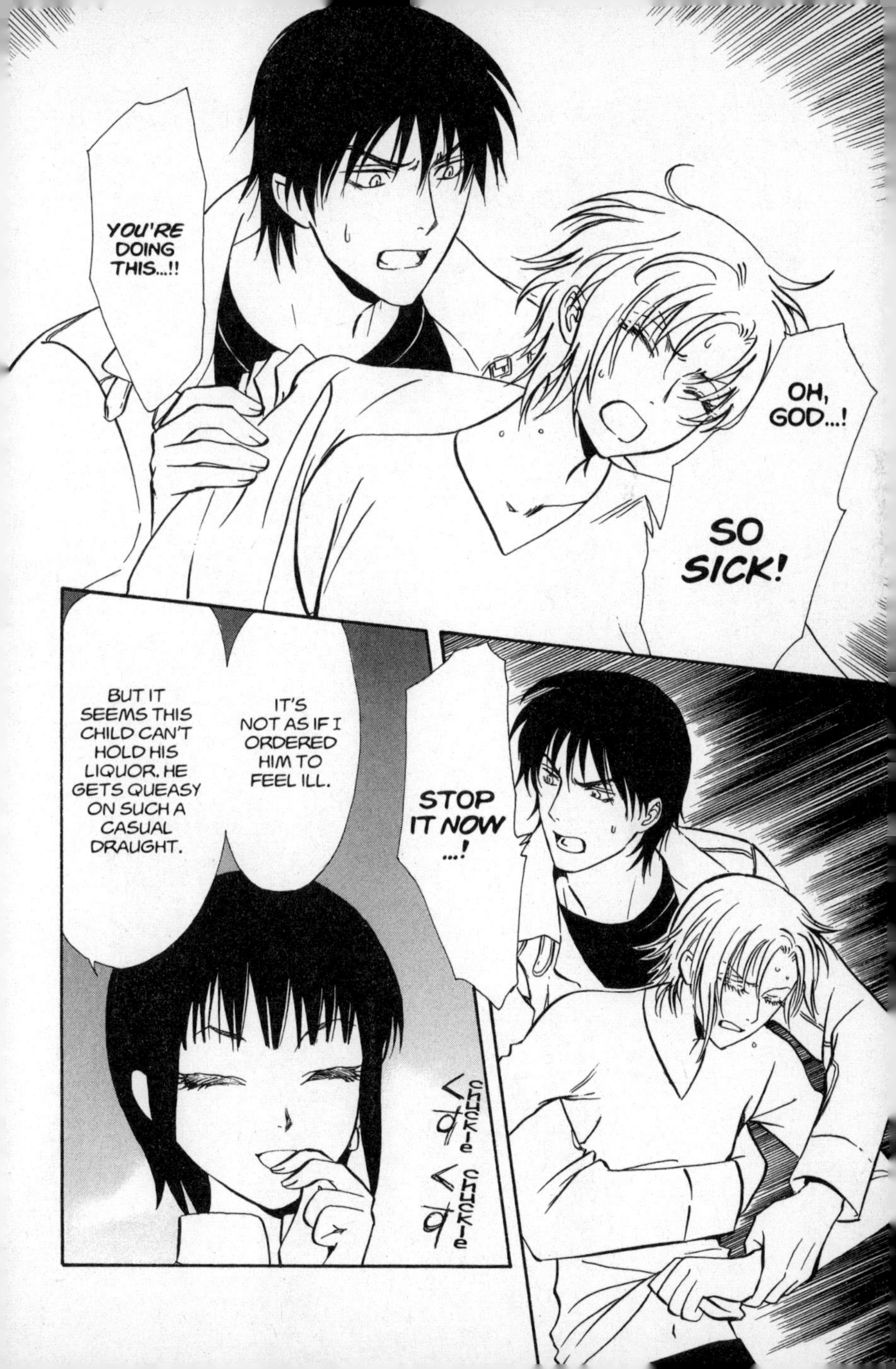
YOU'RE DOING THIS...!!
OH, GOD...!
SO SICK!
STOP IT NOW ...!
IT'S NOT AS IF I ORDERED HIM TO FEEL ILL.
BUT IT SEEMS THIS CHILD CAN'T HOLD HIS LIQUOR. HE GETS QUEASY ON SUCH A CASUAL DRAUGHT.
chuckle chuckle

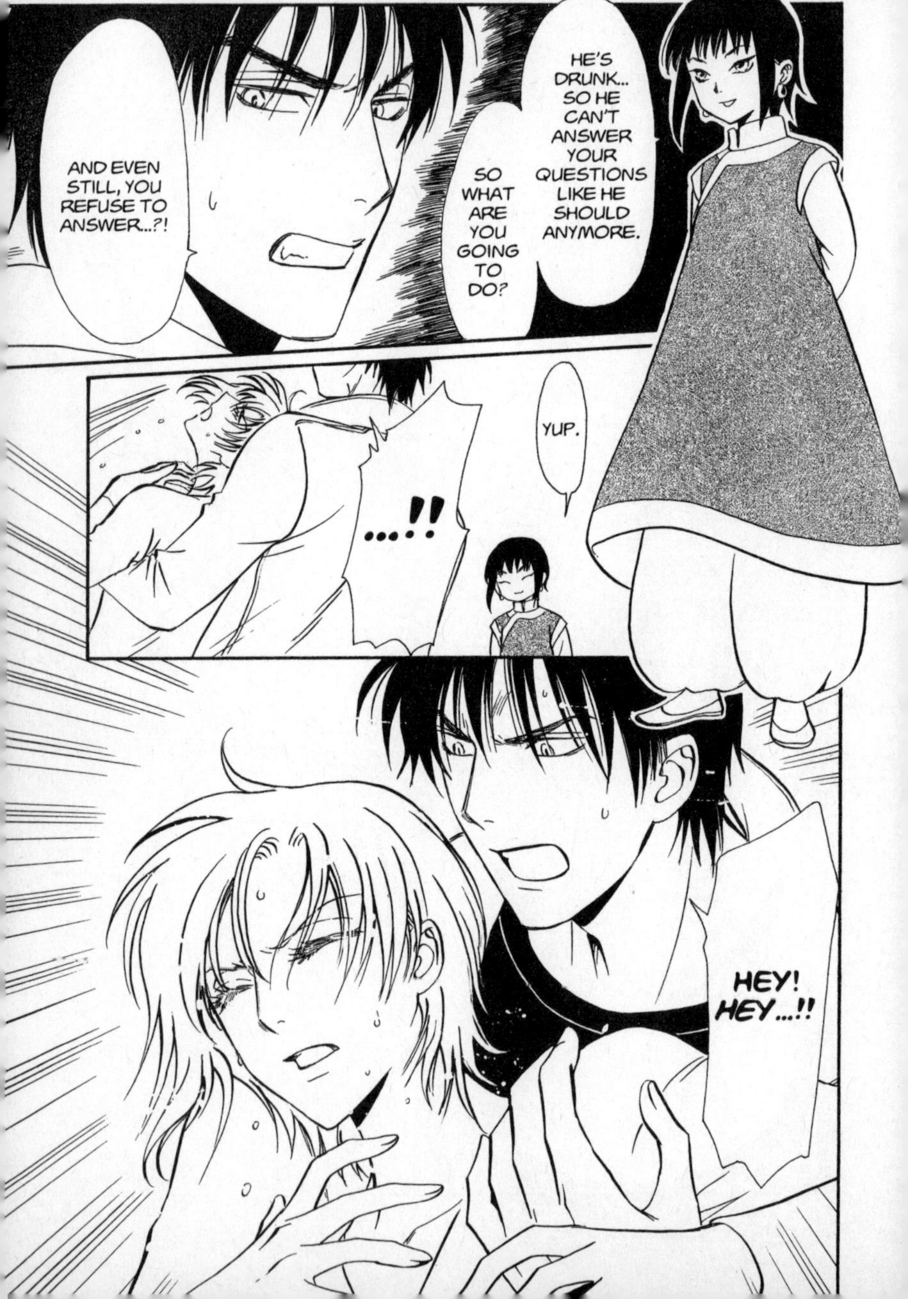
HE'S DRUNK... SO HE CAN'T ANSWER YOUR QUESTIONS LIKE HE SHOULD ANYMORE.
SO WHAT ARE YOU GOING TO DO?
AND EVEN STILL, YOU REFUSE TO ANSWER...?!
YUP.
...!!
HEY! HEY...!!

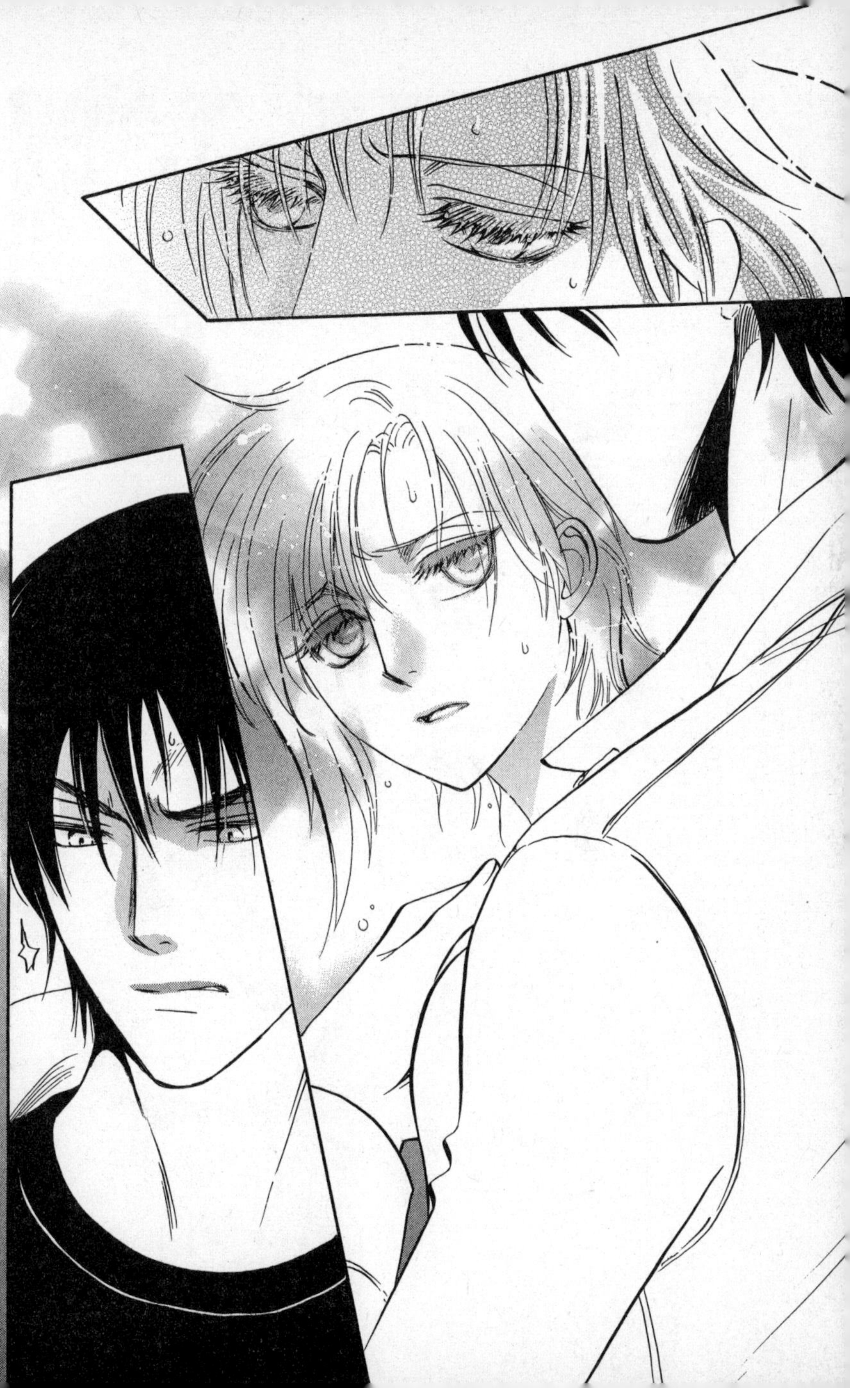

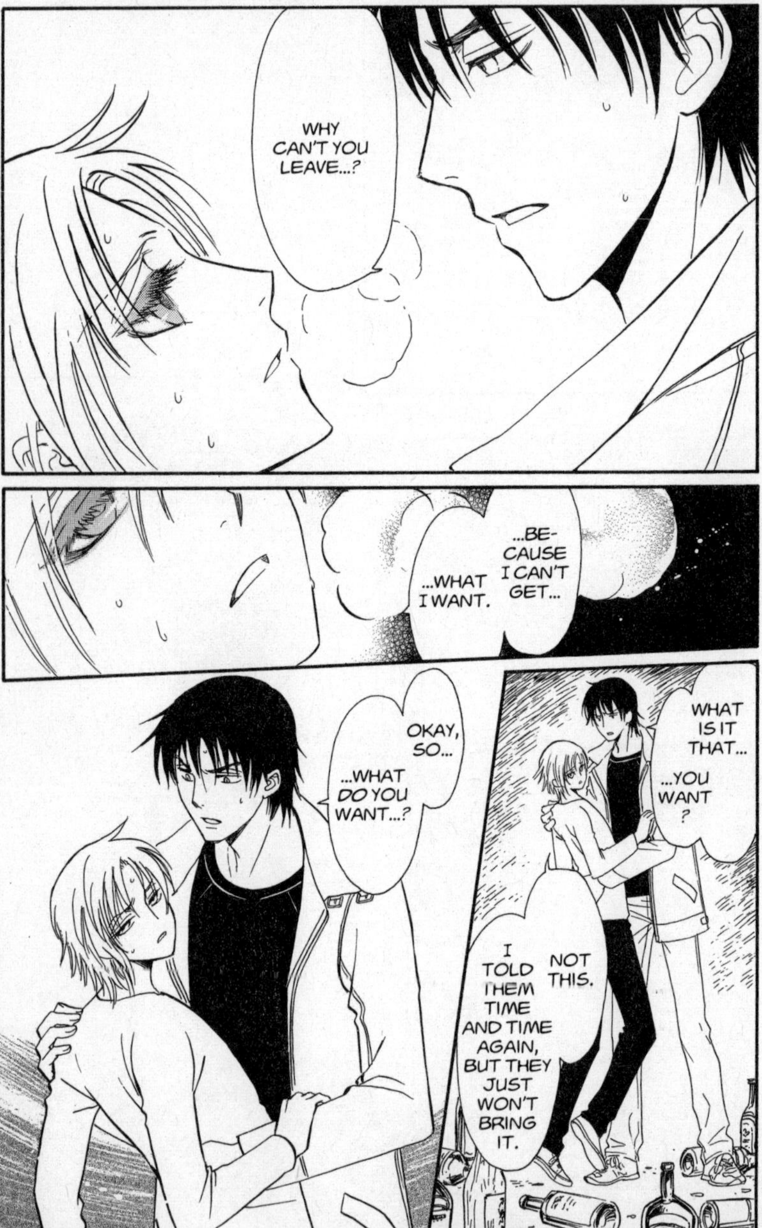
WHY CAN'T YOU LEAVE...?
...BE-CAUSE I CAN'T GET...
...WHAT I WANT.
WHAT IS IT THAT...
...YOU WANT ?
NOT THIS.
I TOLD THEM TIME AND TIME AGAIN, BUT THEY JUST WON'T BRING IT.
OKAY, SO...
...WHAT DO YOU WANT...?

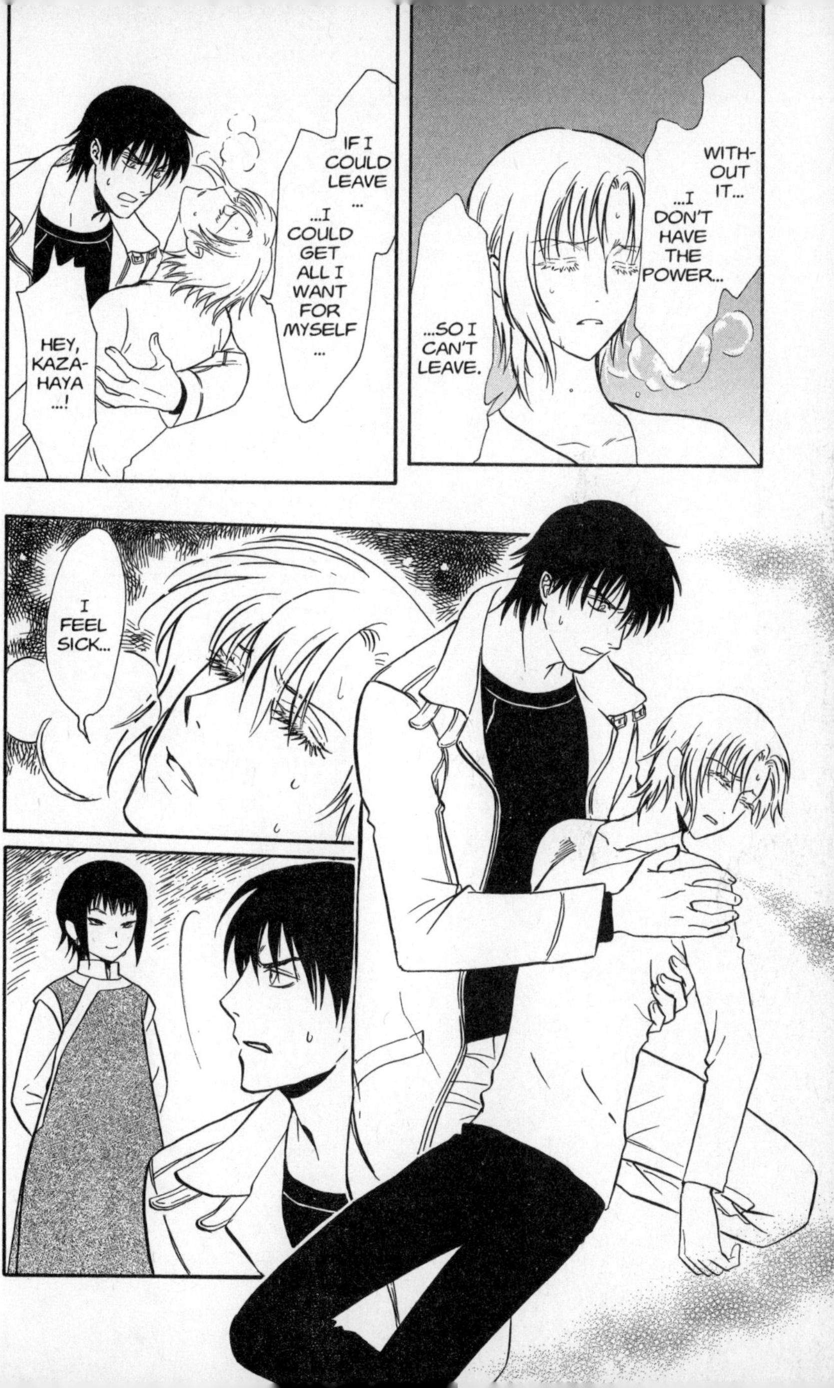
WITHOUT IT... ...I DON'T HAVE THE POWER...
...SO I CAN'T LEAVE.
IF I COULD LEAVE ... ...I COULD GET ALL I WANT FOR MYSELF ...
HEY, KAZAHAYA...!
I FEEL SICK...

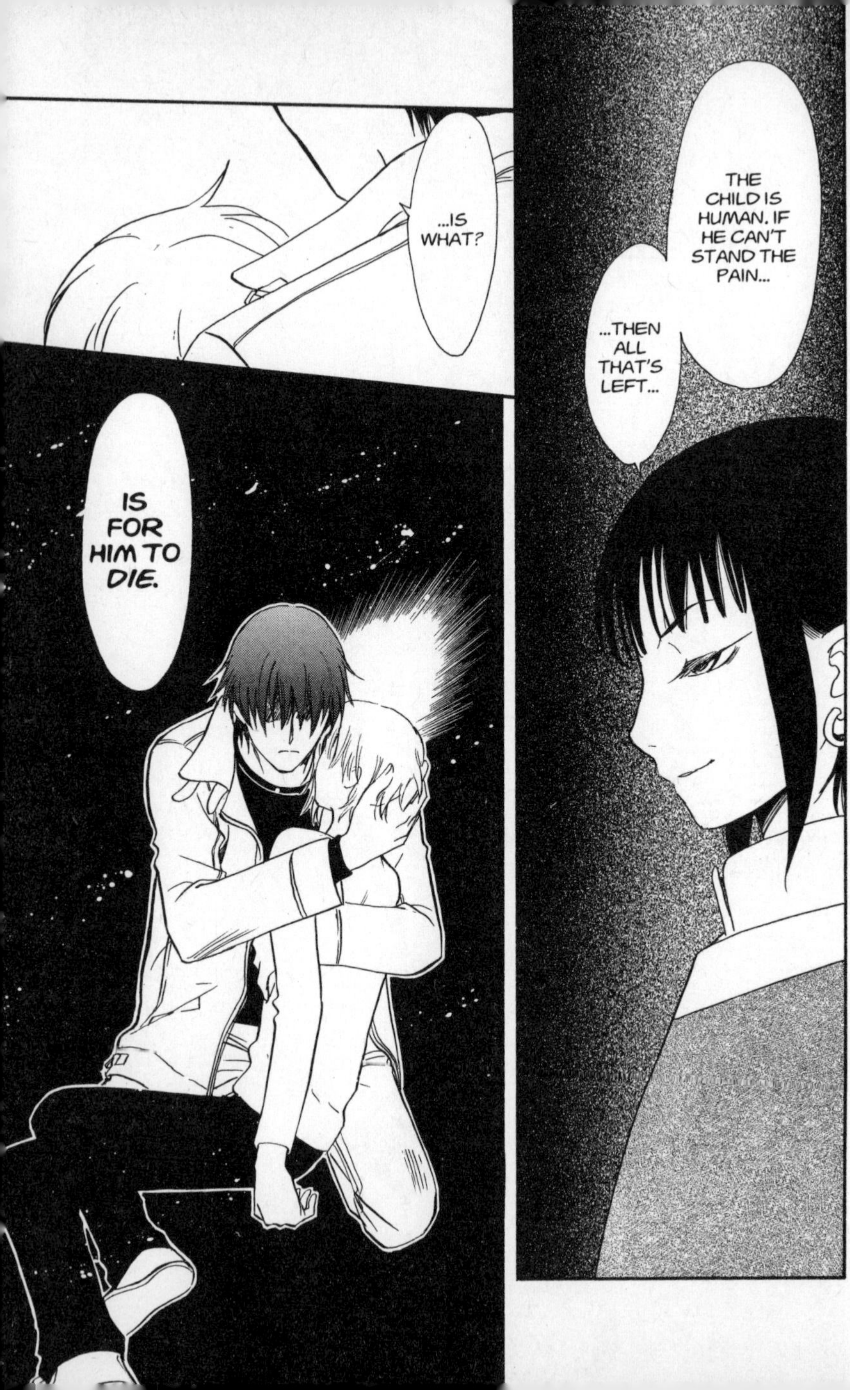
THE CHILD IS HUMAN. IF HE CAN'T STAND THE PAIN...
...THEN ALL THAT'S LEFT...
...IS WHAT?
IS FOR HIM TO DIE.

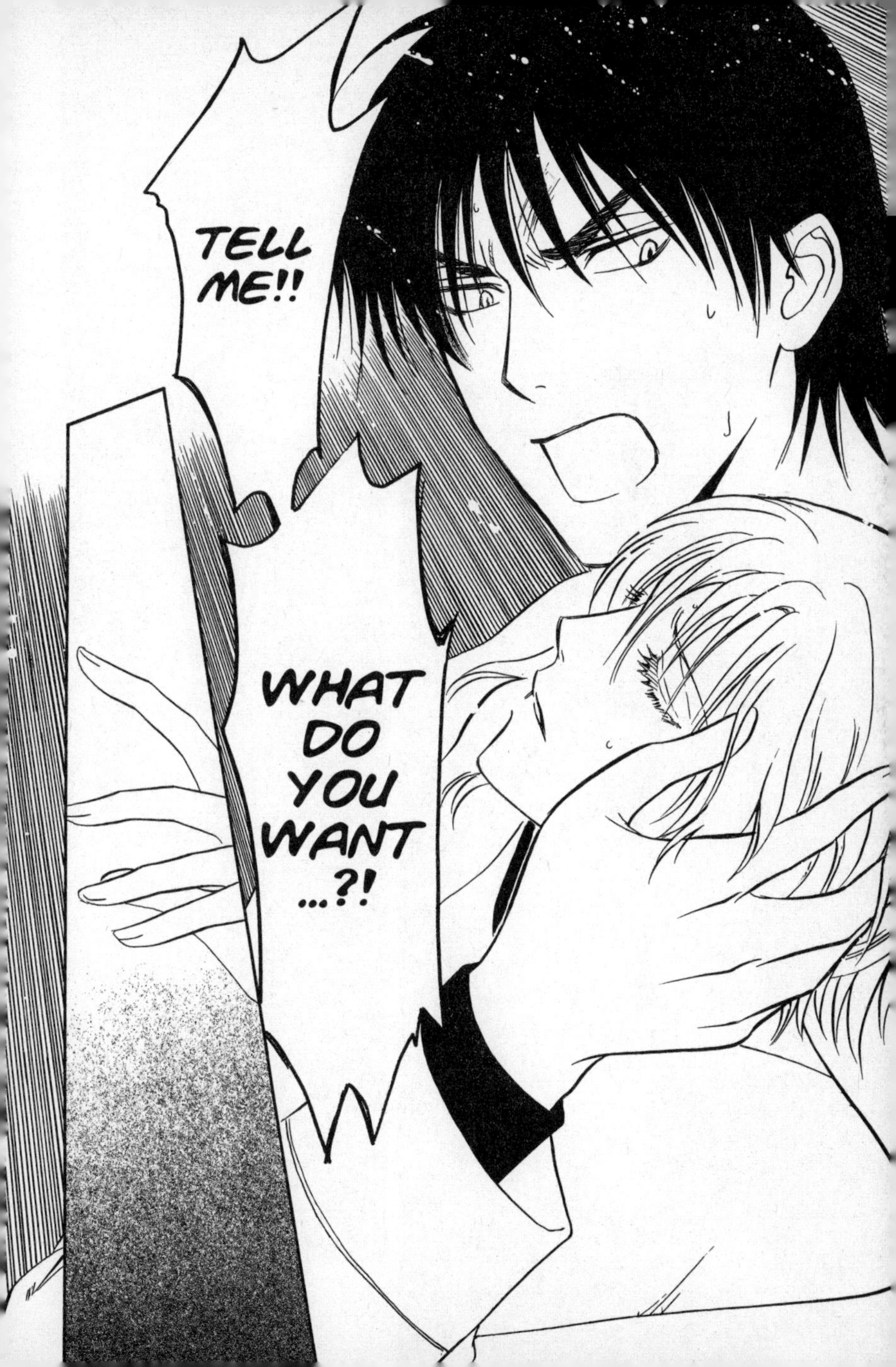
TELL ME!!
WHAT DO YOU WANT ...?!

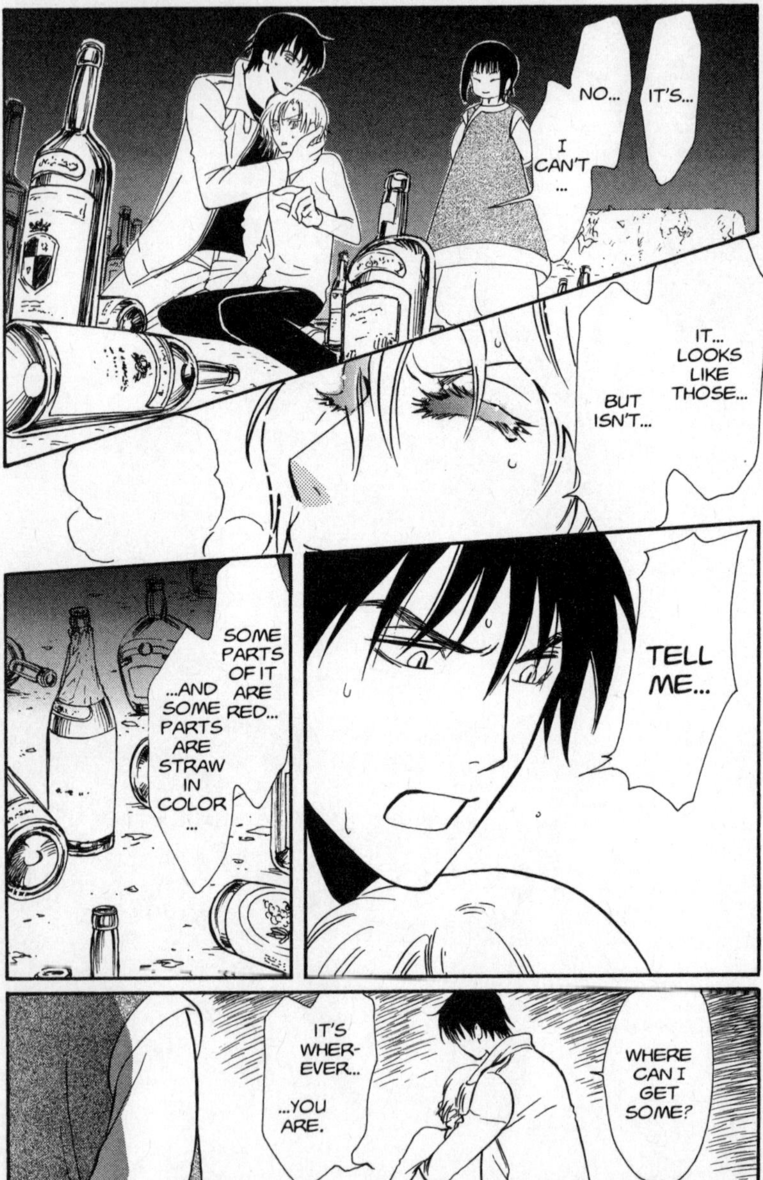
IT'S...
NO... I CAN'T ...
IT... LOOKS LIKE THOSE...
BUT ISN'T...
TELL ME...
SOME PARTS OF IT ARE RED...
...AND SOME PARTS ARE STRAW IN COLOR ...
WHERE CAN I GET SOME?
IT'S WHEREVER...
...YOU ARE.

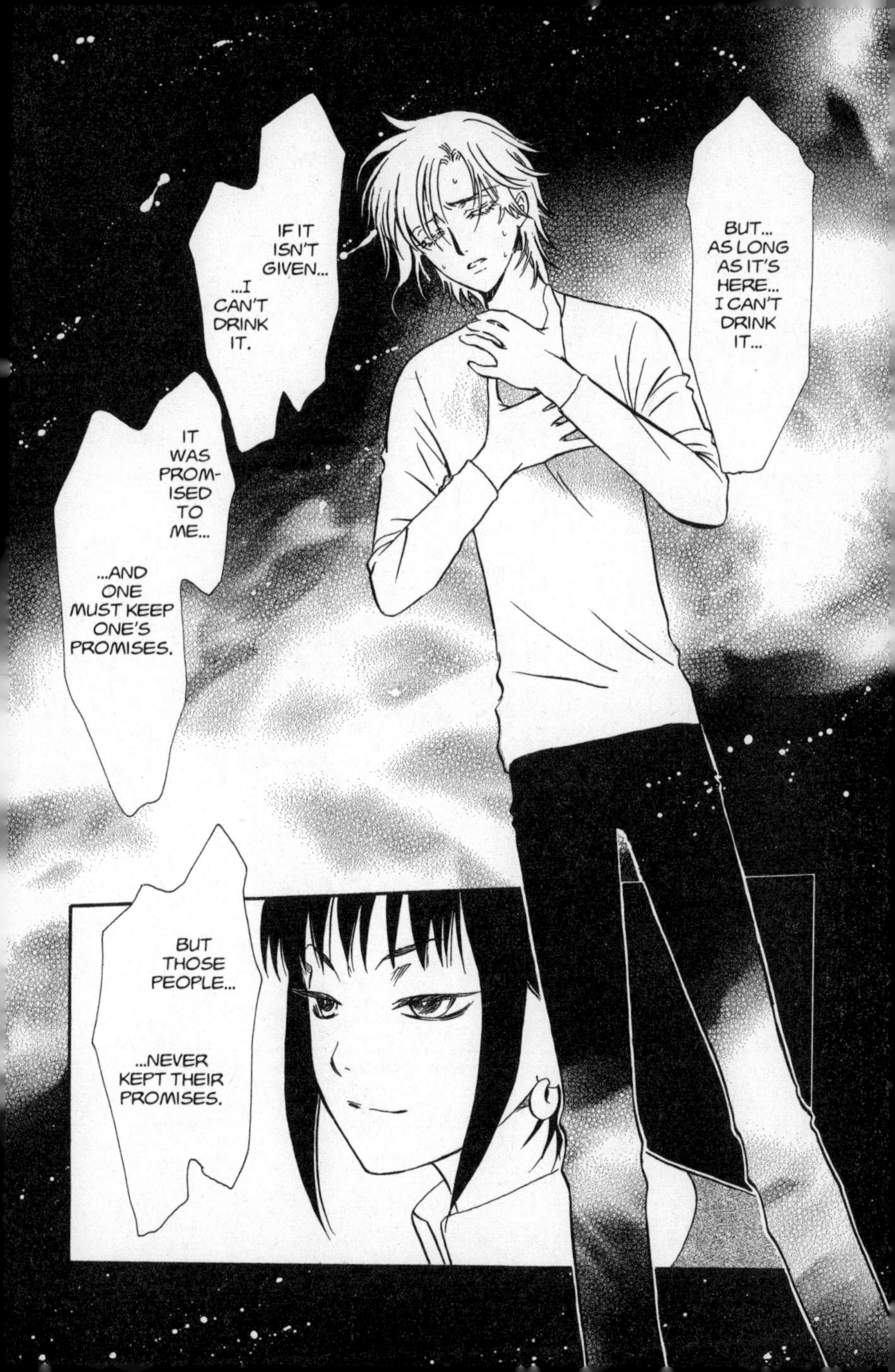
BUT... AS LONG AS IT'S HERE... I CAN'T DRINK IT...
IF IT ISN'T GIVEN... ...I CAN'T DRINK IT.
IT WAS PROMISED TO ME... ...AND ONE MUST KEEP ONE'S PROMISES.
BUT THOSE PEOPLE... ...NEVER KEPT THEIR PROMISES.

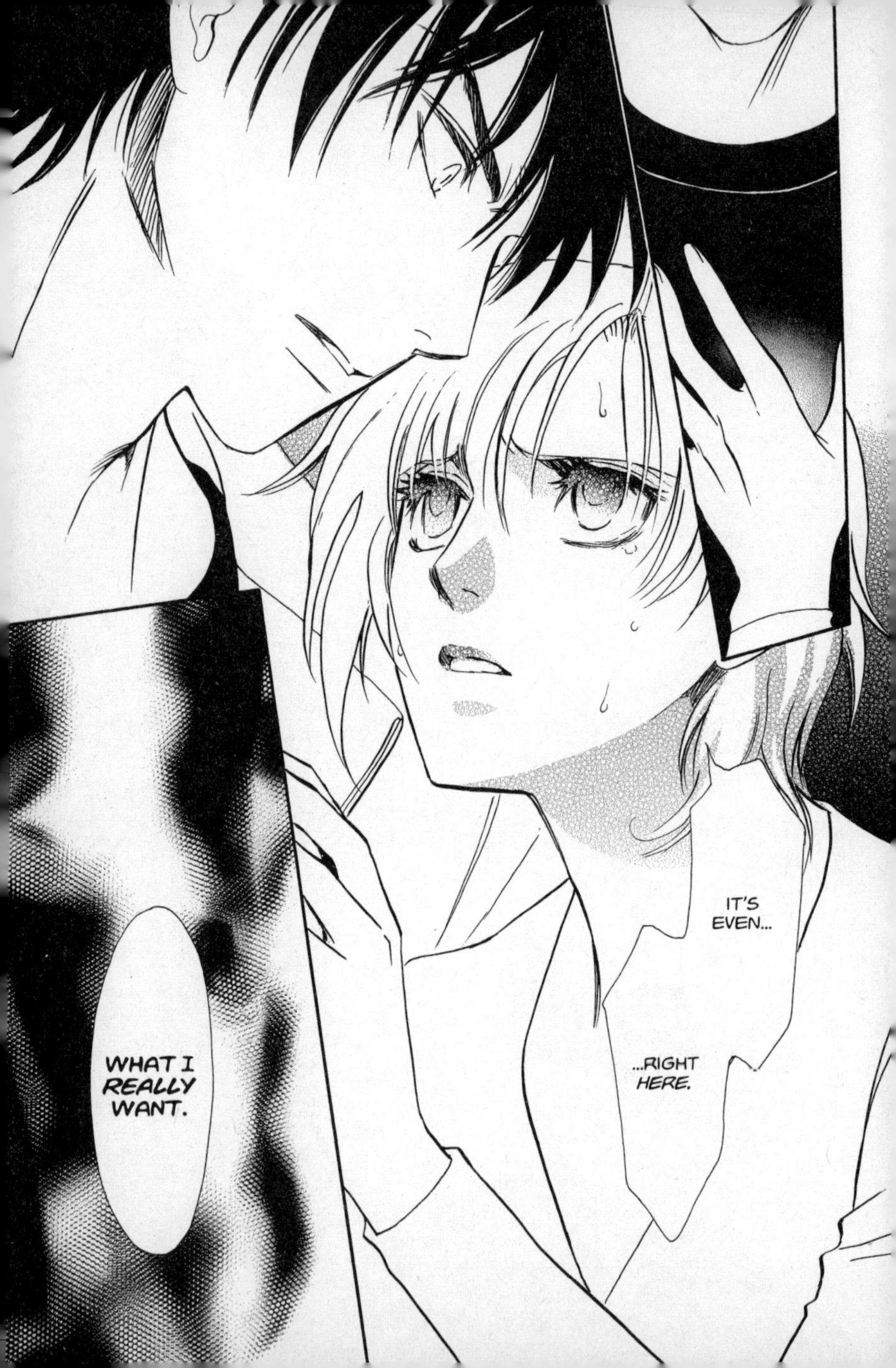
IT'S EVEN...
...RIGHT HERE.
WHAT I REALLY WANT.

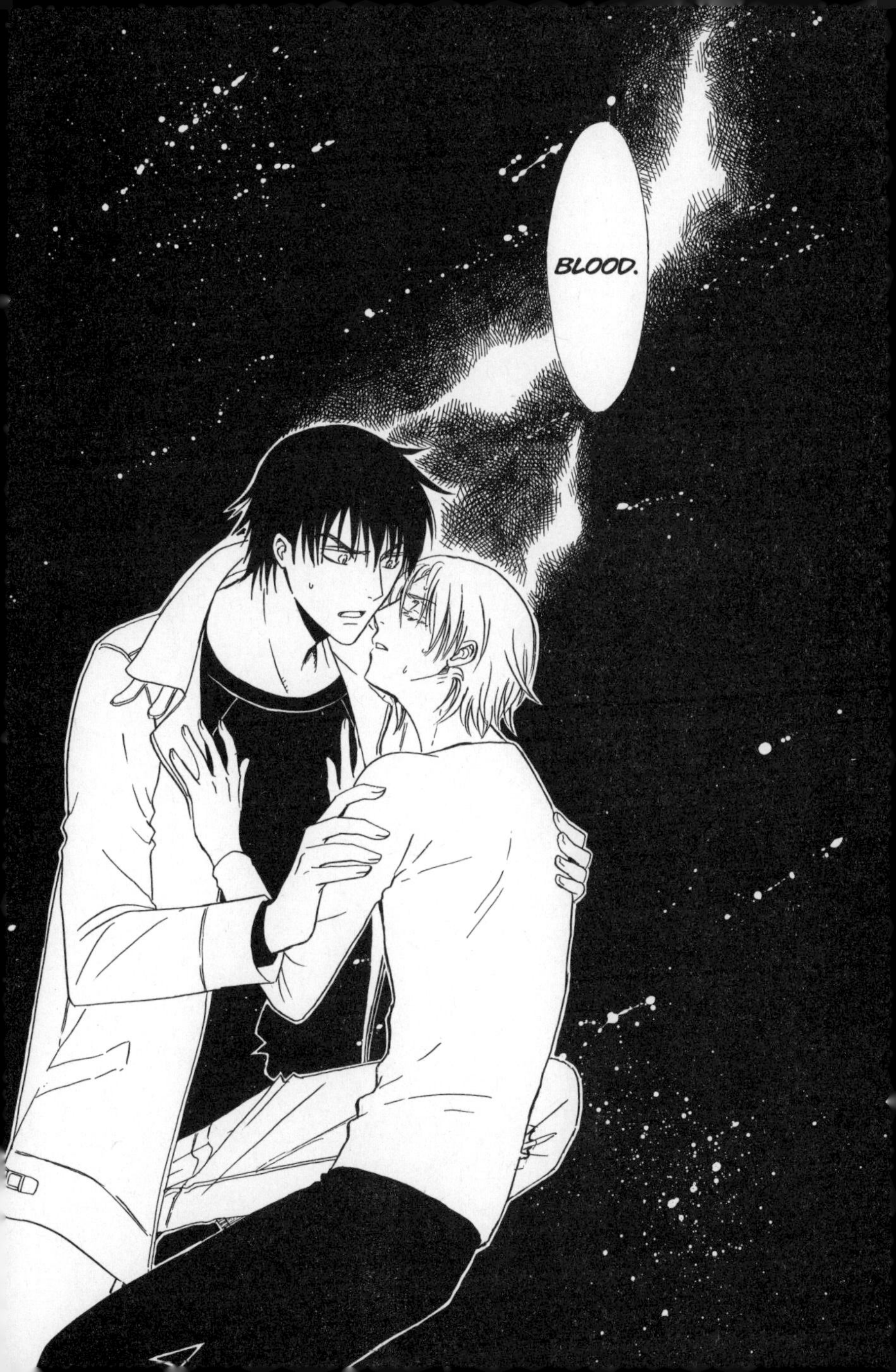
BLOOD.

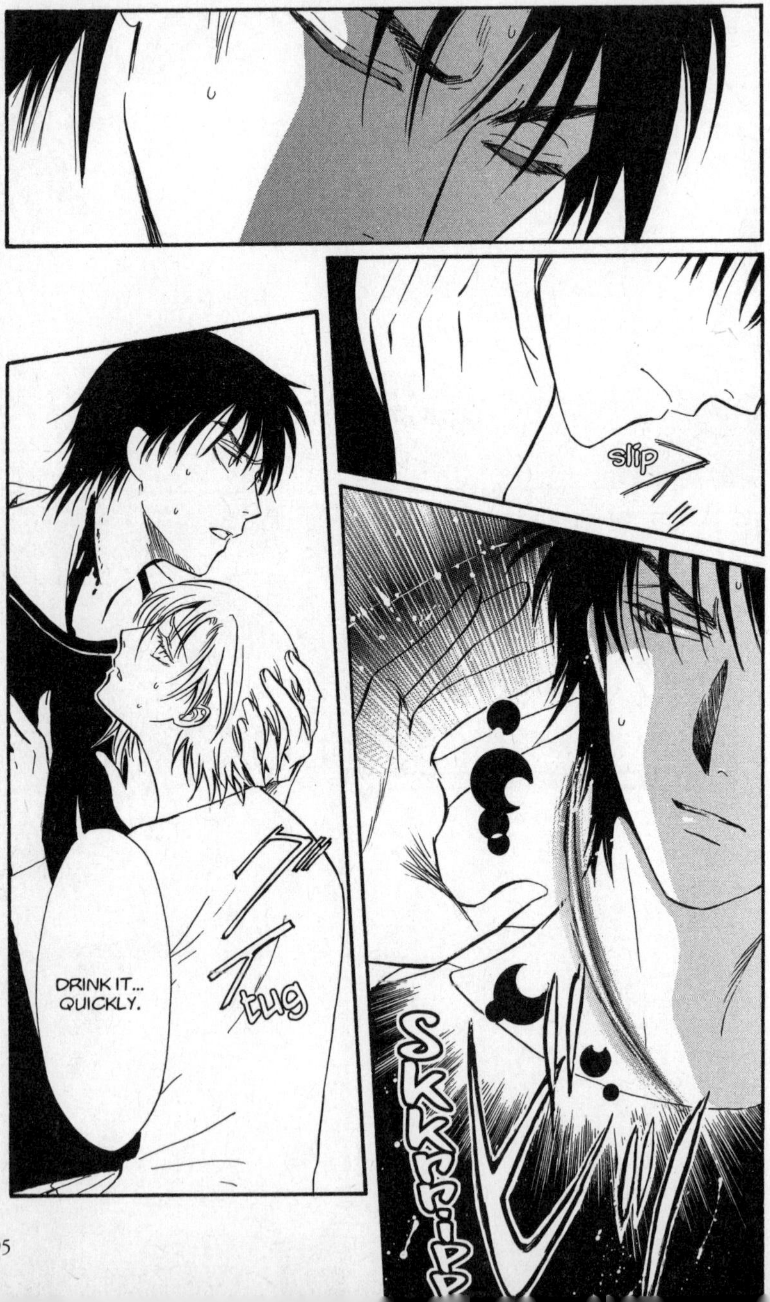
slip
Skkrripp
DRINK IT... QUICKLY.
tug

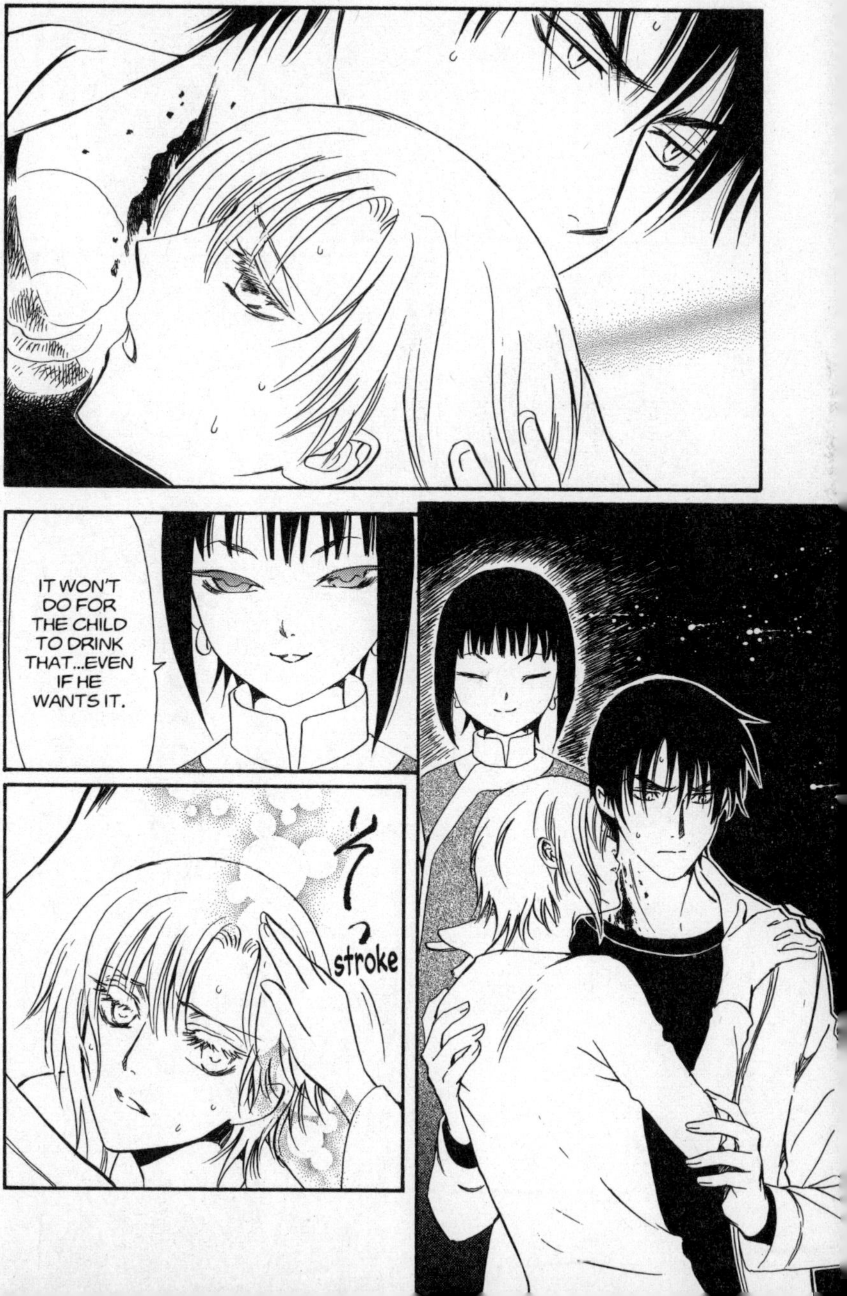
IT WON'T DO FOR THE CHILD TO DRINK THAT...EVEN IF HE WANTS IT.
そっ
stroke

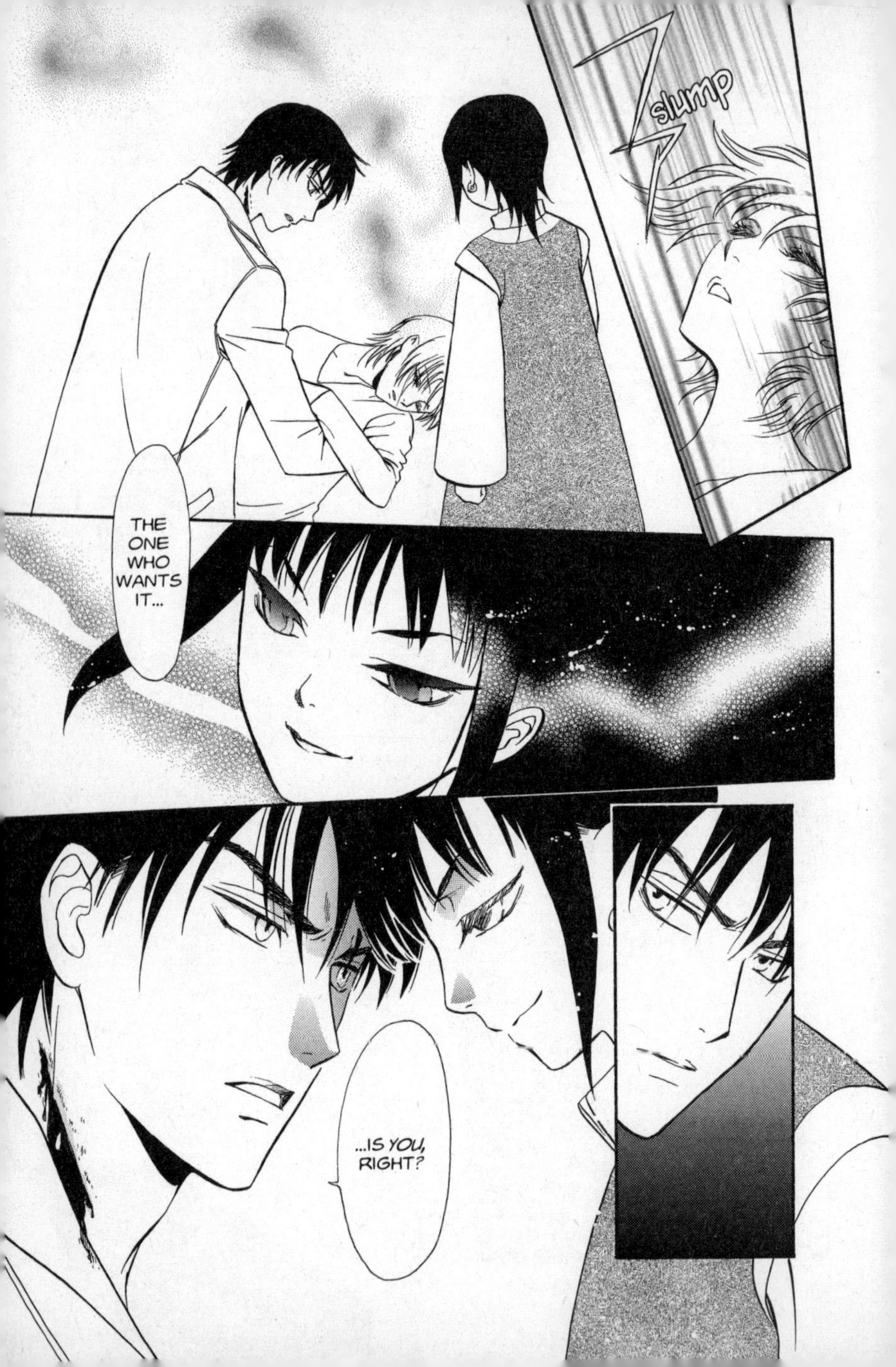
slump
THE ONE WHO WANTS IT...
...IS YOU, RIGHT?

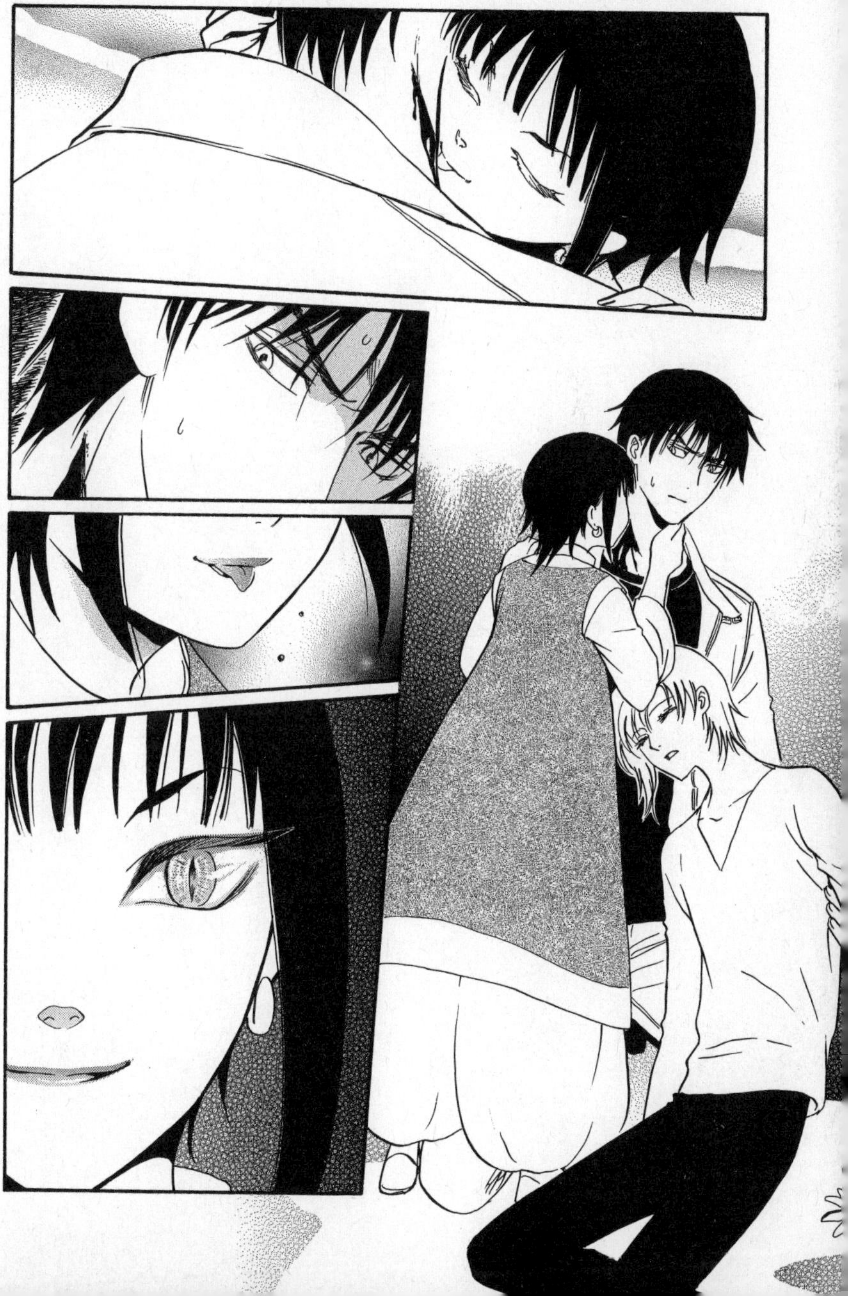

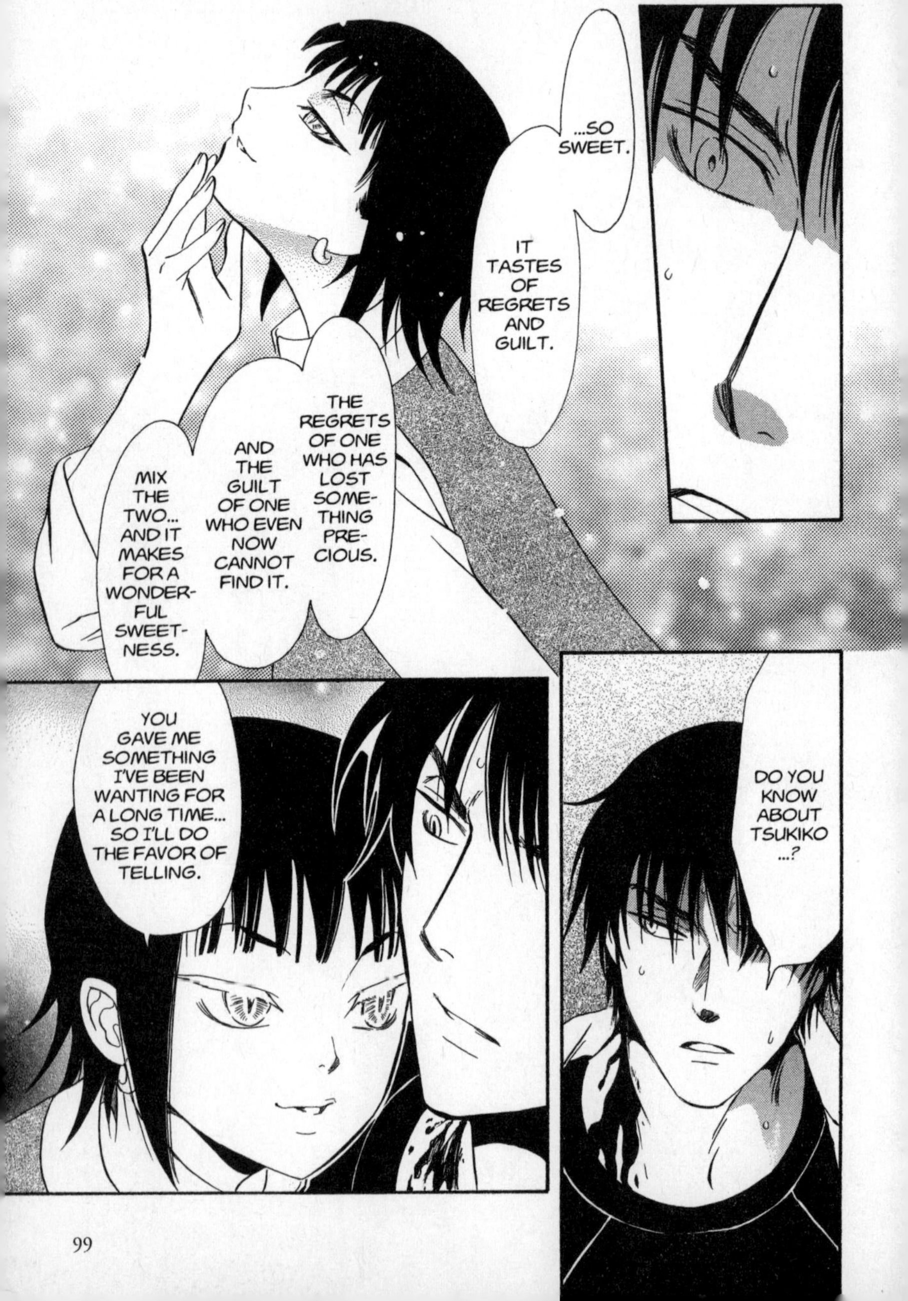
...SO SWEET.
IT TASTES OF REGRETS AND GUILT.
THE REGRETS OF ONE WHO HAS LOST SOME-THING PRE-CIOUS.
AND THE GUILT OF ONE WHO EVEN NOW CANNOT FIND IT.
MIX THE TWO... AND IT MAKES FOR A WONDER-FUL SWEET-NESS.
DO YOU KNOW ABOUT TSUKIKO ...?
YOU GAVE ME SOMETHING I'VE BEEN WANTING FOR A LONG TIME... SO I'LL DO THE FAVOR OF TELLING.

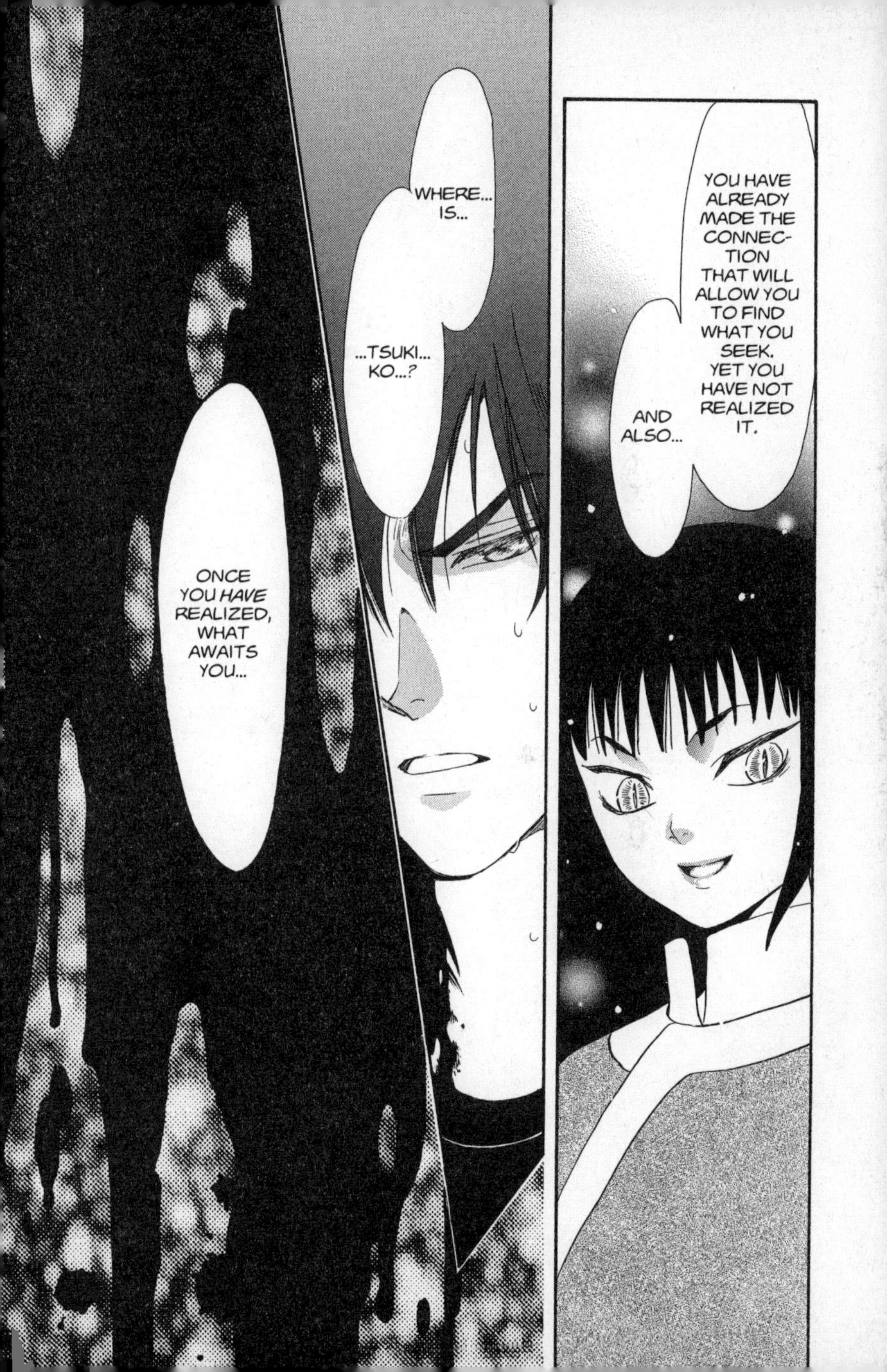
YOU HAVE ALREADY MADE THE CONNEC-TION THAT WILL ALLOW YOU TO FIND WHAT YOU SEEK. YET YOU HAVE NOT REALIZED IT.
AND ALSO...
WHERE... IS...
...TSUKI... KO...?
ONCE YOU *HAVE* REALIZED, WHAT AWAITS YOU...

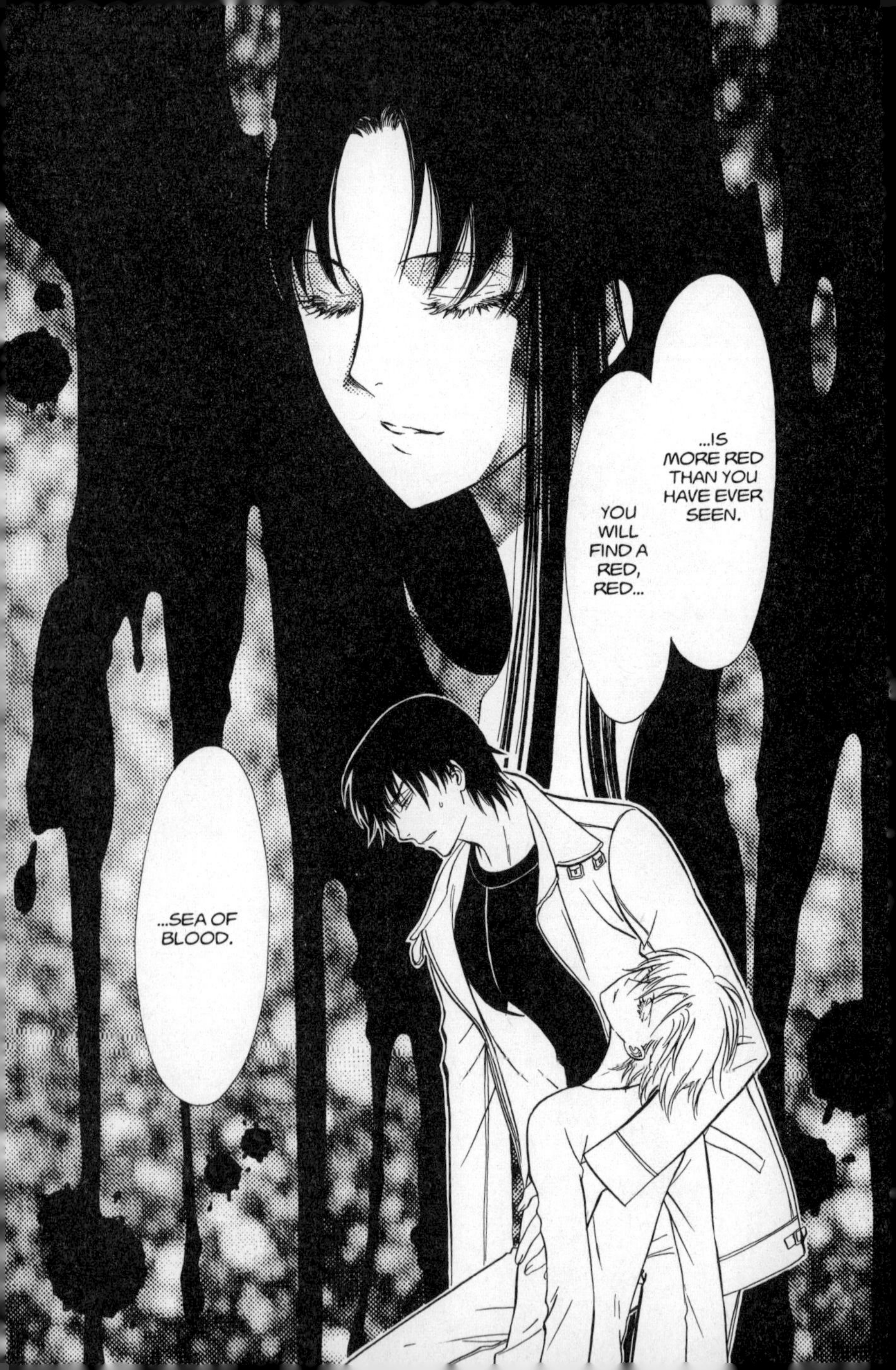
...IS MORE RED THAN YOU HAVE EVER SEEN.
YOU WILL FIND A RED, RED...
...SEA OF BLOOD.

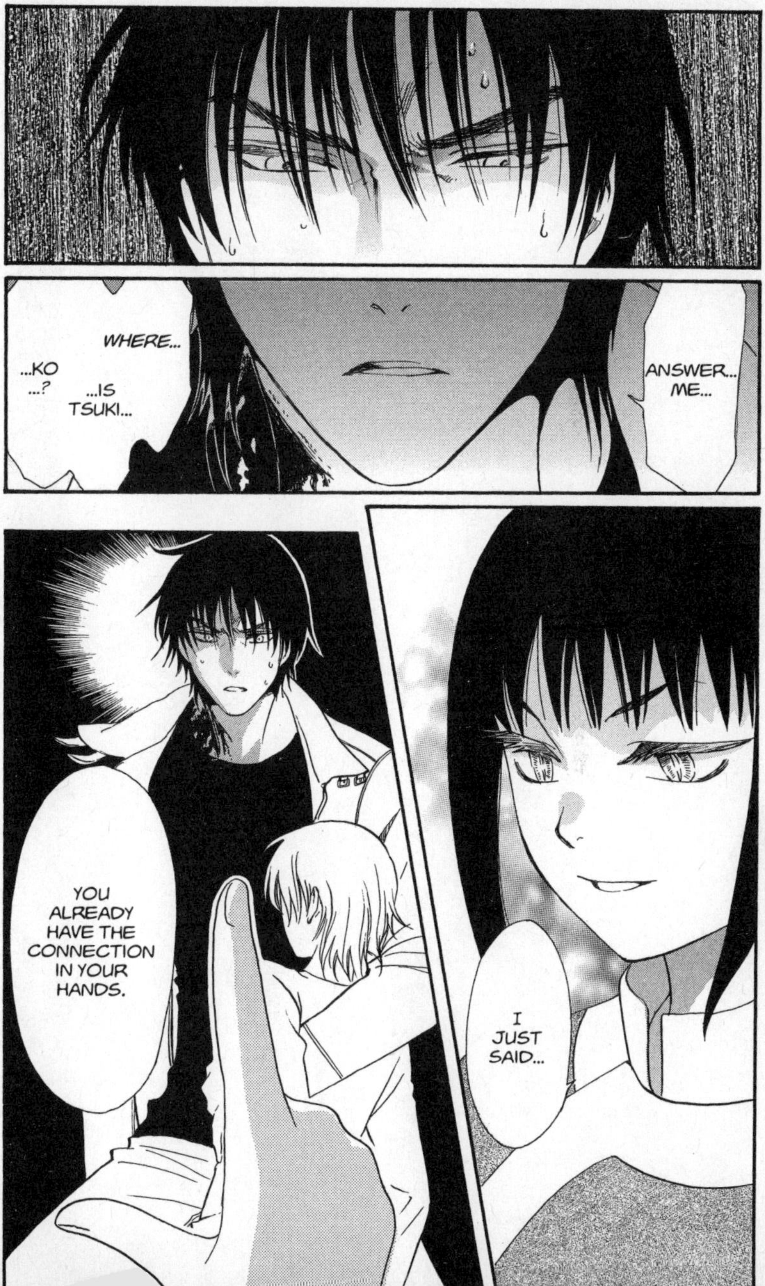
ANSWER... ME...
WHERE...
...IS TSUKI...
...KO ...?
I JUST SAID...
YOU ALREADY HAVE THE CONNECTION IN YOUR HANDS.

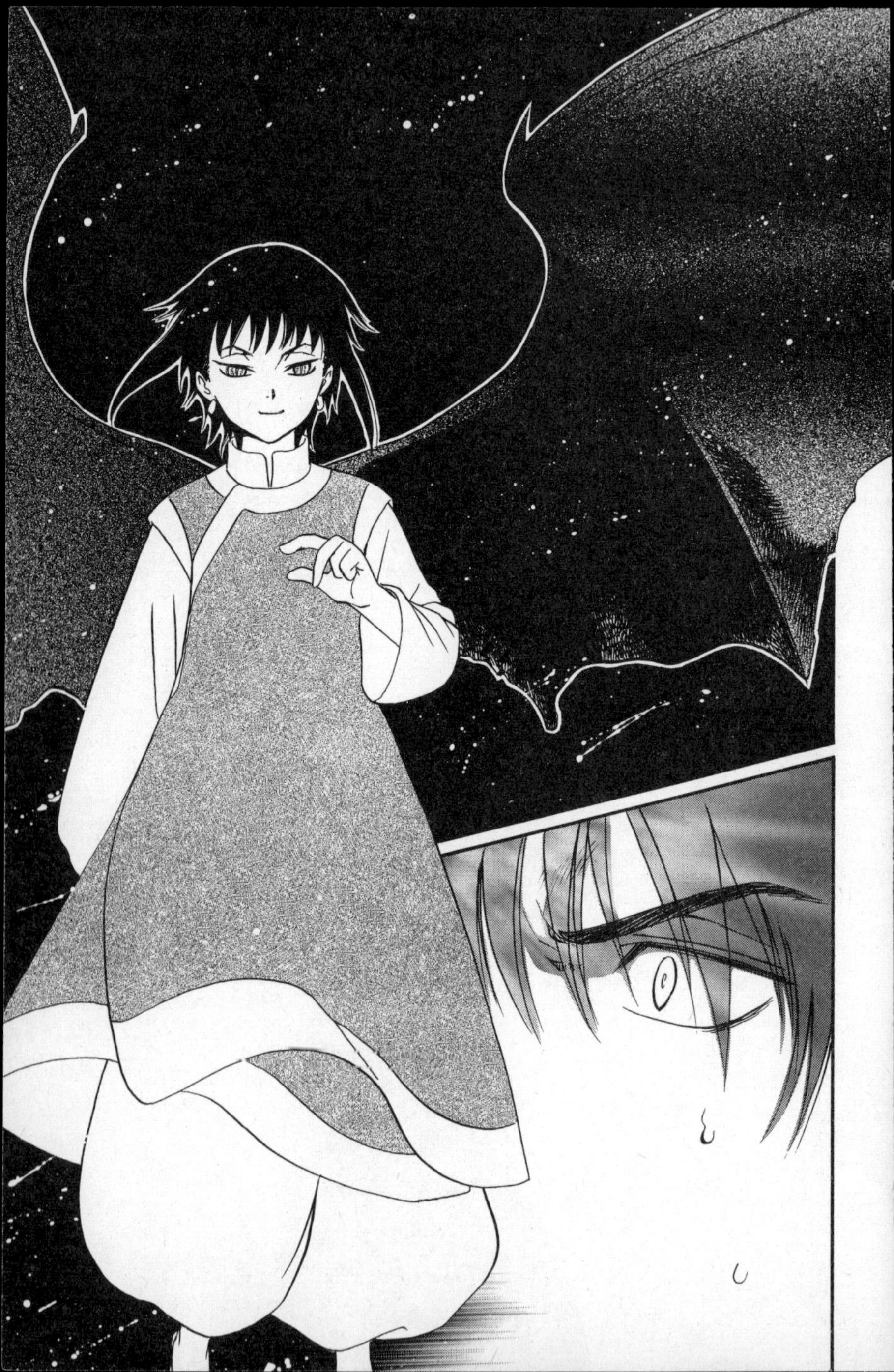

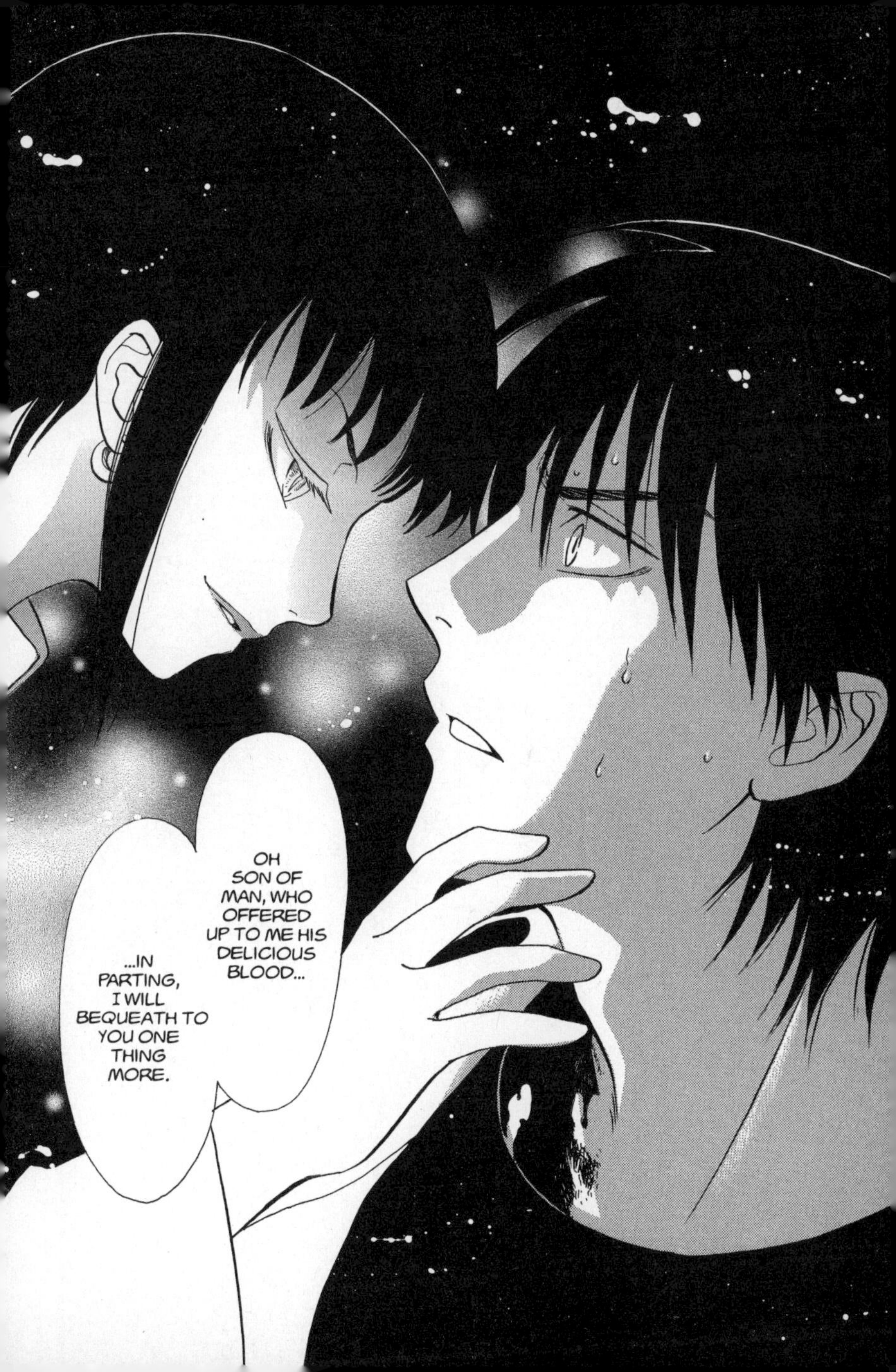
OH SON OF MAN, WHO OFFERED UP TO ME HIS DELICIOUS BLOOD...
...IN PARTING, I WILL BEQUEATH TO YOU ONE THING MORE.

AMIDST THAT RED, RED SEA OF BLOOD, YOU MUST MAKE A CHOICE.
BUT WHATEVER CHOICE YOU MAKE, YOU SHALL LOSE SOMETHING IRREPLACEABLE... AND YOU SHALL NEVER RECOVER IT... UNTIL THE END OF TIME.

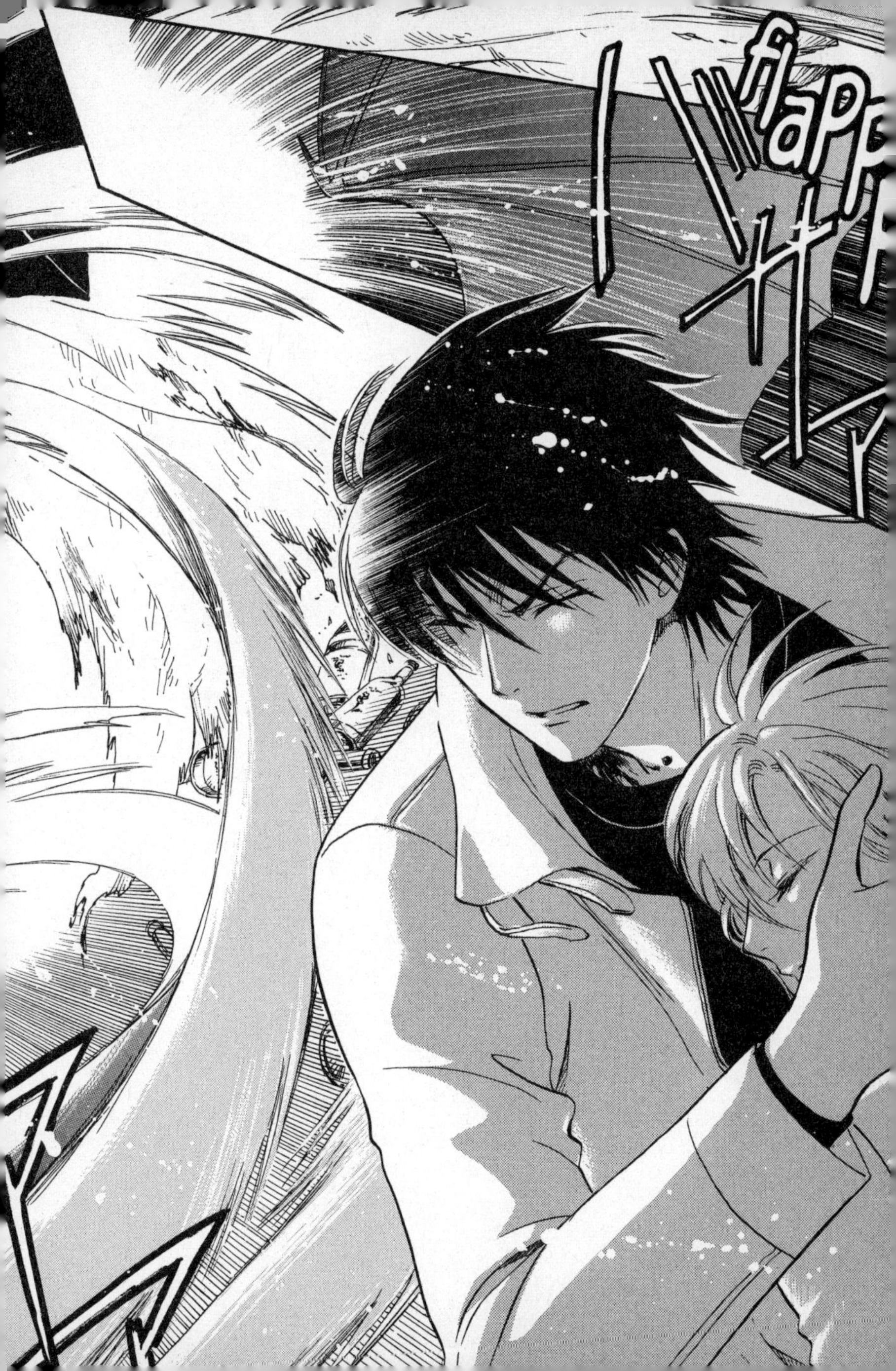
flapp

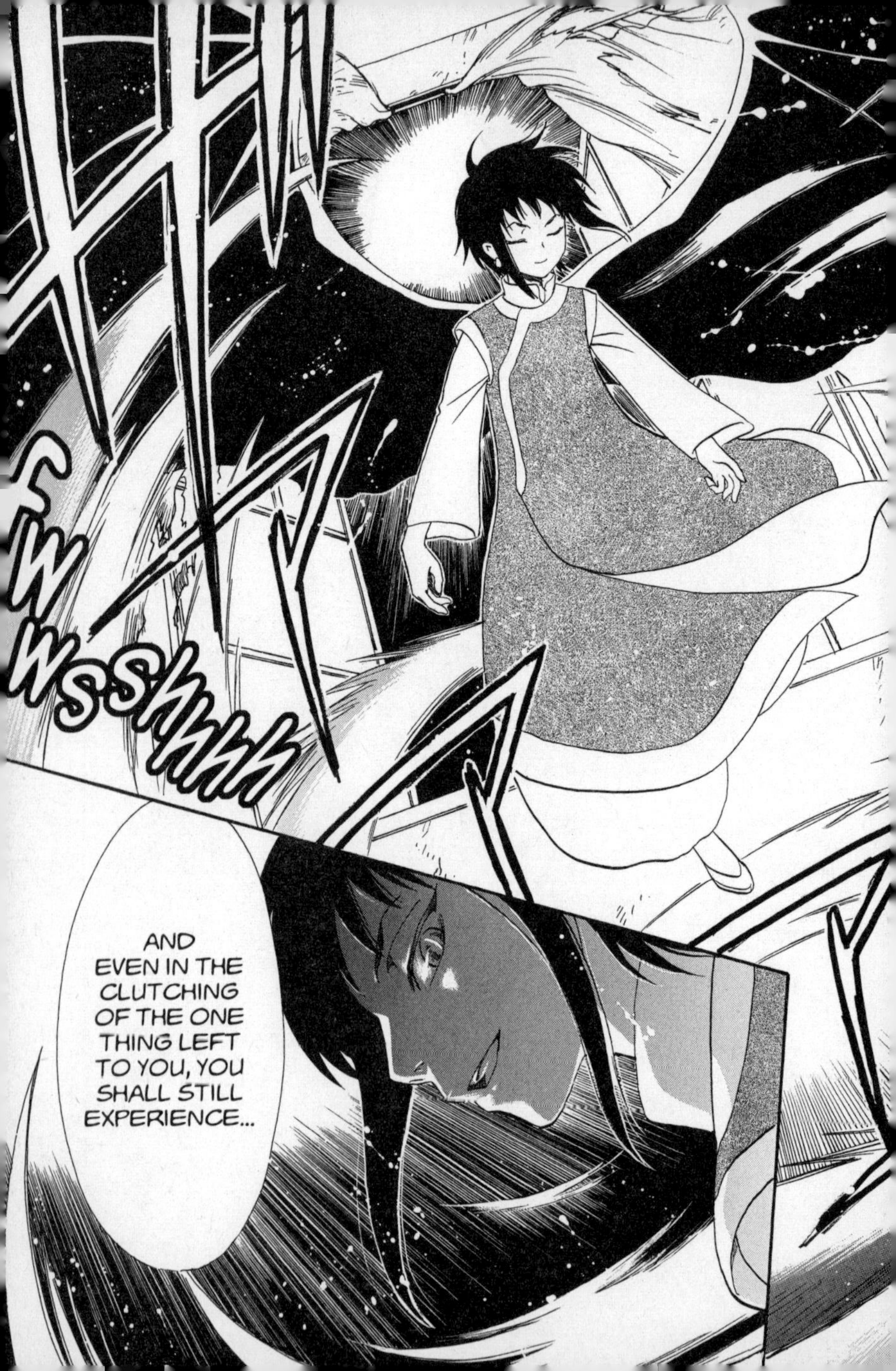
FWWSSHHHH
AND EVEN IN THE CLUTCHING OF THE ONE THING LEFT TO YOU, YOU SHALL STILL EXPERIENCE...

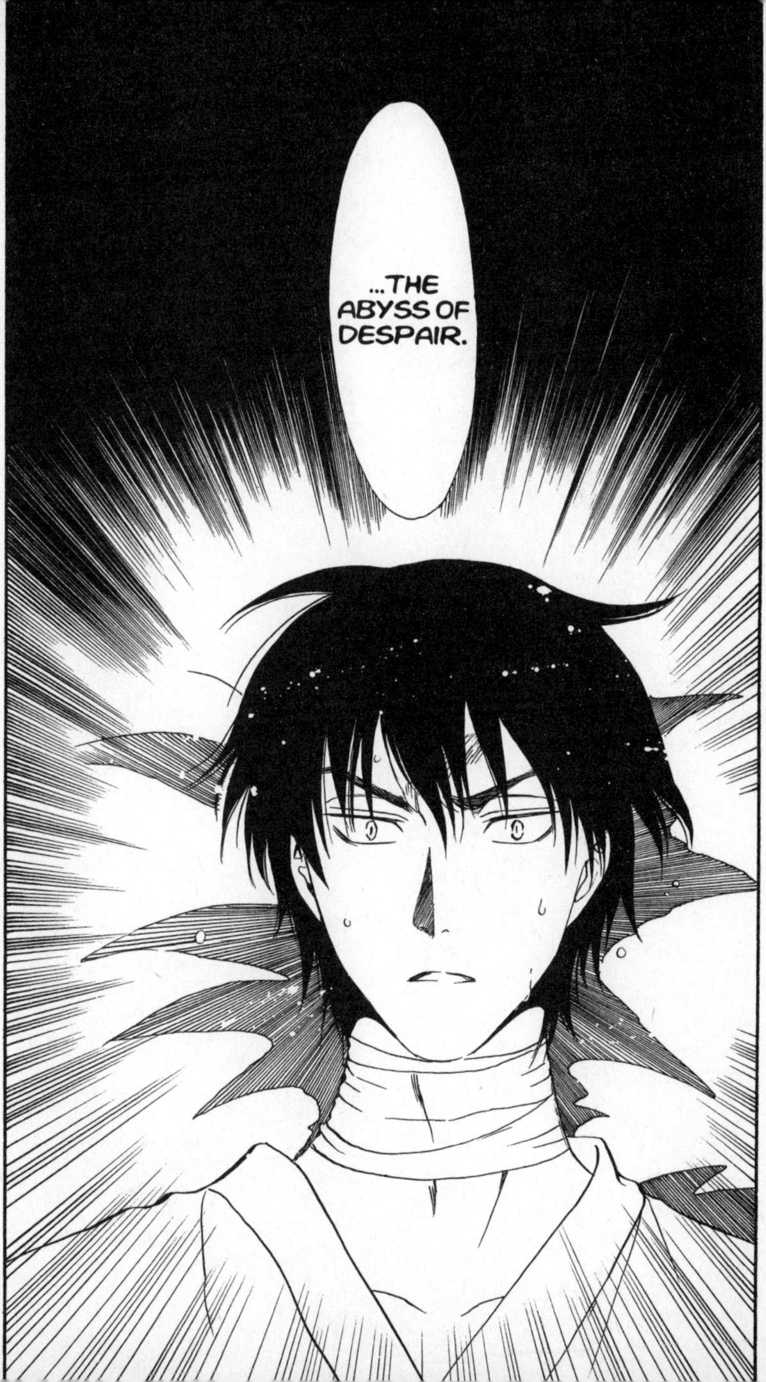
...THE ABYSS OF DESPAIR.

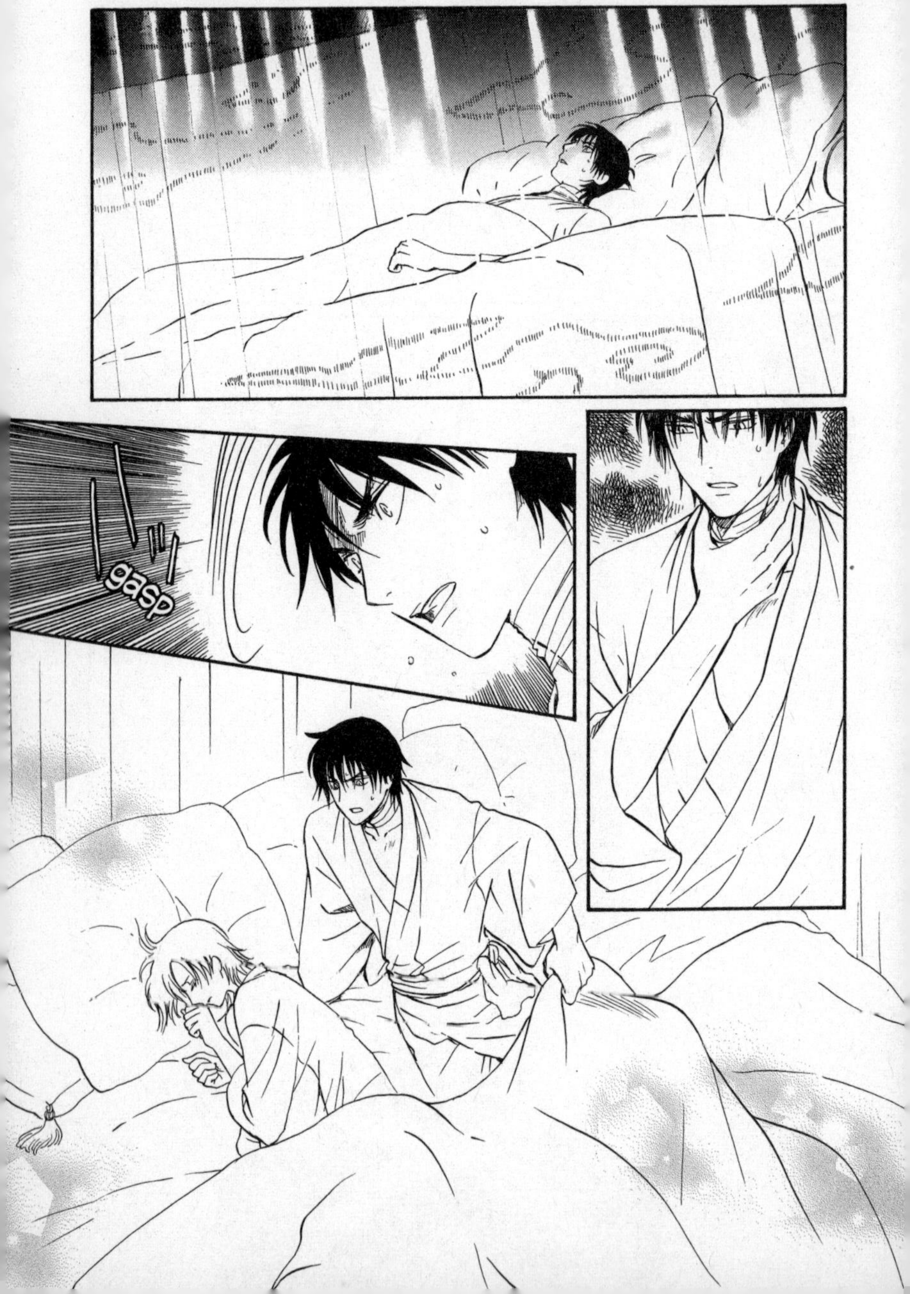
gasp

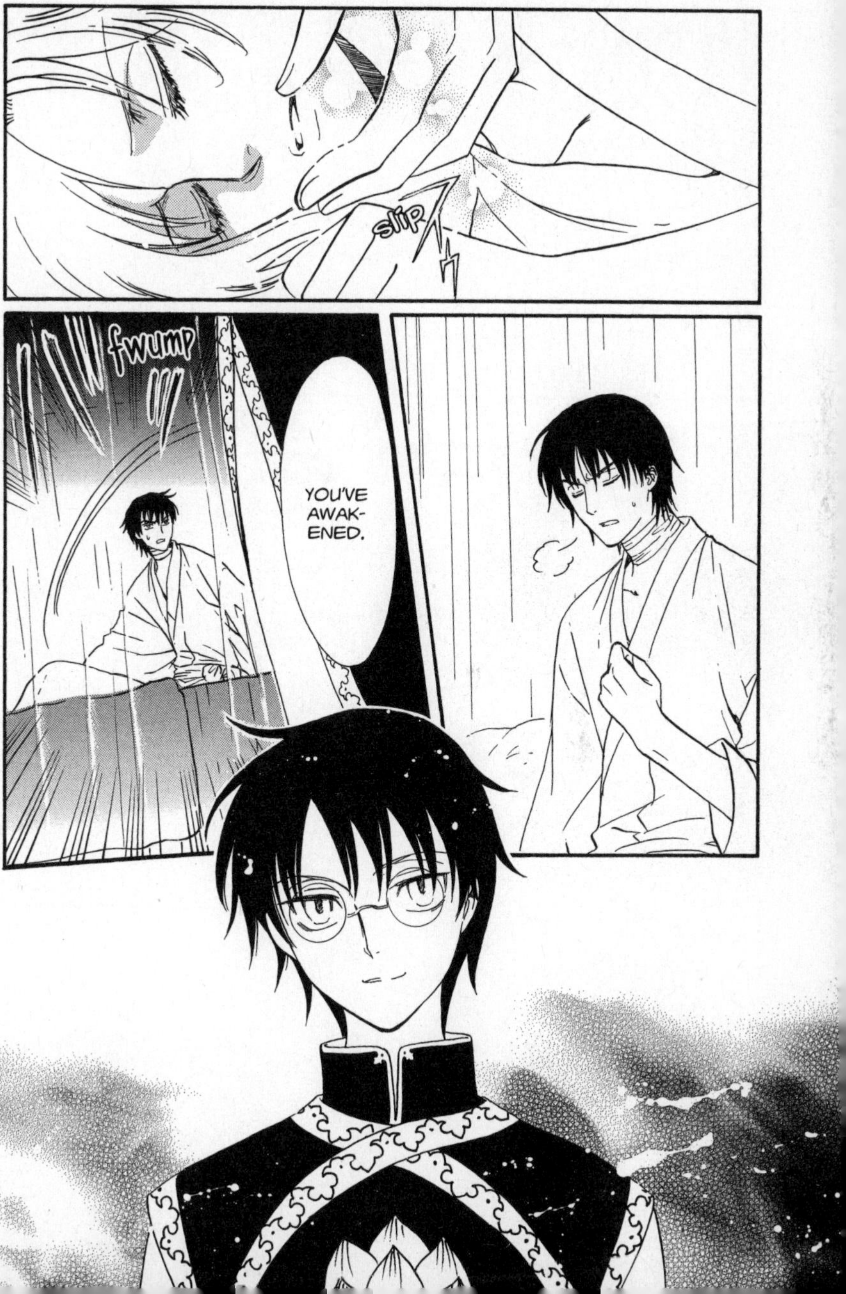
slip
fwump
YOU'VE AWAK-ENED.

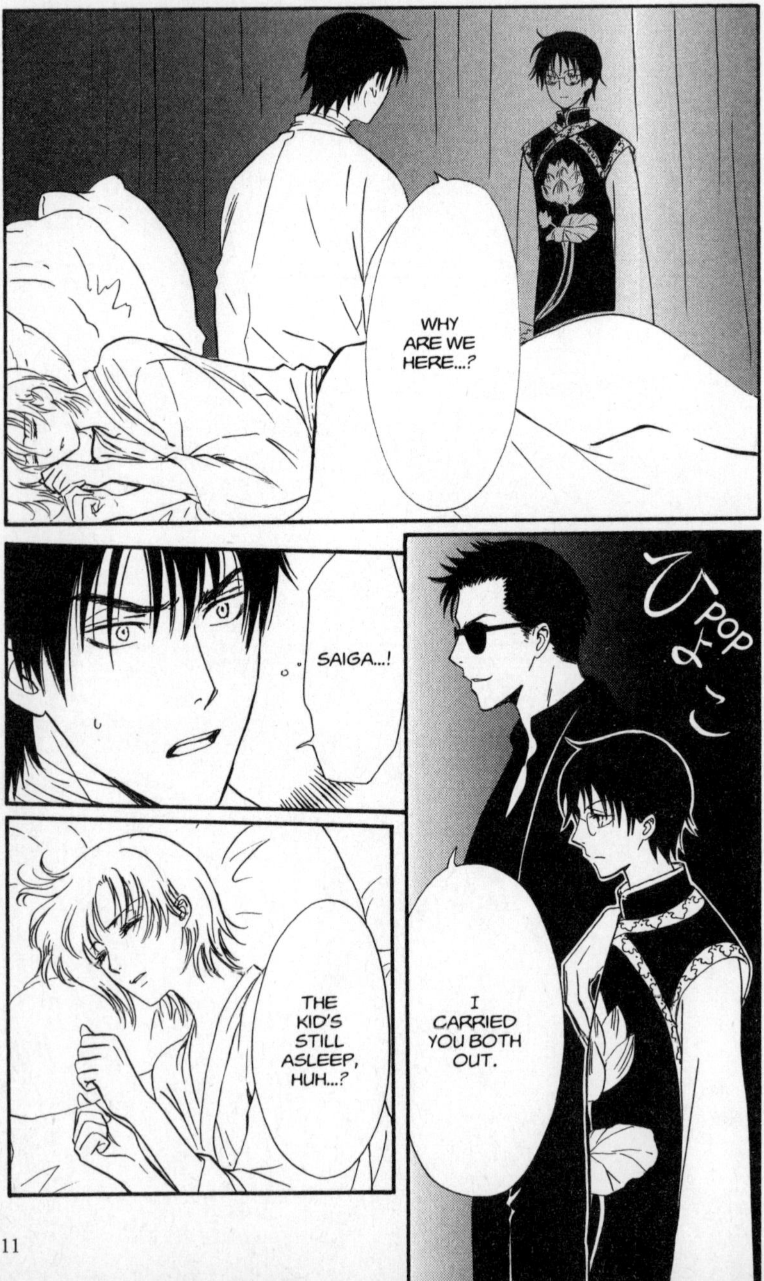
WHY ARE WE HERE...?
ひょこ
POP
I CARRIED YOU BOTH OUT.
SAIGA...!
THE KID'S STILL ASLEEP, HUH...?

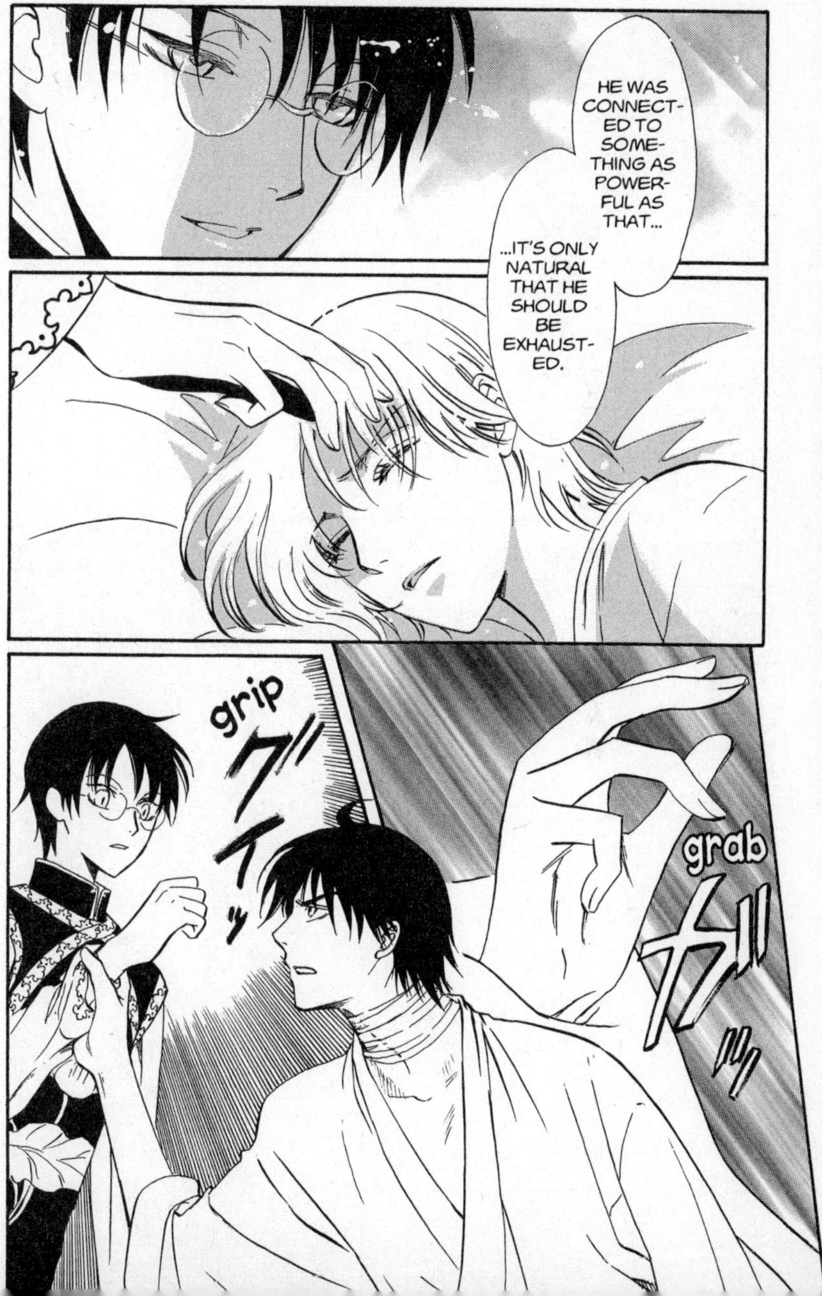
HE WAS CONNECT-ED TO SOME-THING AS POWER-FUL AS THAT...
...IT'S ONLY NATURAL THAT HE SHOULD BE EXHAUST-ED.
grab
grip

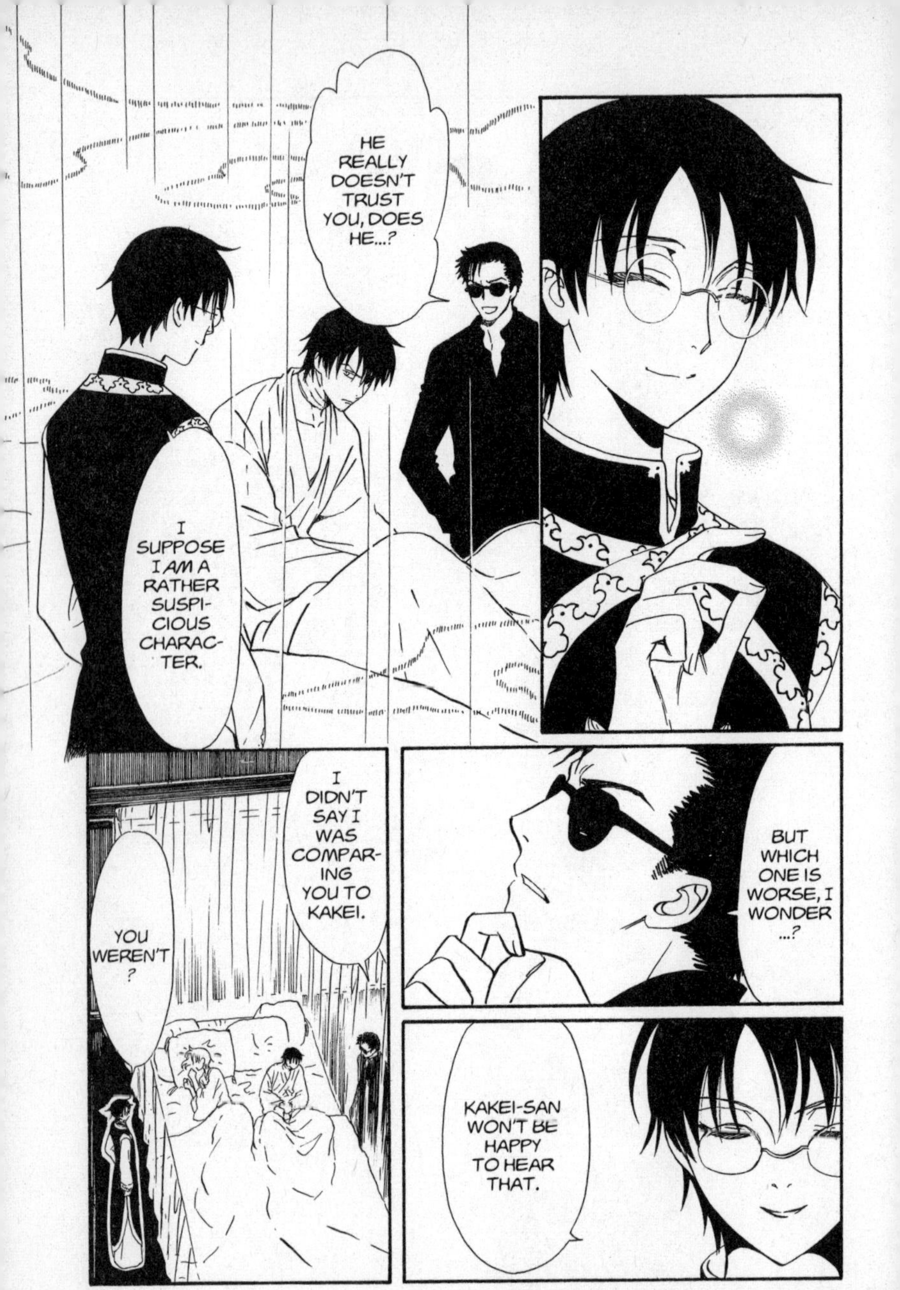
HE REALLY DOESN'T TRUST YOU, DOES HE...?
I SUPPOSE I AM A RATHER SUSPICIOUS CHARACTER.
BUT WHICH ONE IS WORSE, I WONDER ...?
KAKEI-SAN WON'T BE HAPPY TO HEAR THAT.
I DIDN'T SAY I WAS COMPARING YOU TO KAKEI.
YOU WEREN'T ?

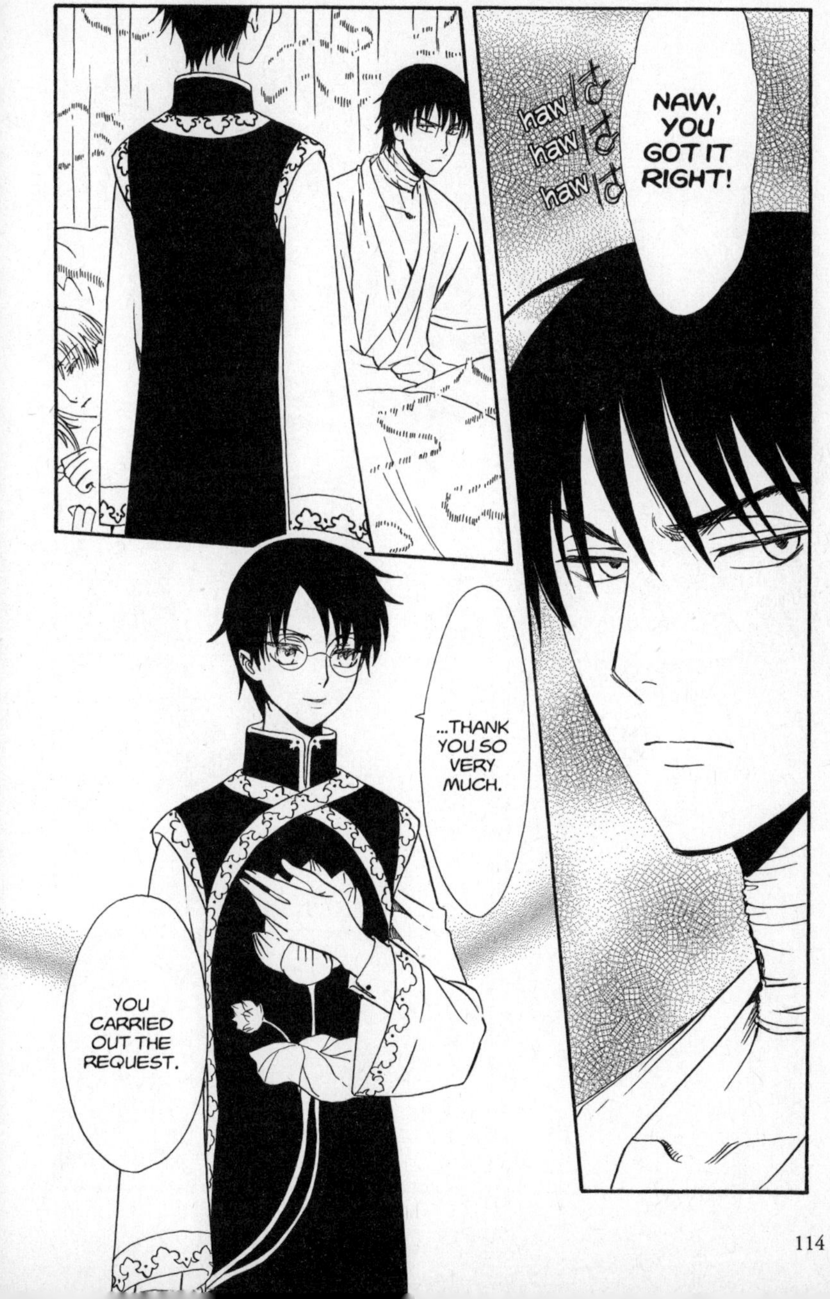
haw haw haw
ははは
NAW, YOU GOT IT RIGHT!
...THANK YOU SO VERY MUCH.
YOU CARRIED OUT THE REQUEST.

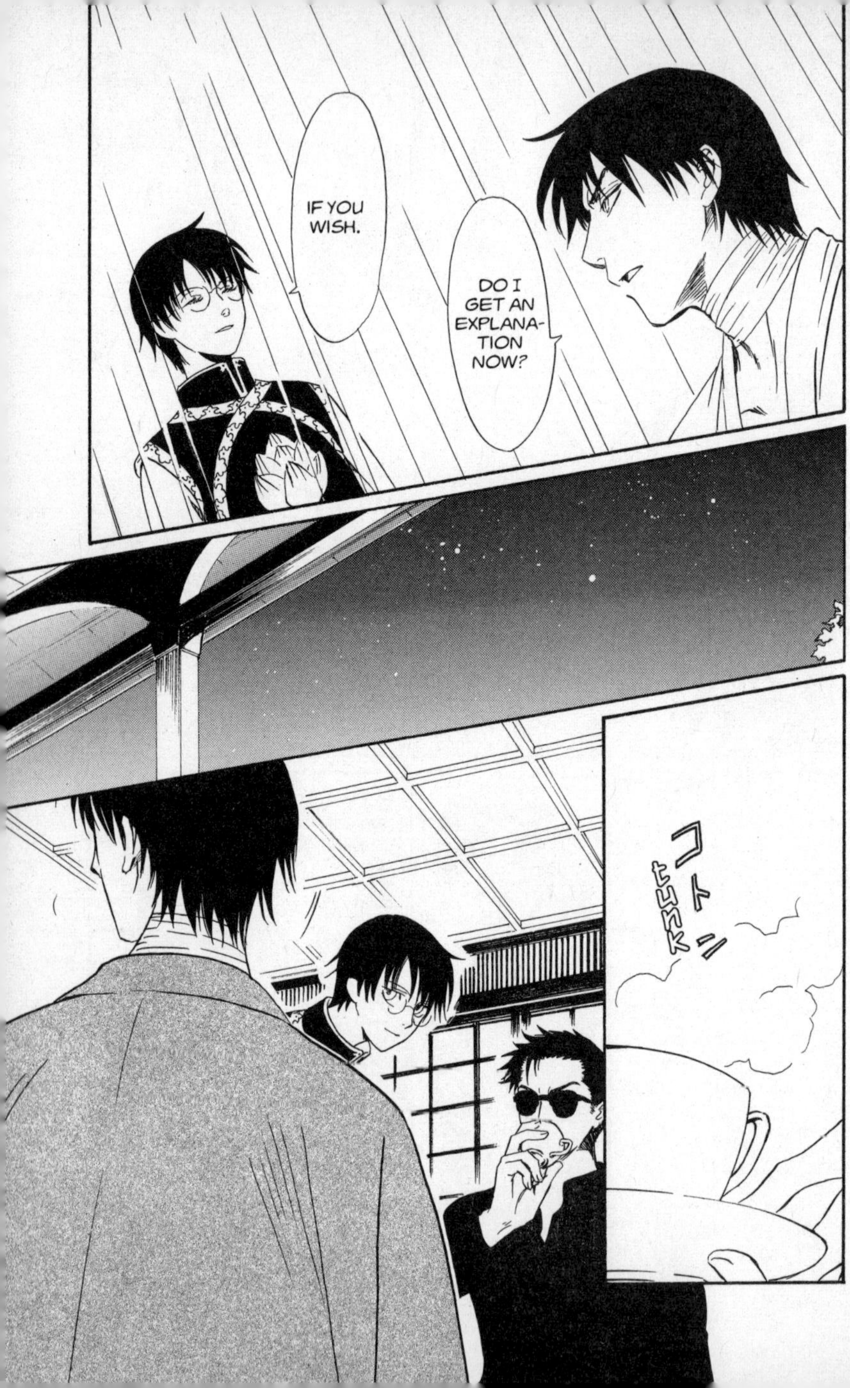
DO I GET AN EXPLANATION NOW?
IF YOU WISH.
コトン
tunk

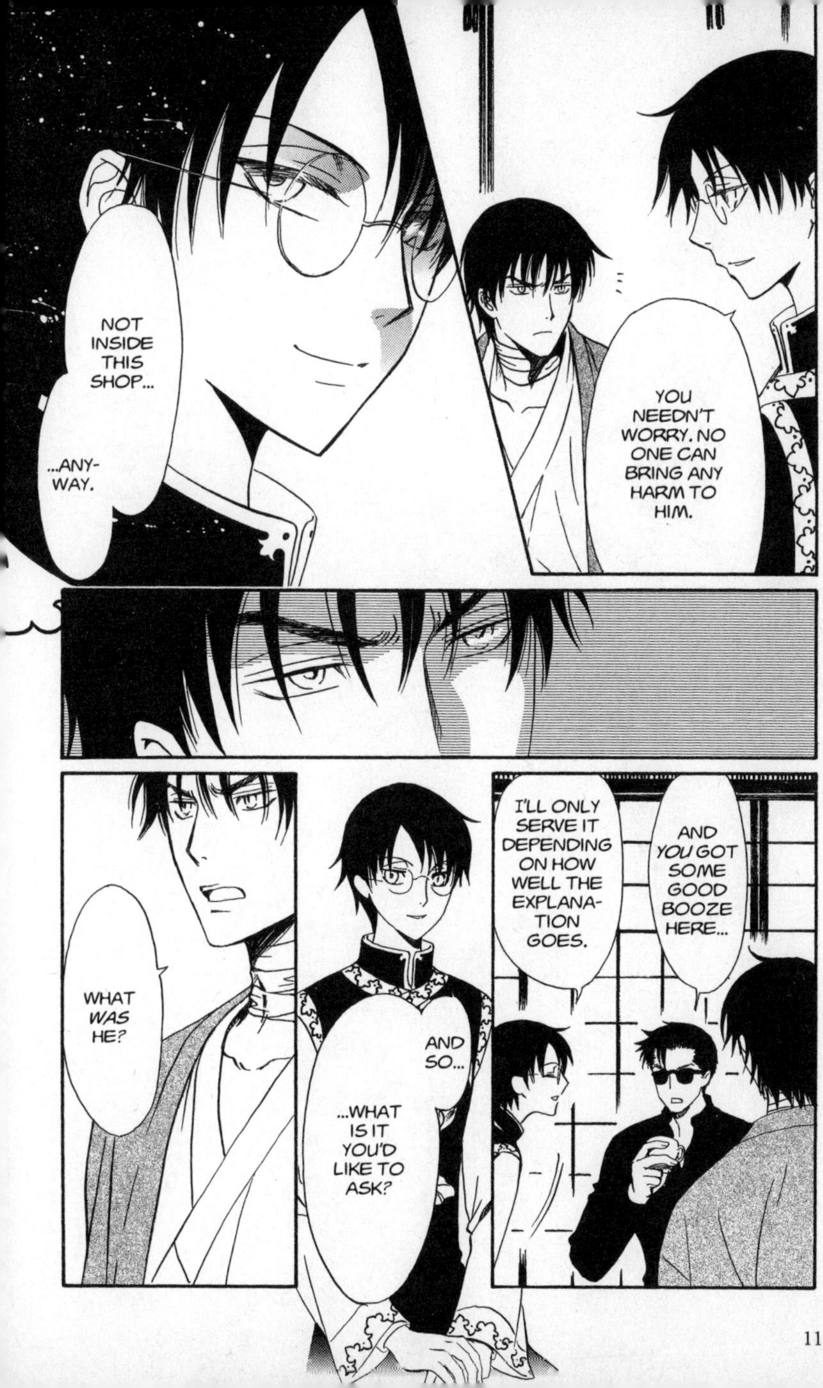
YOU NEEDN'T WORRY. NO ONE CAN BRING ANY HARM TO HIM.
NOT INSIDE THIS SHOP...
...ANY-WAY.
AND *YOU* GOT SOME GOOD BOOZE HERE...
I'LL ONLY SERVE IT DEPENDING ON HOW WELL THE EXPLANA-TION GOES.
AND SO...
...WHAT IS IT YOU'D LIKE TO ASK?
WHAT *WAS* HE?

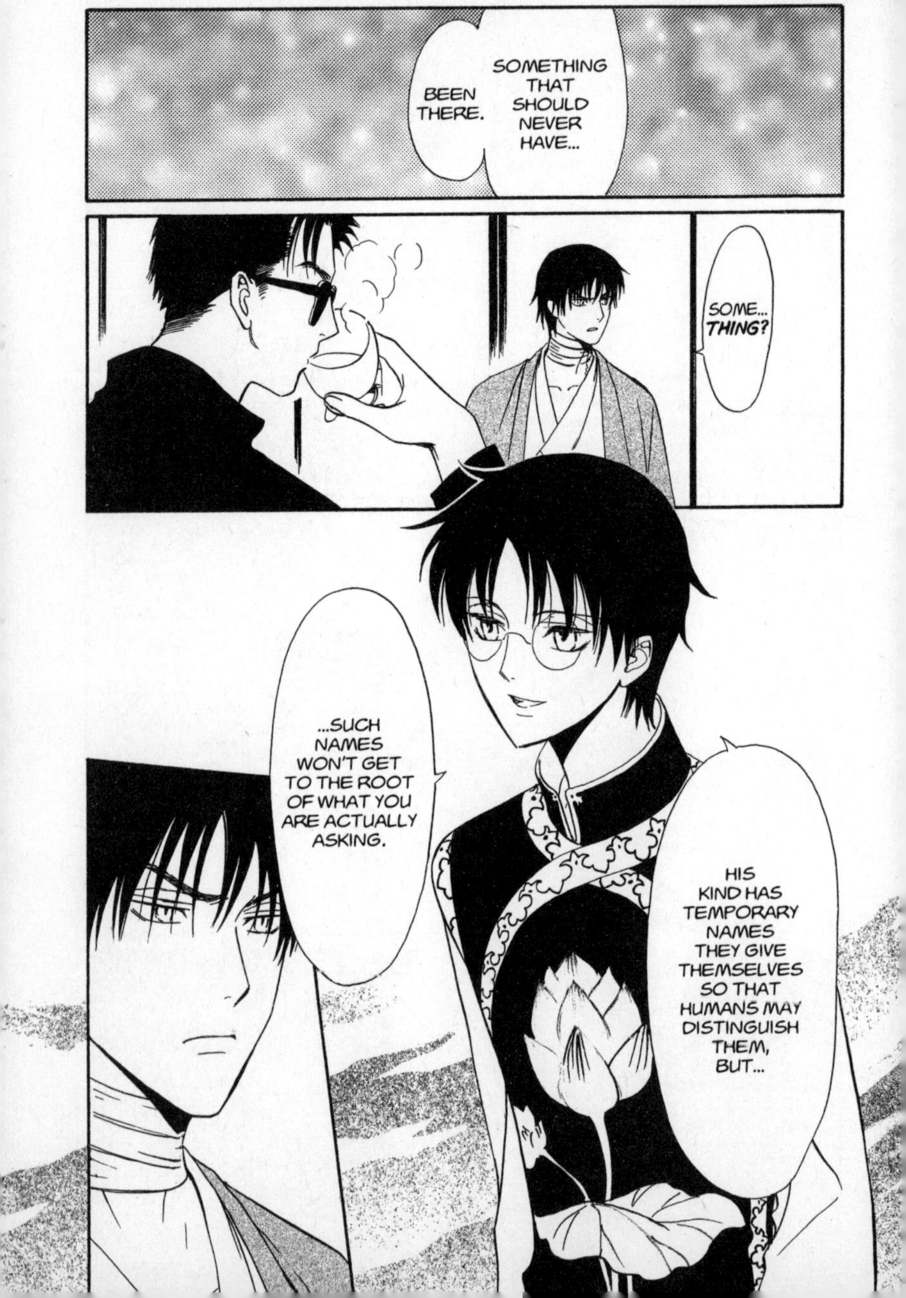
SOMETHING THAT SHOULD NEVER HAVE...
BEEN THERE.
SOME... *THING?*
HIS KIND HAS TEMPORARY NAMES THEY GIVE THEMSELVES SO THAT HUMANS MAY DISTINGUISH THEM, BUT...
...SUCH NAMES WON'T GET TO THE ROOT OF WHAT YOU ARE ACTUALLY ASKING.

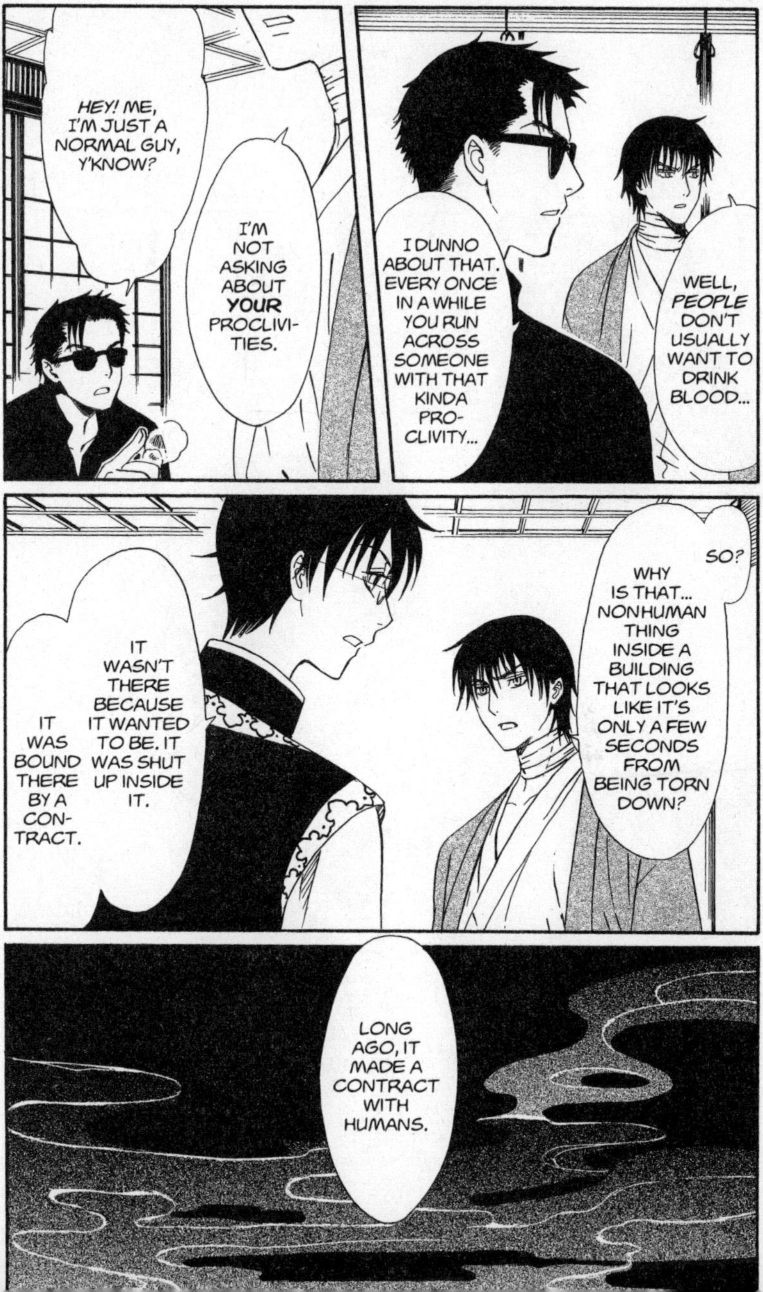
WELL, PEOPLE DON'T USUALLY WANT TO DRINK BLOOD...
I DUNNO ABOUT THAT. EVERY ONCE IN A WHILE YOU RUN ACROSS SOMEONE WITH THAT KINDA PRO-CLIVITY...
I'M NOT ASKING ABOUT **YOUR** PROCLIVI-TIES.
HEY! ME, I'M JUST A NORMAL GUY, Y'KNOW?
SO?
WHY IS THAT... NONHUMAN THING INSIDE A BUILDING THAT LOOKS LIKE IT'S ONLY A FEW SECONDS FROM BEING TORN DOWN?
IT WASN'T THERE BECAUSE IT WANTED TO BE. IT WAS SHUT UP INSIDE IT.
IT WAS BOUND THERE BY A CON-TRACT.
LONG AGO, IT MADE A CONTRACT WITH HUMANS.

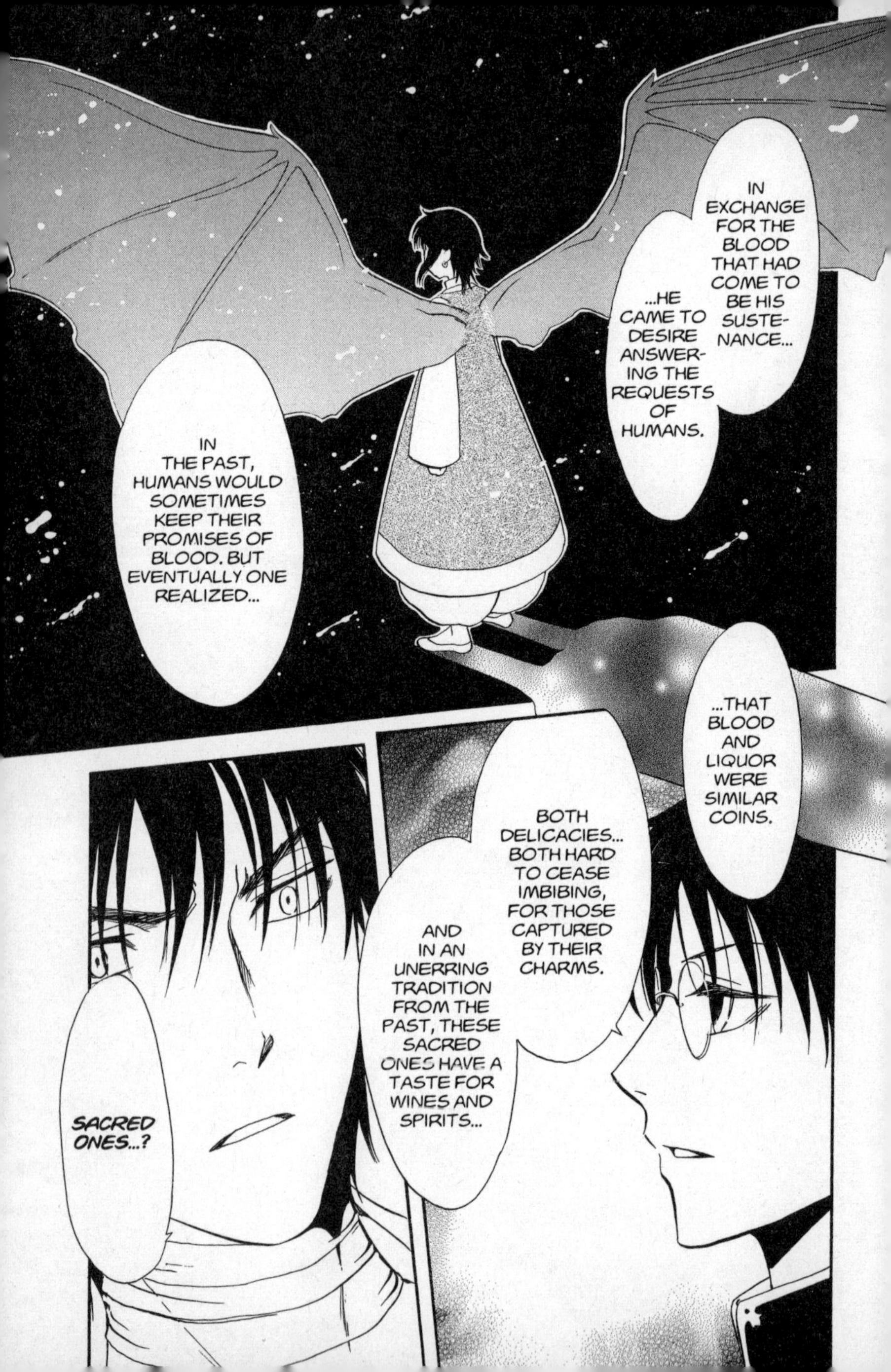
IN EXCHANGE FOR THE BLOOD THAT HAD COME TO BE HIS SUSTENANCE...
...HE CAME TO DESIRE ANSWERING THE REQUESTS OF HUMANS.
IN THE PAST, HUMANS WOULD SOMETIMES KEEP THEIR PROMISES OF BLOOD. BUT EVENTUALLY ONE REALIZED...
...THAT BLOOD AND LIQUOR WERE SIMILAR COINS.
BOTH DELICACIES... BOTH HARD TO CEASE IMBIBING, FOR THOSE CAPTURED BY THEIR CHARMS.
AND IN AN UNERRING TRADITION FROM THE PAST, THESE SACRED ONES HAVE A TASTE FOR WINES AND SPIRITS...
SACRED ONES...?

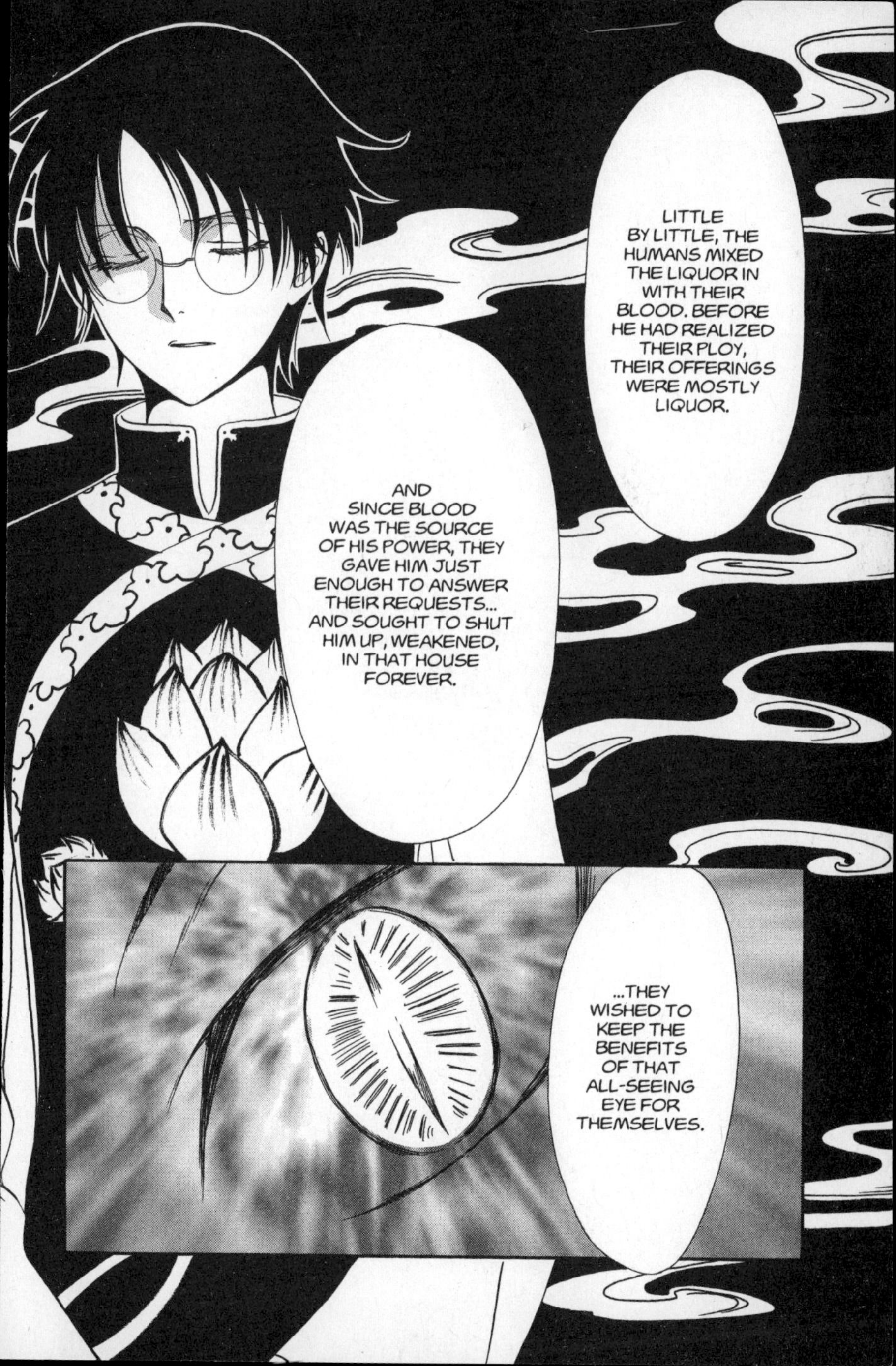
LITTLE BY LITTLE, THE HUMANS MIXED THE LIQUOR IN WITH THEIR BLOOD. BEFORE HE HAD REALIZED THEIR PLOY, THEIR OFFERINGS WERE MOSTLY LIQUOR.
AND SINCE BLOOD WAS THE SOURCE OF HIS POWER, THEY GAVE HIM JUST ENOUGH TO ANSWER THEIR REQUESTS... AND SOUGHT TO SHUT HIM UP, WEAKENED, IN THAT HOUSE FOREVER.
...THEY WISHED TO KEEP THE BENEFITS OF THAT ALL-SEEING EYE FOR THEMSELVES.

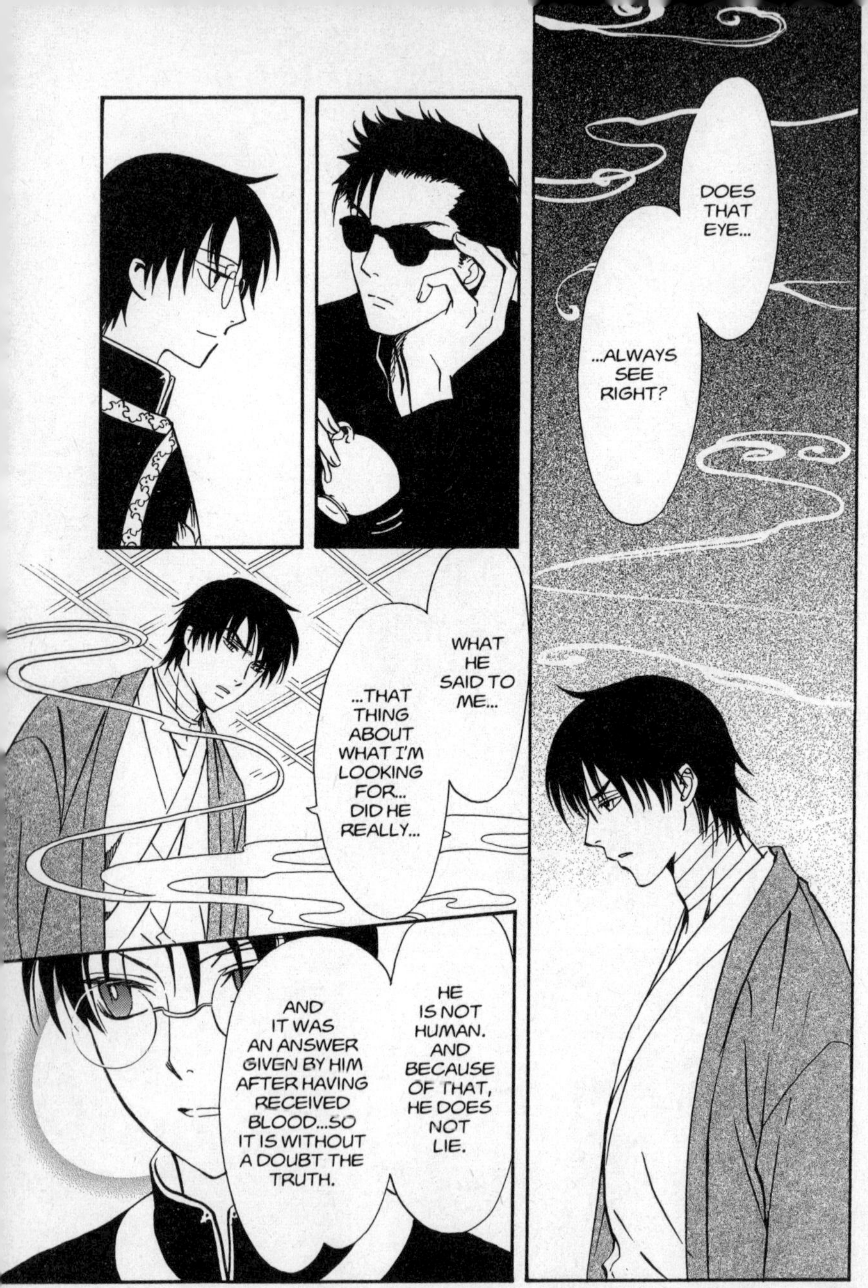
DOES THAT EYE...
...ALWAYS SEE RIGHT?
WHAT HE SAID TO ME...
...THAT THING ABOUT WHAT I'M LOOKING FOR... DID HE REALLY...
HE IS NOT HUMAN. AND BECAUSE OF THAT, HE DOES NOT LIE.
AND IT WAS AN ANSWER GIVEN BY HIM AFTER HAVING RECEIVED BLOOD...SO IT IS WITHOUT A DOUBT THE TRUTH.

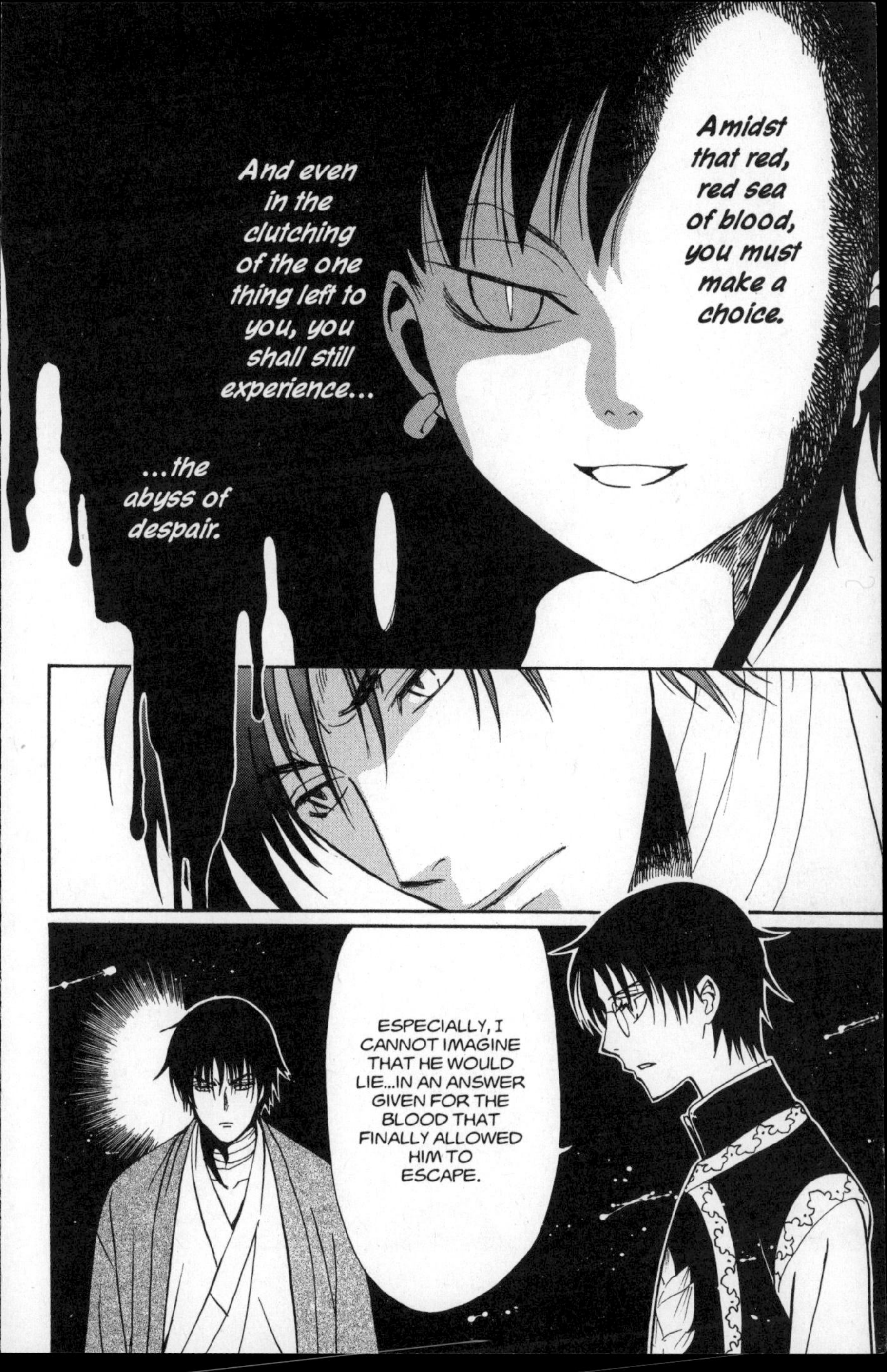
Amidst that red, red sea of blood, you must make a choice.
And even in the clutching of the one thing left to you, you shall still experience...
...the abyss of despair.
ESPECIALLY, I CANNOT IMAGINE THAT HE WOULD LIE...IN AN ANSWER GIVEN FOR THE BLOOD THAT FINALLY ALLOWED HIM TO ESCAPE.

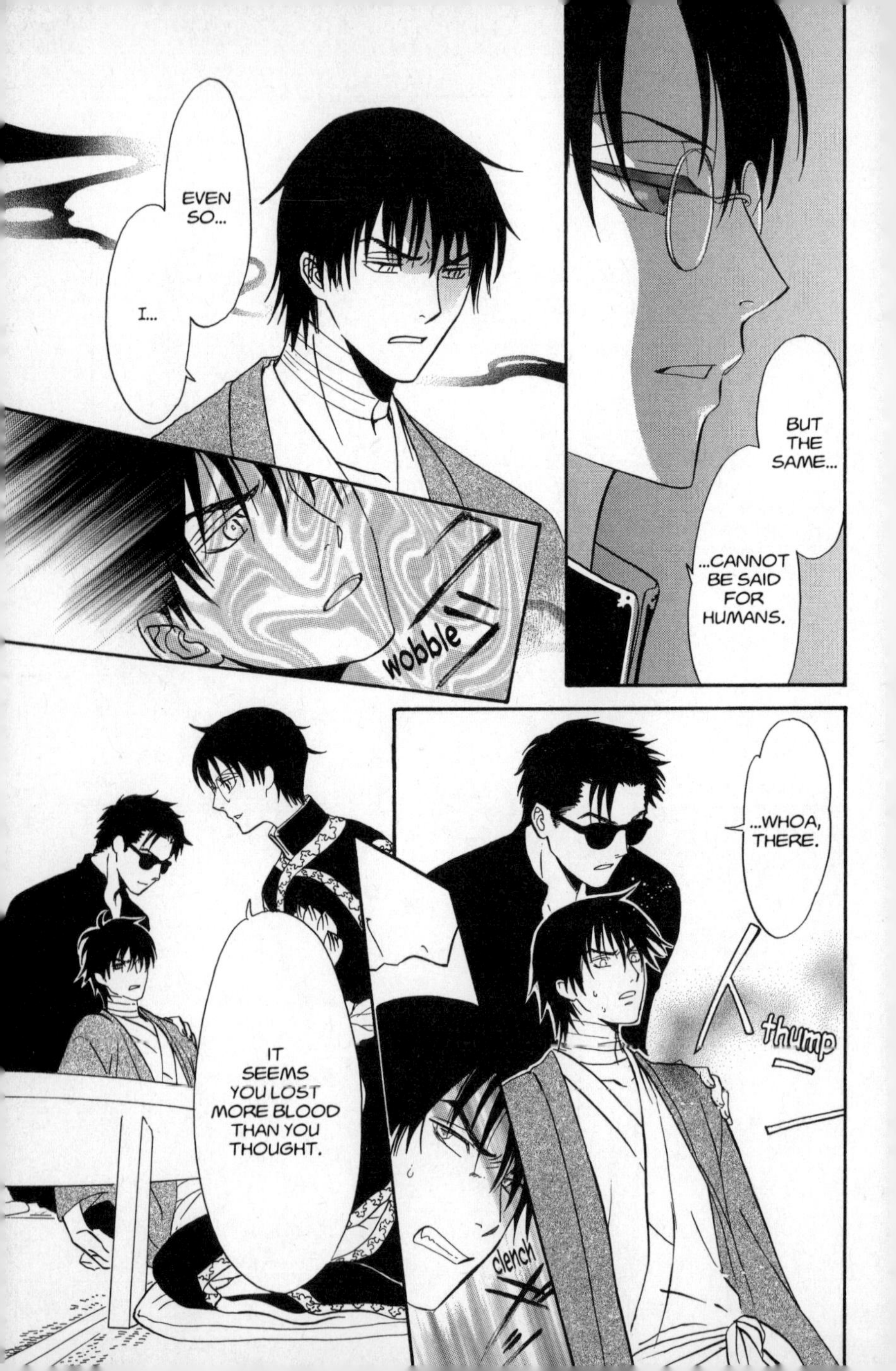
BUT THE SAME...
...CANNOT BE SAID FOR HUMANS.
EVEN SO...
I...
wobble
...WHOA, THERE.
thump
clench
IT SEEMS YOU LOST MORE BLOOD THAN YOU THOUGHT.

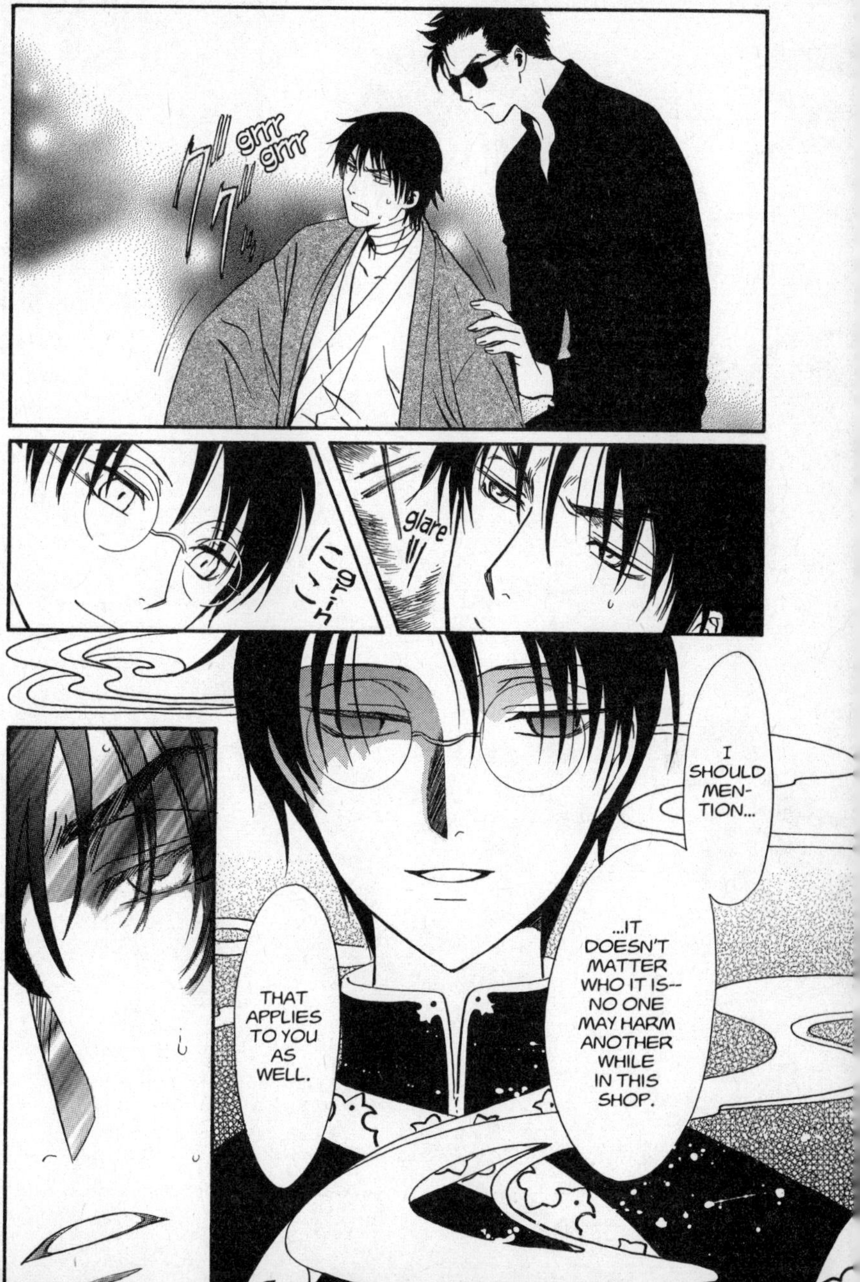
grrr grrr
glare
grin
I SHOULD MEN-TION...
...IT DOESN'T MATTER WHO IT IS-- NO ONE MAY HARM ANOTHER WHILE IN THIS SHOP.
THAT APPLIES TO YOU AS WELL.

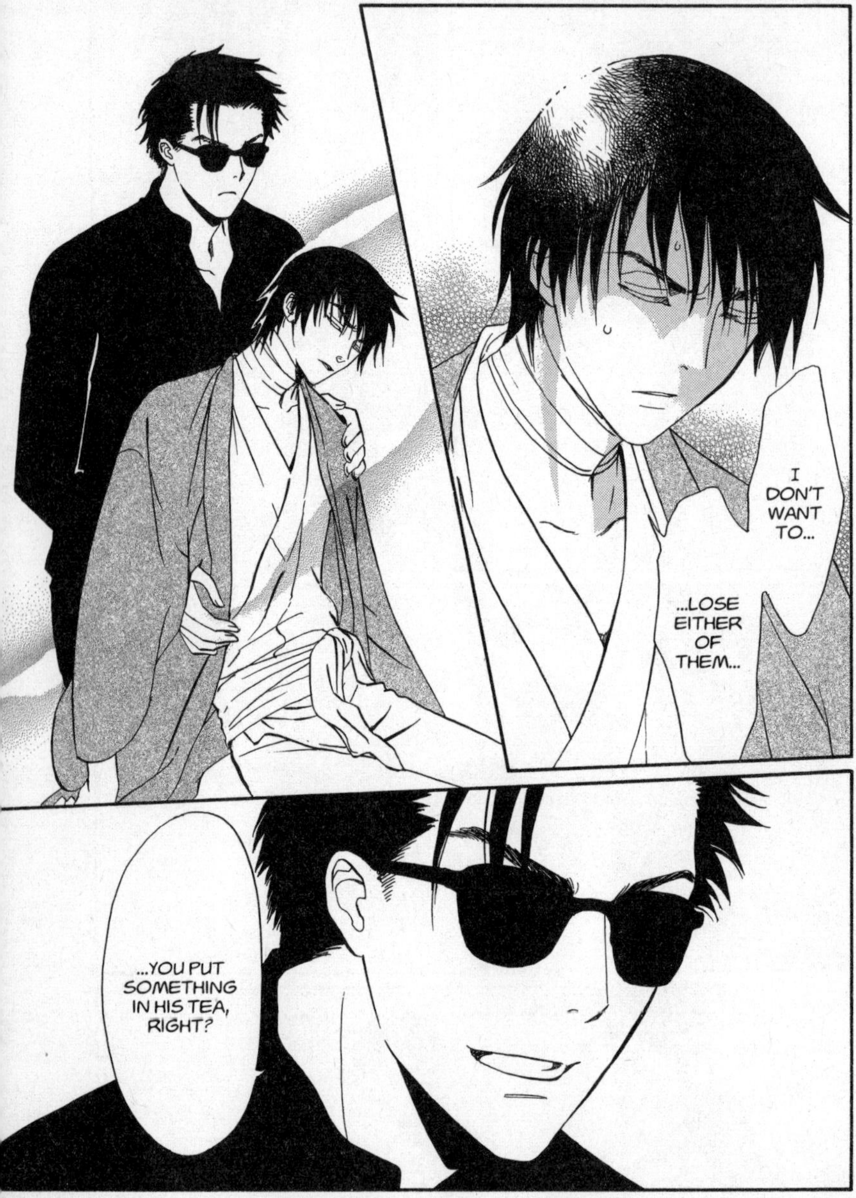
I DON'T WANT TO...
...LOSE EITHER OF THEM...
...YOU PUT SOMETHING IN HIS TEA, RIGHT?

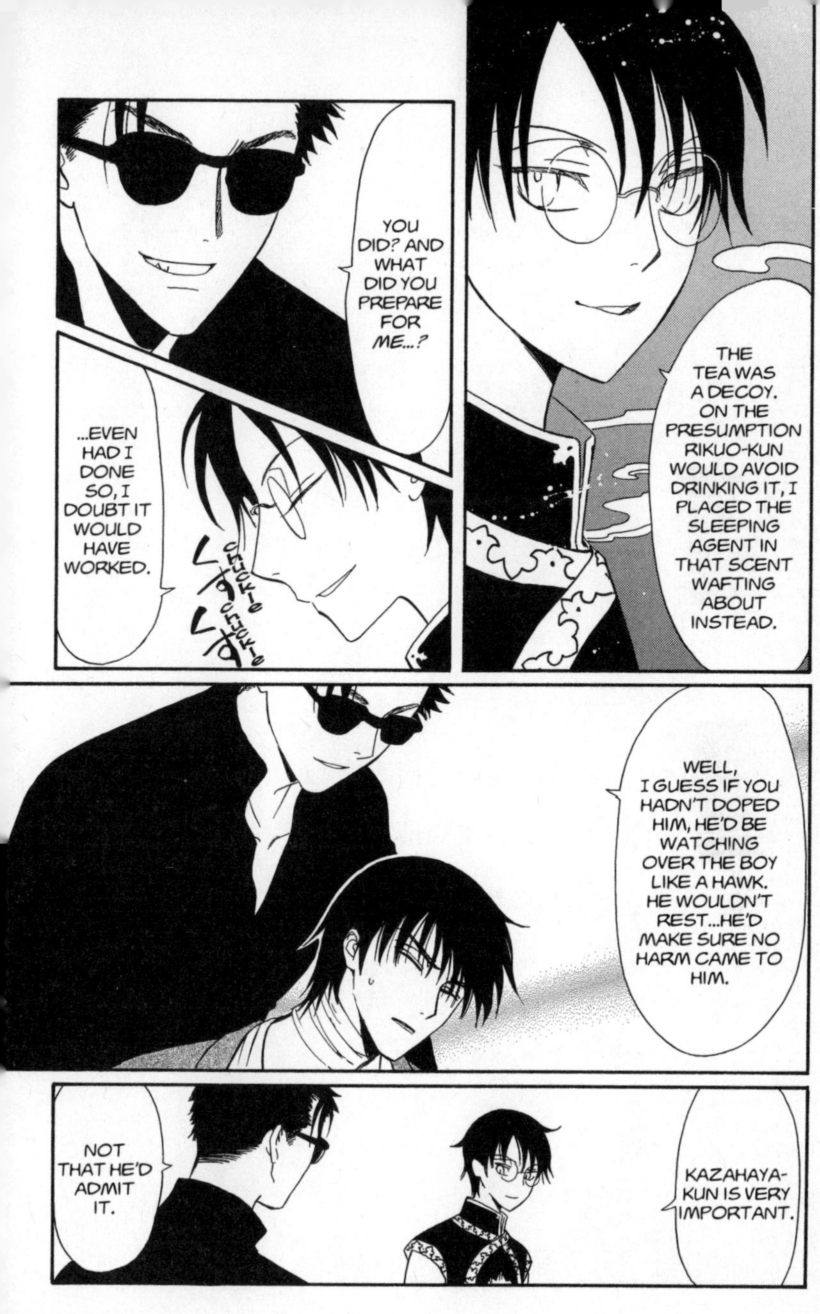
THE TEA WAS A DECOY. ON THE PRESUMPTION RIKUO-KUN WOULD AVOID DRINKING IT, I PLACED THE SLEEPING AGENT IN THAT SCENT WAFTING ABOUT INSTEAD.
YOU DID? AND WHAT DID YOU PREPARE FOR ME...?
...EVEN HAD I DONE SO, I DOUBT IT WOULD HAVE WORKED.
くすくす chuckle chuckle
WELL, I GUESS IF YOU HADN'T DOPED HIM, HE'D BE WATCHING OVER THE BOY LIKE A HAWK. HE WOULDN'T REST...HE'D MAKE SURE NO HARM CAME TO HIM.
KAZAHAYA-KUN IS VERY IMPORTANT.
NOT THAT HE'D ADMIT IT.

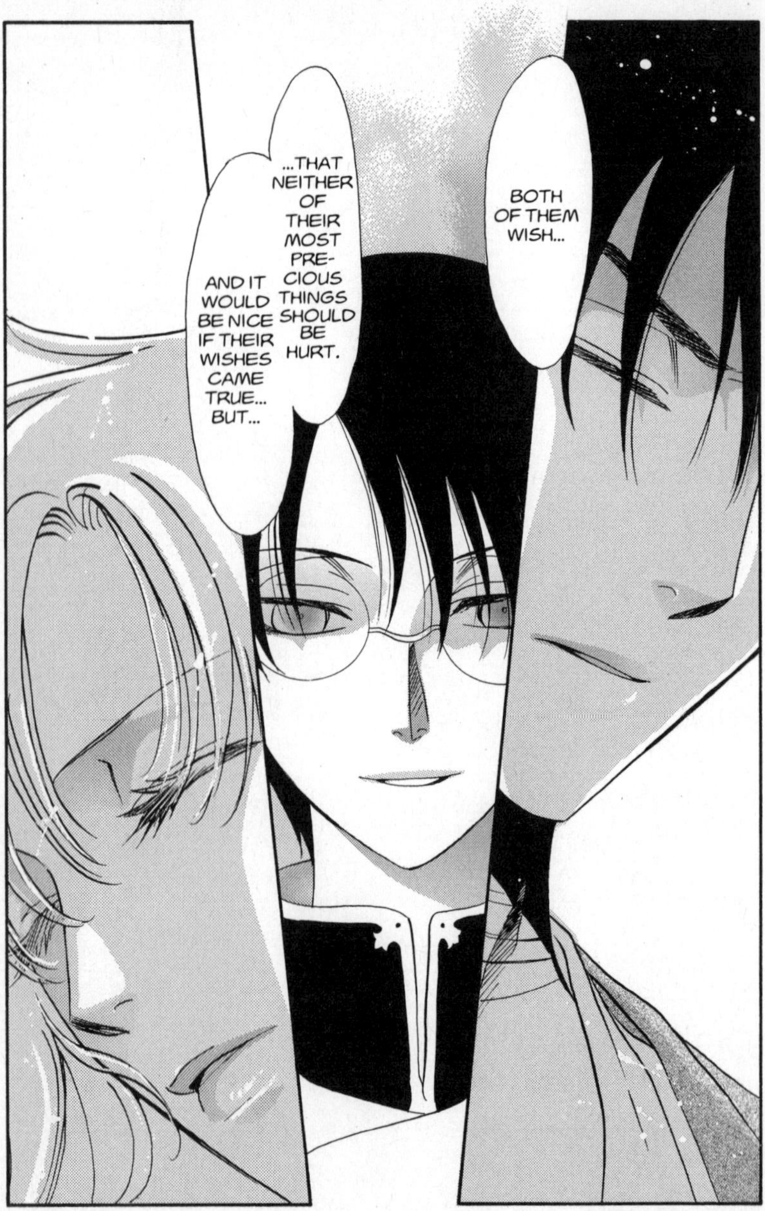
BOTH OF THEM WISH...
...THAT NEITHER OF THEIR MOST PRE-CIOUS THINGS SHOULD BE HURT.
AND IT WOULD BE NICE IF THEIR WISHES CAME TRUE... BUT...

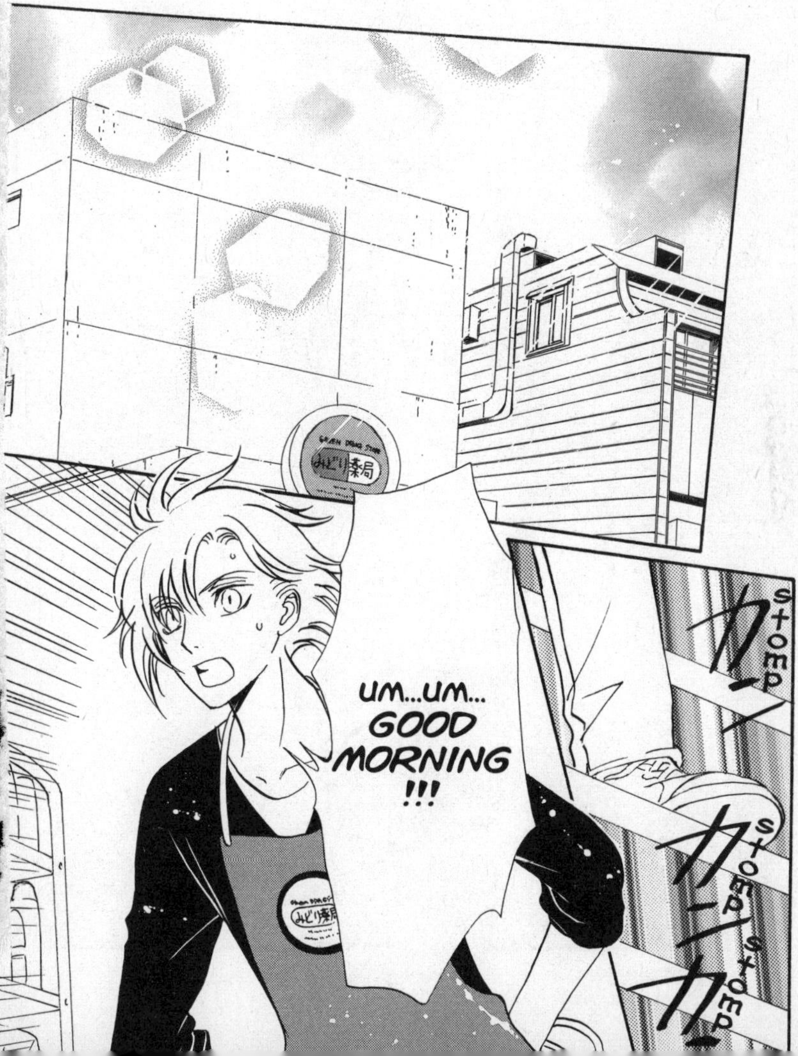

みどり薬局
STOMP
STOMP
STOMP
UM...UM...
GOOD
MORNING
!!!

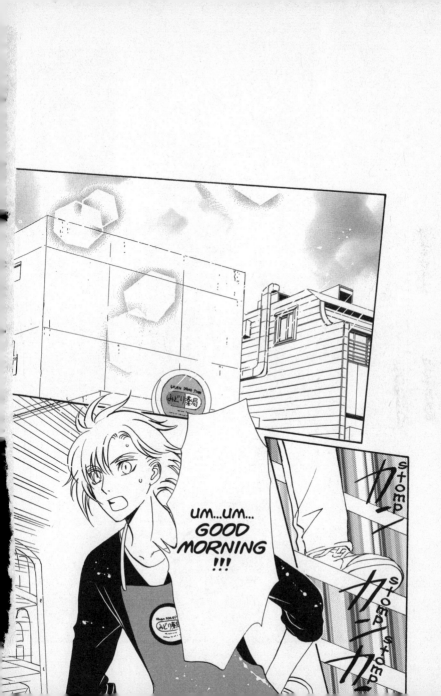

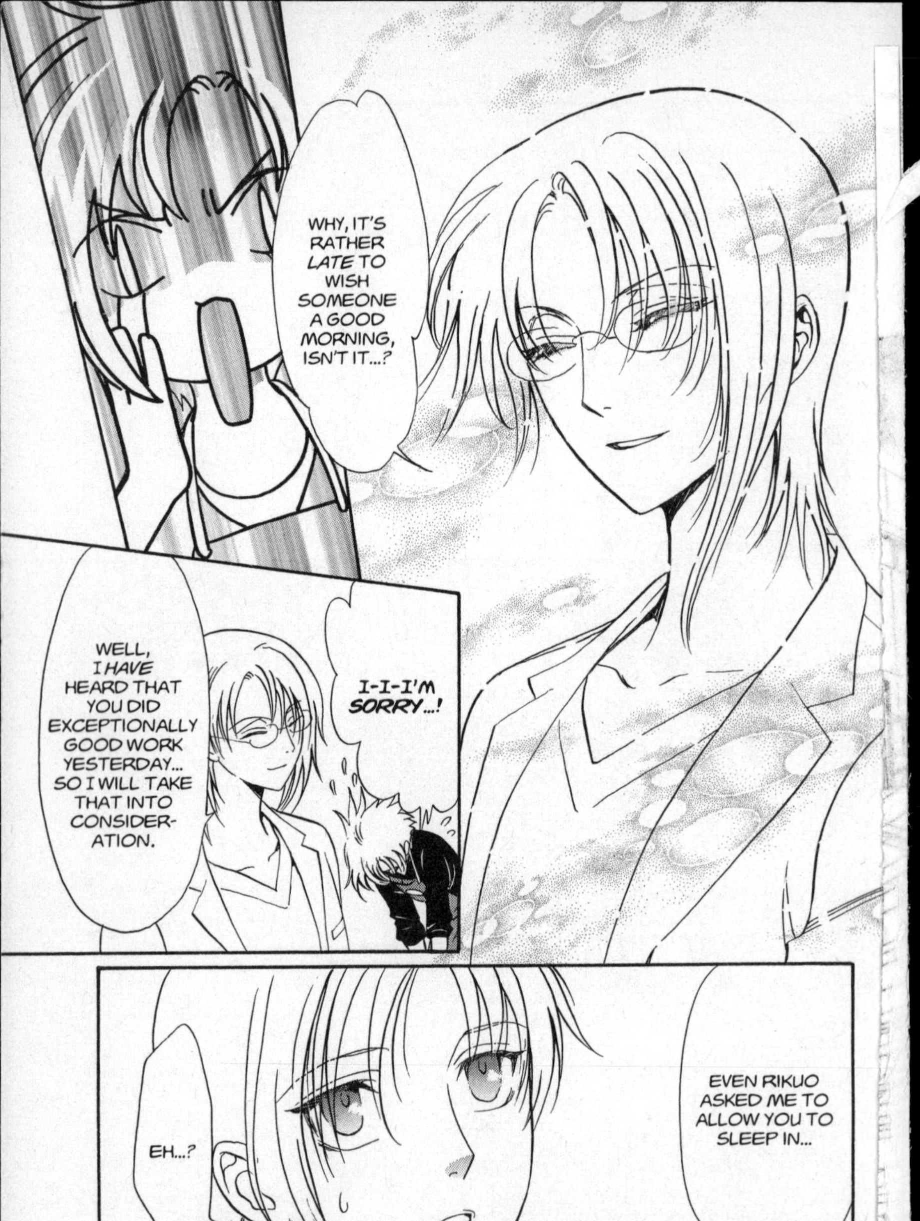
WHY, IT'S RATHER *LATE* TO WISH SOMEONE A GOOD MORNING, ISN'T IT...?
I-I-I'M *SORRY*...!
WELL, I *HAVE* HEARD THAT YOU DID EXCEPTIONALLY GOOD WORK YESTERDAY... SO I WILL TAKE THAT INTO CONSIDER-ATION.
EVEN RIKUO ASKED ME TO ALLOW YOU TO SLEEP IN...
EH...?

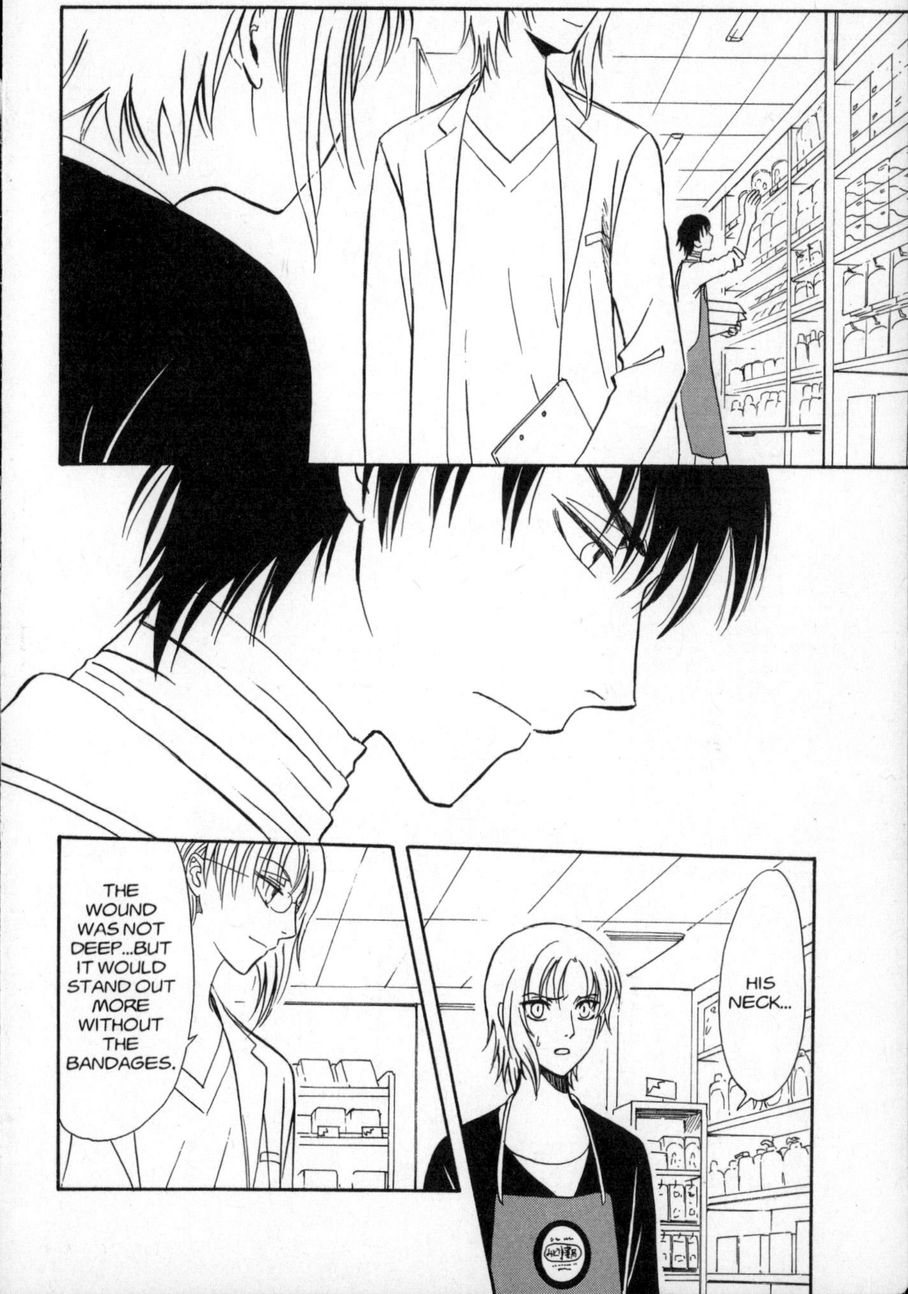
HIS NECK...
THE WOUND WAS NOT DEEP...BUT IT WOULD STAND OUT MORE WITHOUT THE BANDAGES.

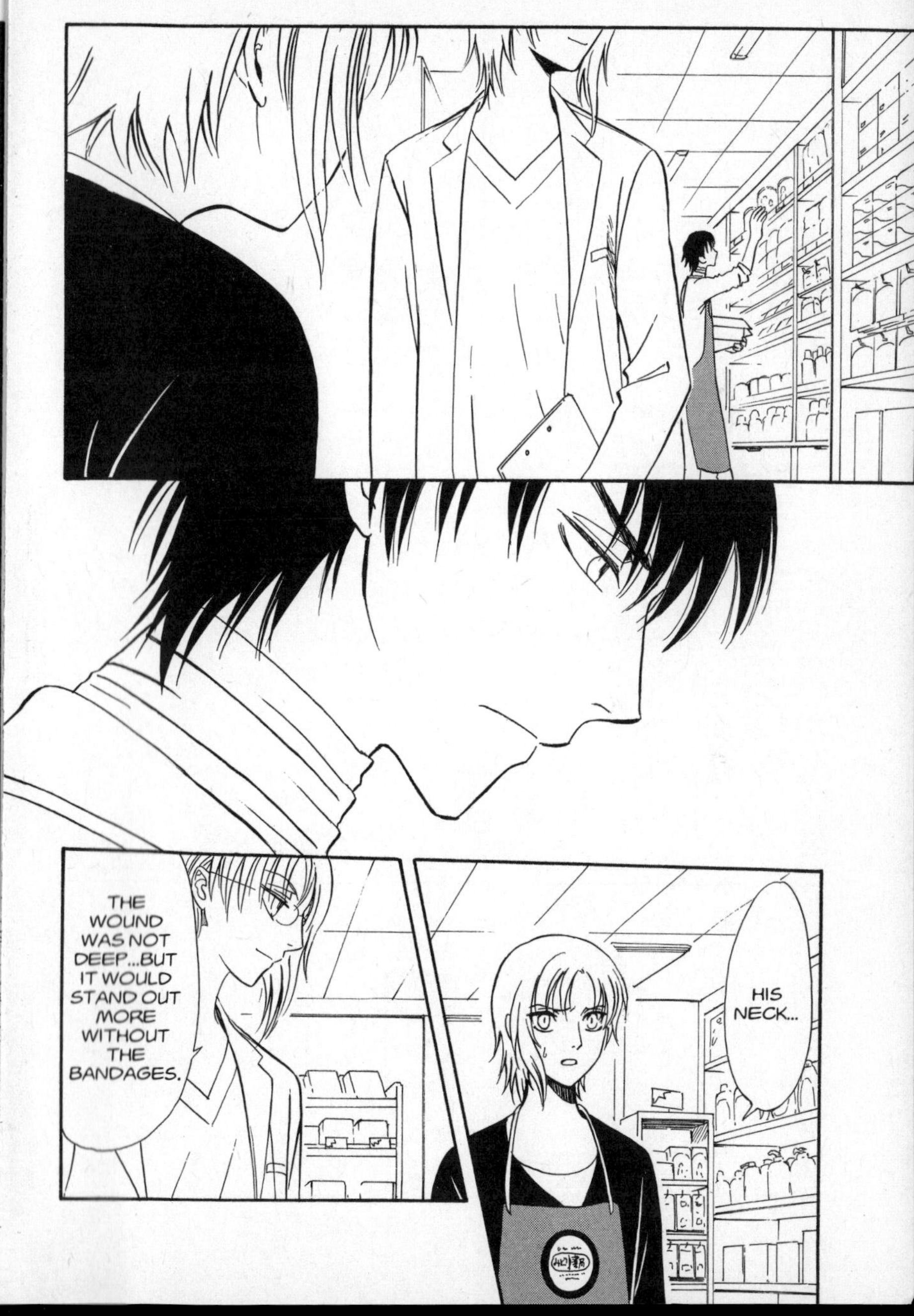
HIS NECK...
THE WOUND WAS NOT DEEP...BUT IT WOULD STAND OUT MORE WITHOUT THE BANDAGES.
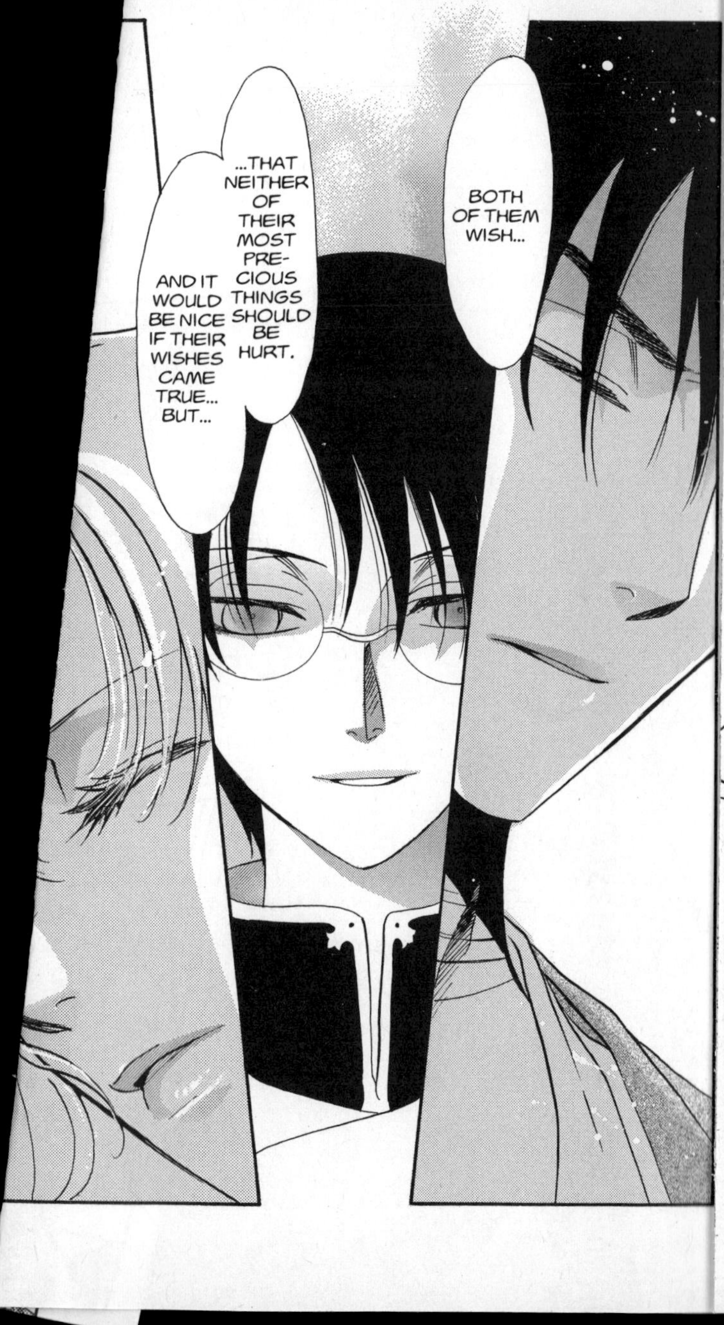
BOTH OF THEM WISH...
...THAT NEITHER OF THEIR MOST PRECIOUS THINGS SHOULD BE HURT.
AND IT WOULD BE NICE IF THEIR WISHES CAME TRUE... BUT...

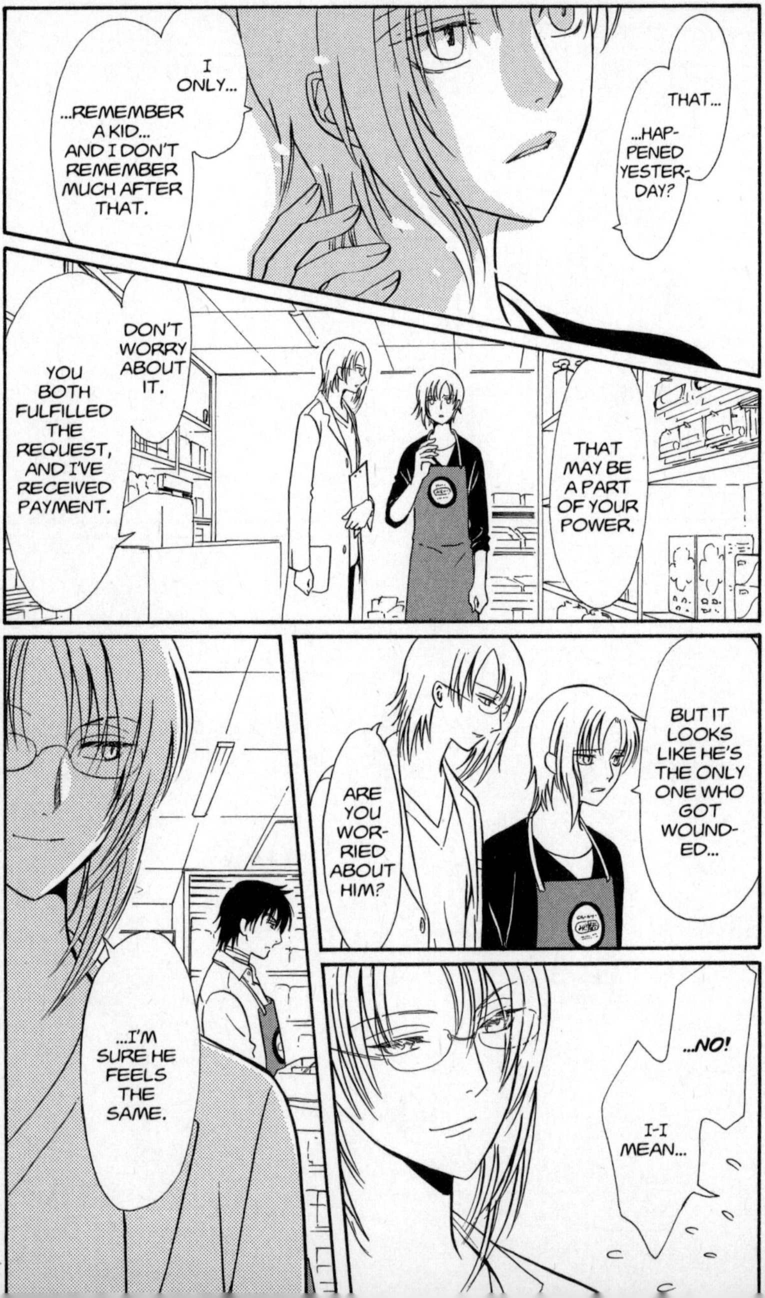
THAT...
...HAP-PENED YESTER-DAY?
I ONLY...
...REMEMBER A KID... AND I DON'T REMEMBER MUCH AFTER THAT.
THAT MAY BE A PART OF YOUR POWER.
DON'T WORRY ABOUT IT.
YOU BOTH FULFILLED THE REQUEST, AND I'VE RECEIVED PAYMENT.
BUT IT LOOKS LIKE HE'S THE ONLY ONE WHO GOT WOUND-ED...
ARE YOU WOR-RIED ABOUT HIM?
...NO!
I-I MEAN...
...I'M SURE HE FEELS THE SAME.

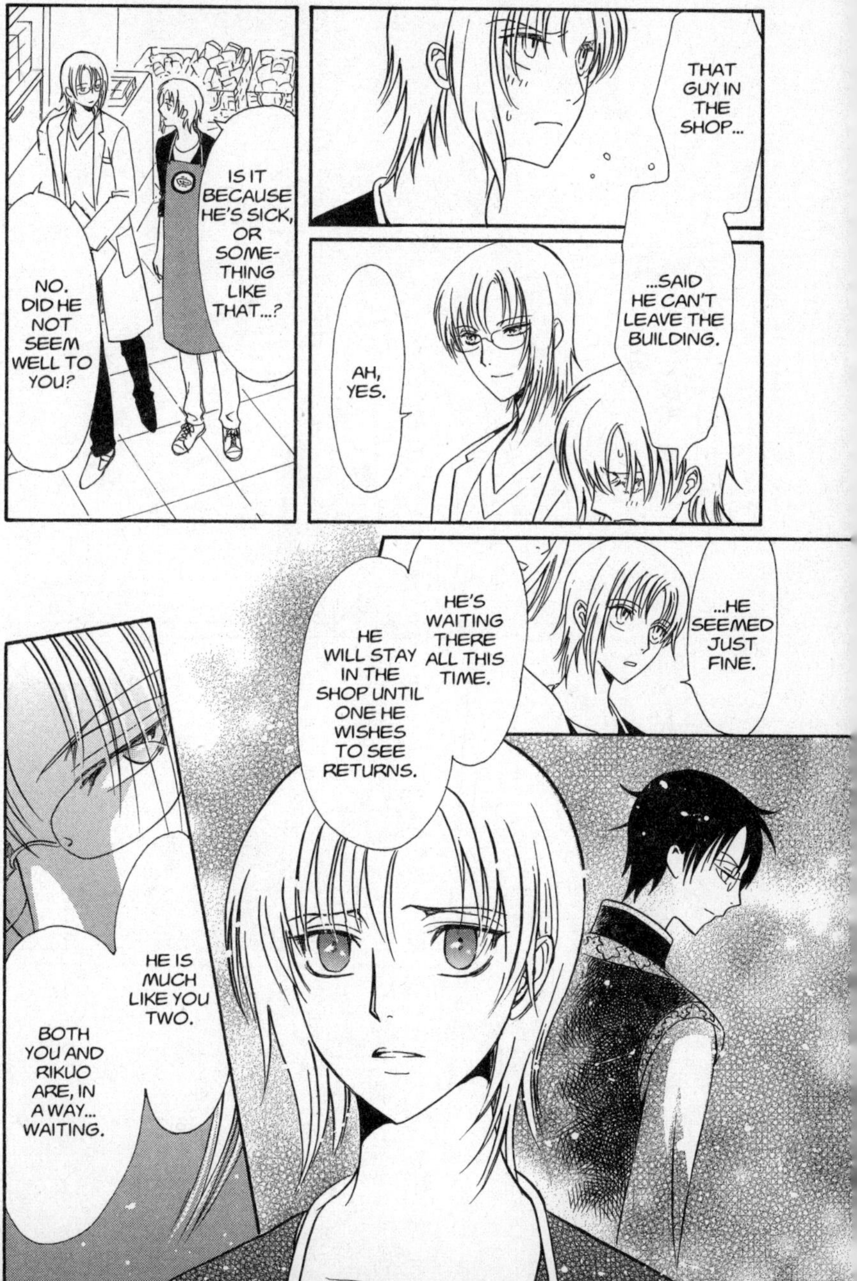
THAT GUY IN THE SHOP...
...SAID HE CAN'T LEAVE THE BUILDING.
AH, YES.
IS IT BECAUSE HE'S SICK, OR SOMETHING LIKE THAT...?
NO. DID HE NOT SEEM WELL TO YOU?
...HE SEEMED JUST FINE.
HE'S WAITING THERE ALL THIS TIME.
HE WILL STAY IN THE SHOP UNTIL ONE HE WISHES TO SEE RETURNS.
HE IS MUCH LIKE YOU TWO.
BOTH YOU AND RIKUO ARE, IN A WAY... WAITING.

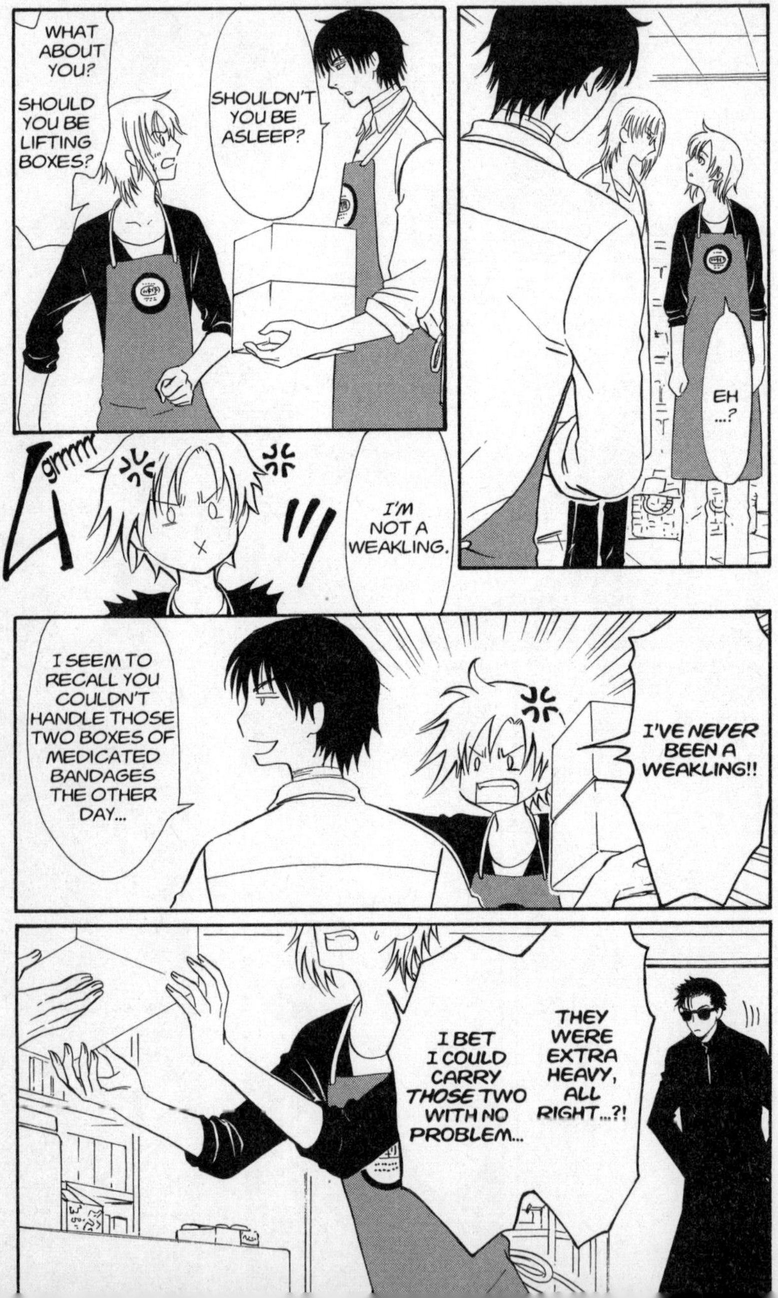
EH ...?
SHOULDN'T YOU BE ASLEEP?
WHAT ABOUT YOU? SHOULD YOU BE LIFTING BOXES?
I'M NOT A WEAKLING.
grrrrr
I SEEM TO RECALL YOU COULDN'T HANDLE THOSE TWO BOXES OF MEDICATED BANDAGES THE OTHER DAY...
I'VE *NEVER* BEEN A WEAKLING!!
THEY WERE EXTRA HEAVY, ALL RIGHT...?!
I BET I COULD CARRY *THOSE* TWO WITH NO PROBLEM...

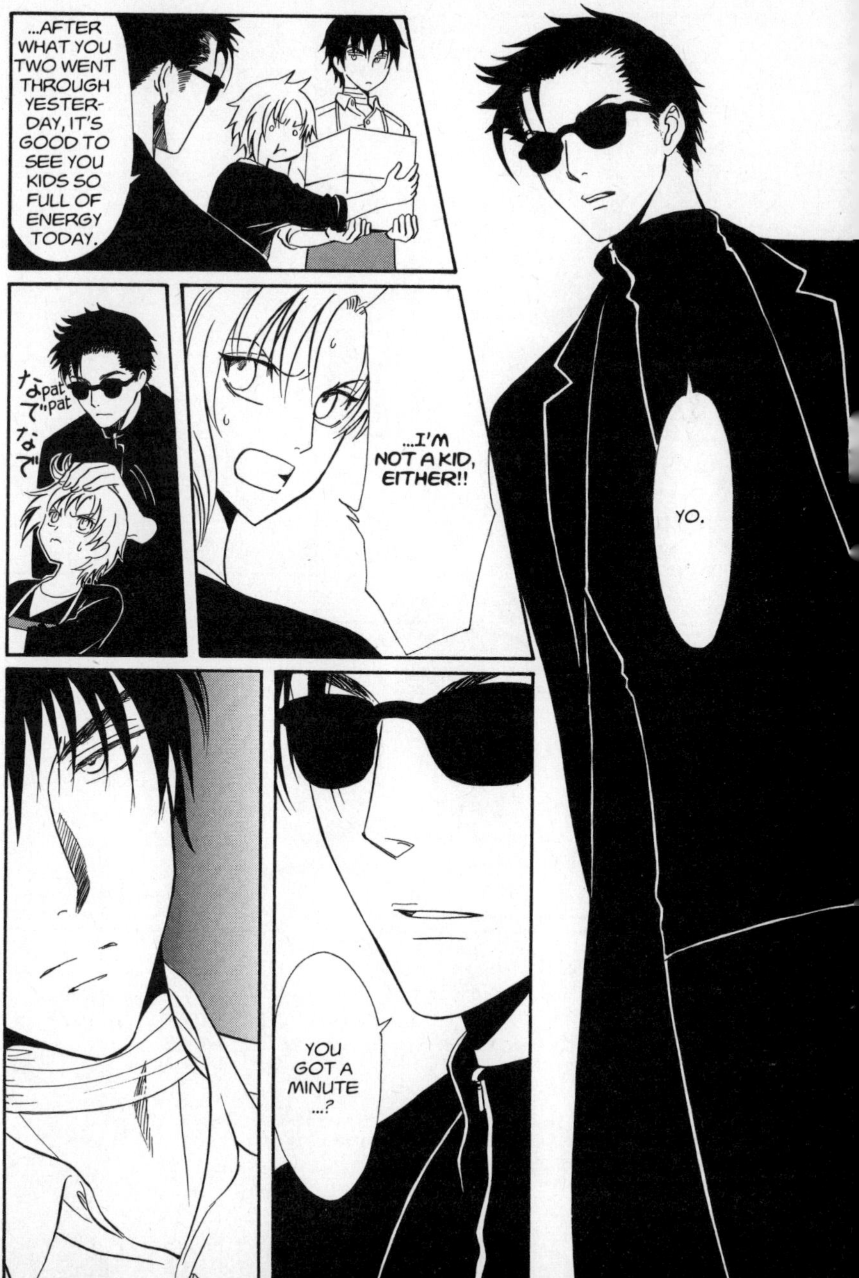
YO.
...AFTER WHAT YOU TWO WENT THROUGH YESTER-DAY, IT'S GOOD TO SEE YOU KIDS SO FULL OF ENERGY TODAY.
...I'M NOT A KID, EITHER!!
なで pat
なで pat
YOU GOT A MINUTE ...?

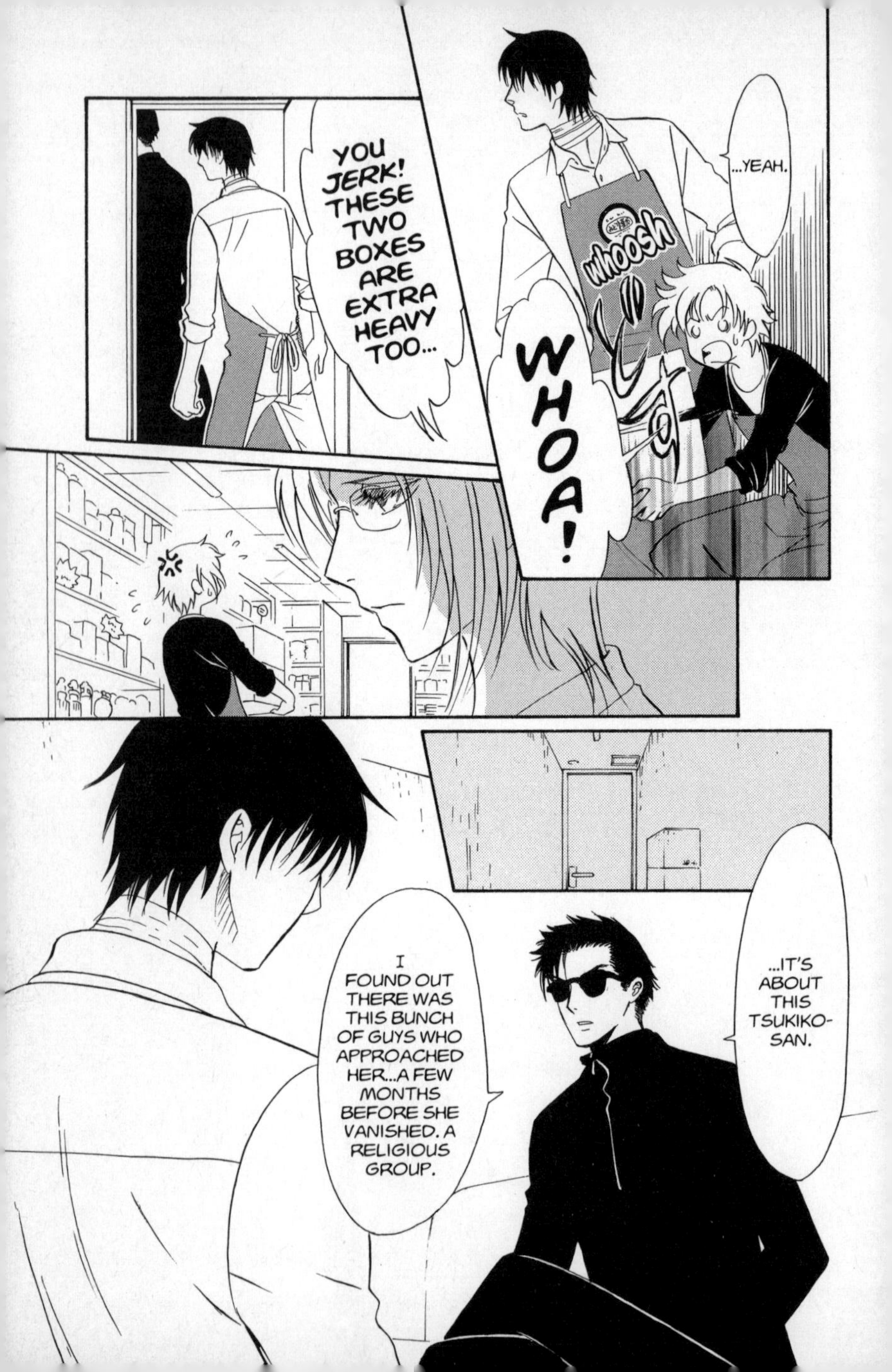
...YEAH.
whoosh
WHOA!
YOU JERK! THESE TWO BOXES ARE EXTRA HEAVY TOO...
...IT'S ABOUT THIS TSUKIKO-SAN.
I FOUND OUT THERE WAS THIS BUNCH OF GUYS WHO APPROACHED HER...A FEW MONTHS BEFORE SHE VANISHED. A RELIGIOUS GROUP.

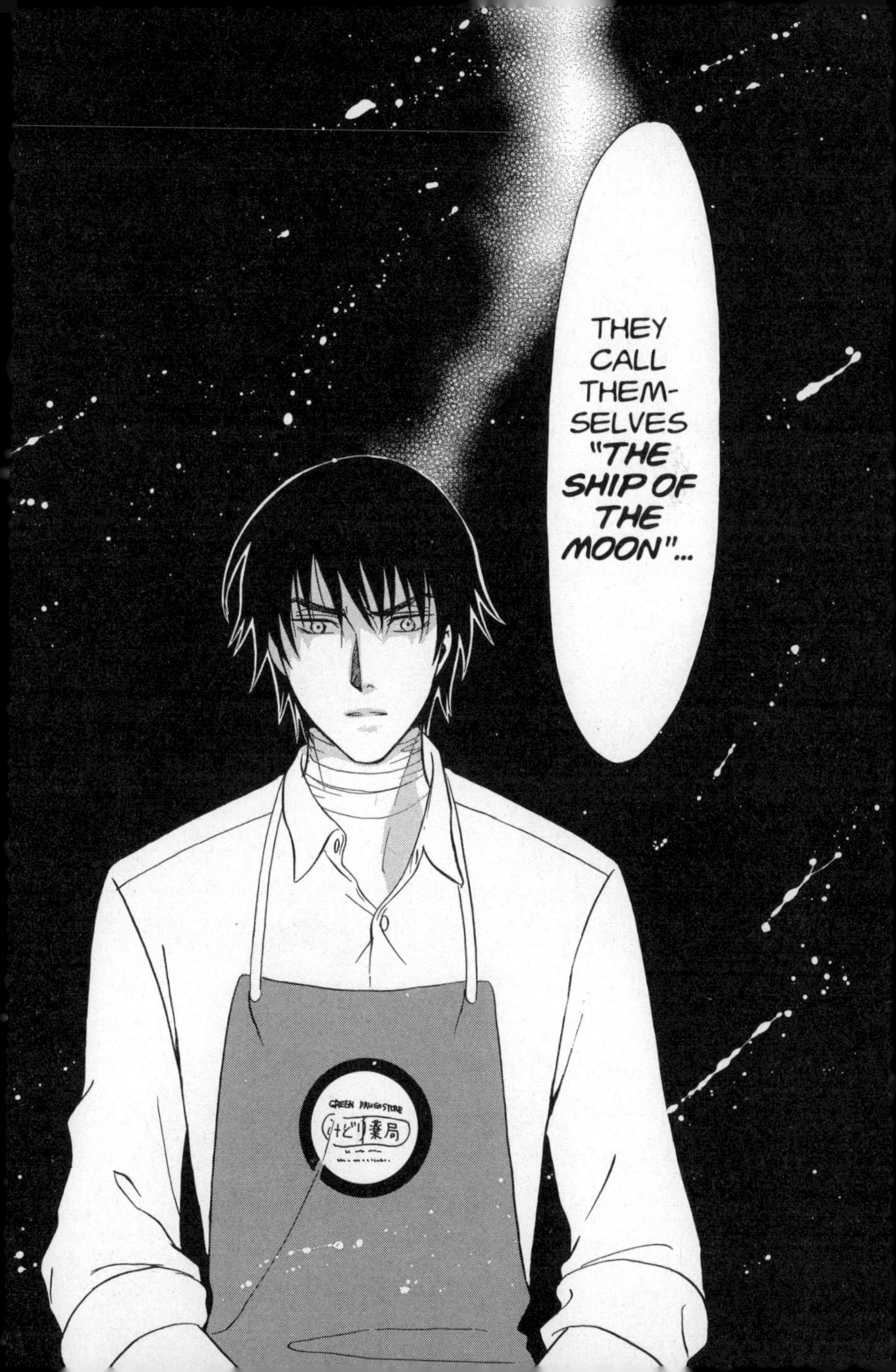
THEY CALL THEM-SELVES "THE SHIP OF THE MOON"...
GREEN DRUGSTORE

DRUG
& DROP

a drugstore with medicine and a danger

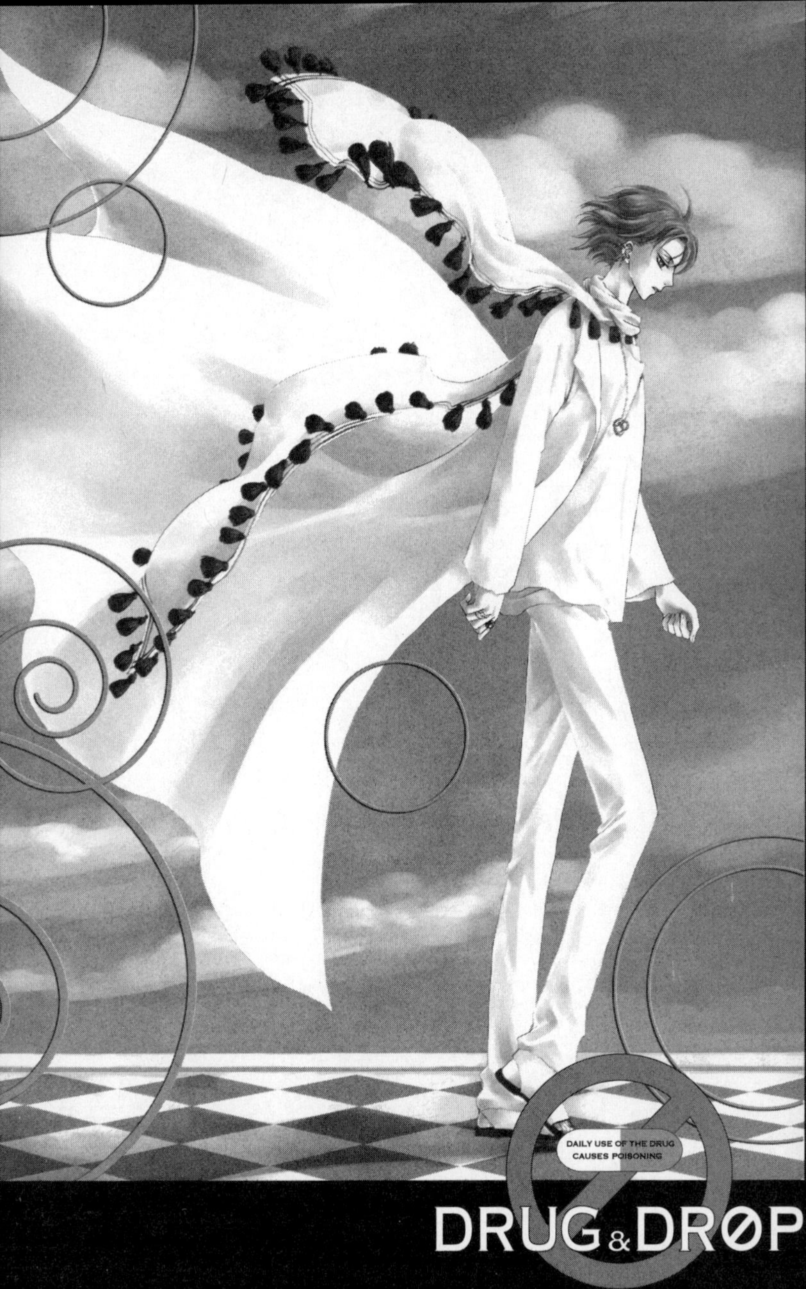
DAILY USE OF THE DRUG
CAUSES POISONING
DRUG&DRØP

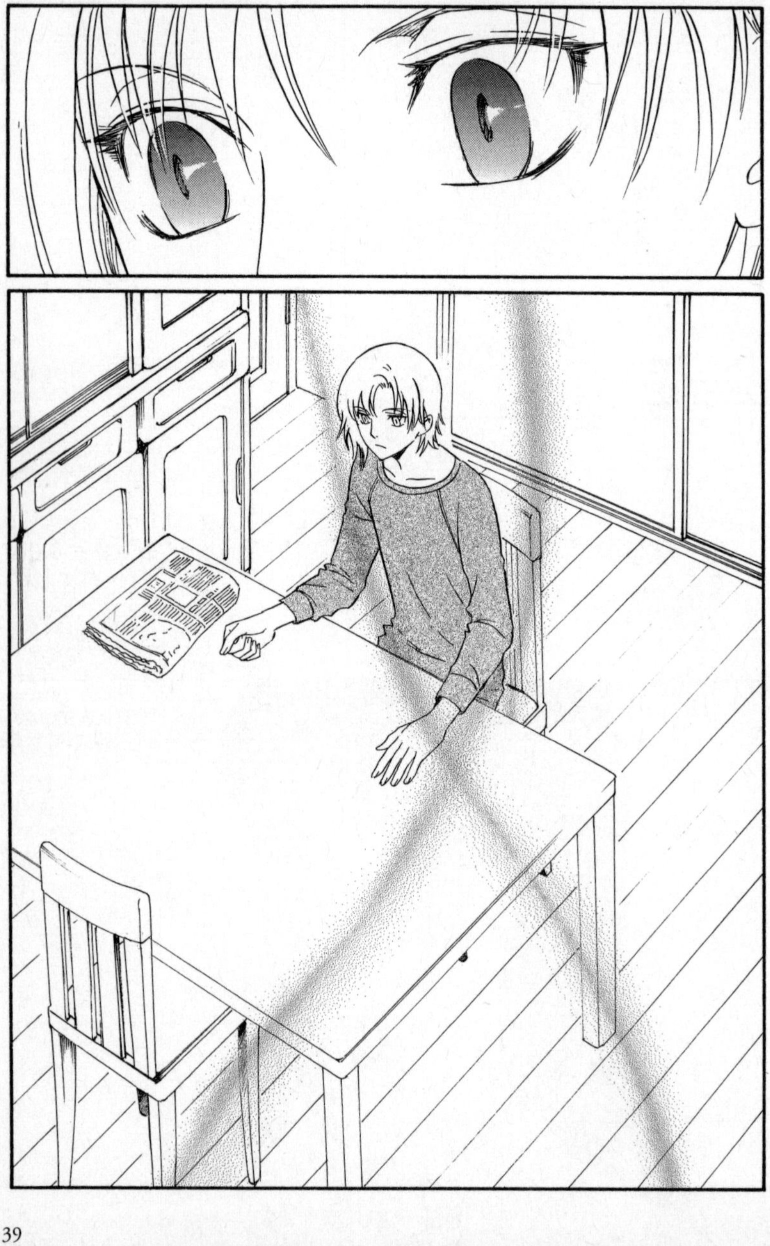

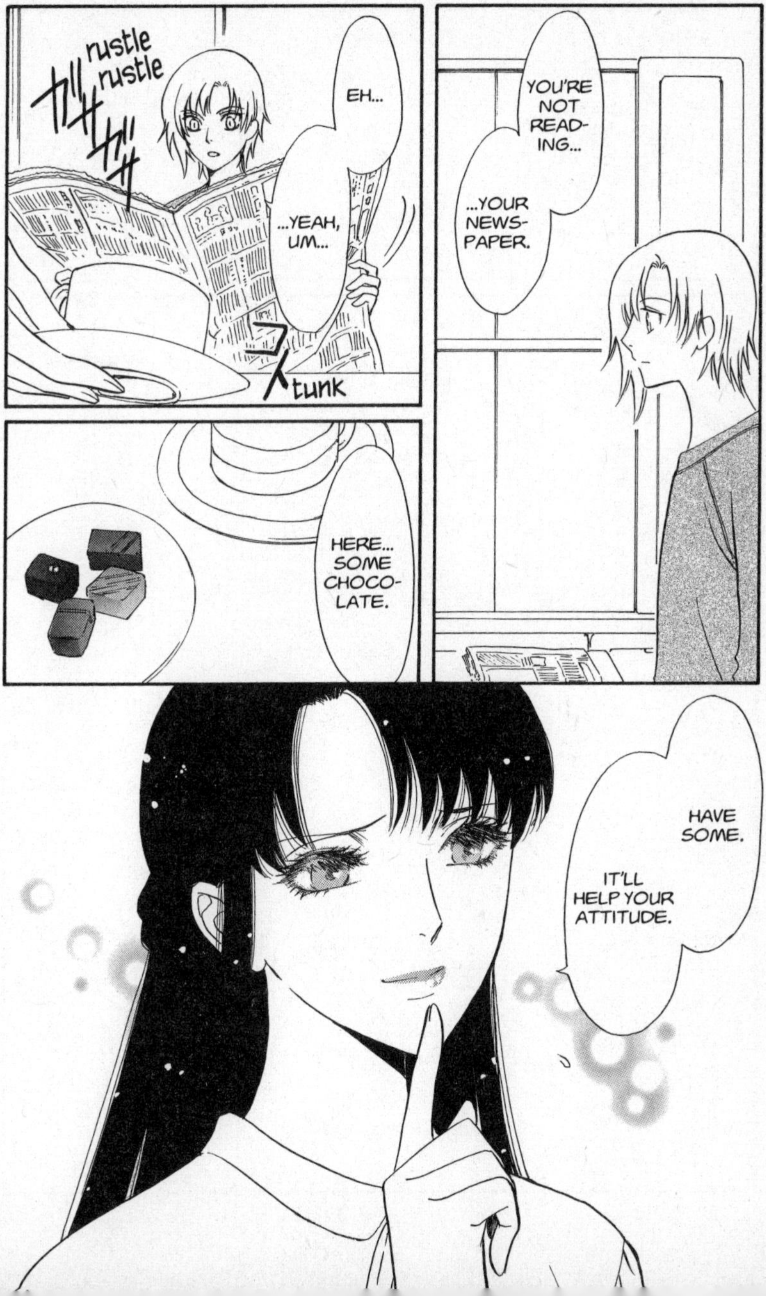
YOU'RE NOT READING...
...YOUR NEWSPAPER.
rustle rustle
EH...
...YEAH, UM...
tunk
HERE... SOME CHOCOLATE.
HAVE SOME.
IT'LL HELP YOUR ATTITUDE.

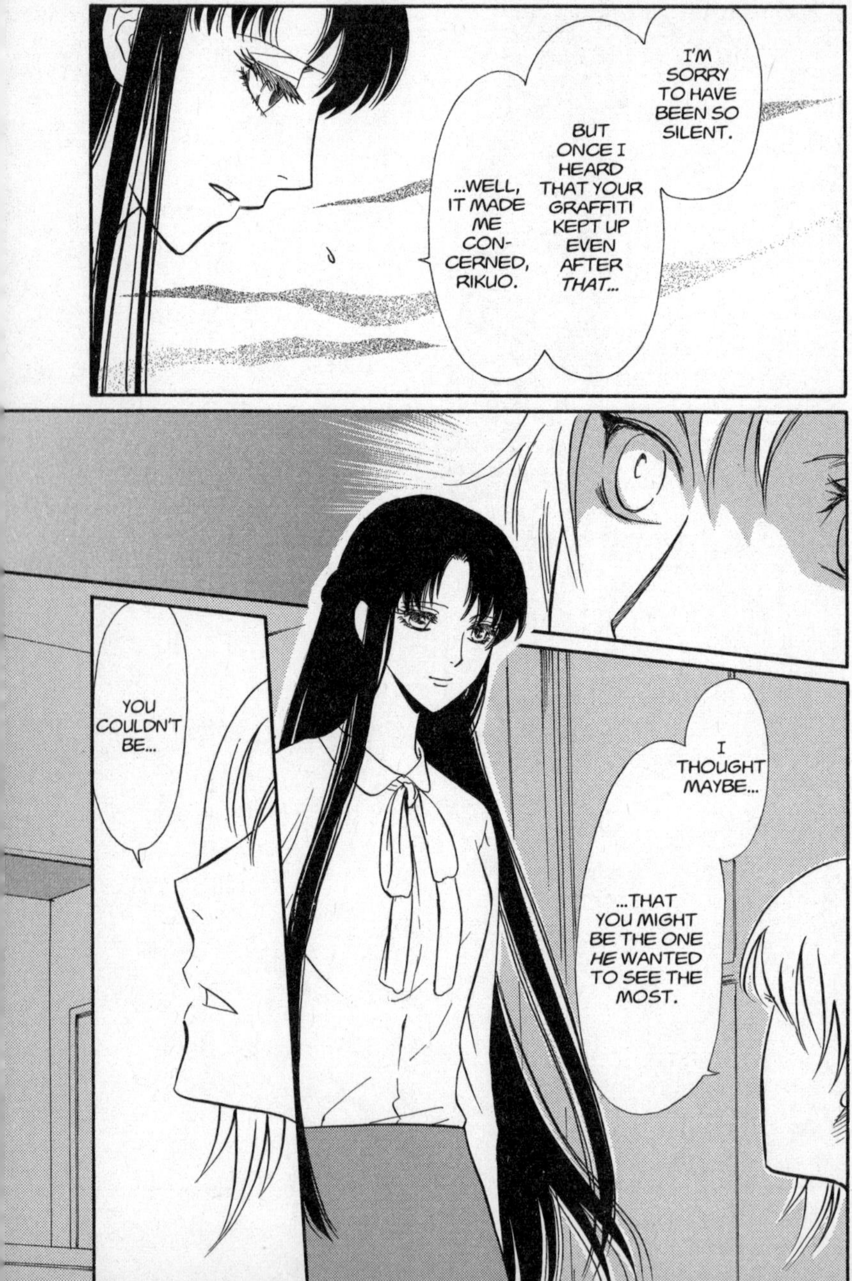
I'M SORRY TO HAVE BEEN SO SILENT.
BUT ONCE I HEARD THAT YOUR GRAFFITI KEPT UP EVEN AFTER *THAT*...
...WELL, IT MADE ME CON-CERNED, RIKUO.
I THOUGHT MAYBE...
...THAT YOU MIGHT BE THE ONE *HE* WANTED TO SEE THE MOST.
YOU COULDN'T BE...

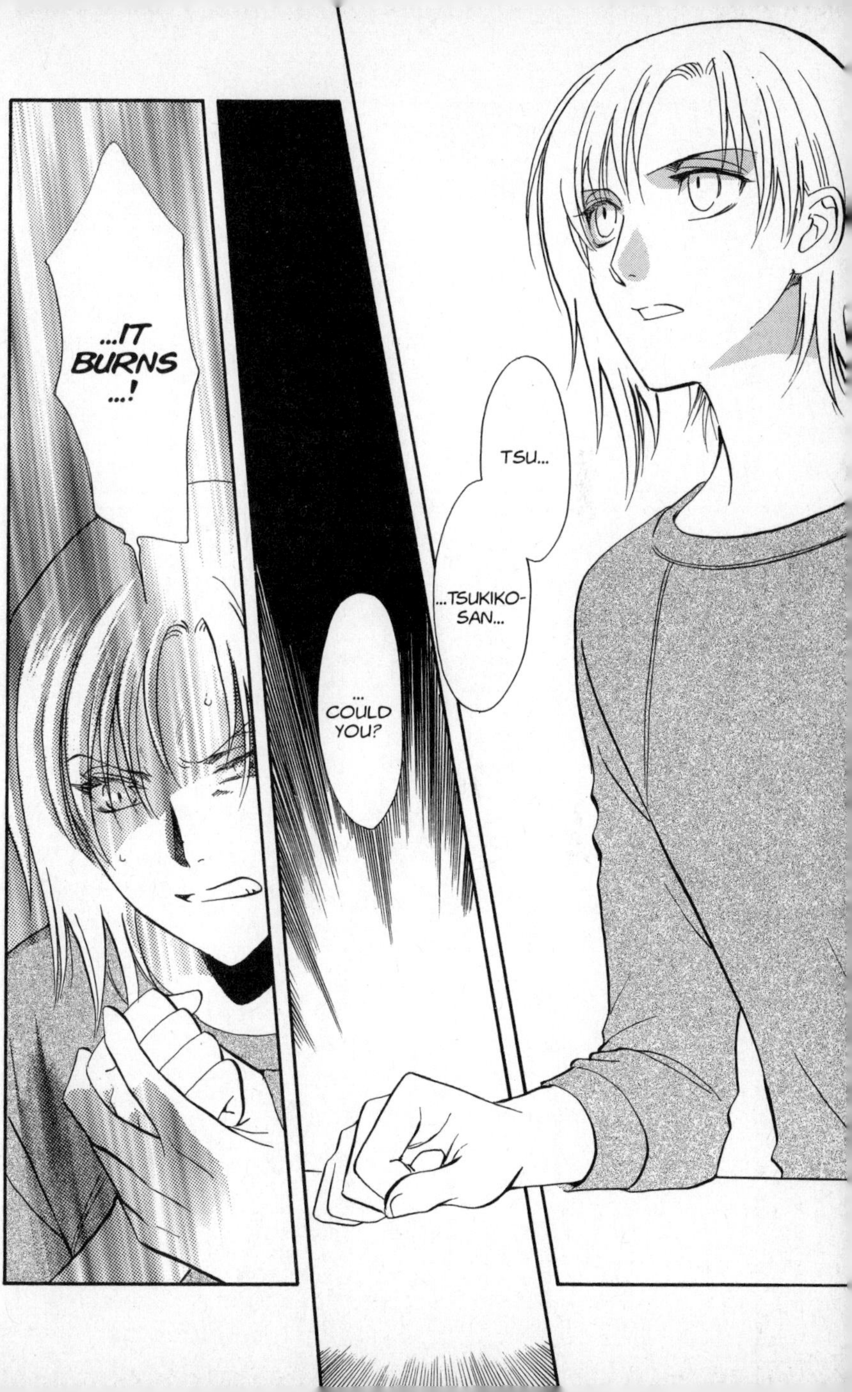
TSU...
...TSUKIKO-SAN...
...COULD YOU?
...IT BURNS ...!

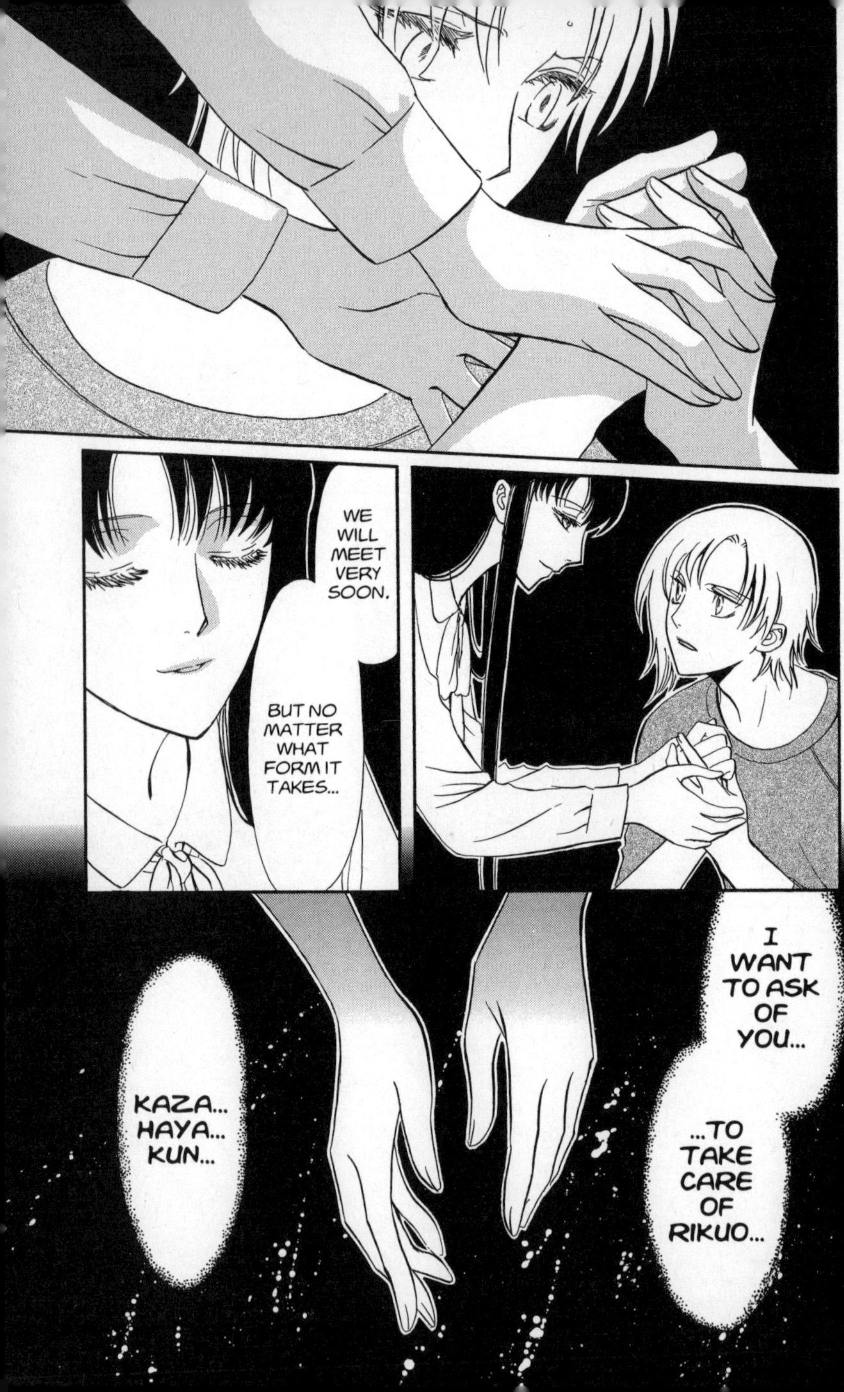
WE WILL MEET VERY SOON.
BUT NO MATTER WHAT FORM IT TAKES...
I WANT TO ASK OF YOU...
...TO TAKE CARE OF RIKUO...
KAZA... HAYA... KUN...

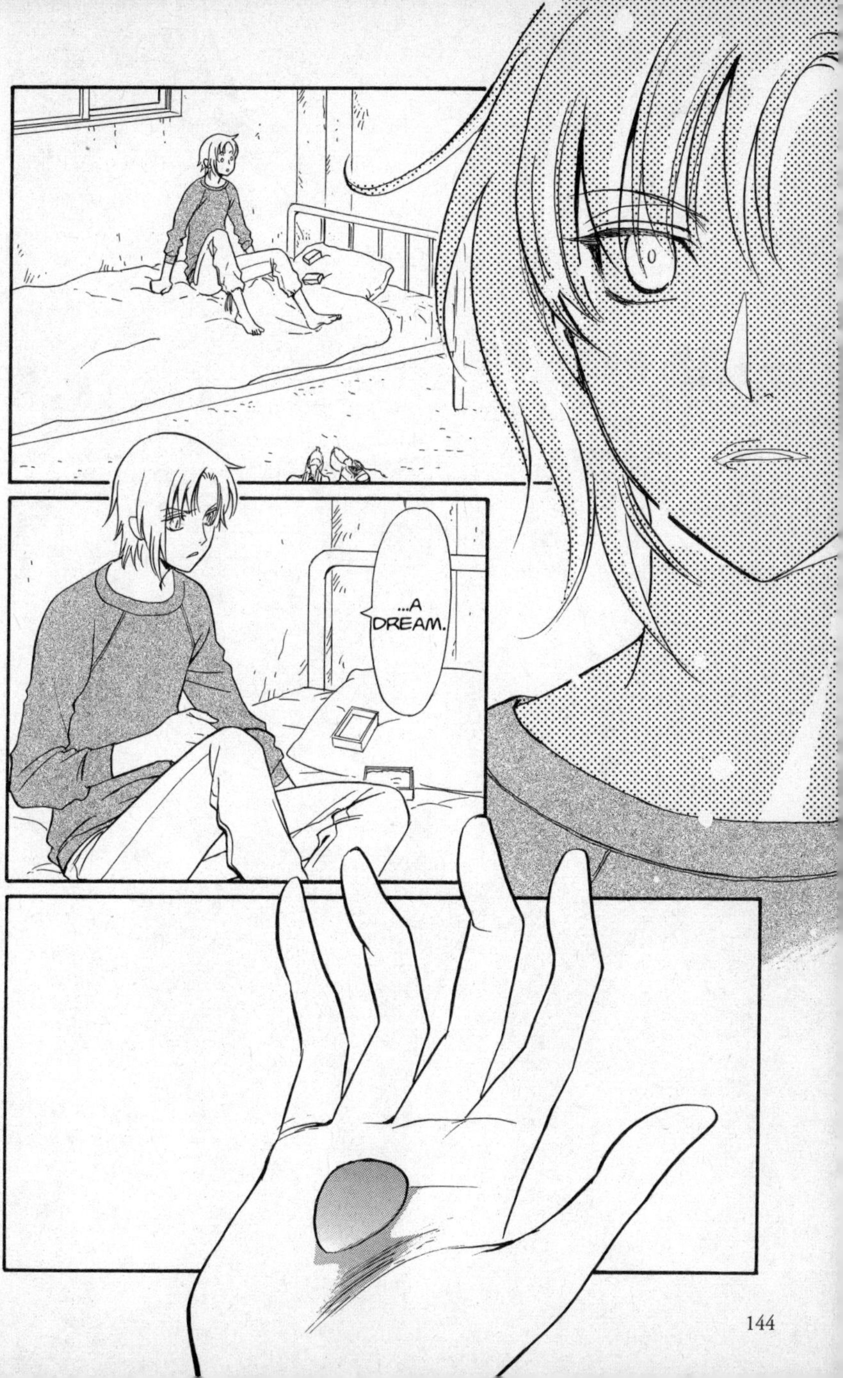
...A DREAM.

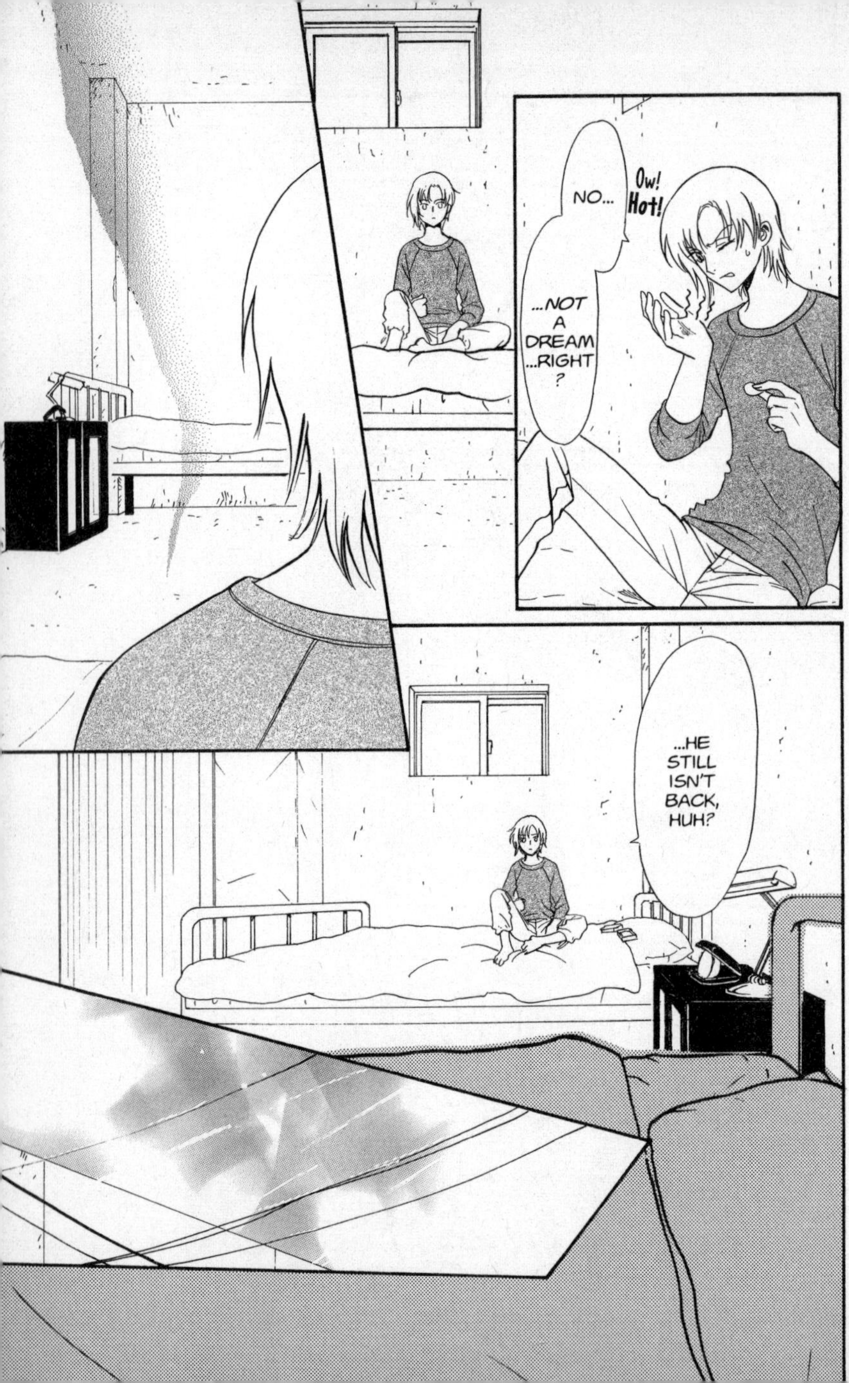
Ow! Hot!
NO...
...NOT A DREAM ...RIGHT?
...HE STILL ISN'T BACK, HUH?

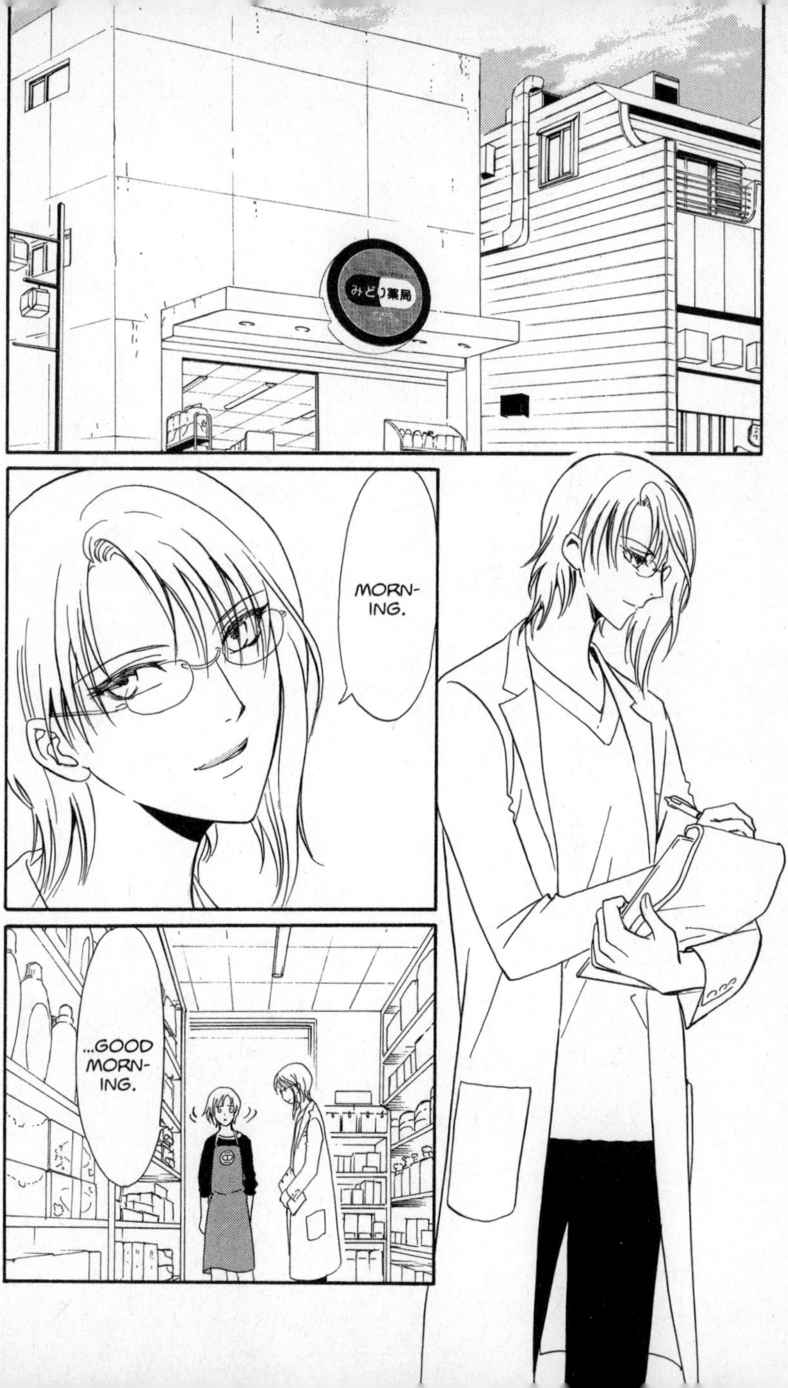
みどり薬局
MORN-
ING.
...GOOD
MORN-
ING.

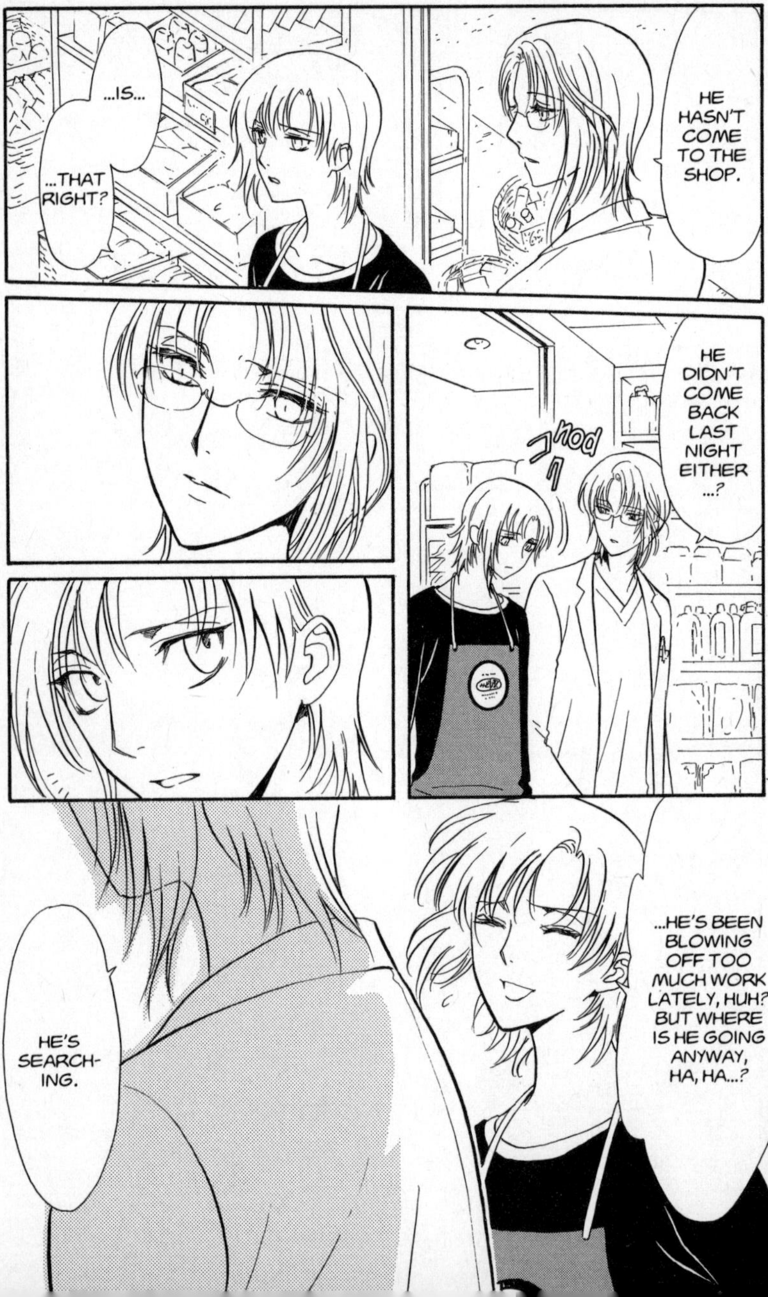
HE HASN'T COME TO THE SHOP.
...IS...
...THAT RIGHT?
HE DIDN'T COME BACK LAST NIGHT EITHER ...?
nod
...HE'S BEEN BLOWING OFF TOO MUCH WORK LATELY, HUH? BUT WHERE IS HE GOING ANYWAY, HA, HA...?
HE'S SEARCH-ING.

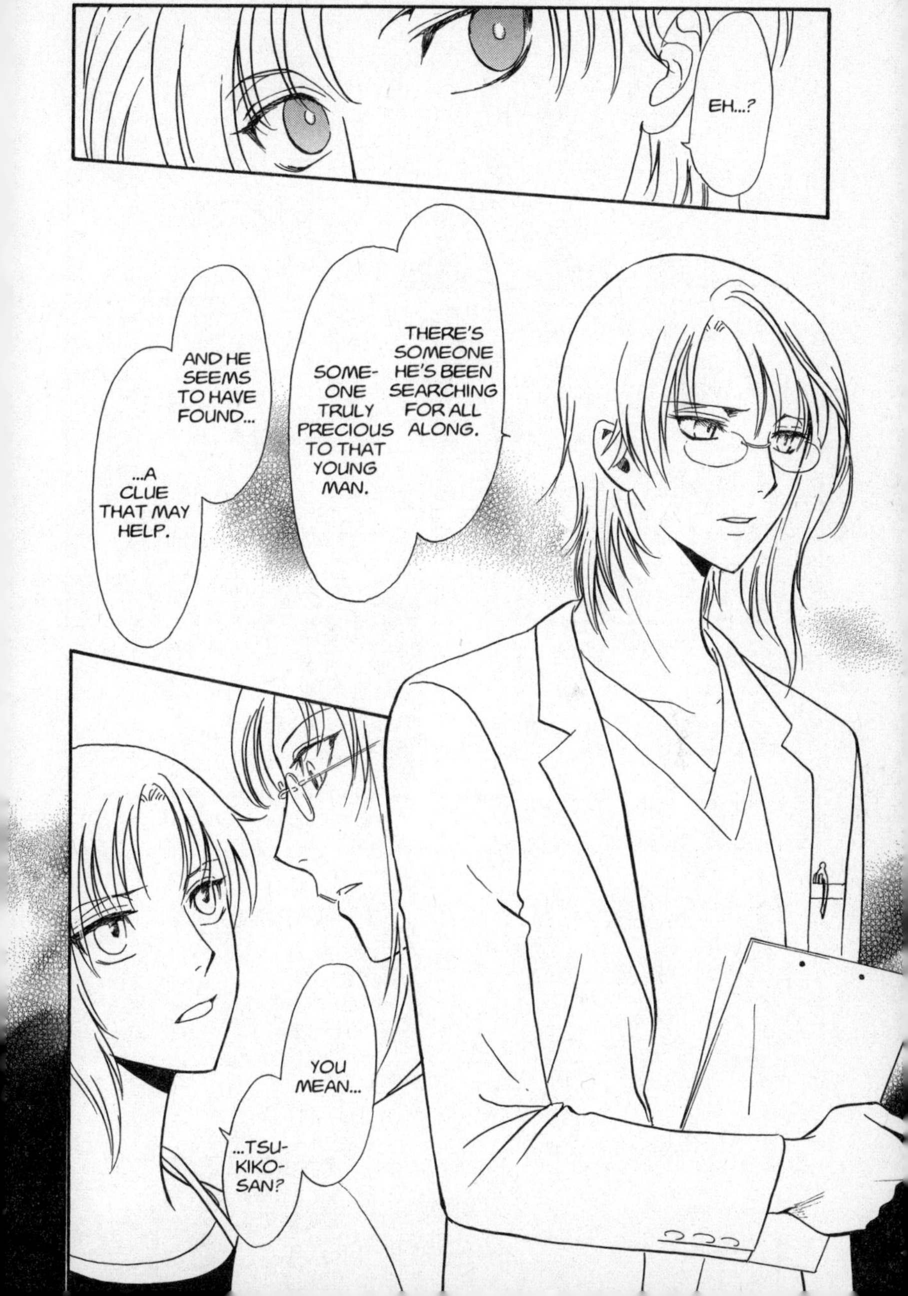
EH...?
THERE'S SOMEONE HE'S BEEN SEARCHING FOR ALL ALONG.
SOME-ONE TRULY PRECIOUS TO THAT YOUNG MAN.
AND HE SEEMS TO HAVE FOUND...
...A CLUE THAT MAY HELP.
YOU MEAN...
...TSU-KIKO-SAN?

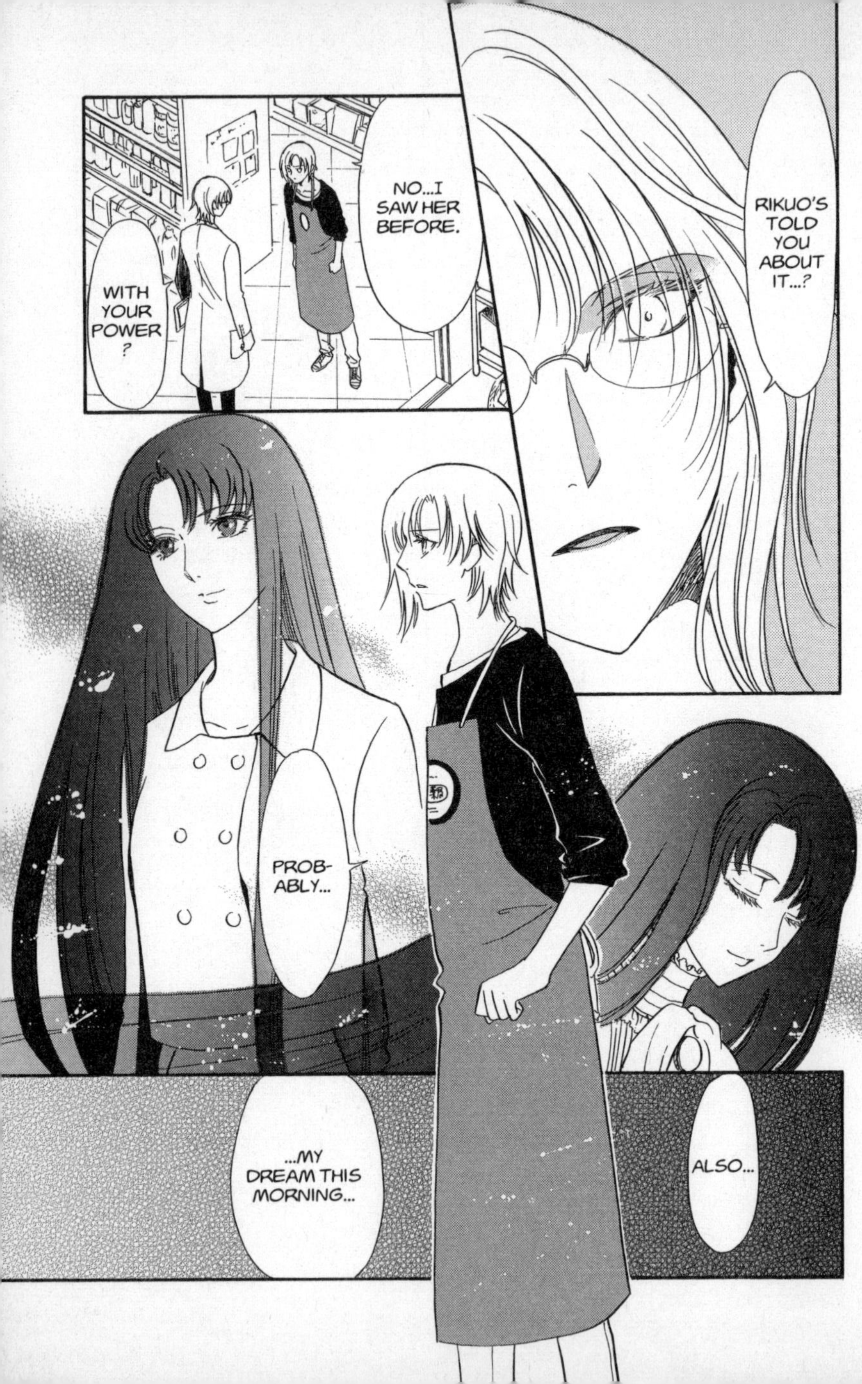
RIKUO'S TOLD YOU ABOUT IT...?
NO...I SAW HER BEFORE.
WITH YOUR POWER?
PROBABLY...
ALSO...
...MY DREAM THIS MORNING...

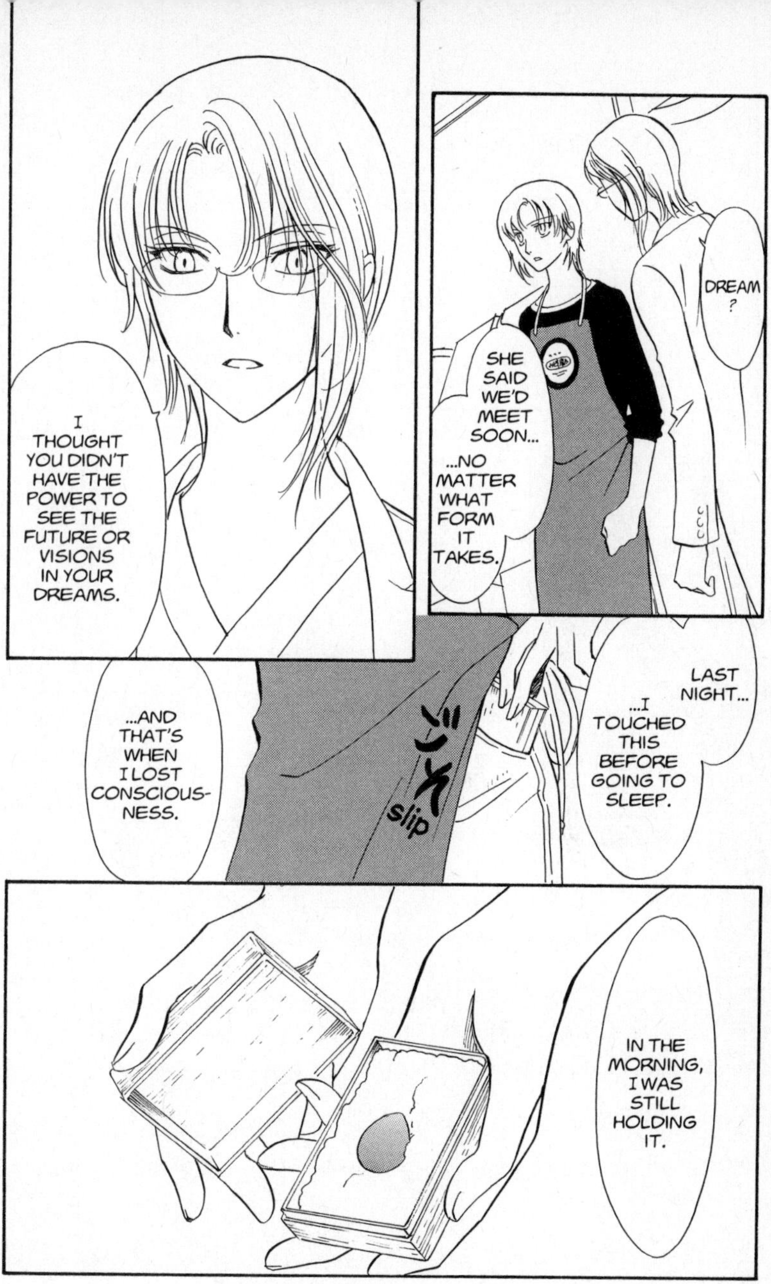
DREAM?
SHE SAID WE'D MEET SOON...
...NO MATTER WHAT FORM IT TAKES.
I THOUGHT YOU DIDN'T HAVE THE POWER TO SEE THE FUTURE OR VISIONS IN YOUR DREAMS.
LAST NIGHT...
...I TOUCHED THIS BEFORE GOING TO SLEEP.
slip
...AND THAT'S WHEN I LOST CONSCIOUSNESS.
IN THE MORNING, I WAS STILL HOLDING IT.

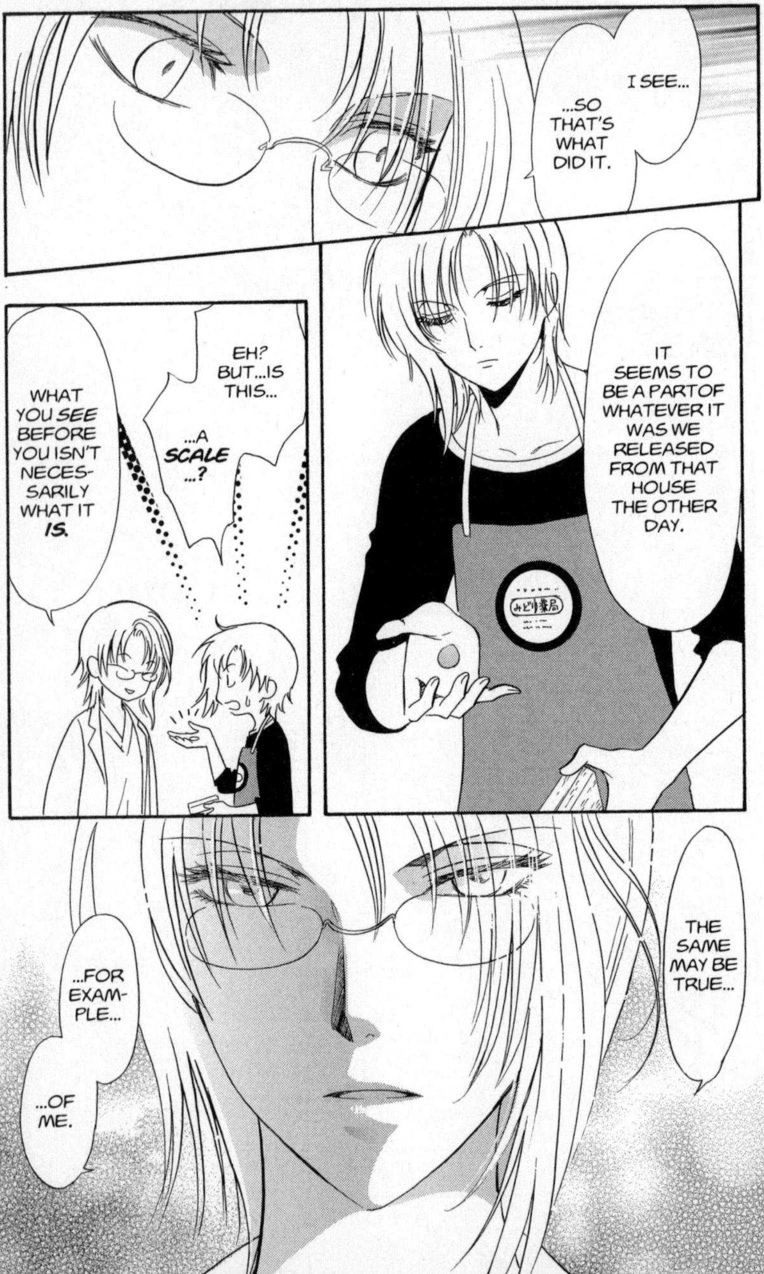
I SEE...
...SO THAT'S WHAT DID IT.
IT SEEMS TO BE A PART OF WHATEVER IT WAS WE RELEASED FROM THAT HOUSE THE OTHER DAY.
みどり薬局
EH? BUT...IS THIS...
...A *SCALE*...?
WHAT YOU *SEE* BEFORE YOU ISN'T NECES-SARILY WHAT IT ***IS.***
THE SAME MAY BE TRUE...
...FOR EXAMPLE...
...OF ME.

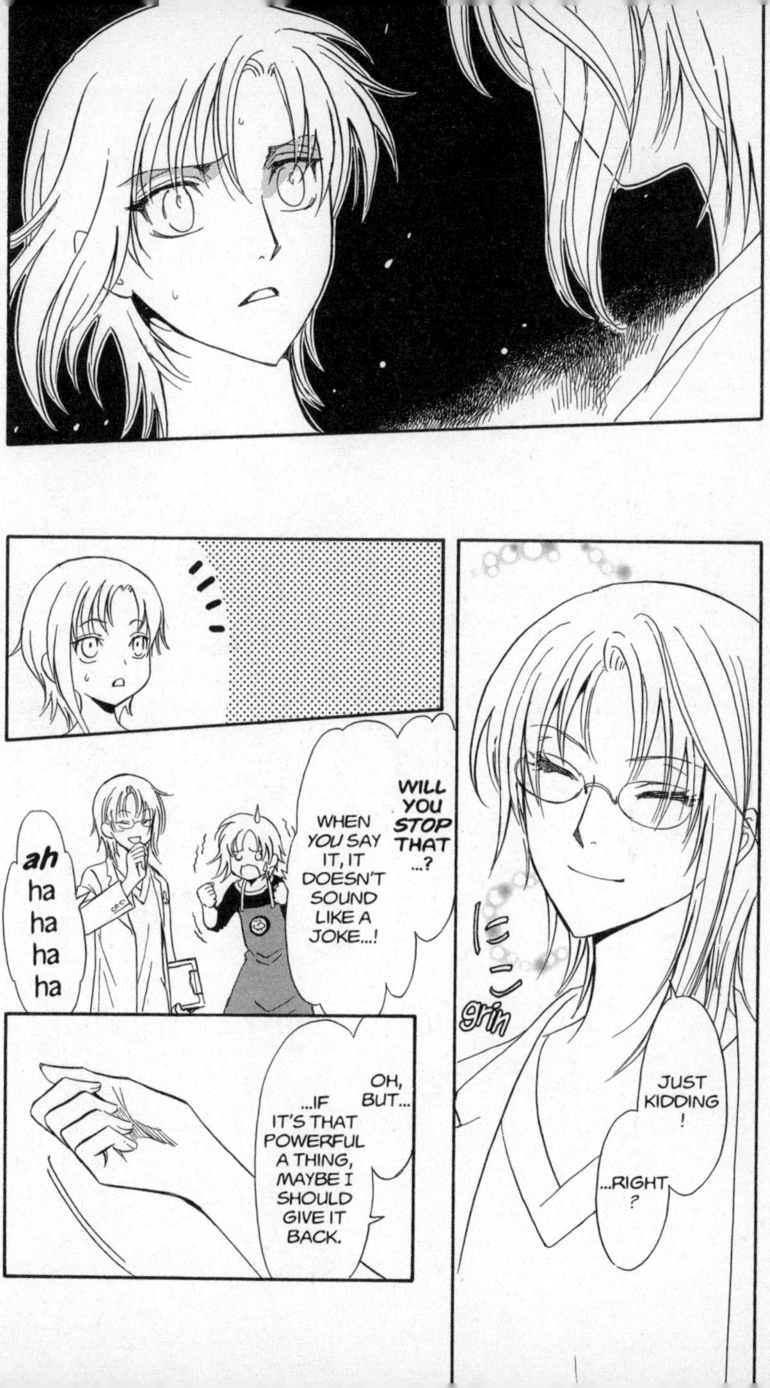
grin
JUST KIDDING!
...RIGHT?
WILL YOU STOP THAT...?
WHEN YOU SAY IT, IT DOESN'T SOUND LIKE A JOKE...!
ah ha ha ha ha
OH, BUT...
...IF IT'S THAT POWERFUL A THING, MAYBE I SHOULD GIVE IT BACK.

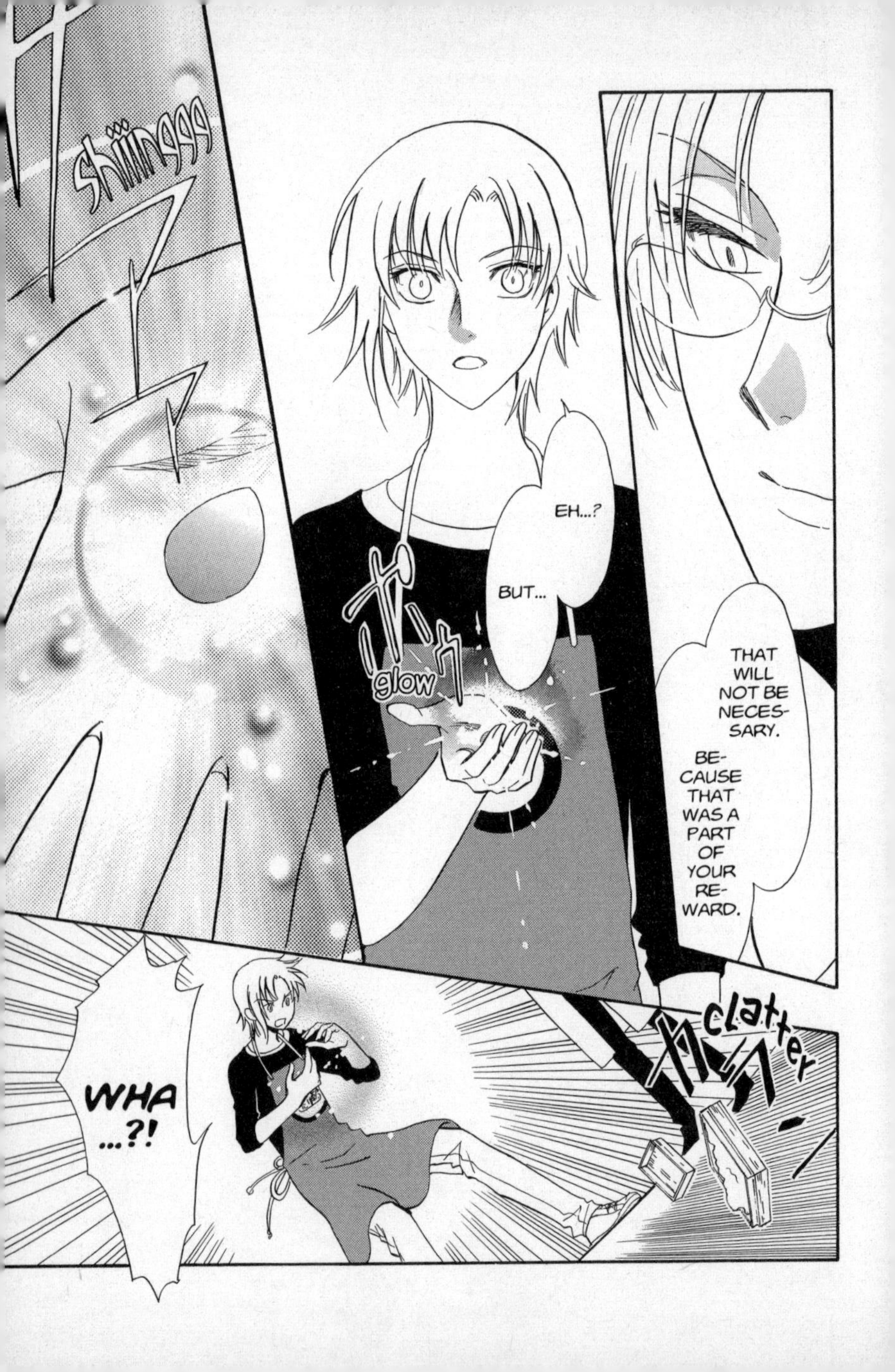
EH...?
BUT...
glow
THAT WILL NOT BE NECES-SARY.
BE-CAUSE THAT WAS A PART OF YOUR RE-WARD.
shiiinggg
clatter
WHA ...?!

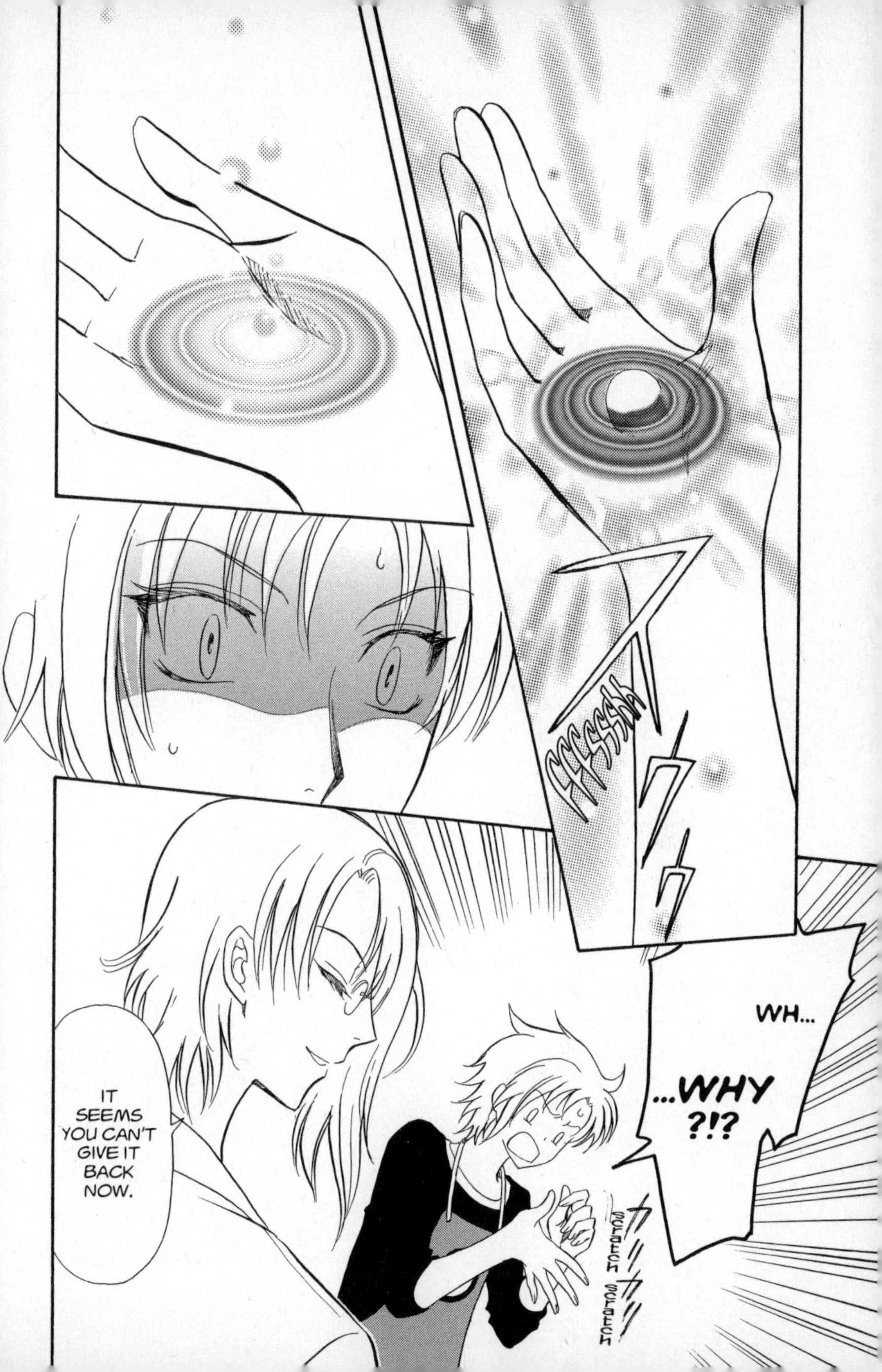
FFSSSH
WH...
...WHY ?!?
SCRATCH SCRATCH
IT SEEMS YOU CAN'T GIVE IT BACK NOW.

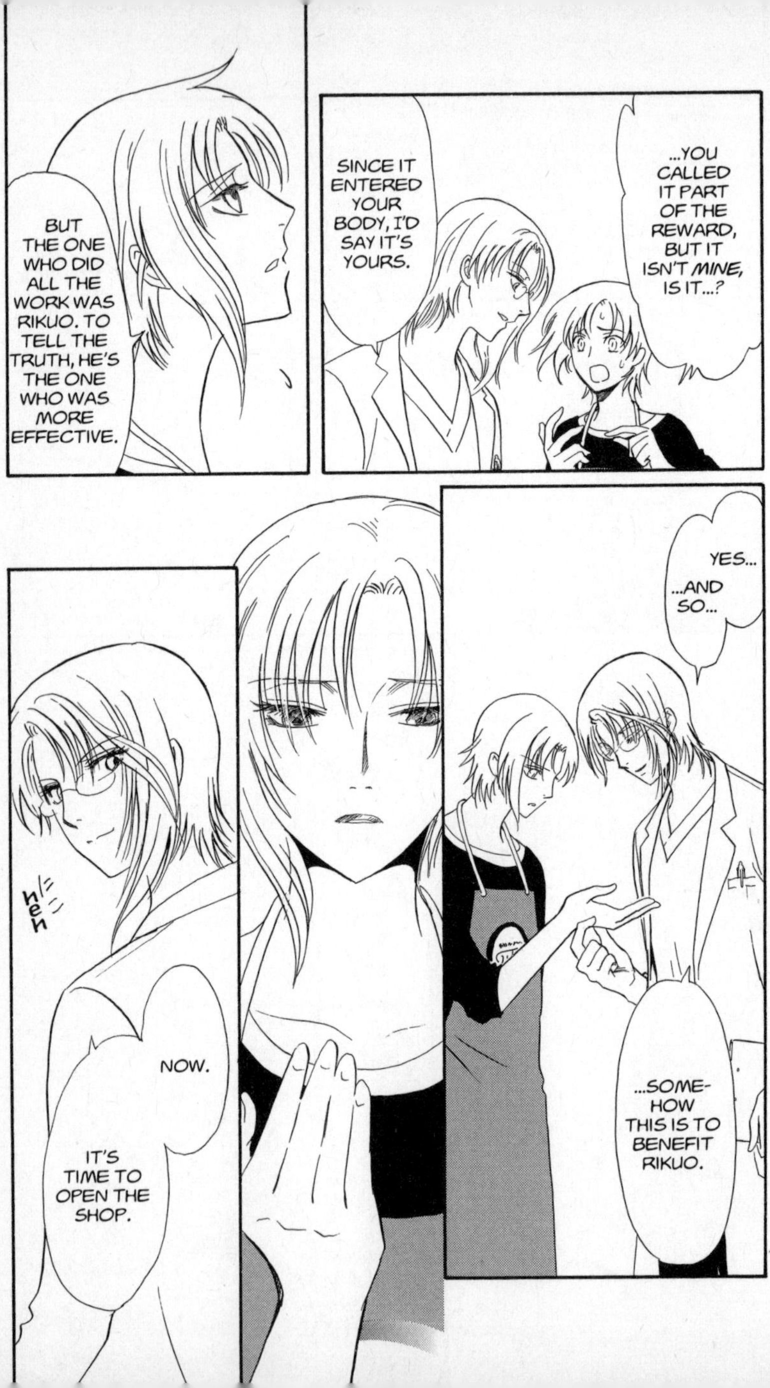
...YOU CALLED IT PART OF THE REWARD, BUT IT ISN'T *MINE*, IS IT...?
SINCE IT ENTERED YOUR BODY, I'D SAY IT'S YOURS.
BUT THE ONE WHO DID ALL THE WORK WAS RIKUO. TO TELL THE TRUTH, HE'S THE ONE WHO WAS MORE EFFECTIVE.
YES... ...AND SO...
...SOME-HOW THIS IS TO BENEFIT RIKUO.
heh
NOW.
IT'S TIME TO OPEN THE SHOP.

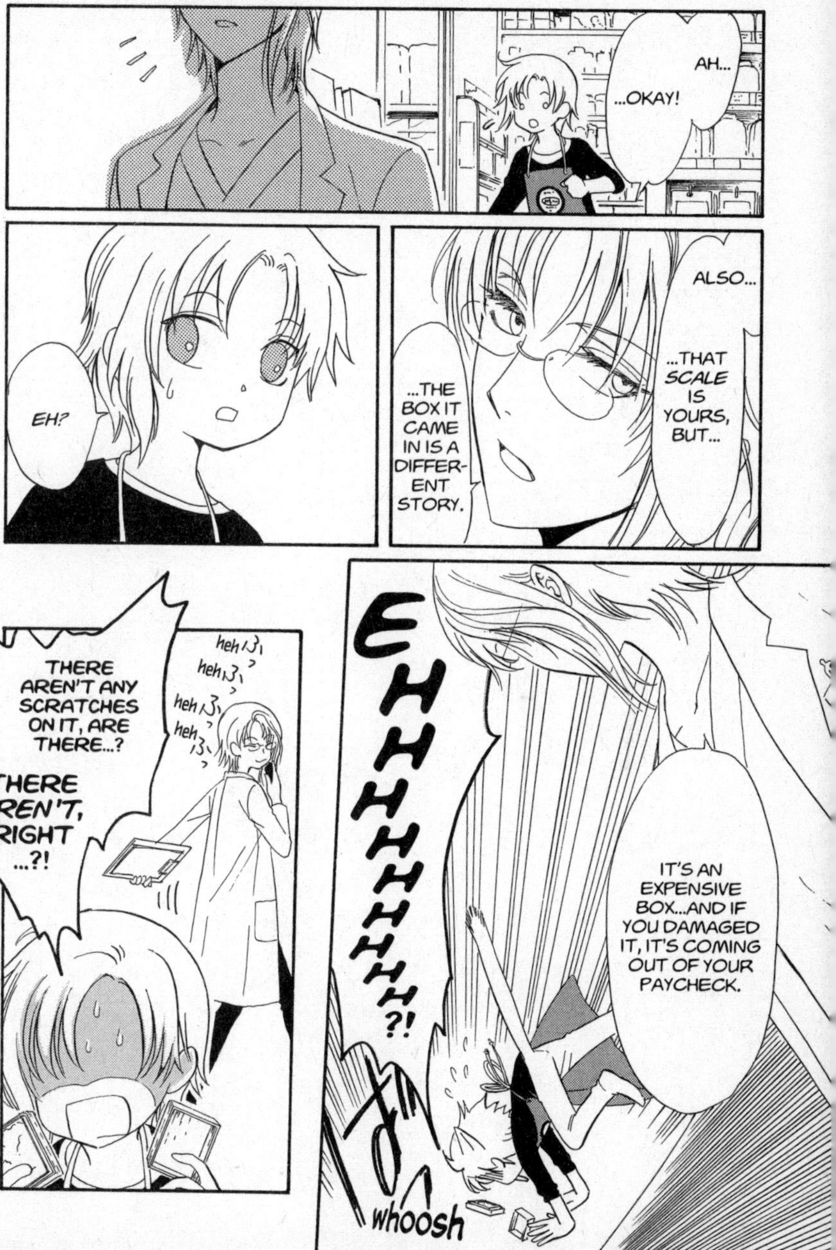
AH...
...OKAY!
ALSO...
...THAT SCALE IS YOURS, BUT...
...THE BOX IT CAME IN IS A DIFFERENT STORY.
EH?
IT'S AN EXPENSIVE BOX...AND IF YOU DAMAGED IT, IT'S COMING OUT OF YOUR PAYCHECK.
EHHHHHHHH?!
whoosh
heh ふ
heh ふ
heh ふ
heh ふ
THERE AREN'T ANY SCRATCHES ON IT, ARE THERE...?
THERE AREN'T, RIGHT...?!

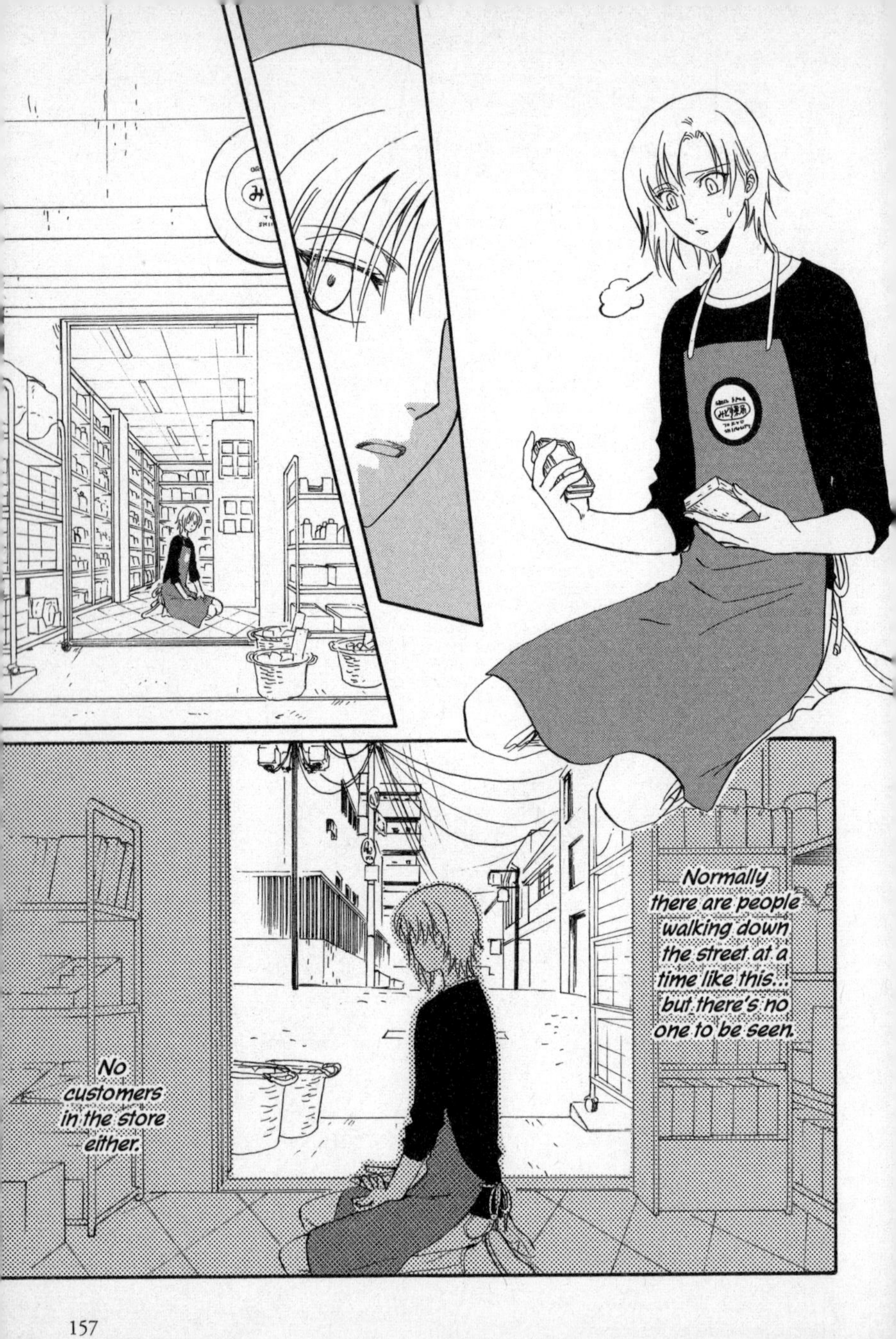
Normally there are people walking down the street at a time like this... but there's no one to be seen.
No customers in the store either.

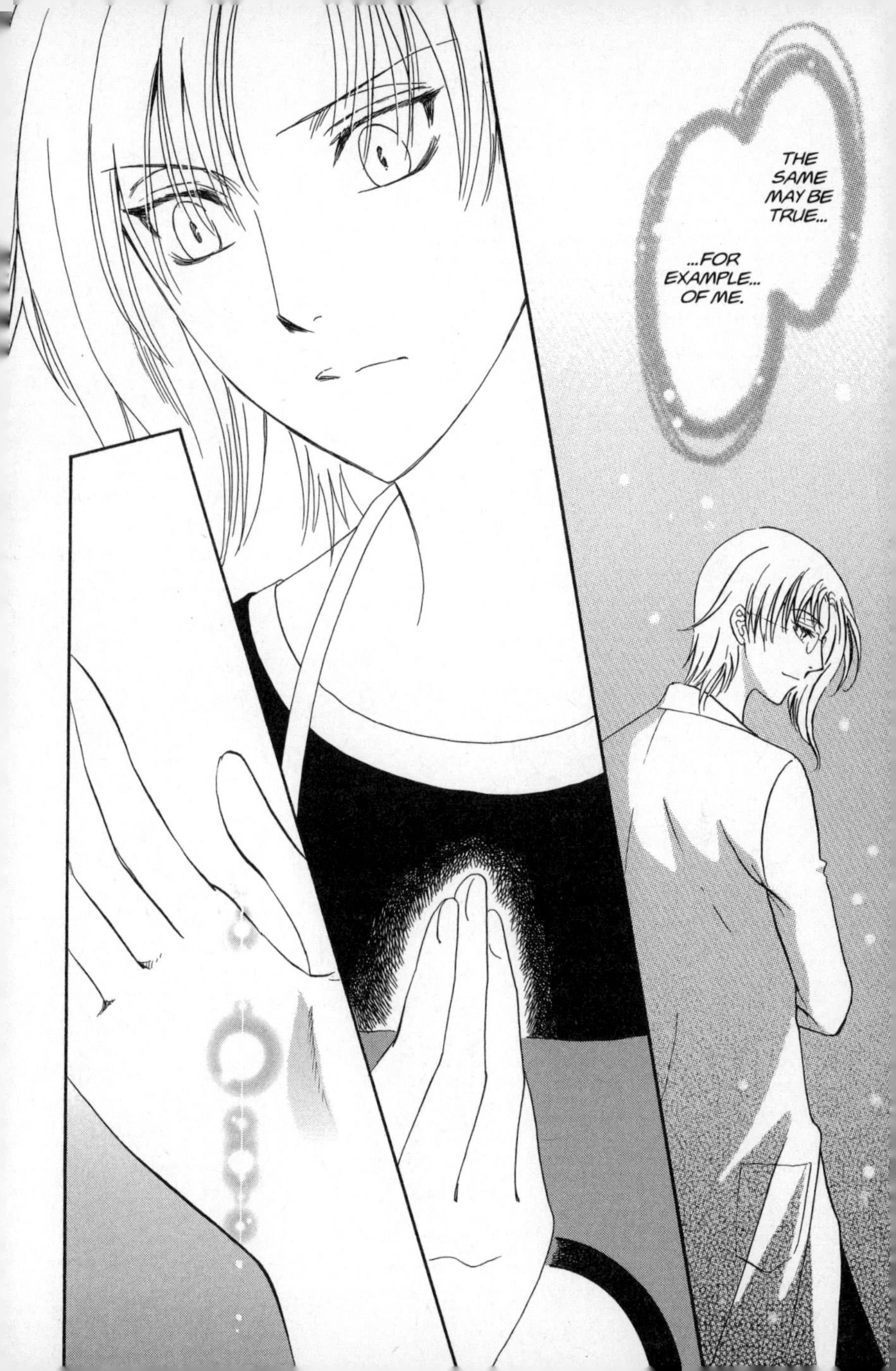
THE SAME MAY BE TRUE...
...FOR EXAMPLE... OF ME.

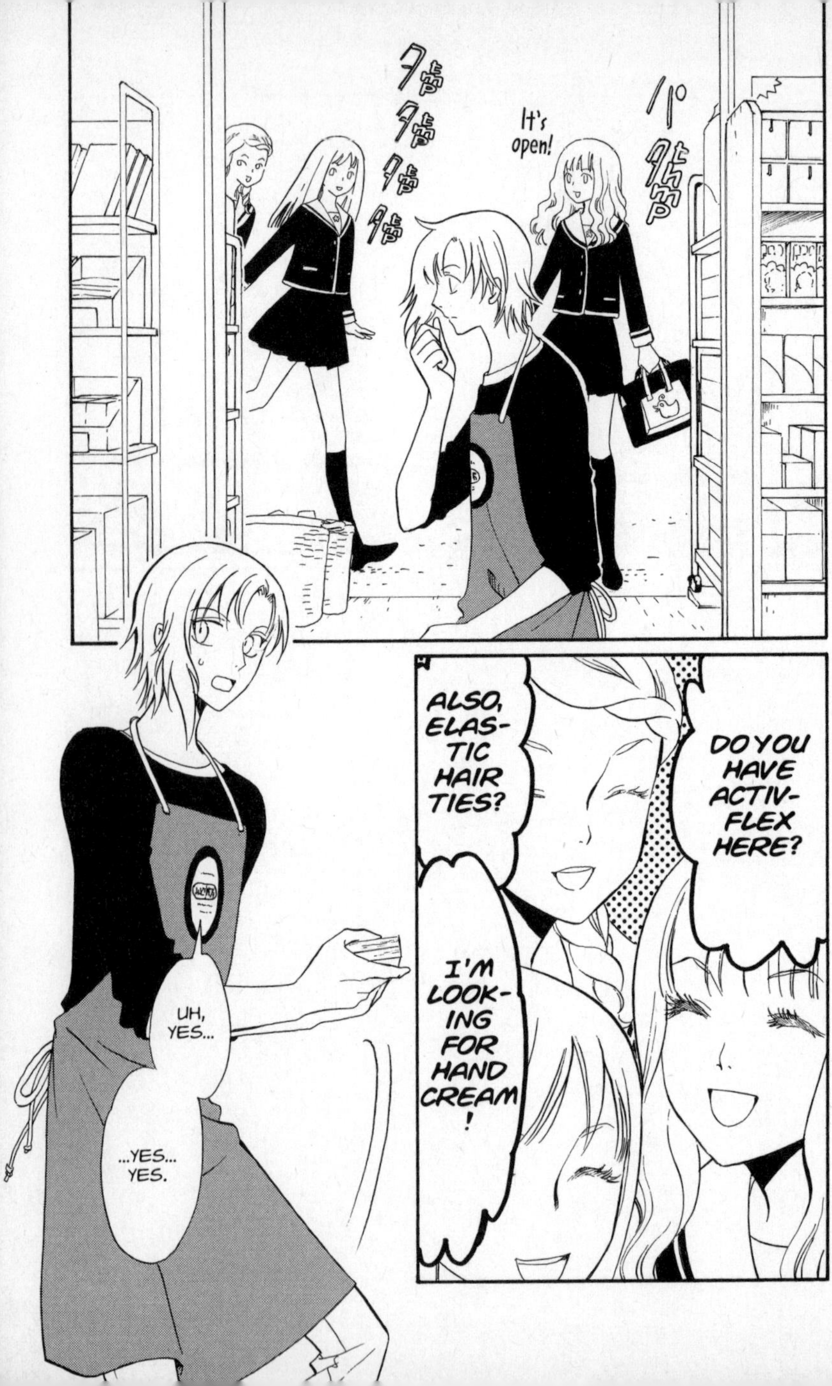
It's open!
DO YOU HAVE ACTIV-FLEX HERE?
ALSO, ELAS-TIC HAIR TIES?
I'M LOOK-ING FOR HAND CREAM!
UH, YES...
...YES... YES.

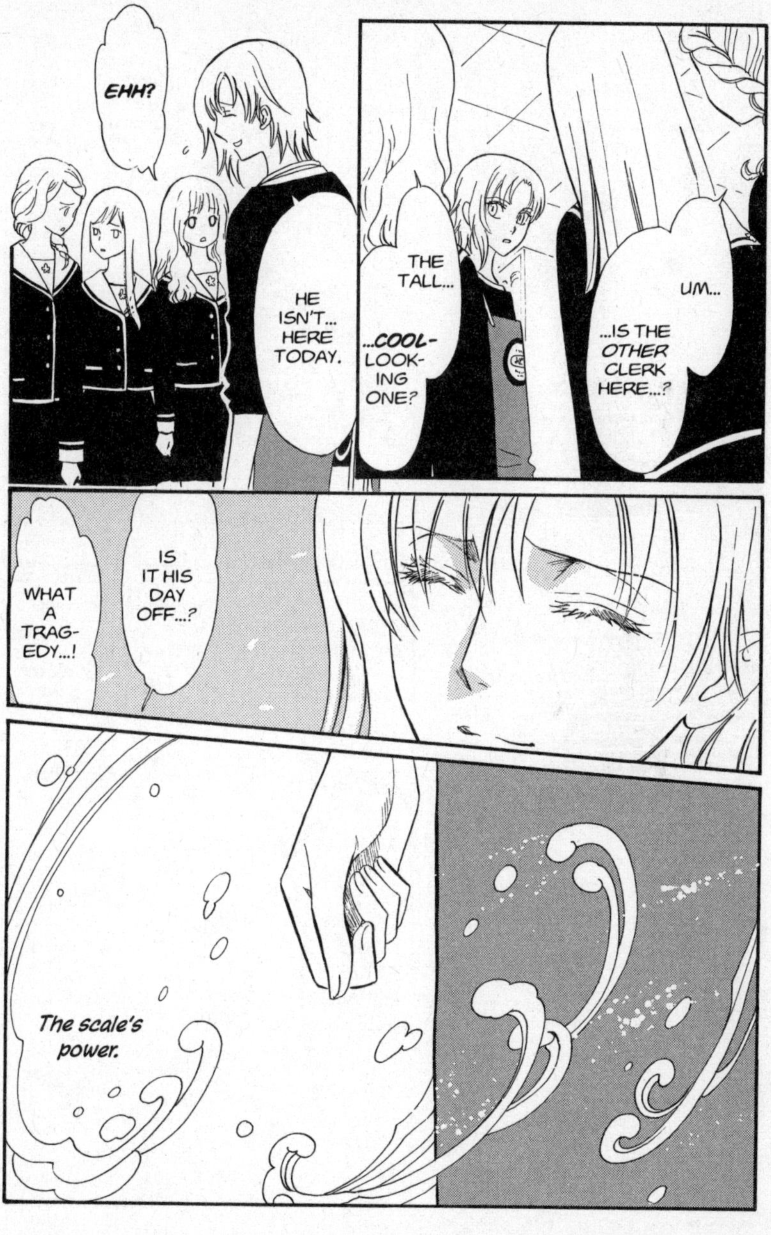
UM...
...IS THE OTHER CLERK HERE...?
THE TALL...
...COOL-LOOKING ONE?
HE ISN'T... HERE TODAY.
EHH?
IS IT HIS DAY OFF...?
WHAT A TRAG-EDY...!
The scale's power.

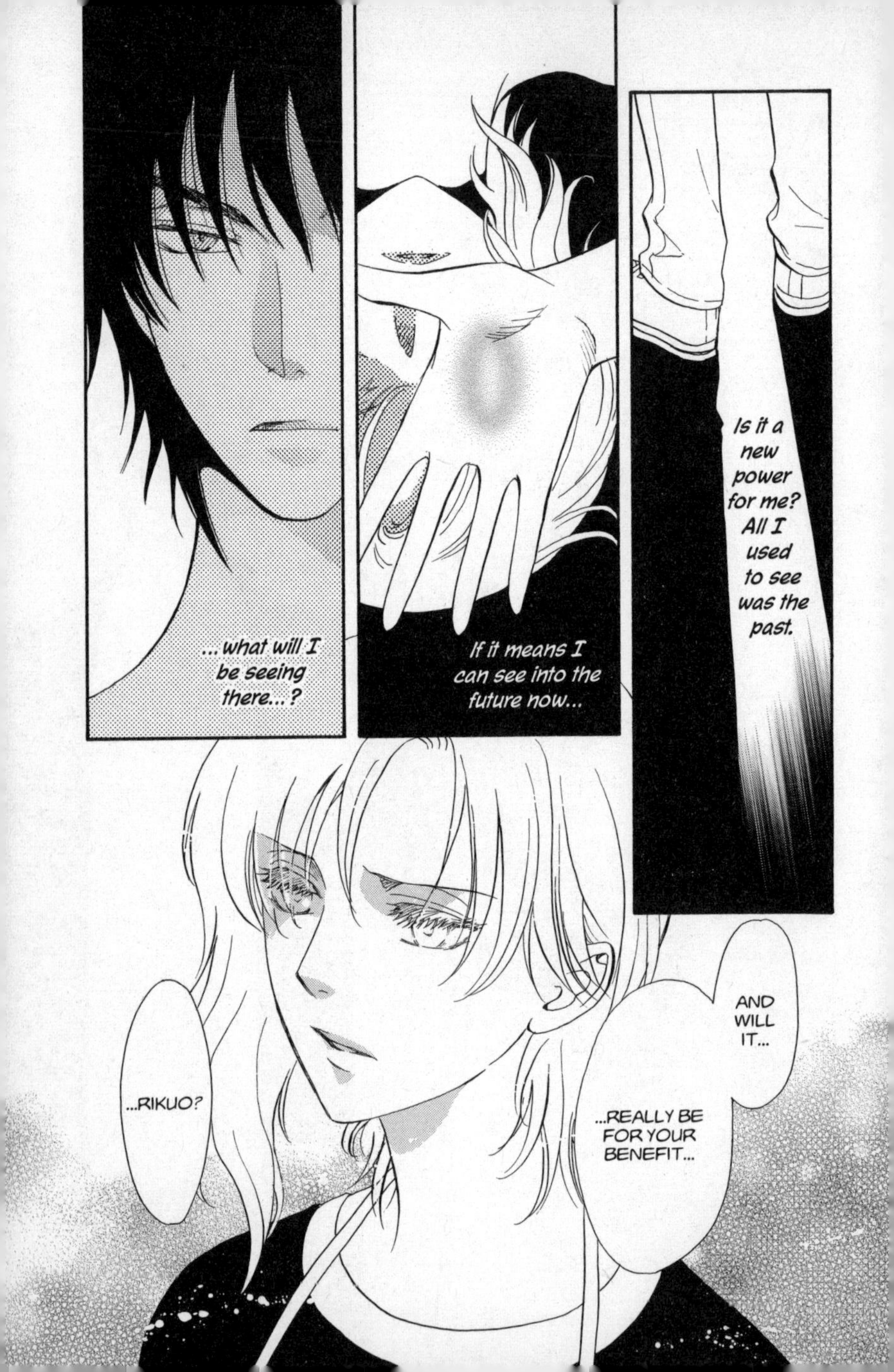
Is it a new power for me? All I used to see was the past.
If it means I can see into the future now...
...what will I be seeing there...?
AND WILL IT...
...REALLY BE FOR YOUR BENEFIT...
...RIKUO?

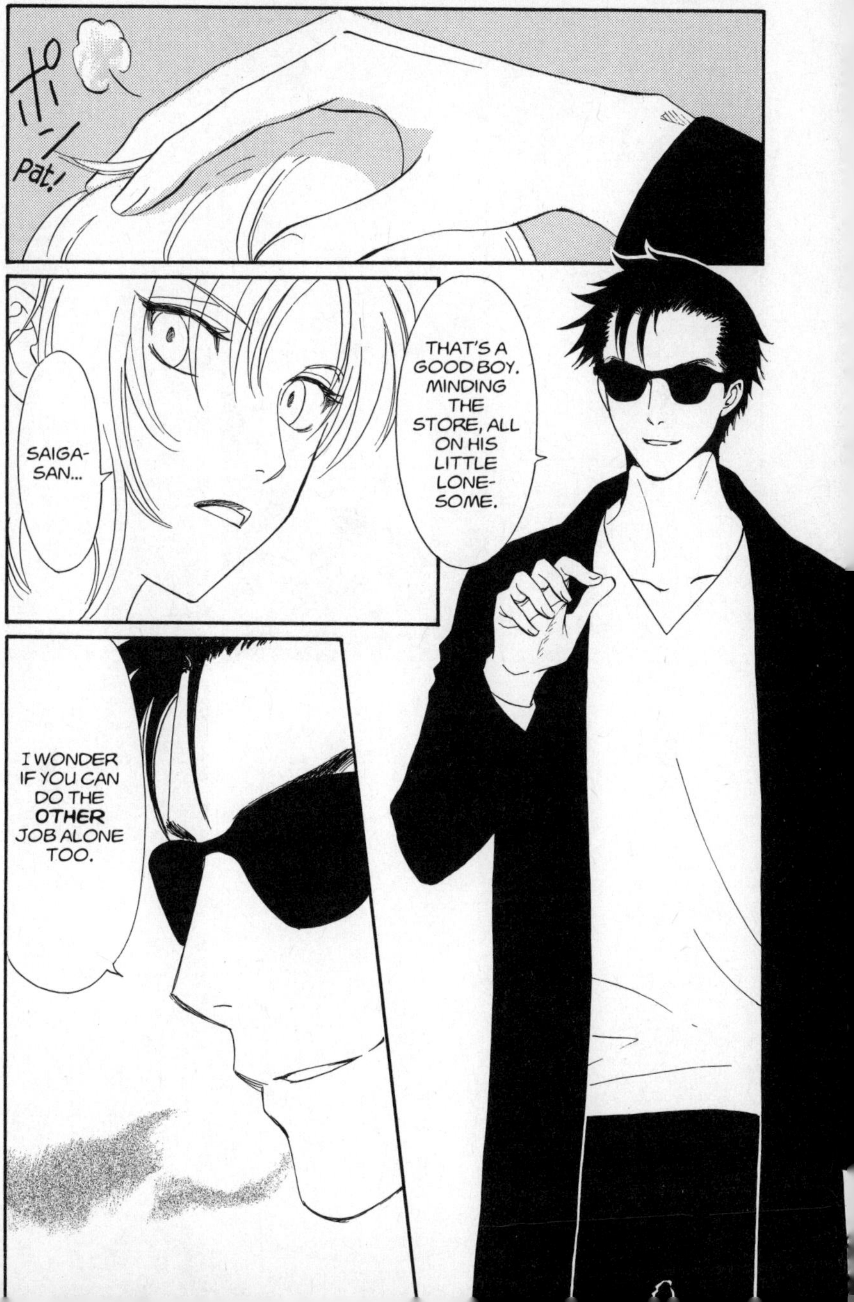
Pat!
THAT'S A GOOD BOY. MINDING THE STORE, ALL ON HIS LITTLE LONESOME.
SAIGA-SAN...
I WONDER IF YOU CAN DO THE **OTHER** JOB ALONE TOO.

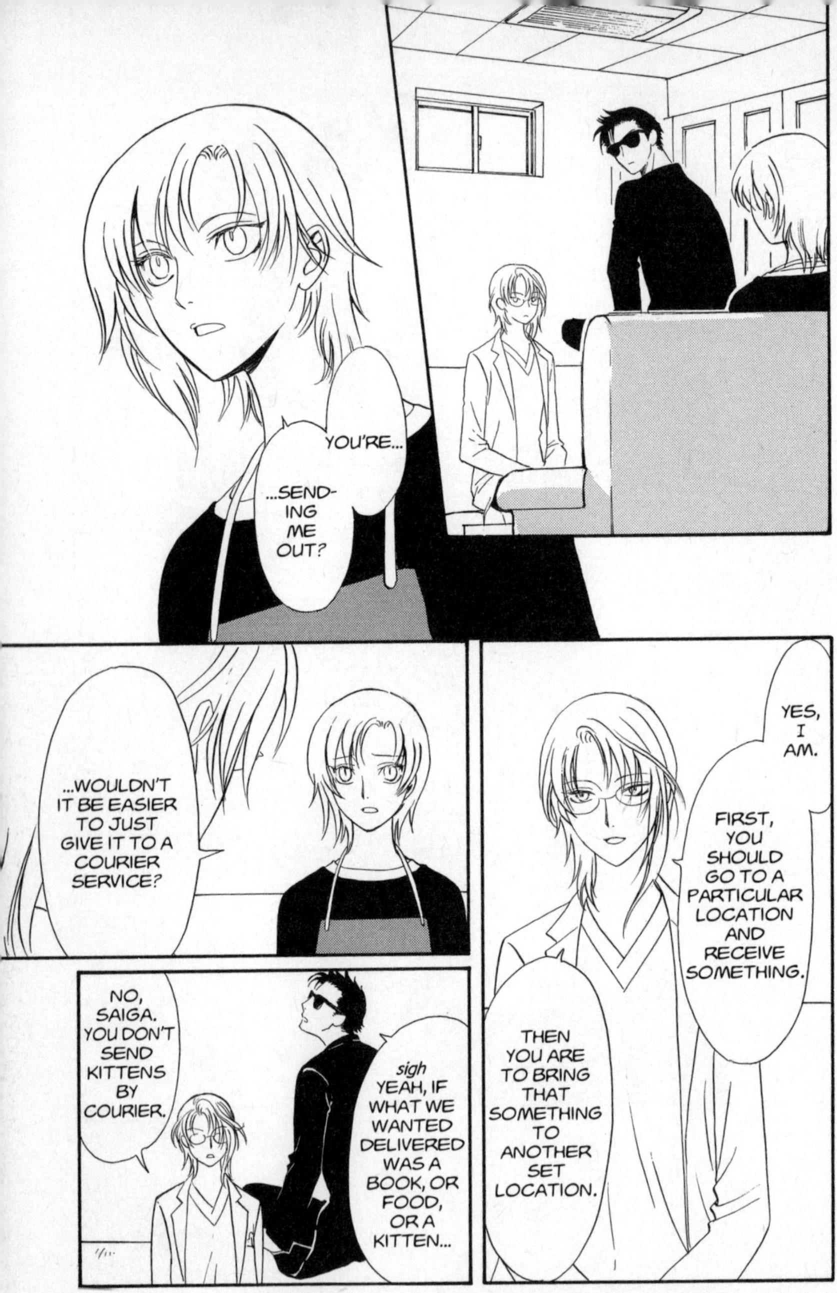

YOU'RE...
...SEND-ING ME OUT?
YES, I AM.
FIRST, YOU SHOULD GO TO A PARTICULAR LOCATION AND RECEIVE SOMETHING.
THEN YOU ARE TO BRING THAT SOMETHING TO ANOTHER SET LOCATION.
...WOULDN'T IT BE EASIER TO JUST GIVE IT TO A COURIER SERVICE?
sigh
YEAH, IF WHAT WE WANTED DELIVERED WAS A BOOK, OR FOOD, OR A KITTEN...
NO, SAIGA. YOU DON'T SEND KITTENS BY COURIER.

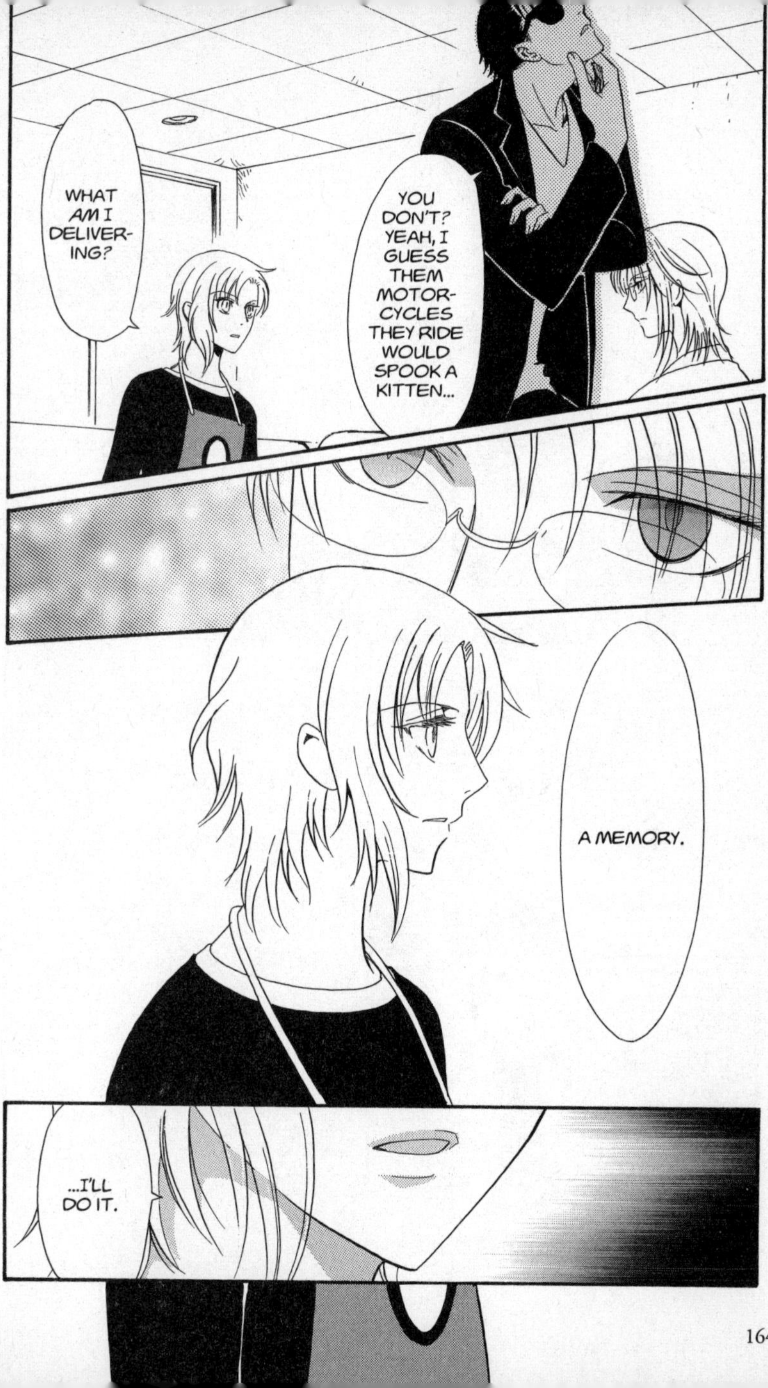
YOU DON'T? YEAH, I GUESS THEM MOTORCYCLES THEY RIDE WOULD SPOOK A KITTEN...
WHAT AM I DELIVERING?
A MEMORY.
...I'LL DO IT.

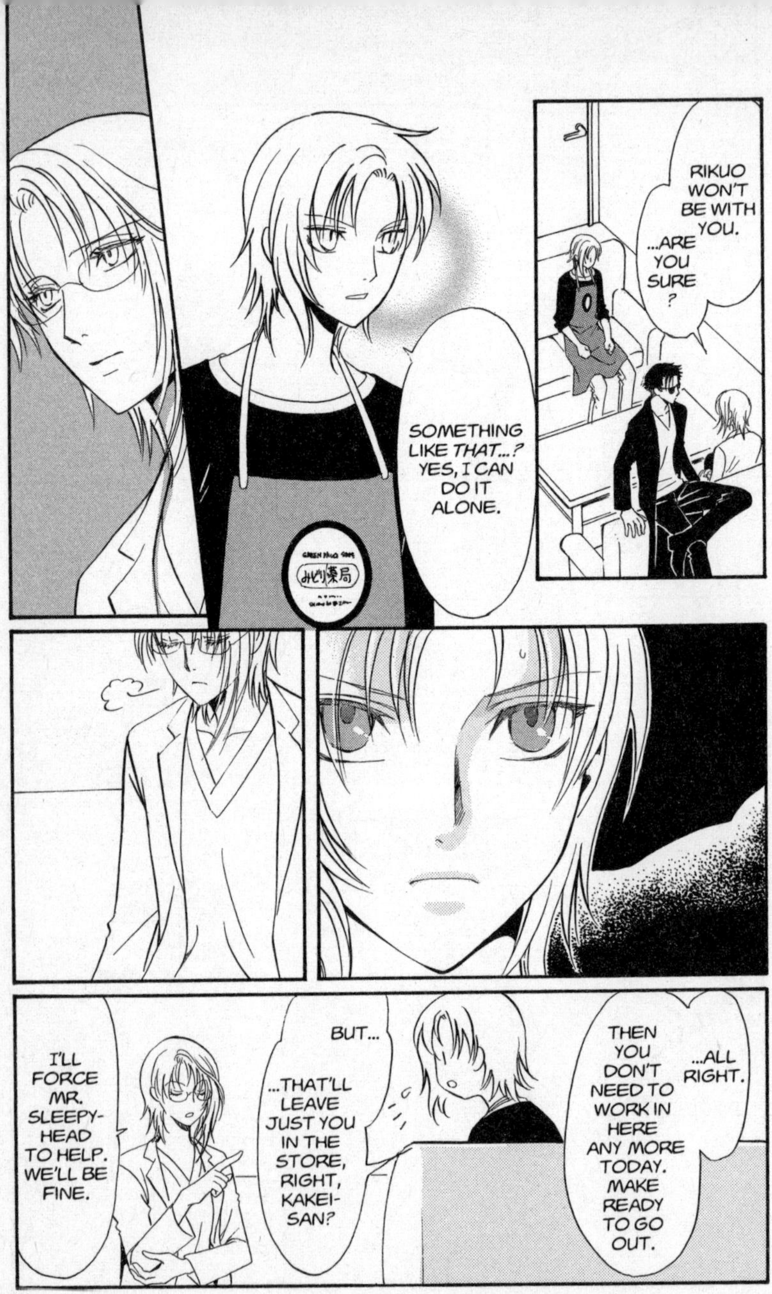

RIKUO WON'T BE WITH YOU.
...ARE YOU SURE?
SOMETHING LIKE *THAT*...? YES, I CAN DO IT ALONE.
みどり薬局
THEN YOU DON'T NEED TO WORK IN HERE ANY MORE TODAY. MAKE READY TO GO OUT.
...ALL RIGHT.
BUT...
...THAT'LL LEAVE JUST YOU IN THE STORE, RIGHT, KAKEI-SAN?
I'LL FORCE MR. SLEEPY-HEAD TO HELP. WE'LL BE FINE.

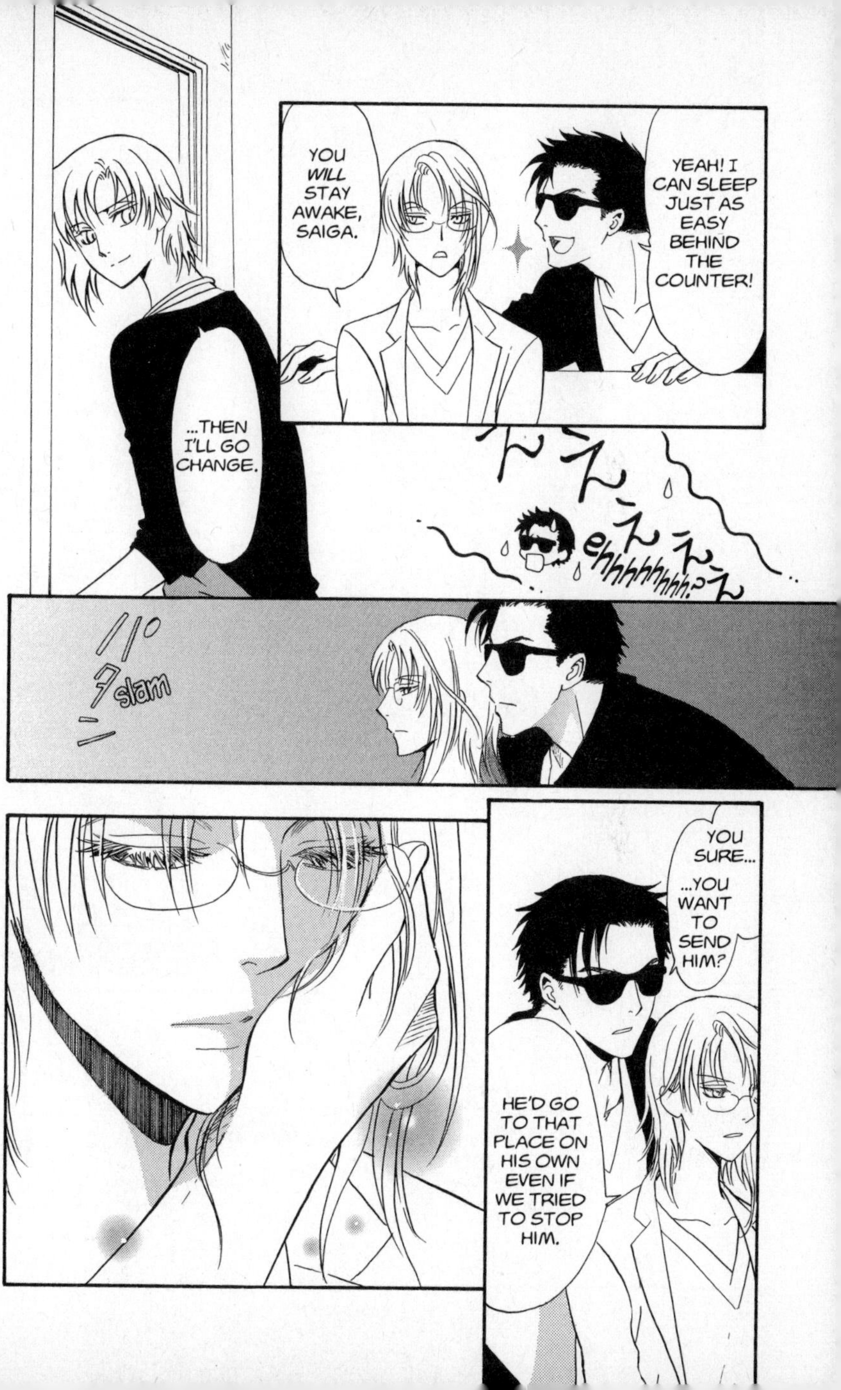
YEAH! I CAN SLEEP JUST AS EASY BEHIND THE COUNTER!
YOU WILL STAY AWAKE, SAIGA.
ehhhhhhhh?
...THEN I'LL GO CHANGE.
slam
YOU SURE...
...YOU WANT TO SEND HIM?
HE'D GO TO THAT PLACE ON HIS OWN EVEN IF WE TRIED TO STOP HIM.

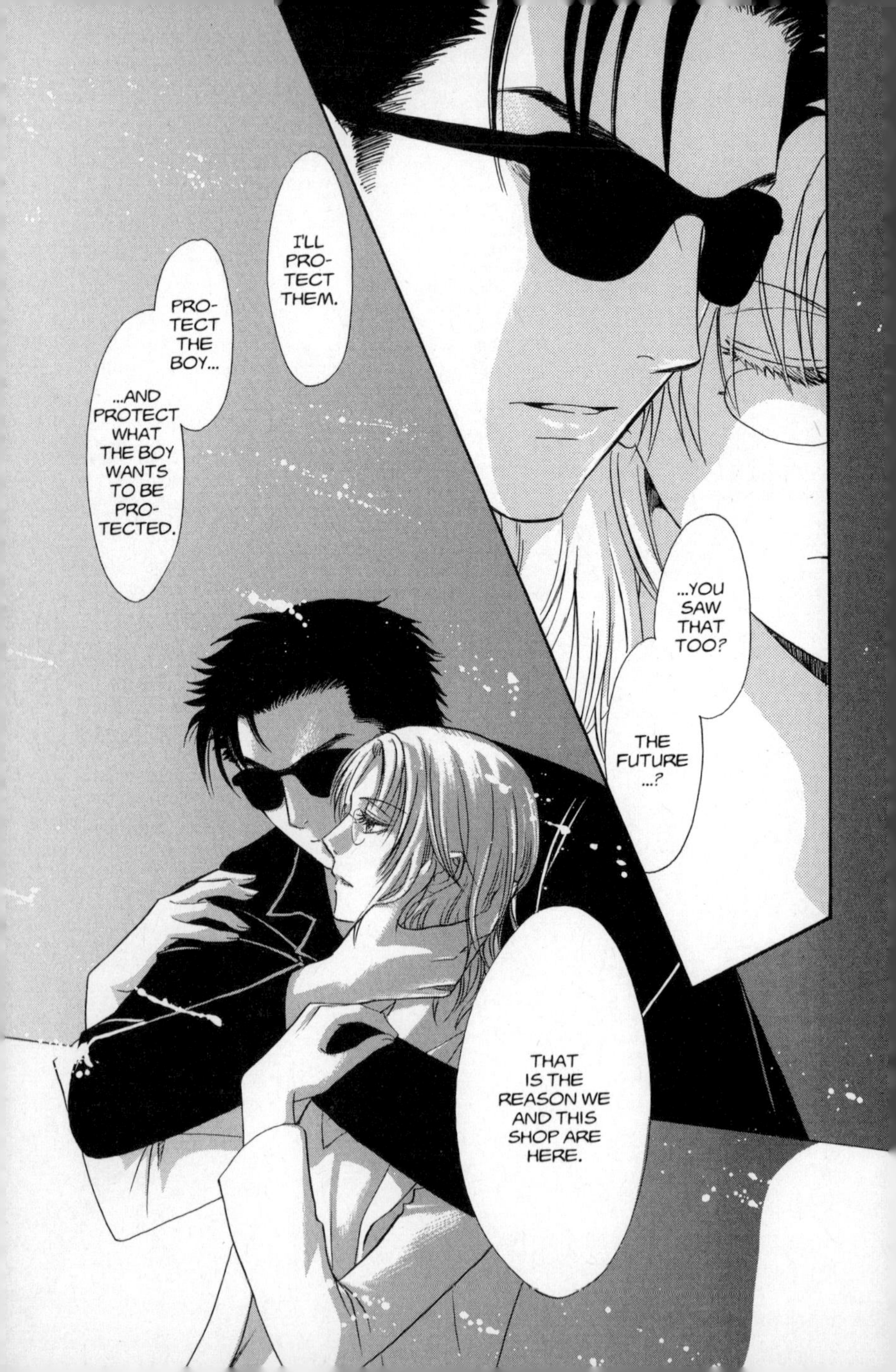
...YOU SAW THAT TOO?
THE FUTURE ...?
I'LL PROTECT THEM.
PROTECT THE BOY...
...AND PROTECT WHAT THE BOY WANTS TO BE PROTECTED.
THAT IS THE REASON WE AND THIS SHOP ARE HERE.

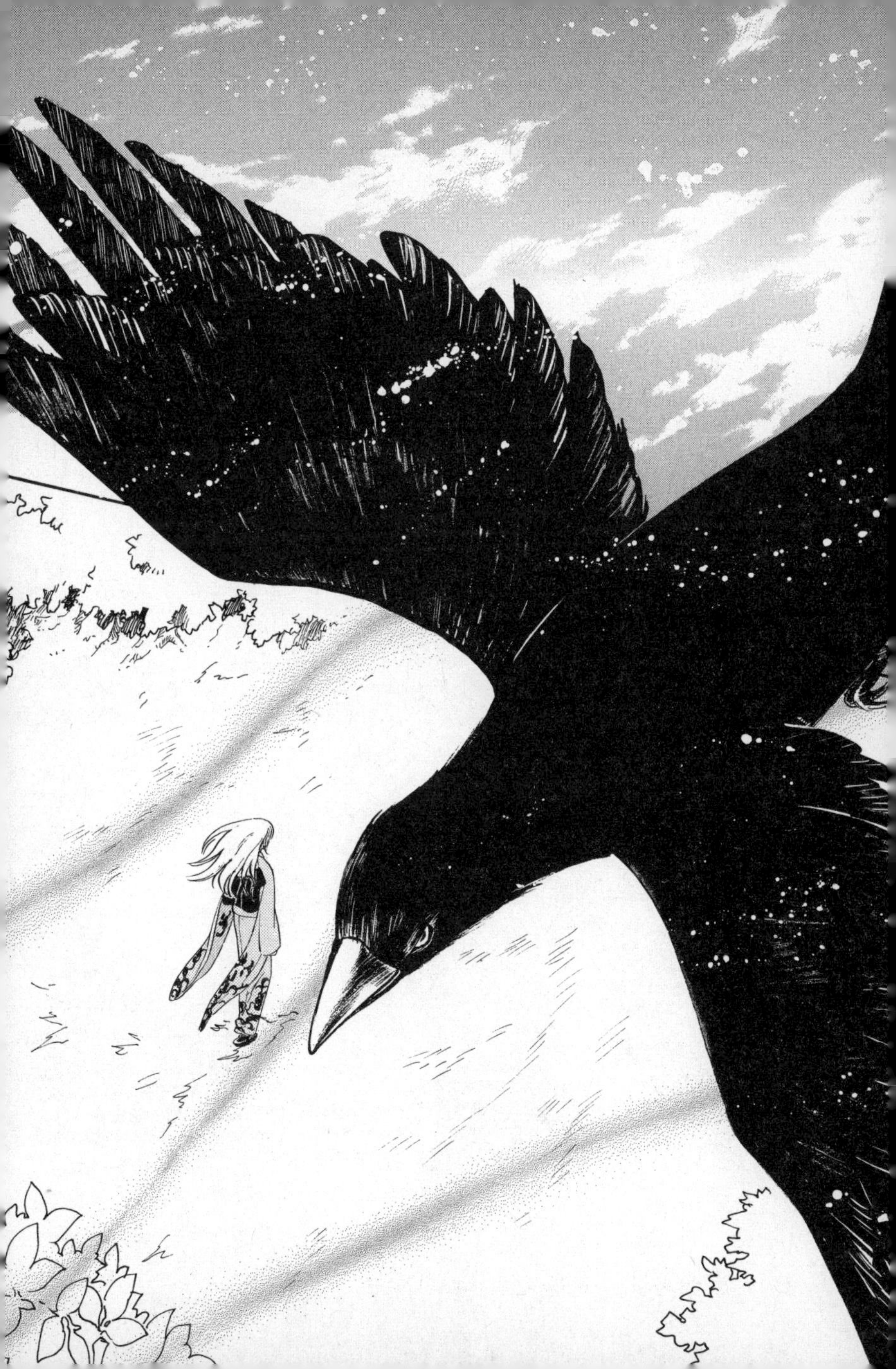

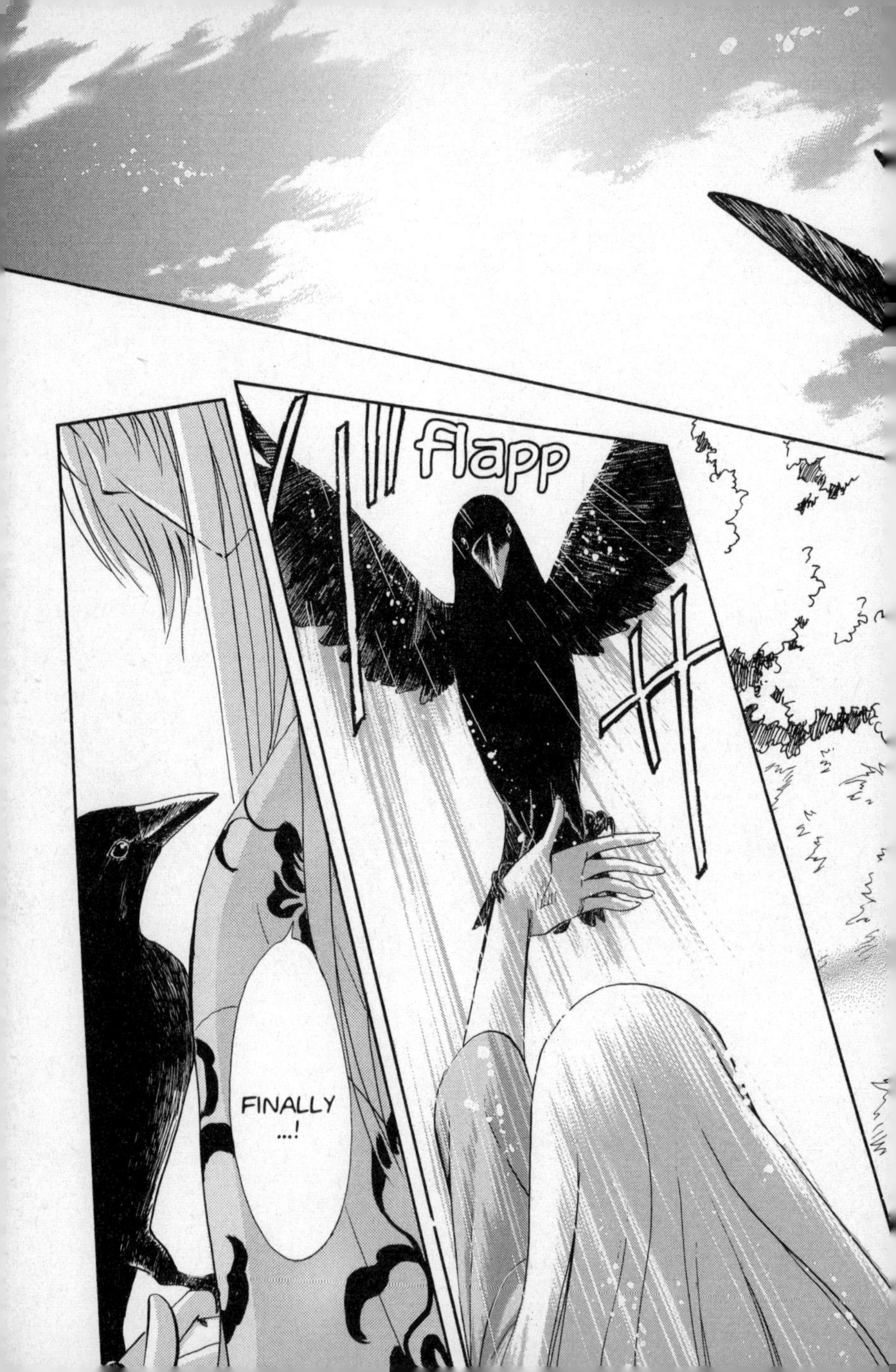
flapp
FINALLY ...!

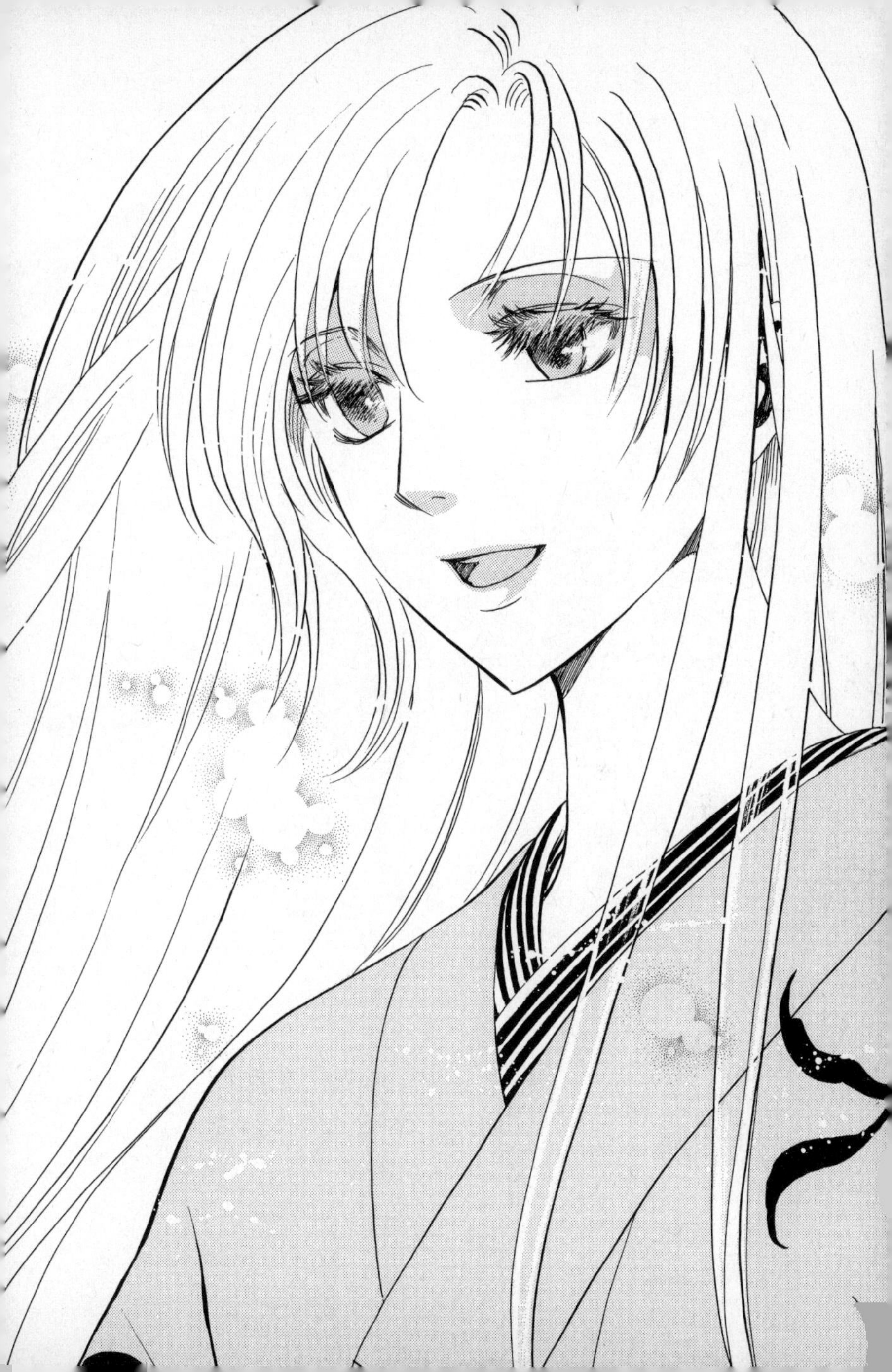

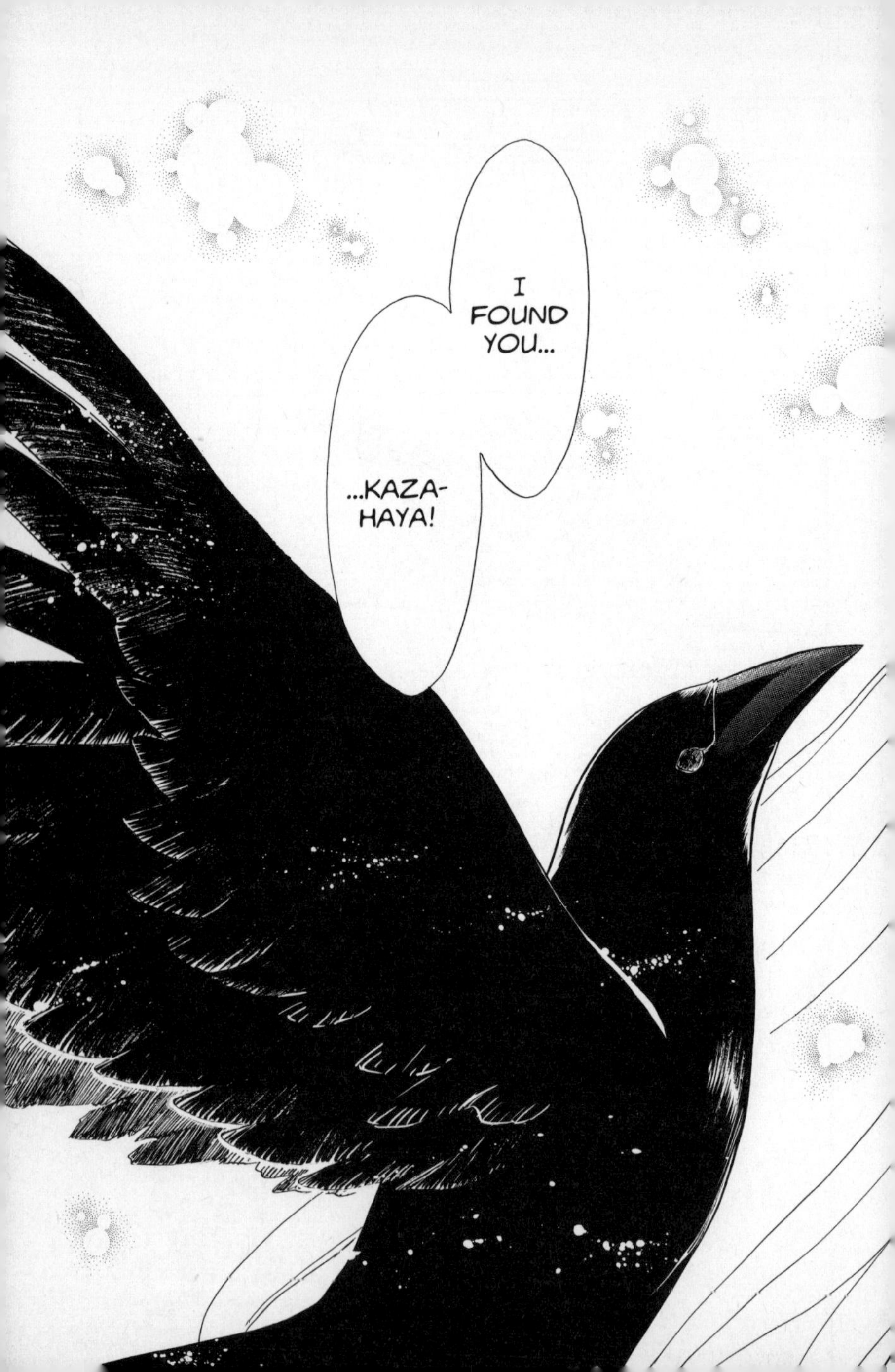
I FOUND YOU...
...KAZA-HAYA!

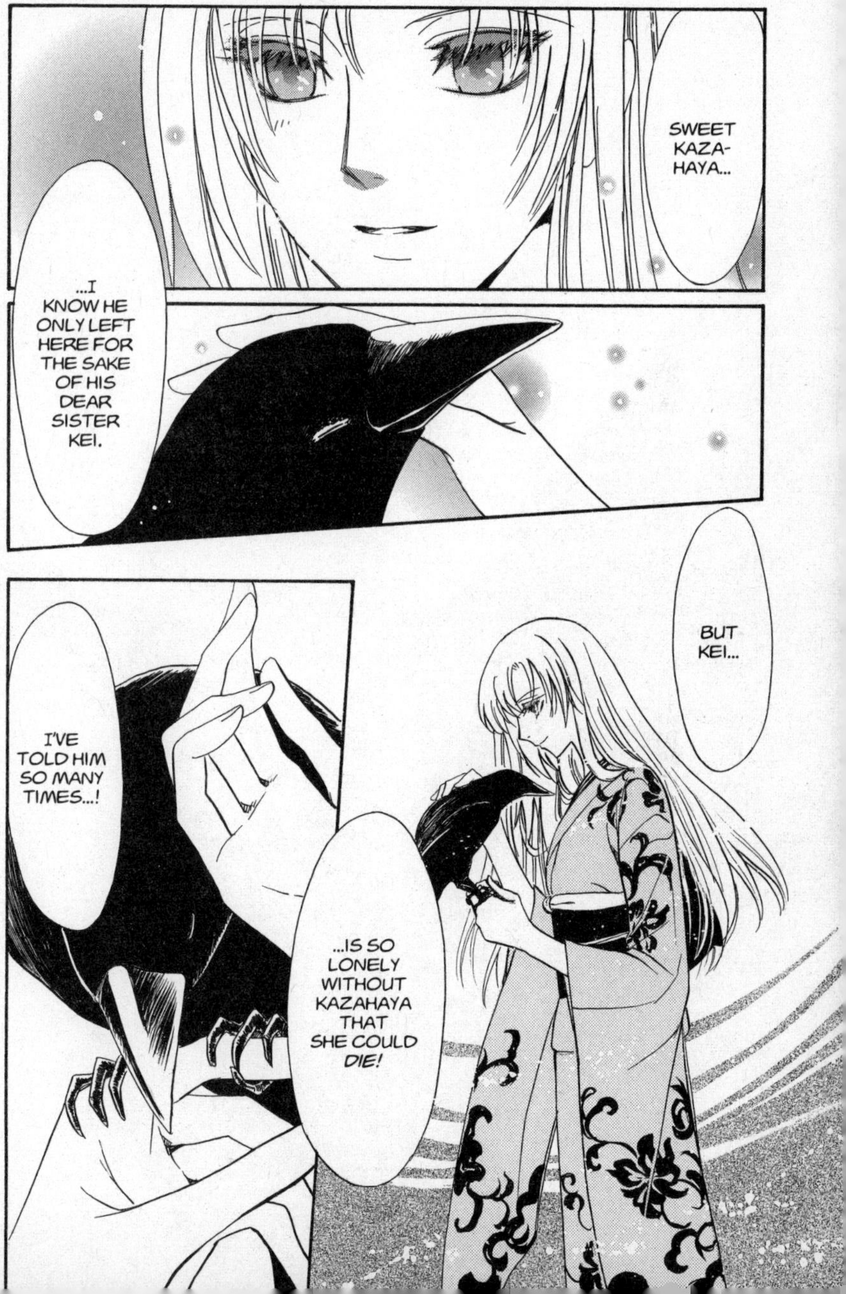
SWEET KAZA-HAYA...
...I KNOW HE ONLY LEFT HERE FOR THE SAKE OF HIS DEAR SISTER KEI.
BUT KEI...
...IS SO LONELY WITHOUT KAZAHAYA THAT SHE COULD DIE!
I'VE TOLD HIM SO MANY TIMES...!

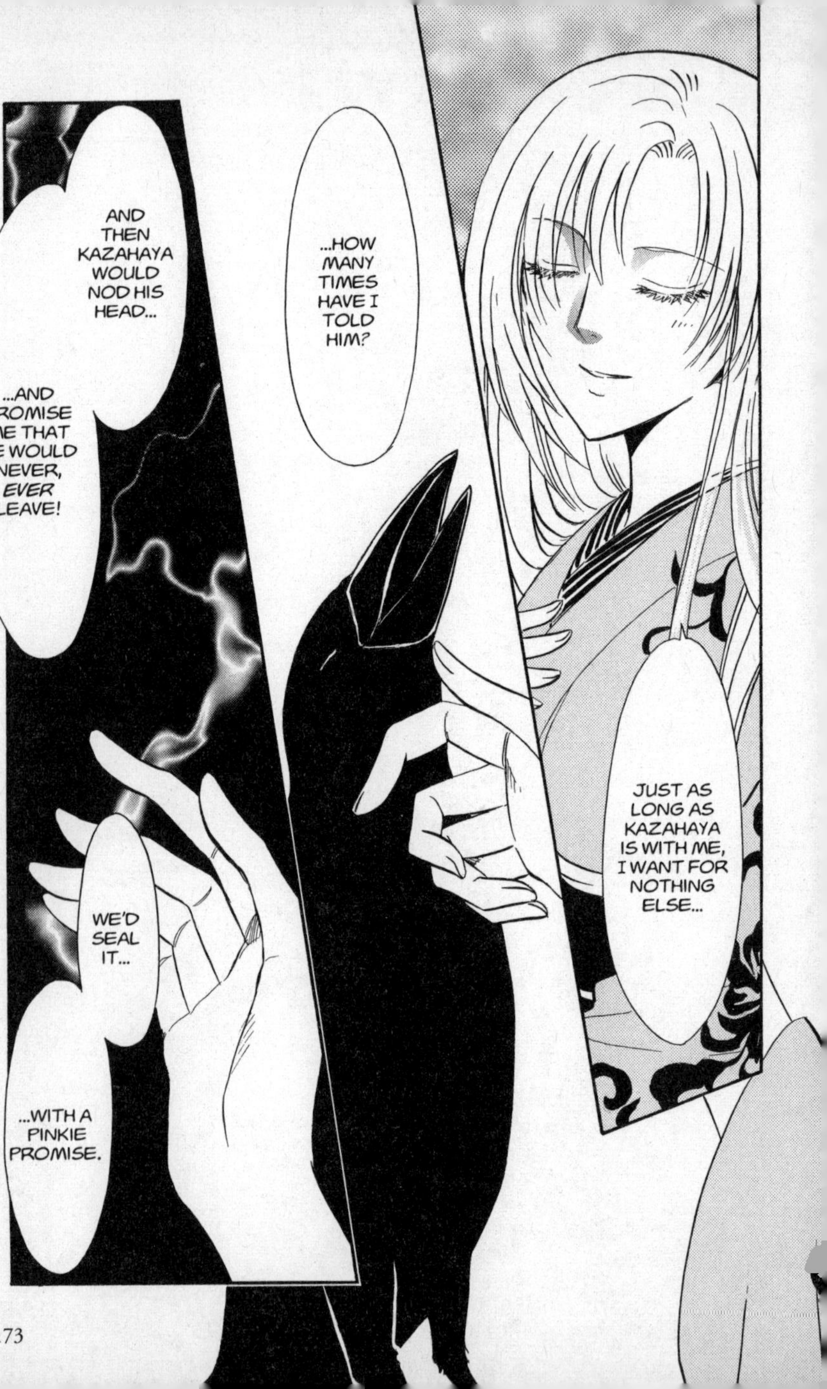
...HOW MANY TIMES HAVE I TOLD HIM?
JUST AS LONG AS KAZAHAYA IS WITH ME, I WANT FOR NOTHING ELSE...
AND THEN KAZAHAYA WOULD NOD HIS HEAD...
...AND PROMISE ME THAT HE WOULD NEVER, *EVER* LEAVE!
WE'D SEAL IT...
...WITH A PINKIE PROMISE.

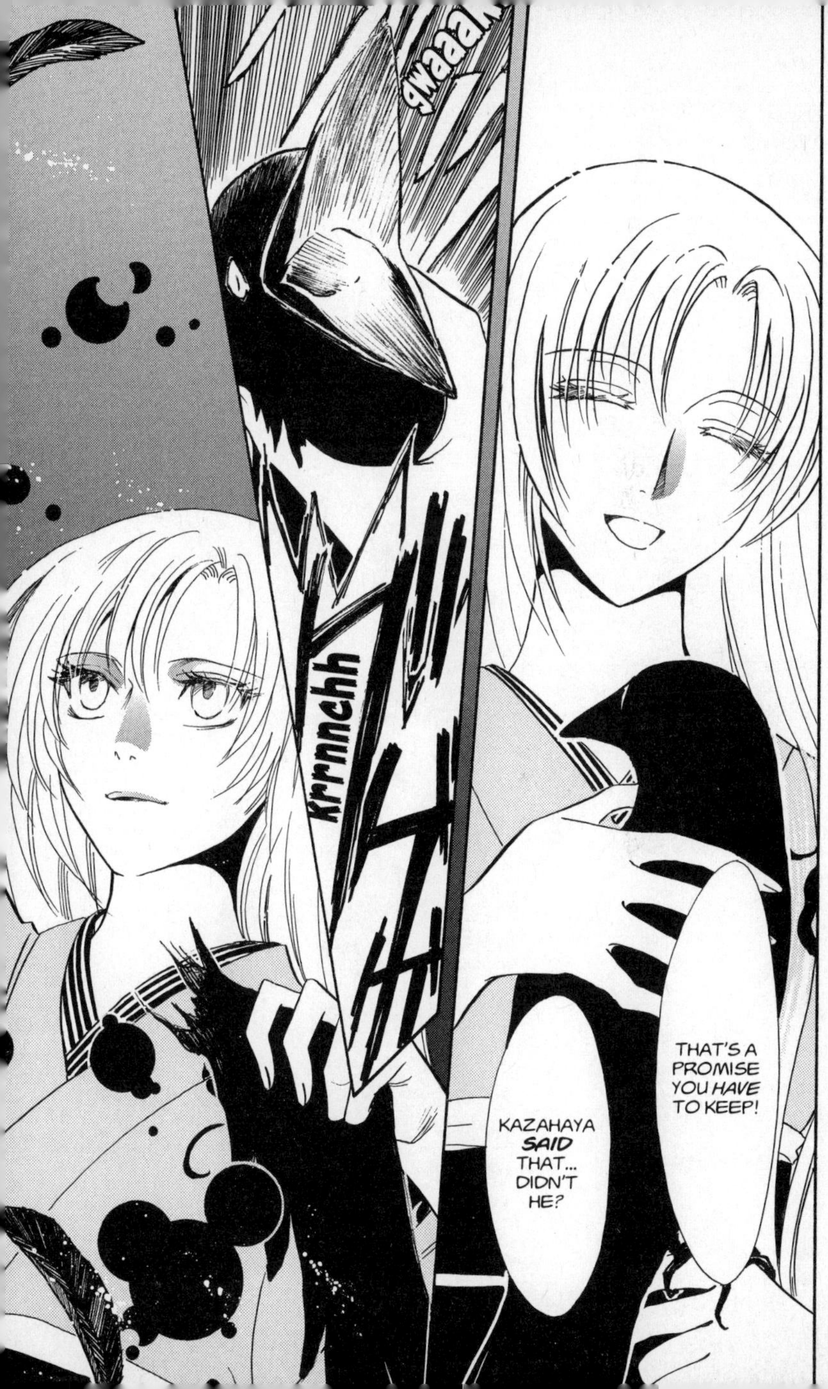

gwaaa
Krrnnchh
THAT'S A PROMISE YOU *HAVE* TO KEEP!
KAZAHAYA ***SAID*** THAT... DIDN'T HE?

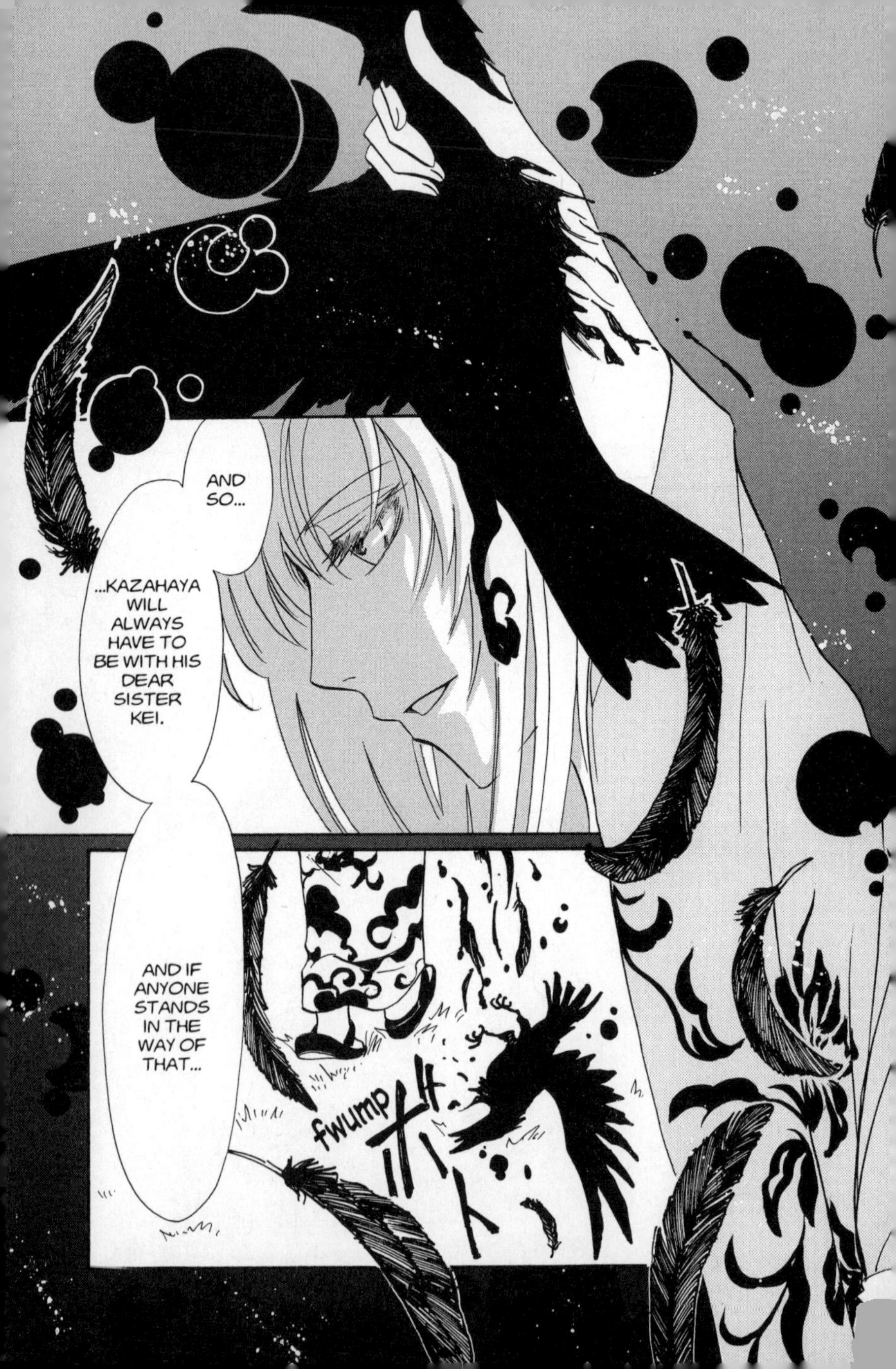
AND SO...
...KAZAHAYA WILL ALWAYS HAVE TO BE WITH HIS DEAR SISTER KEI.
AND IF ANYONE STANDS IN THE WAY OF THAT...
fwump

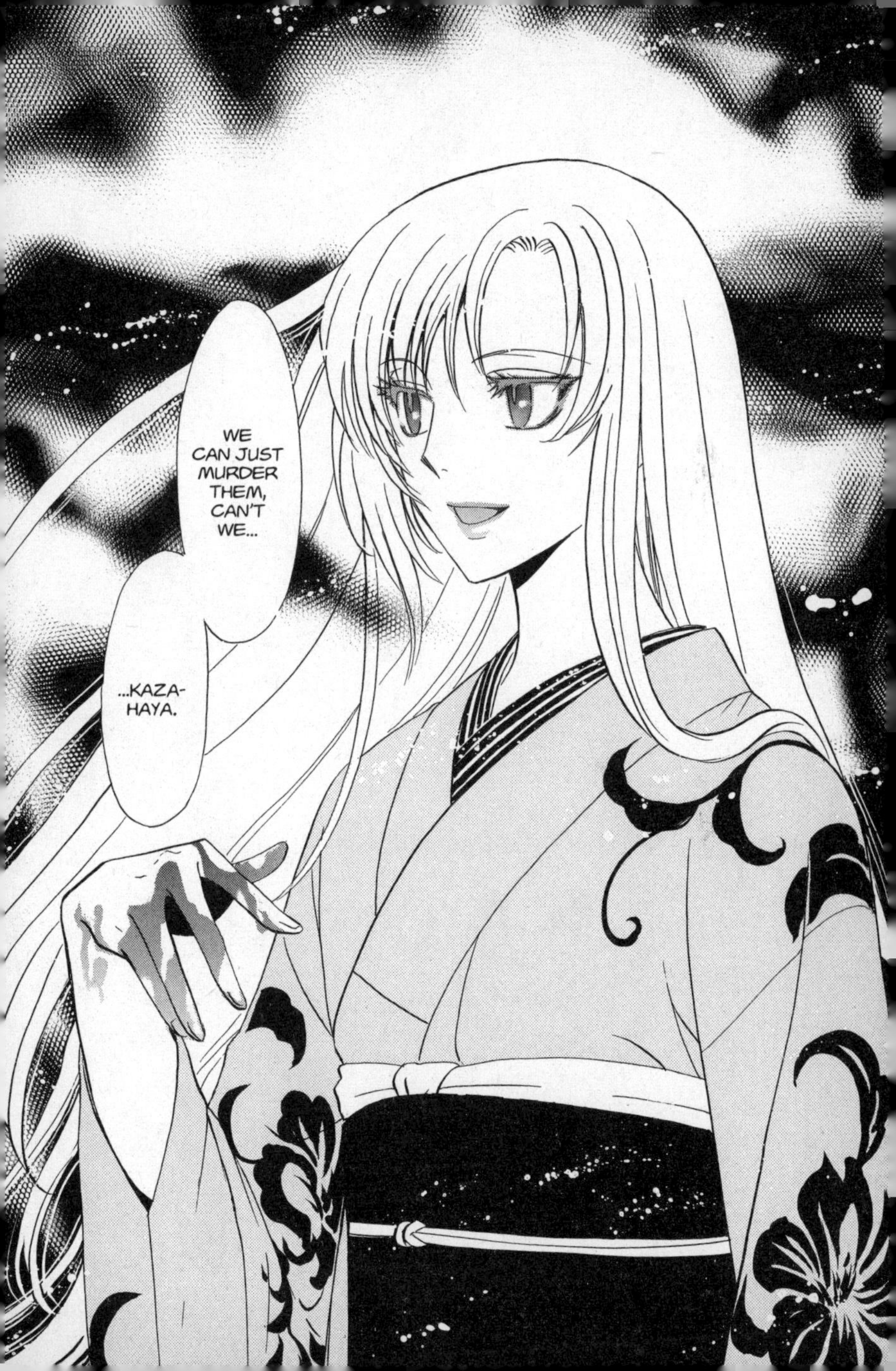
WE CAN JUST MURDER THEM, CAN'T WE...
...KAZA-HAYA.

DRUG
& DROP

a drugstore with medicine and a danger

TO BE CONTINUED

colophon drug

PLANNING AND PRESENTED BY
CLAMP

STORY BY
NANASE OHKAWA

ART BY
TSUBAKI NEKOI

ART ASSISTANTS
SATSUKI IGARASHI
MOKONA

Editor
Carl Gustav Horn

Translation by
William Flanagan

Lettering and Retouch by
John Clark

Special Thanks to
Michael Gombos

Designer
Brennan Thome

President and Publisher
Mike Richardson

English-language version produced by Dark Horse Comics

Published by
Dark Horse Manga
A division of Dark Horse Comics, Inc.
10956 SE Main Street
Milwaukie, OR 97222

DarkHorse.com

To find a comics shop in your area, call the Comic Shop Locator Service toll-free at 1-888-266-4226.

First edition: January 2015

ISBN 978-1-61655-595-5

10 9 8 7 6 5 4 3 2 1

Printed in the United States of America

東京 TOKYO BABYLON

CLAMP

**CLAMP's early epic of dangerous work
—and dangerous attraction!**

It's 1991, the last days of Japan's bubble economy, and money and elegance run through the streets. So do the currents of darkness beneath them, nourishing the evil spirits that only the arts of the onmyoji—Japan's legendary occultists—can combat. The two most powerful onmyoji are in the unlikely guises of a handsome young veterinarian, Seishiro, and the teenage heir to the ancient Sumeragi clan, Subaru—just a couple of guys whom Subaru's sister Hokuto has decided are destined to be together!

"Tokyo Babylon is CLAMP's first really great work."
—Manga: The Complete Guide

**Each omnibus-sized
volume features over
a dozen full-color
bonus pages!**

VOLUME ONE
ISBN 978-1-61655-116-2
$19.99

VOLUME TWO
ISBN 978-1-61655-189-6
$19.99

AVAILABLE AT YOUR LOCAL COMICS SHOP OR BOOKSTORE!
To find a comics shop in your area, call 1-888-266-4226
For more information or to order direct: • On the web: DarkHorse.com
E-mail: mailorder@darkhorse.com • Phone: 1-800-862-0052 Mon.–Fri. 9 AM to 5 PM Pacific Time
Tokyo Babylon © CLAMP. Dark Horse Manga™ and the Dark Horse logo are trademarks of Dark Horse Comics, Inc.
All rights reserved. (BL 7033)
DarkHorse.com

DARK HORSE MANGA

CLAMP artist Mokona loves the art of traditional Japanese kimono. In fact, she designs kimono and kimono accessories herself and shares her love in *Okimono Kimono*, a fun and lavishly illustrated book full of drawings and photographs, interviews (including an interview with Onuki Ami of the J-pop duo Puffy AmiYumi), and exclusive short manga stories from the CLAMP artists!

From the creators of such titles as *Clover*, *Chobits*, *Cardcaptor Sakura*, *Magic Knight Rayearth*, and *Tsubasa*, *Okimono Kimono* is now available in English for the first time ever!

ISBN 978-1-59582-456-1

$12.99

AVAILABLE AT YOUR LOCAL COMICS SHOP OR BOOKSTORE
To find a comics shop in your area, call 1-888-266-4226
For more information or to order direct: • On the web: DarkHorse.com
E-mail: mailorder@darkhorse.com • Phone: 1-800-862-0052 Mon.–Fri. 9 AM to 5 PM Pacific Time.
CLAMP MOKONA NO OKIMONO KIMONO © 2007 CLAMP Mokona. Original Japanese edition published by Kawade Shobo Shinsha, Publishers. English translation copyright © 2010 Dark Horse Manga. Dark Horse Manga™ is a trademark of Dark Horse Comics, Inc. All rights reserved.
DarkHorse.com (BL 7089)

Cardcaptor Sakura

カードキャプターさくら

Story and Art by

CLAMP

Fourth grader Sakura Kinomoto has found a strange book in her father's library—a book made by the wizard Clow to store dangerous spirits sealed within a set of magical cards. But when Sakura opens it up, there is nothing left inside but Kero-chan, the book's cute little guardian beast... who informs Sakura that since the Clow cards seem to have escaped while he was asleep, it's now her job to capture them!

With remastered image files straight from CLAMP, Dark Horse is proud to present *Cardcaptor Sakura* in omnibus form! Each book collects three volumes of the original twelve-volume series, and features thirty bonus color pages!

OMNIBUS BOOK ONE
ISBN 978-1-59582-522-3 $19.99

OMNIBUS BOOK TWO
ISBN 978-1-59582-591-9 $19.99

AVAILABLE AT YOUR LOCAL COMICS SHOP OR BOOKSTORE!

To find a comics shop in your area, call 1-888-266-4226

For more information or to order direct: • On the web: DarkHorse.com

E-mail: mailorder@darkhorse.com • Phone: 1-800-862-0052 Mon.–Fri. 9 AM to 5 PM Pacific Time

STOP!

THIS IS THE BACK OF THE BOOK!

This manga collection is translated into English, but arranged in right-to-left reading format to maintain the artwork's visual orientation as originally drawn and published in Japan. If you've never read comics this way before, take a look at the diagram below to give yourself an idea of how to go about it. Basically, you'll be starting in the upper right-hand corner, and will read each word balloon and panel moving right to left. It may take a little getting used to, but you should get the hang of it very quickly. Have fun! If this is the millionth manga you've read this way, never mind. ^_^

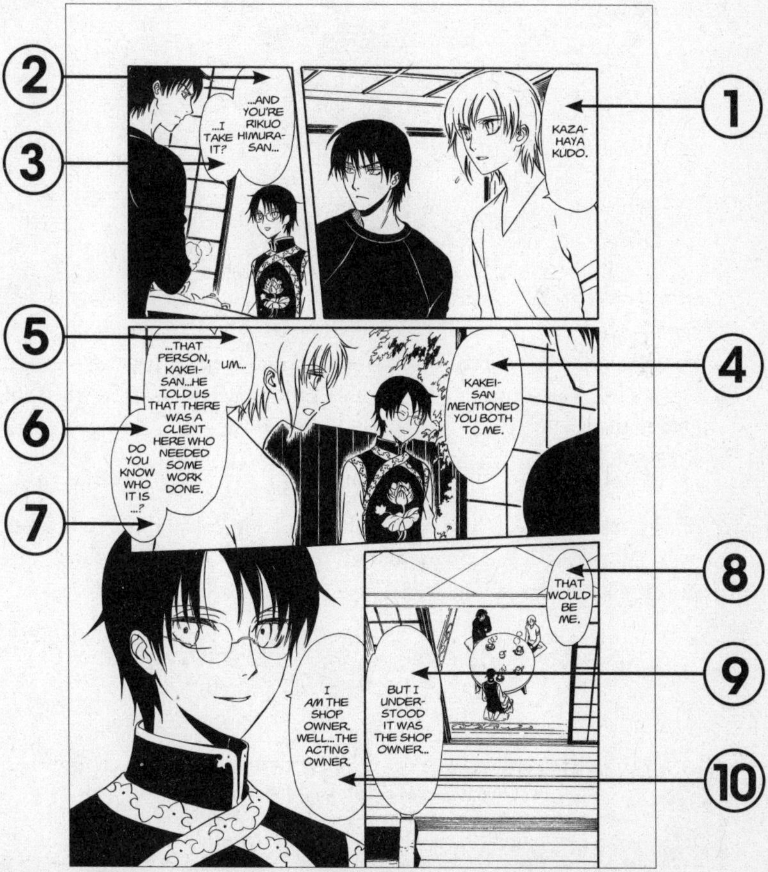
1
KAZAHAYA KUDO.
2
...AND YOU'RE RIKUO HIMURA-SAN...
3
...I TAKE IT?
4
KAKEI-SAN MENTIONED YOU BOTH TO ME.
5
UM...
6
...THAT PERSON, KAKEI-SAN...HE TOLD US THAT THERE WAS A CLIENT HERE WHO NEEDED SOME WORK DONE.
7
DO YOU KNOW WHO IT IS ...?
8
THAT WOULD BE ME.
9
BUT I UNDERSTOOD IT WAS THE SHOP OWNER...
10
I AM THE SHOP OWNER. WELL...THE ACTING OWNER.